BY HIS OWN LABOR
THE BIOGRAPHY OF DARD HUNTER

Cathleen A. Baker

OAK KNOLL PRESS
NEW CASTLE, DELAWARE
2000

First Trade Edition
Published by Oak Knoll Press
310 Delaware Street, New Castle, Delaware, USA

ISBN 1-58456-020-7

BY HIS OWN LABOR: THE BIOGRAPHY OF DARD HUNTER
Cathleen A. Baker

This work was first published as a fine press book by Red Hydra Press,
Northport, Alabama, in a handmade limited edition of 155 copies.

Typography, book design & cover design: Steve Miller
Wood engraved frontispiece: John DePol
Publishing Director: J. von Hoelle

Library of Congress Cataloging-in-Publication Data
Baker, Cathleen.
By his own labor : the biography of Dard Hunter / Cathleen A. Baker.
p. cm.
Includes bibliographical references (p.) and index.
ISBN 1-58456-020-7
1. Hunter, Dard, 1883-1966. 2. Papermakers—United States—Biography.
3. Papermaking—History. I. Title.

TS1098.H8 B34 2000   676'.2'092—dc21   [B]   00-020692

Printed in the United States of America on 60 lb. archival, acid-free
paper meeting the requirements of the American Standard for
Permanence of Paper for Printed Materials.

This book is respectfully dedicated to
Patricia Scott, Stephen Rees Jones, Dard Hunter III
and E. Shirley Baker.

To Love a Craft
TIMOTHY D. BARRETT

To be able to determine the locality and period of old papers it is necessary to make a minute study of the ancient papermaking appliances, as the succession of innovations, occurring in different countries at various periods, caused changes in the character of paper throughout the ages. To the casual observer these changes are insignificant, but to the student of papermaking they are clues that, followed, lead to the secrets of the craft he loves. Dard Hunter

At the age of 16, more than 30 years ago, I was a casual observer of paper. I found it a rather peculiar, curious material. My father answered my first general questions about how paper had been made by hand before the paper machine was invented. I was interested in how difficult it might be to make handmade paper myself, and I learned a good deal from an article by Henry Morris in *The Paper Maker*.

I first saw paper made by hand as a boarding school student during a visit to Laurence Barker's printmaking studio at the Cranbrook Academy of Art. I kept picking up pieces of information here and there, but all things considered, I was still naive and had little sense of the history of the craft or its intricacies. Then one day, bothered by questions that refused to go away, I went to the Academy Library. After a few moments in the card catalogue, I had my first encounter with the work of Dard Hunter. I clearly remember opening a copy of Hunter's *Papermaking Through Eighteen Centuries*. I had never imagined papermaking had a history of such richness and depth. I immediately knew that I had encountered a treasure trove of information that would be of tremendous help to me in my desire to learn more. Most importantly, Hunter's work helped validate my private fascination with hand papermaking and gave me confidence that I was on to something meaningful. Not long thereafter, I began carrying a piece of Japanese handmade paper around in my checkbook. Its warmth and character puzzled me, and I could not help wondering why it was so different from other papers.

Years later, at Antioch College, I set up a small papermaking workshop while pursuing a host of other interests. After graduating in 1973, I joined Kathryn and Howard Clark at Twinrocker Handmade Paper in Brookston, Indiana, where Hunter's *Papermaking: The History and Technique of an Ancient Craft* was our guiding light. By 1975, I felt I had to learn more about papermaking traditions and techniques, and perhaps with Dard Hunter's own travels in mind, I decided to try to arrange to study abroad with artisans who had grown up in the midst of the craft. I set my sights on Japan. A year and a half later, I found myself totally immersed in the Japanese craft, funded by a Fulbright Fellowship. During my study, I began to understand the source of character in Japanese paper that I had found so intriguing ten years earlier. I could see that part of it came from the use of traditional techniques that required exceptional raw materials and careful processing by experienced hands, but there were still elusive qualities that I yearned to understand more completely. At the age of 27, as a result of my interactions with Katsu Tadahiko and other teachers, I came to realize that working to understand character in paper could keep me busy and satisfied for the rest of my life. After two very valuable years in Japan, without knowing if any of what I had learned would allow me to earn a living, I returned to America. (In retrospect, there are odd similarities with Hunter's own younger years filled with rambling paper-related travels and work, all pursued energetically but with future income a minimal consideration.)

I settled in my parents' barn in Michigan, built a workshop for paper-making, and went on lecture/workshop tours to try to keep the wolf from the door. Henry Morris published my first book, *Nagashizuki: The Japanese Craft of Hand Papermaking*, and did an exquisite job, printing it on his own handmade paper. Once while visiting Henry, he paid me one of the more memorable compliments of my professional life. We were sitting in his car at an intersection, waiting for the light to change. Henry was peering out the windshield, listening to me talk about how tight money was. Suddenly he turned and, jabbing his finger at me, said, "Listen, kid, let me tell you something! I knew that guy Dard Hunter at the end of his career. His shirts were all frayed and worn at the collar—he had spent all his family money traveling all over the place studying papermaking, and if you don't watch out, you're going to end up just like him!" I felt a little concerned and yet honored at the same time.

For seven years, I lived and worked in the barn workshop making western and Japanese-style papers, developing tools and techniques, and undertaking a study of early European papers. In 1985, Kim Merker and colleagues brought me to the University of Iowa to join the Center for the Book. Since then everything has come round full circle. Now I teach others about the richness of the history of the craft, and I ask them to help me uncover the many secrets to the subtleties of character in handmade paper. It has been a fascinating and rewarding journey, with Dard Hunter, somehow, always in the background.

Recently, I joined Kathryn and Howard Clark and about twenty others at Twinrocker's 25th year reunion. During the event, we talked about the tremendous commitment it took on everyone's part, about the Clarks' devotion to the craft, and about the rewards that can come from persistence and determination. For weeks after the event, I wondered: What accounted for all that energy at Twinrocker? Why did we all work so hard then, and why does everyone still work so hard there? Why have so many of us, after leaving Twinrocker, gone on to do things that require the same kind of devotion? And lastly, why did Dard Hunter invest himself so heavily in the study and making of paper when he could have chosen from a number of other, perhaps more lucrative, careers? I think the answer to all these questions is the same: it was and is the paper itself. Hunter, and all of us since, have found ourselves totally absorbed by the making of this ordinary, plain, flat, utilitarian material. But why? Paper is not usually considered the finished product; it is something other artisans use to make a completed piece. It is as if we all had become intoxicated with making leather, or colored glass, or specialty clays, or printing inks. Why all this tremendous effort directed at handmade paper?

The answer to this question, I think, brings us to the essence of Hunter's work. Dard Hunter realized, long before anyone else, the enormity of paper's contribution to humankind, its tremendous range of character, and its central role in the quality of a book, drawing, or print. More important than anything else, Hunter came to understand how a single piece of paper could bring alive the moment of its own making and the presence of its makers. In his life and work, he found a way to pay homage to the craft and to honor those who practiced it. Almost out of thin air, he gave us a sense of the heritage of the craft, and for this, we will always be in his debt.

University of Iowa
Iowa City, Iowa

The Quintessential Roycrofter
MARIE VIA

At what moment does one realize that an interest has become a passion and the passion a life work? Both Dard Hunter and Cathleen Baker have experienced that moment, his culminating in the renaissance of hand papermaking, hers in the scholarly examination of his achievements. She properly credits the late Patricia Scott with launching work on a Hunter biography, but it was Cathy's recognition of the true scope of the project that has brought into being this definitive biography of an American giant.

My own introduction to the work of Dard Hunter came through research on the Roycroft community of artisans, of which he was a central figure for a brief but influential period of its forty-three-year history. Young Dard was in many ways the quintessential Roycrofter. Like many of Elbert Hubbard's craftsmen, he accepted the opportunity to test his skill in several different Roycroft shops. Unlike any other, however, he mastered each enterprise to which he applied his head, heart, and hand. Whether the medium was wood, copper, ceramic, glass, leather, or paper, Hunter's marvelous sense of design rendered objects more beautiful, more graceful, and more inventive than any others bearing the Roycroft cross and orb.

As he matured, Hunter focused his intellect and his artistic gifts upon the one field in which he was to gain his greatest glory: the book arts. Although he eventually dismissed those Roycroft years as a fairly insignificant detour in his life journey, he nonetheless absorbed one important lesson from Elbert Hubbard and other proponents of the Arts & Crafts Movement: the necessity of learning through firsthand experience, which in turn inspires a reverence for the very act of "making." These twin beacons, coupled with his own curiosity and creativity, led Dard Hunter down a path of experimentation that continues to stimulate and inform students of the book arts nearly one hundred years later.

In a strikingly similar fashion, Cathy Baker calls upon a singular battery of talents to help us understand Hunter's genius. Her scholarly research is evident in the meticulous detail of the historical record she has compiled from Hunter family correspondence, period newspapers, school records, and other primary sources. Many years of working as a professional conservator of paper artifacts, along with hands-on experience as a papermaker, lend real authority to her understanding of the medium Hunter made his own. And her total involvement in the production of this book—for not only did she research and write the text, but also helped print the limited edition—demonstrates her affinity for Hunter's own goal of an intimate relationship with the fruits of one's own labor.

A few years ago, I had the opportunity to spend a memorable Thanksgiving weekend with Cathy and Dard III at Mountain House, when I appreciated for the first time her remarkable commitment to this project. A few months before, she had resigned her tenured position and moved to Chillicothe to devote her full efforts to this biography. She was soon immersed in the heroic task of sifting, sorting, and cataloguing the voluminous personal papers of five generations, and the whole house had become a sort of research laboratory for her inquiry into the life and work of Dard I. When it came time to serve the Thanksgiving feast, boxes of books and piles of papers that had settled into residence on the enormous dining room table had to be relocated. An entire wall of the room was soon lined with cartons and files and stacks of history.

As we sat down to our dinner of roasted turkey, baked carrots and chestnuts, and homemade cinnamon rolls, there was no question but that Dard I was there in the room with us. We felt his presence as we raised our glasses in tribute, and then I'm certain he stole quietly into the studio across the hall where his printing presses still stand ready for use, or down into the basement where his moulds are still used to make paper, or into the library where his extensive collection of books on art and paper still lines the walls. His legacy is a living one, and through this first comprehensive biography of his life and career, we can at last discover the full meaning of the work he so lovingly produced by his own hand.

Memorial Art Gallery
Rochester, New York

A Friend of Dard Hunter
KENNETH BREIDENBAUGH

This foreword provides a chance to remember my late colleague and friend, Patricia Scott, who before her death in 1989 was devoted to the subject of Dard Hunter, and whose work has been the inspiration for this book.

Pat became interested in Hunter sometime after 1980. She was new to Chillicothe, had heard his name mentioned here and there, and so decided to learn, with characteristic determination, just who Dard Hunter was. This was an activity carried out casually, and in conjunction with sorting out the town in general. But it was also with an eye increasingly turned toward the sort of artistic production in which, she began to understand, Hunter had been engaged.

Pat had heard from the first about his one-man books. When she discovered, however, that Hunter was first an artist, and next a scholar, Hunter's early years began to intrigue her, this portion of his life suiting Pat's idea of what a young mind and spirit are supposed to do: look for some creative truth. Her interest was stirred and she began reading in some earnestness. Turning to his own bibliography, she started what would become a thorough search of the Hunter literature.

The 1983 centennial exhibition in Columbus and Chillicothe lent legitimacy to Pat's curiosity. It introduced her to other Hunter scholars and illuminated for her, probably for the first time, the scope of her subject. Her catalogue essay for the exhibition opened an activity that would make her inquiries into Hunter unique, as she sought out his family and his papers to begin to understand what was to become her subject.

From here she pursued Hunter in full seriousness. A book project was the logical result.

Pat referred to the book, this book, as a critical biography. She recognized that while a number of people had written on Hunter throughout Hunter's career(s), no writer had given the subject either full biographical treatment or real art historical analysis.

Her working manuscript covered Hunter in ten chapters. Chapter one, "An American Phenomenon," placed Hunter in his context of domestic erudition. The households in Steubenville and Chillicothe excited her: she approved of their bookishness and stream of activity, as understood by her through Hunter's own autobiographical account.

Pat then moved to the Roycroft years. The American Arts & Crafts Movement appealed to Pat because of its truthful premise, its reliance in decoration upon abstracted natural forms, and in architecture for its open-ness and freedom. Thus Hunter's involvement with the movement appealed to her. She marveled at the young man's absorption of the style's basic tenets, and his quick move to European influences which would soon bloom in his graphic work, filtered albeit through his own American attitude. Pat found the result really quite wonderful.

But she also found Hunter's later disdain for the Roycroft years good news. For Pat, his mild scorn showed Hunter's willingness to self-evaluate, and proved his need to get on to bigger and better, deeper and more diffi-cult, things.

Following Roycroft, Pat's conceived book moved to Hunter's paper-making ventures, his books (the major emphasis of Pat's outline), his travels (where she discovered him to have been as much a sensitive observer of the local scene as a researcher bent on discovery), his widening and unique knowledge of papermaking by hand, and finally, to the museum.

Here, in the museum venture, Pat (and Hunter) shone. The museum years were not golden for Hunter. Pat discovered that he had been treated less than fairly on a matter or two, and in a sense rallied to his cause. She came to know Hunter through his correspondence from those years, in a way she of course had not known him before. Pat found him to have been a gen-tleman, and was pleased. She warned against eulogizing the subject, but here felt her admiration justified.

When Pat was told in 1988 what was to be her allotment of time, she set to work in earnest. Like the rest of us, she had counted on some leisure to check those questions she felt her book must address and suggest answers to. Finding that to be impossible, she filled in her outline and began assembling smoother initial drafts, working late in the day. Our conversations from this time were punctuated with her need for an assurance of the book's future.

Responsible for finding a scholar interested in Pat's work, I was indeed fortunate that Cathy stepped forward, to examine Pat's work and then pain-stakingly move the biography and research to her own interests and direction. Through her contact with Dard Hunter III, Cathy availed herself of resources unknown to Pat, and Cathy's book is the better for it. The final form of this book of course belongs to Cathleen Baker.

Hunter was three things to Patricia Scott: artist, scholar, and humanist, the highest of her orders. That he was a Chillicothean, and that his Mountain House is occupied by his grandson—and stands only a short walk from my own home—is a good and comforting thought.

Ohio University
Chillicothe, Ohio

A Short History of this Book with a Note to the Reader
CATHLEEN A. BAKER

The exact date, of course, does not come to mind, but the first time I heard Dard Hunter's name was in 1976 in the British Museum's paper conservation laboratory, where I was an advanced intern on leave from the University of London's Courtauld Institute Galleries. It was my supervisor who asked if I had ever read Hunter's classic book *Papermaking: The History and Technique of an Ancient Craft*. I had to say no. This was an embarrassing confession to make in light of the fact that I had been working as a conservator of works of art on paper for a number of years. I immediately borrowed a copy and read it. I could not believe what I learned about paper from that book. A few months later, I was back at the Courtauld and began teaching a mini-course in paper conservation to the paintings conservation students. A major component of that annual course was a field trip to J. Barcham Green's Hayle Mill in Maidstone, Kent, which was still making paper by hand using traditional techniques and materials. Each year, as I watched the vatman form paper on the large moulds, I became more fascinated by the process. After each visit, I went back to *Papermaking* and applied what I had seen to what I read.

In 1978, after a ten-year stay in England, I decided to return to the United States to teach paper conservation full-time. Selfishly, I wanted the luxury of studying all I could about papermaking so that in the process of explaining its technology to students, I would gain more insight into the subject. I was fortunate to find exactly the position I wanted in the Conservation of Historic and Artistic Works graduate program in the State University of New York's College at Oneonta located in Cooperstown. Hunter's book became *the* textbook for my courses.

Three years passed during which time my desire to actually make paper steadily increased. In 1981, I met Timothy Barrett when he demonstrated Japanese hand papermaking at a meeting of the newly formed Book & Paper Group of the American Institute for Conservation. I will never forget the thrill of seeing the techniques that Hunter described—which I had read over and over again but until that day had not comprehended—come to life as Tim formed sheet after sheet of paper, using traditional Japanese techniques. At the same conference, the Friends of the Dard Hunter Paper Museum (FDHPM) was formed. Tim was elected president; I was secretary. That summer, accompanied by Tim, I made my first visit to the Institute of Paper Chemistry in Appleton, Wisconsin, which housed Hunter's museum. Most of the papermaking appliances illustrated in his book were there. I was surprised to discover that the printing arts were also well represented;

this was a component of Hunter's work of which I was only vaguely aware. His wonderful limited edition books on papermaking were also exhibited; little could I have known then the impact those books would have on my life's work.

Oddly enough I cannot remember when or where it was that I first took up a papermaking mould and pulled a sheet. But when I attended Syracuse University from 1984–85, I finally had the opportunity to make editions of handmade papers, each sheet, as nearly as possible, the same. I was there to earn a terminal degree for tenure, an M.F.A. in the book arts. (I was ultimately awarded an M.A. in art history, but that's another story.) That period at Syracuse was a turning point. I learned not only how to make consistent sheets of paper from fiber processed from rags, but also printed letterpress from hand-set type. An added bonus was that the library of SUNY's College of Forestry, Paper Science & Engineering, affiliated with Syracuse University, had a number of Hunter's private press books, and it was there that I first handled and examined them closely.

After graduation, teaching again became my primary focus and making books was pushed down my list of priorities. However, the invaluable experience I had gained about practical papermaking vastly increased my understanding of the material and the craft, and this further augmented my conservation course instruction.

I first met Patricia Scott in 1983 in conjunction with the centennial celebration of the birth of Dard Hunter. It was clear then that she had more than a passing interest in Hunter, which was reflected in the essay she wrote for the exhibition catalogue, *The Compleat Bookman*. In 1986, I was elected president of the FDHPM, and during my first two-year term, Patricia was one of the vice presidents. Over the next few years, she and I were in contact either about Friends's business or her developing biography project. Sadly, she was also coping with breast cancer. In early 1989, her fight ended; she left behind a family and her unfinished manuscript. Six months or so following Patricia's death, Dard Hunter II passed away. Tim Barrett and I attended the funeral in Chillicothe, and that evening, we sat with Dard III in the Chinese Room in Mountain House and talked well into the early morning hours. It was then that I began to understand the unique accomplishments of the Hunters, Senior and Junior.

At the time of the funeral, Ken Breidenbaugh and Ron Salomone, colleagues of Patricia and executors of her biography project, contacted me to discuss advertising in the FDHPM newsletter for an author to finish Patricia's book. Although Tim does not remember discussing this on our way back to the airport, I clearly remember his suggesting that I be that person. He also reminded me that I had never had a sabbatical and that the biography project would be a perfectly relevant activity for the leave.

I mulled this idea over for a few weeks and then called Dard III; I needed to know if he wanted a biography published (his late father had not been particularly happy about the idea). I do not remember him hesitating as he said, "Yes," and then added, "Cathy, I can't think of anyone I would rather have write this book than you, and I'll do all I can to help you." And with that generous and supporting sentence, *By His Own Labor* was launched.

My sabbatical began in autumn 1991. I had planned to work from my home in Buffalo as Dard confirmed the existence of only a few boxes of letters, which his father had used to write his magnificent two-volume work, *The Life Work of Dard Hunter* (1981, 1983). He agreed to ship them to me as needed. I was surprised then when, in early October, Dard invited me down to Mountain House for the weekend. That first evening, after a delicious meal that he had prepared, Dard led me into the vault, full of books about books, including the family's copies of the Mountain House Press editions. To that point, very few people had ever been in the vault, and I felt honored to have been included in that select minority. And as if that were not enough, Dard then showed me boxes, packages, and files, all crammed full of letters. And, he assured me, there was more. He explained that in the process of inspecting the nooks and crannies of the house for structural problems, he discovered letters that his father had carefully hidden away.

As I looked over the soon-to-be-augmented treasure trove laid out on the dining room table, I remember feeling both elated and dejected. I was elated because Dard was offering me exclusive access to the Hunter archives, the bulk of which had not been read by anyone alive. I was dejected because I realized that the letters, which were in no order, would first have to be organized before any research could begin. It was clear that much more than one year would be required to finish the biography.

Putting aside my feelings of dejection, I focused on the positive. I moved into an apartment in Chillicothe and went to Mountain House nearly every day for the next nine months. My first priority was to organize the material into chronological order. Once most of the hidden correspondence was found, I estimated there were about 10,000 items, not counting any books, in the Hunter archives.

By August 1992, I was back in Buffalo preparing for the upcoming semester. I thought that I could work on the biography and teach at the same time, but that proved to be impossible. By early 1993, after fifteen years of teaching, I decided to resign my tenured position and devote myself to Hunter's biography. Even though I had no prospect of an income from this activity, I relished the thought of being able to completely immerse myself in the project, no matter what it might cost me financially. Then Dard did an extraordinary thing: he invited me to live in Mountain House for as long as I wanted. After spending the summer commuting to East Aurora from Buffalo to research Hunter's years with the Roycrofters, I moved into Mountain House's northeast tower with its grand view of Chillicothe, spread out at the foot of Carlisle Hill. For over two and a half years in my rather large room, I lived and slept, read letters, books, and newspapers, and wrote. I cannot begin to say how important it was for me and essential to the book to have lived in Mountain House. If I had a question about a Hunter book, one of the handpresses, or his type, all I had to do was go downstairs to find the answer. Living in the house also helped me understand the Hunters, as well as establish a lasting relationship with Dard III and Cornell Hunter and his family. Unfortunately, Cornell died before the publication of this book.

My routine was established early on. I read letters for a week or so, making brief notes about the contents, and while they were still fresh, I wrote at the computer. Reading those deeply personal letters was not an easy task. Often, when sharing a meal with Dard, I was either happy or depressed, depending on what his grandfather had "done" that day. Once writing began, I decided to include everything that I thought was important to Hunter's story. Of course, without reading all of the letters, I could not know what would be pivotal and what would be merely interesting. Finally, on the evening of 15 April 1996, I finished the first draft (it was nearly twice as long as the book you are holding). The next step was to send it out to my readers, and they all agreed, among other things, that there was simply too much information. Although I dreaded losing even one word, once I started to edit, I found it relatively easy.

Editing and reorganization of the text took another year and a half. One key to making sense of Hunter's life was to give up the idea of relating it in a strictly chronological order. Because he was always involved in a number of concurrent activities, I decided to deal with each significant project from its conception to its conclusion. This approach also presents problems, and in order to give the reader a concise overview of Hunter's life, a chronology has been provided.

While revising the manuscript, I moved from Chillicothe to Tuscaloosa, Alabama, to be closer to Steve Miller, the publisher. Once the second draft was completed, it was sent to the copy editor. Finally, after working on the project for over six years, I wrapped up the finished manuscript and gave it to Steve as a New Year's present on 31 December 1997. Only a few weeks before, I had completed my first semester in The University of Alabama's

Book Arts Program. This decision to go back to school was a natural outcome of my previous encounters with the book arts. My experiences at Syracuse had never been completely forgotten, and while living in Mountain House, I had made paper with Hunter's moulds and printed a few things with his type and presses. While researching this book, I came to realize how amateurish my previous efforts had been compared with those of the Hunters and their private press contemporaries. I wanted to improve my skills in these crafts, and the M.F.A. program seemed the ideal solution. By the time printing of the limited edition of *By His Own Labor* commenced—at the beginning of my second year—I was an accomplished enough printer to assist Steve, who was also my professor. Being intimately involved in printing my own book was an unforgettable experience and a fitting culmination of an exciting and enriching project.

But there were problems associated with the project, too. By the end of 1994, my savings were running low. I applied for a number of grants and fellowships, and three were successful. My deep appreciation goes to the Sandy Hill Foundation, the Ludwig Vogelstein Foundation, and the Foundation for the Study of the Arts and Crafts Movement at Roycroft. Before a job could become a necessity, I decided that I would try to raise additional funds myself. Swallowing my pride, I sent out letters to my family, personal friends, and the membership of the Friends of Dard Hunter. To facilitate fund-raising, Dieu Donné Papermill, Inc. offered to act as the project's fiscal sponsor, which allowed tax-exempt donations to be made through it. I would like to extend my deep gratitude to Susan Gosin, Mina Takahashi, and the Dieu Donné board of directors for making this possible. I sent out about six hundred letters asking for any donation, large or small, and in the end, approximately $17,000 was raised, including a substantial grant from the Margaret L. Wendt Foundation. Today, it astounds me that I managed to live for almost three years on what was left of my savings and those donations. If I have gained nothing else from this project, I have experienced the freedom that comes with living simply.

As a small token of my deep appreciation of their support for this project, I gratefully acknowledge the following individuals and organizations for their donations of money, services, or in-kind support: Archivart Products, Dan P. Ashton, Carolyn N. Audi, Bruce A. Austin, J. Quentin & E. Shirley Baker, Tom Balboa, Dr. Prof. Gerhard Banik, Bark Frameworks, Inc., Timothy D. Barrett, Phil Bishop, Tom Bojanowski, Merrill Brown, Irene Brückle, Lore F. Burger, Elizabeth Buschor, Denise Carbone, Lilias F. Cingolani, Marion E. Cluff, Marjorie B. Cohn, Wavell Cowan, Angela & Michael Cronk, Kathy Crump, Elizabeth Curren, Donna M. Demmick, Deda Divine, Wayne T. Dodge & Larry Kreisman, Susan Mackin Dolan, Mindell Dubansky, the late Jerry Durand, Michael Durgin, August W. Engel, Helga M. Evans, Jane M. Farmer, Dorothy Field, David Findley, Elisabeth West FitzHugh, Jennifer & Bob Futernick, Karen Garlick, Georgetown & Scott County Museum, Sara Gilfert, Gomez Foundation for Mill House, Ken Grabowski, Maria Grandinette, Patricia Grass, Arnold E. Grummer, Hugh B. Hanson, Marc W. Harnly, Patricia & Gary Harrington, the late Roy H. Homans, Cathy S. Hunt, the late Cornell C. Hunter, Dard Hunter III, Earl S. & Jean K. Ide, Lois James, Helen B. Jarman, Charlotte Johnson, Hendrika Kamstra, Michael S. Kaufman, Carol Kazwick, Joyce Kierejczyk, David Kimball, Dr. Yoshinari & Mrs. Kazue Kobayashi, Susan L. Koss, Dr. Gabriela Krist, the late Jeanette and Irving Kushel, Dan A. Kushel, Hedi Kyle, Murray Lebwohl, Jeannine Love, Giselle & the late Georg Mandl, Sam A. Marks, the Mary Roelofs Stott Roycroft Fund, Bobbi Mastrangelo, Jean McDaniel, Janice McDuffie, William Messer, Julia V. Miller, Leslie Miller, Timothy Moore & Pati Scoby, Jobe B. Morrison, Cynthea J. Moiser, Ralph Ocker & Ocker and Trapp Library Bindery, Inc., Charles Rand Penney, Ann Cooper Penning, E. Jack Prather, Lois Olcott Price, Winifred Radolan, Charles & D.J. Raney, Sara Reid-Plumb, Robert & Kitty Turgeon Rust, Scott & Marjorie Searl, Fred H. Shihadeh, Gertrude Simon, Dolph Smith, Merrily Smith, Kezia Sproat & the South Central Ohio Preservation Society, Inc., Moyna Stanton, Nellie Stavisky, Lynn Sures, Marilyn Sward, Chris & Tay Tahk, Ellen Riggs Tillapaugh, Raymond Tillman, Marjorie Tomchuk, Caroline Pool Turoff, Walter P. Underwood, David L. Vander Meulen, Jim & Marie Via, Jean-François Vilain & Roger S. Wieck, John & Mona Waterhouse, Doris Wolverton, Martha & Ed Zimmer, and a number of others who prefer to remain anonymous.

I have dedicated this book to four remarkable people without whose inspiration, faith, and love this book would never have materialized. The first is Patricia Scott. Her vision gave this project life; my debt to her is deep.

Stephen Rees Jones was head of the Courtauld's restoration department when I was hired as his secretary in 1970. Betraying my Americanness in the first moments of our meeting, I blurted out that for years I had dreamed of becoming a restorer. Mr. Rees Jones promptly replied, "Fine, I'll give you a painting to work on in your spare time." But it did not take me long to decide that I was not cut out to work on paintings and was far more interested in restoring works of art on paper. For the next year, I watched and eventually treated a few paper artifacts under the supervision of Kasia Szeleynski before she left the Courtauld for the Tate Gallery. Within a few years, I had taken over her position. I realize now that Mr. Rees Jones's offer to teach me just because I wanted to learn was tantamount to a surgeon letting an interested stranger have a go on a patient! I do not know why he did it, but he did, and because of his generosity of spirit, this book exists. Regrettably, he did not live to share in the celebration of its publication.

Dard III was a shy fifteen-year-old when I first saw him at Mountain House during the 1983 centennial celebration. The next time we met was on the occasion of his father's funeral, six years later. A soft-spoken, poised college student, "young" Dard seemed mature beyond his years. Over the intervening years, we have become great friends, almost family. I will never be able to adequately thank him for opening up his home and the life of his family to me. It could not have been easy for him to learn that his grandfather did or did not do something that was contrary to what he had heard all his life, but which I could substantiate beyond doubt. I hope he feels, as I certainly do, that the real Dard Hunter was a far more interesting, humorous, talented, and dedicated man than the one we had been previously allowed to know.

E. Shirley Baker, my mother, heads the list of people who steadfastly supported this labor of love. Always putting my well-being first, she was alarmed when I told her that I was going to leave teaching and try to live without any appreciable financial means. But she understood me well enough to know that nothing would deter me from my plan. She is not only my biggest fan but also my toughest critic. I gave her a copy of the edited manuscript to read and then waited anxiously until she pronounced, "It is very good, dear. I really enjoyed it." I breathed a sigh of relief. We then discussed, sometimes heatedly, statements and phrases that she thought were unclear; more often than not, she was right. She has an uncanny eye for mistakes and was invaluable in proofing the copy-edited text. She has stood by me through a very difficult period in my life, always making sure that I kept my "eye on the prize."

I want to gratefully acknowledge my readers: Marie Via, Michael Durgin, and Jean-François Vilain. David Marshall was my very capable copy editor. Tim Barrett generously helped me with Appendix A. James Via took many of the photographs for the plates.

And finally, there is Steve Miller. When Steve heard about my fledgling project in mid-1993, he told me that he was going to print my book. I was very flattered that such a fine printer—he had been co-proprietor of the respected Red Ozier Press—was interested in publishing a book of which neither of us had a clear idea. For three years, Steve stood quietly in the background, urging me forward without prodding. In early 1996, we started talking seriously about what the book would be—paper, typeface, dimensions, binding, etc. Initially, it was to be printed from photopolymer plates, but

independently we both changed our minds. During one meeting, we
danced around the subject, until Steve pronounced that this book had to be
printed in as traditional a manner as possible, and that meant metal, not
plastic, type; I happily concurred. This is but one example of how similar are
our sensitivities to the many facets of books. From then on, Steve has involved me in every decision about the book's production. I did fear that our
friendship would change once we became professor and student, then printer
and assistant. But because of our mutual respect, and abundant senses of humor, it did not, and we remain the best of friends and respected colleagues.

Appreciation and thanks also goes to a number of individuals who provided
essential information and research assistance. These include Martin Anto-
netti; Richard Blacher; Judy Brewton; William H. Loos, Buffalo and Erie
County Public Library; Dr. Andreas Lehne, Bundesdenkmalamt, Vienna; the
staff, Carl Geyling's Erben, Vienna; the editor and staff, *Chillicothe Gazette*;
Kathryn & Howard Clark; Alexander Yale Goriansky, Club of Odd Vol-
umes; Tom Conroy; Muir Dawson, Dawson's Book Shop; Bruce Bland and
Gen Steffen, Elbert Hubbard-Roycroft Museum; Babette & Daniel Gehn-
rich; Lydia M. Giancotti; Gladys E. Godding; Gomez Foundation for Mill
House; Grolier Club; Dr. Erika Patka, Hochschule für Angewandt Kunst,
Vienna; Dr. Werner Sobotka, Höhere Graphische Bundes Lehr- und Versuch-
sanstalt, Vienna; Tom Lange and Alan Jutzi, The Huntington Library; J.B.
Lankes; Tom Lord; Boice Lydell, Roycroft Arts Museum; the staff, Institute
Archives, Special Collections, and Museum, MIT; Mary Anne McKay; Paul
McKenna; Edwards Metcalf; the staff, American Decorative Arts Depart-
ment, Metropolitan Museum of Art; John & Lois Minsker; the staff, Ohio
Historical Society; the late Georg Mandl; Patricia Medert, Evelyn Walker, and
Thomas Kuhn, McKell Library; Marie Via and Marjorie Searl, Memorial Art
Gallery; Virginia Moskowitz; Helena E. Wright, R. Stanley Nelson, and Joan
Boudreau, National Museum of American History; Herr. Prof. & Frau Chris-
tian M. Nebehay; Paul Gehl, Newberry Library; the staff, Österreichische Na-
tionalBibliothek, Vienna; the late Ronald H. Pearson; Neeta Premchand; John
Bidwell, Princeton University Libraries; the late Ward Ritchie; Cindy Bow-
den, Melanie Lynch, David Bell, and Robert Patterson, Robert C. Williams
American Museum of Papermaking; Jean McDaniels, Robbins Hunter Mu-
seum; David Pankow, Cary Collection, RIT; Anthony W.C. Phelps, Rowfant
Club; Robert C. Rust; Mildred Starin; Mark Stevenson; Douglas Stone; Gil-
more Stott; Warren C. Moffett, Town of Aurora, East Aurora; Evelyn
Walker, University of Rochester Library; Lynne Veatch; James M. Via; Jean-
François Vilain; Bernie Vinzani; the late Arno Werner; Thomas L. Vince,

Western Reserve Academy; and the many staff members in small public and historical libraries throughout Ohio and Pennsylvania. If I have left anyone out, please accept my apologies.

A Note to the Reader:
In an effort to make this book as readable as possible without sacrificing its scholastic nature, the traditional footnote format has been modified. Quotation references that contain only bibliographical information are not denoted within the text. These references are located in the Notes by page number and the beginning words of the quote. A second type of reference, which contains supplemental, and occasionally bibliographical, information, is denoted within the text by one of three marks * † ‡. These references are also located in the Notes by page number and corresponding mark. In each quote, the original spelling and punctuation have been retained.

Chapter 1

His life-long achievements as represented by the books issued from his Mountain House Press and in the collection at the Paper Museum certainly have enriched our lives and give us a renewed respect for hand craftsmanship in a world dominated by technology and machine-made progress. Technology eases the tasks of every day life, but the work of Dard Hunter reminds us that the products of our own hands and toil can be beautiful and rewarding. Men and women of the future will be inspired by Hunter's example to respect and preserve the traditions of hand craftsmanship.
Patricia Scott

As the next millennium approaches, we find ourselves at the beginning of the information age. Computers and the Internet allow unprecedented access to information, but some sacrifices may have to be made for this technology. For example, bibliophiles fear that the electronic book will render the physical one redundant. This threat to what we would consider the "traditional" book is not a new one. One hundred fifty years ago, as a result of the Industrial Revolution, handmade books were almost entirely replaced by ones made by machines. Fortunately, English author and socialist John Ruskin recognized the importance of reviving the hand crafts, including bookmaking, before they completely disappeared. His arguments provided the resulting Arts & Crafts Movement with its philosophical foundation, while William Morris (among others) provided it with physical objects. One of Morris's projects was the Kelmscott Press (1891–1896), which provided bibliophiles with his conception of the "ideal" book. Although Morris's typefaces were cast by machine, the Kelmscott Press books were printed on handmade paper or animal parchment with manually operated presses.

Deeply influenced by Morris's vision, Dard Hunter sought to bring the "book harmonious" to its ultimate conclusion—to produce it by his own labor. As far as can be known, he was the first to create a one-man book: he made the paper, cut the punches and hand-cast a font of type of his own design, and printed it. This first book, finished in 1916, was authored and published by others, and in 1923, Hunter completed the cycle by writing and publishing *Old Papermaking*, the first in his series of limited edition books about the history and technology of paper.

Hunter's interest in paper actually began many years earlier, in the first decade of this century, when he worked as a graphic designer for the Roycroft Press. As he examined books printed on both handmade and machine-made papers, he soon appreciated their differing tactile and visual qualities. This sensitivity heightened in 1911 when he first made paper by hand. Five years later, with the completion of his one-man book, Hunter made the momentous decision to devote his life to the revival of hand papermaking. His erudition, augmented by practical experience and firsthand observation, has contributed incalculably to our present knowledge about this ancient craft as practiced around the world. Dard Hunter's legacy far exceeded this knowledge, however, and he would be gratified to know that within the decade following his death in 1966 a renaissance in hand papermaking and the book arts commenced, due largely to his scholarship and example.

HIS HERITAGE

Dard Hunter spent most of his life traveling, figuratively and literally, down obscure paths to rediscover the technology of the handmade book, but he was not the first in his family to be a pathfinder. The irrepressible urge to lead the way down trails of discovery was in his blood. Like many thousands of Scotch-Irish who populated America's hinterlands in the eighteenth and nineteenth centuries, Hunter's forebears displayed all of the characteristics described by his father, William Henry Hunter, in *The Pathfinders of Jefferson County Ohio*, "[The Scotch-Irish were] the most determined, the most stubborn, the most religious, the most persistent men who ever colonized a new country." Hunter's ancestors left the north of Ireland to settle in the Commonwealth of Virginia in the late seventeenth century. A few members of the next generation moved westward into new territory, taming dangerous lands and establishing homes and churches. Wherever they went, the Hunters were productive, leading citizens.

Joseph R. Hunter, Dard Hunter's grandfather, was no exception. He was born in western Pennsylvania in 1802, and his family settled in Ohio in 1816. By then, the fourteen-year-old Joseph knew that he was not interested in being a farmer like his father, and he went to Pittsburgh to learn cabinetry. After completing his apprenticeship, Joseph set up a chair business in Mt. Pleasant, Ohio. Although not much more than a quaint village now, Mt. Pleasant was then an industrial and literary center of eastern Ohio. It was home to the first Abolitionist newspaper, and the town's citizens provided "underground railroad" stations used to hide runaway slaves en route to Canada.

Although Joseph found the intellectual and political climate of Mt. Pleasant stimulating, his business soon outgrew the town. He relocated to the thriving city of Cadiz, Ohio in 1834 and set up a large factory for the manufacture of fine furniture. (A family joke is that one of his apprentices was the young George Armstrong Custer, who made his "first stand" in Joseph's workshop.) It was in Cadiz that Joseph met Letitia Stafford McFadden, the daughter of a prominent Scotch-Irish merchant, and they were married in 1835. The Joseph Hunters had seven children, four sons and three daughters. William Henry, Dard Hunter's father, was the sixth child. In the 1850s, Joseph retired from his business, as he had no wish to compete with machine-made furniture. He spent his retirement years actively supporting the anti-slavery cause, and he was also part owner of the local newspaper, the Cadiz *Sentinel*.

When he was 84, he fell ill for the first time in his life and died within a few weeks. Letitia, completely exhausted after nursing him, died nine days later. Like his father and grandfather, Joseph left a considerable estate, valued at over $21,000, which was divided among the five surviving children. This money provided income for the Hunter families to expand their respective businesses. However, the more important, intangible inheritance of Joseph and Letitia Hunter was imbued in the personalities and appearance of their sons and grandsons, including Dard Hunter. "[They were] men of strong character and became outstanding in their communities. They all looked alike, all had rugged features and Roman noses. All had decided views on every important question."

PARENTS WILLIAM AND HARRIET HUNTER

William Henry Hunter, born in 1852, was about twelve years old when he was apprenticed to his brother-in-law, W.H. Arnold, editor of the Cadiz *Sentinel*. William started out as the printer's devil. This job entailed performing menial tasks such as preparing the ink and cleaning and distributing the metal type back into the cases after printing. Working his way up from the bottom, William eventually studied journalism under Arnold. When he was twenty-two years old, he learned that the Steubenville [Ohio] *Gazette* was for sale. He borrowed $1100 from his father, and in partnership with his cousin, H.H. McFadden, purchased the newspaper. Under their ownership, the first issue of the politically Democratic *Gazette* was published on 1 February 1875.

As far as marriage was concerned, William started courting Harriet Rosamond Browne when they were both living in Cadiz. Born in 1855, "Hattie" was the only child of William Courtney Browne and Margaret Roseman (the maternal surname had a number of spelling variations). Margaret had a delicate constitution, and when Harriet was just eleven months old, she died of tuberculosis. Fortunately for his daughter, Harriet's father considered education a valuable asset even for a woman. Harriet not only went to high school but attended the female seminary in Steubenville—the first to be established west of the Alleghenies.

William Hunter thought Harriet would make an ideal wife, but his father did not.

> Dear Will, . . . Matty [sic] Brown would be very unsuitable for you, as she has no health, would never to be able to do anything & you would have a sick wife to nurse as long as she lived. All her Mother's family died of consumption . . . Yours affectionately, JR Hunter (destroy this when you read it)

Displaying characteristic family stubbornness and persistence, William not only did not destroy the letter, he married Harriet four months later on 7 June 1876. Two years later, William began the construction of their home "River Side," an elegant brick and stone structure. The house was located at the corner of Fifth Street and Steubenville's LaBelle Park and overlooked the Ohio River.* On 12 December 1881, Harriet gave birth to their first son, Philip Courtney. By early 1883, Harriet was pregnant again. In late November, even though his wife was due to give birth at any moment, William had to leave her to attend the marriage of his younger brother, George. The wedding took place on Thanksgiving Day, 29 November 1883. And as fate would have it, that same day, Harriet gave birth to a second son. As was common for that period, the child's name did not appear on the birth certificate. It is possible that during the first month or so of his life, the unnamed baby was simply referred to as "darling." According to family tradition, two-year-old Philip could not pronounce that word, and instead said, "dard."† Eventually, the baby was christened William Joseph, after his father and grandfather. Willie's parents and brother had a number of nicknames for him, but they rarely used "Dard." However, other relatives and friends often referred to him by that unusual name.

WILLIAM'S ARTISTIC ENDEAVORS

The Centennial Exhibition, held in Philadelphia in 1876, attracted displays of the decorative arts, as well as the latest technological advances, from America and around the world. At the Exhibition, large numbers of Americans first saw the work of the English designer, William Morris. Although it is not known whether William Hunter attended the Exhibition, in the family library, there is a well-thumbed book devoted to it. In this way, at least, he was familiar with the exhibits. In particular, the Japanese and Chinese porcelains with simple, elegant forms and beautiful glazes caught his eye.

In 1879, he and a friend, Steubenville druggist and chemist William A. Long, attended the Cincinnati Industrial Exposition. Displayed alongside the newest machinery were local handmade wares: Rookwood art pottery (modeled after Oriental ceramics) and the woodcarving of Benn Pitman, Henry and William Fry, and their students, including Laura A. Fry. On their return from the Exposition, both Hunter and Long began woodcarving. Ultimately, William's mahogany panels decorated two fireplace mantels in his home. That December, he ordered ceramic tiles for these mantels from the newly established Steubenville Pottery Company. No doubt, he and Long looked on as the tiles were formed, decorated, and fired.

This introduction to the production of ceramics whetted their appetites, and they decided to experiment with underglaze-decorated faience pottery. To aid in their efforts, Long built a kiln behind his drug store. Eleven years later, the results of their experiments became public on 21 March 1891, when the *Gazette* printed a lengthy announcement that Long, Hunter, and Alfred Day (secretary of the Steubenville Pottery Company) had formed the Lonhuda Art Pottery; the name was made up of the beginning letters of their surnames.* By October, Lonhuda ware, which rivaled Rookwood's art pottery, was being sent to New York, Chicago, Philadelphia, and San Francisco, where it was met with high praise. At the end of March 1892, there were one hundred seventy-five pieces of Lonhuda ware for sale.

The opportunity to show Lonhuda to large numbers of prospective buyers came with the company's successful application to exhibit at the World's Columbian Exposition, popularly known as the Chicago World's Fair. The Exposition marked the 400th anniversary of Columbus's discovery of America and was scheduled to open in May 1893. A few months before this, Laura A. Fry, who had been an innovative decorator at the Rookwood pottery, arrived in Steubenville to step up production of Lonhuda ware. Taking the subject of the Exposition to heart, Fry designed a new line of Lonhuda based on the shapes of Pre-Columbian pottery. To further emphasize

this, she designed a new mark, a native Indian head. This was stamped
into the base of all Lonhuda pottery made after her arrival. Unfortunately,
many of the pieces based on Fry's new style were ruined in the kiln. Nevertheless, Lonhuda pottery achieved critical success, and by the time the
Exposition closed, more than twenty-seven million people may have seen it.
(plate 1) However, the public was not prepared to buy the pottery in sufficient quantities to keep the small, costly business going. As a consequence,
when S.A. Weller of Zanesville, Ohio made an offer to buy Hunter and
Day's interests in the business in late 1894, they accepted. Long did not sell
out, however, and together with Weller, he formed the Lonhuda Faience
Company, which made art pottery until late 1895.

Once out of the pottery business, William Hunter devoted the next few
years to scholarly endeavors. He had already written a series of articles titled
"Local History," and they served as the basis for *The Pathfinders of Jefferson
County Ohio*, published by the Ohio State Archaeological and Historical
Society in 1898. The critical success of *The Pathfinders* established William as
a scholar, and he continued to write about early Ohio history and the Scotch-
Irish in America.

YOUNG PHILIP AND DARD HUNTER

In this heady atmosphere of arts, crafts, and scholarship, Philip and
William "Dard" Hunter grew up. (For purposes of clarity, "Dard" will be
used except when quoting from letters.) Dard's earliest extant letter was
written in 1893 when he was nine years old.

> Dear Maw I know to boys from Steubenville. Ones name is Philip ands
> tother Will. The big one is 10 and the other eleven. Fill ways 65 and
> Will 97. . . . We are going to dinner at Aunts Hates to help eat a 20 pond
> turkey. I will write to you what they had. . . . Tot ways 70 and I way 97½
> Willie Hunter [the name is repeated five times]

From this letter and photographs, it is clear that there was a pronounced
physical difference between the brothers. (plate 2) Even though he was two
years younger, Dard was taller and more stout than Philip. Dard took after
his father in nearly every respect, even to the Hunter men's pronounced
Roman nose. Philip, on the other hand, favored his mother except that he
inherited his father's almond-shaped eyes.

Dard was an adventurous boy who loved physical activity. In his autobiography, he recalled:

. . . when the care of my father's two spirited horses was finally entrusted to me I found that task no hardship, as I have always been a lover of horses. The *Gazette* printing-office was about one mile from the house, and when I was not cleaning the stable and currying the horses or hoeing corn and cutting grass, I was occupied at the printing-office or my father's pottery. . . . For me, working days started early in life; my parents were filled with energy and could not tolerate indolence. My brother . . . and I were busy from morning until night— indeed, on some nights when the great kiln at [Long's] was being fired with the white-hot gas flames, father and we two boys did not return home until the small hours of the morning.

Dard also had his share of misadventures.

Dear Philip, . . . Dard could ride Roxy as good as I could till to-day at noon. When we was coming out Fifth St., Roxy ran off with Dard and slung him off and cut his head and hurt his hip badly. . . . Just before it happen Dard was joking as usual. The blood poured out of his head by the buckets full . . . Your special friend, Harry Gladfelter.

After Philip, Harry was Dard's closest friend. His father worked at the nearby Hartje Paper Mill, and no doubt Dard and Harry visited the mill often. (Perhaps Hunter's life-long dislike of modern paper mills was the result of visits to that unbearably hot and noisy place.) A much more pleasant activity that occupied Philip, Dard, and Harry was located in the Hunter home. Nearly thirty years later, in a shaky hand, Harry's mother wrote to Dard, "I can't think of you as grown up but just three happy boys always busy. Tot and yourself and Harry. Do you remember the little printing press that the three of you worked so hard printing cards. Those were happy days for all of us." Home printing presses were very popular during this period, and when promotional cards for Philip's sideline business in magic were required, the boys dashed them off with ease. William was pleased with his sons' interests in printing and impressed on both the virtues of this noble profession: "There is no branch of mechanism wherein so much artistic taste is required and displayed as in the typographical." Of course, he expected at least one of his sons to follow in his footsteps, and even at an early age, it was apparent that Philip was the more likely of the two boys.

Philip was bright, with a real love and talent for writing. When he was about twelve, he started composing long, highly amusing stories, some of which were published in the *Gazette*. He was also the editor and proprietor of *The Fifth Ward Tribune*, a weekly "sheet" printed by him on the home printing press; no doubt, Dard and Harry were reporters. This paper was published from about August 1894 to the end of January 1895. While the comings and goings of the Hunters' relatives were routinely published, "W.J." Hunter is mentioned only once: while attending a "Hard Times Social," Dard was fined ten cents for "being fat."

Harriet Hunter, writing under the pen name "Rosa Rosemond," wrote poetry and an occasional column for the *Gazette*. Despite her father-in-law's prediction that she would die young of tuberculosis, Harriet had not shown any signs of the disease. As her paternal grandmother died at the age of ninety-one, it was obvious that Harriet took after her father's side of the family. However, there was the ever-present fear that either Philip or Dard might be stricken later on. Both boys endured the normal childhood diseases, but in 1889, they contracted scarlet fever, and the already frail Philip suffered a lasting effect, a weakened heart.

Philip started high school in 1895. Besides English, he took Science (mostly physics), Latin, and German. While Philip was getting a good classical education, Dard stopped going to school when he was about fourteen or fifteen. Although his grades were not too bad, he had absolutely no interest in formal education. He felt there were better ways to occupy his time, and he far preferred doing chores and helping out the neighbors. When boys his age would have been apprentices or schoolboys, Dard was neither. This lack of interest in his own future caused concern. His Grandfather Browne echoed the general feeling about Dard when he wrote, "I am fearful that Will . . . [is] taking the chestnuts as they fall and not making much effort to thresh them from the limbs." There was something about him, though; Dard exuded such an air of confidence and *joie de vivre* that his family knew that, some day, he would make them proud.

Because Dard was an easy-going boy who loved the outdoors and rough play, he had lots of friends. Philip, on the other hand, was introspective and erudite beyond his years, and as a consequence, he had only one close friend, Dard. The following essay was written by Philip in about 1897. It is the first good description of the young Dard Hunter, and of the special relationship that existed between the Hunter brothers.

MY BEST FRIEND

The first characteristic of my best friend—or rather of the person who is as good a friend to me as any body else—that would likely be noticed by a stranger is his slowness, or what at first sight appears to be slowness. Possibly he isn't as speedy as the average mortal, but anyhow he does as much and more in a given period of time than some people who tear around like a whirlwind. He is a living proof of the old adage: "Make haste slowly." I venture that each setting sun sees more accomplished by him than by any half dozen of those who ridicule his deliberate manner. These persons may *appear* to have more get up about them than my friend, but speed is what speed does.

My friend may not be particularly bright in what is called book learning and he never did stand at the head of his class as far as I know, but he has a great passion for reading and reads like all possessed. And he reads everything. He has borrowed from me everything from Shakespeare to Haggard's "She,"—and he always brings the books he borrows back without waiting a coon's age like some others.

His best friends are his guitar and his tools. Everyday his guitar comes in for a couple of hours' practice. I don't know anything about music myself, but have been told that he is all right, so we will take for granted that he is.

However it doesn't take a musical education to be able to form an opinion as to his wood carving and carpentry. Without doubt he can handle tools to perfection. Some of the articles that have come forth from his workshop are marvels of mechanical ingenuity.

He is a great lover of flowers and raises chrysanthemums, asters, sweet peas and all sorts of posies by the wagon load. Last Summer he built himself a greenhouse, of no mean dimensions, that looks nice enough for the most delicate orchids in creation. His plans are to extend this conservatory until he has one fit for a king, and his plans are not mere air-castles.

In this essay, Philip described a number of attributes that foretold the man Dard Hunter would become. The first was his perspicacity. From a relatively early age, Dard was known for his determination to accomplish anything to which he had set his mind (and nothing to which he had not). The second was his voracious appetite for reading. This characteristic was to serve him well all of his life as he sought knowledge about obscure subjects (although once an adult, he no longer had the time or inclination to read classical literature). The third was his love of tools, and by extension, the creation of handcrafted objects. His interest in woodcarving was certainly an activity his father would have encouraged; he also had a proven ability in drawing, his best subject at school. The only exception was that Dard Hunter did not play any musical instruments later in life.

FAMILY MOVES TO CHILLICOTHE, OHIO

In late 1899, William told his family that they would soon move about two hundred miles west to the historic town of Chillicothe, Ohio.

Chillicothe was the first capital of Ohio when it became a state in 1803. Although the state government was later established in Columbus, Chillicothe's importance did not fade. By the 1820s, boat trade to New Orleans via the local Scioto River, which flowed to the Ohio River and thence to the Mississippi, was booming. In 1831, the last section of the Ohio & Erie Canal was completed, linking Chillicothe with the Great Lakes. The railroad arrived in 1852, and although canal traffic waned, the town continued to grow. By 1900, Chillicothe had a population of 13,000, about the same size as Steubenville.

The family was moving because William had decided to become partners with his brother George in a Chillicothe newspaper. In 1882, George F. Hunter, after acquiring experience at the Cadiz *Sentinel*, purchased the Chillicothe *Advertiser* with a partner. Upon the latter's retirement, George invited William to join him. Although William was one of Steubenville's prominent citizens, he liked his brother's grand ambition to consolidate Chillicothe's *Advertiser, Daily News,* and the *Ross County Register* to form a new Democratic paper, the *News-Advertiser*.

In February 1900, William went to Chillicothe to attend to business while the family remained behind so that Philip could finish his last year of high school. After graduation that June, the family moved into a rented house on the brow of Carlisle Hill, which provided a marvelous view of the town below.* Later, William bought a large house at 188 North High Street.

Following the practice established at the *Gazette*, the entire family had different jobs on the *News-Advertiser*. William was the editor; Harriet wrote occasional articles for the home under her new pseudonym, "Peggy Spriggs." Philip was proofreader and occasional editor, and seventeen-year-old Dard was the paper's artist. The first time one of his drawings appeared in the *News-Advertiser* was in the 18 June 1900 issue. This political cartoon, "The Evolution of the Elephant," a depiction of a grotesque animal with a human head, was a condemnation of the various "trusts," or monopolies, which threatened free enterprise. It was signed "W.J. Hunter," the "unter" placed between the bottom stems of the "H." This was just one of a number of signatures Dard used from 1900–1904: "Hunter," "W.J.H.," "Dard Hunter," a script "W.J. Hunter," and a wide "H." In addition to cartoons, he also drew portraits of the newsworthy and designed column headings. (The method used by the newspaper to print Dard's drawings was the quick, though somewhat crude, chalk plate technique.†)

The Hunters were immediately accepted into society thanks to William's reputation as an influential newspaper editor and author. For example, he instigated a project to plant trees and flower beds, to bring in fresh water for a lake, and to establish a small zoo in the park he named Yoctangee, meaning "painted creek." He was involved in starting up a new business to enhance the town's economy, the Florentine Pottery Company, which was modeled after the Steubenville Pottery Company and the Lonhuda Art Pottery. By 1903, the new pottery was in full swing. In September of that year, a Viennese artist, Rudolf Lorber, was named head of the Decorative Department. Lorber, a graduate of Austrian technical schools, specialized in geometric designs, which he toned down for American tastes. (Considering Dard's later fascination with the designs of the Viennese Secessionists, it is an intriguing notion that his introduction to this new art style might have come from Lorber.) Although the Florentine company's art pottery was exhibited at the 1904 St. Louis Exposition, in 1905 this line was discontinued, perhaps because Lorber left for parts unknown.

In 1905, William Hunter was among a group of influential citizens who backed young George Houk Mead's successful efforts to reorganize the Mead Paper Company's Chillicothe plant, the town's largest employer. (Some thirty years later, Dard Hunter and the same George Mead planned to establish a paper museum in Chillicothe, but the project fell through when Hunter's collection went instead to the Massachusetts Institute of Technology.)

But the event that crowned William's role as an important town father was Ohio's centennial celebration, which he arranged to be held in Chillicothe, rather than Columbus. The celebration was held in May 1903, and the entire Hunter family participated, including Philip and Dard who wrote and illustrated, respectively, a fanciful page "The Chilikofa Nus–Advertiser, Ma 20, 2003," for a special edition of the *News-Advertiser*. (plate 3) While Dard's fanciful drawings of airships, rockets, and women wearing trousers are not particularly sophisticated in their design or technique, more accomplished efforts were drawn for the article that his father wrote on the history of Ohio. Here for the first time, Dard's monogram, ⊂H, appears on most of these drawings and designs; the rest are signed with a simple "H."

The most extraordinary of these designs is the masthead for "Ohio History Notes and Comments Compiled by W.H. Hunter." (plate 4) The lettering style Dard incorporated in this design was based on so-called Rugged display fonts popular at the time, although Hunter did exaggerate some of these letters, notably the *s*. Also interesting are the white, uppercase letters in black rectangles creating a cameo effect and the "high-waisted" *Hs*.

But being the artist for the *News-Advertiser* was not the teenager's sole occupation in the early years of the new century. Dard was, in fact, a seasoned entertainer in Philip's magic show.

Chapter 2

This hotel is positively the finest thing I ever saw. It is exactly as I would have made it. You can't imagine how it makes me feel to look at it. It almost drives me crazy. It is "Old Mission" until you can't rest. Dard Hunter

Philip was ten when he first described himself as a magician. Six years later, in 1897, he and thirteen-year-old Dard were putting on public shows featuring magic tricks and hypnotism. Their act was described in a small pamphlet, probably printed on their home press.

COMING SOON! COMING SURE!
in their own special traveling chariots
The Brothers Hunter
Philip Courtney   William Joseph
The Wonder Workers

. . . One of the brothers, William Joseph, has made a study of the manifestations of spirit mediums and has discovered that they are, to speak plainly, all rank fakes, and in his performance each evening repeats the experiments of the most famous mediums. Many of these he explains so that any person visiting the exhibition will be able to repeat them himself, so simple are they when the secrets are once fathomed. One of the features of the show is the explanation of a number of tricks in magic which are extremely puzzling, and yet so simple that anyone can do them.

To further enhance their performances, the boys printed songbooks as well as leaflets explaining some of Philip's tricks. After moving to Chillicothe, Philip became known as The Buckeye Wizard, or The Wizard. His first Chillicothe performance was in October 1900 at a benefit for his family's church, the Walnut Street Methodist-Episcopal Church. The next day, the performance was reviewed in the *News-Advertiser*, not without some bias, "there was not a feature of the [Wizard's] programme which was not perfect in its way, and every illusion was presented with a skill and dexterity which surpassed the best acts of either the renowned Kellar or Herrmann. Mr. Hunter is certainly a master magician, and his skill amounts to genius." Philip was an elegant performer. Always appearing in a formal cutaway coat, his out-of-the-ordinary appearance was enhanced by his almond-shaped eyes.

In late 1901, Philip decided to go professional, and he was contracted by a lyceum bureau for a long tour. The Phil Hunter Company included Dard, who took that as his professional name. His primary role on stage was as the spiritualist "Karmos"; off stage, he was the magician's assistant. In this latter role, he was responsible for packing, unpacking, and setting up the paraphernalia at each venue—a particularly demanding and exhausting job when the company was doing one-night stands. They often had to catch the midnight train to the next stopover; this was referred to as a "jump."

As the tour proceeded, Dard's talents as an artist were increasingly exploited. He became the company's "chalk talker," then a popular form of entertainment. Dard described his act: "With square sticks of colored chalk I drew pictures on large sheets of rough paper held upon upright easels, and at the same time carried on a line of 'patter' supposed to be both humorous and instructive." While Dard's performances were popular components of the act, they served the more important purpose of giving Philip crucial rest periods. On the tour, Philip "had been losing weight and was pale and fatigued. But [they] went on from one town to another, with little sleep, tired and worn." In mid-September 1902, the tour was finally over. Even though Philip had been in fragile health all of his life, his parents were appalled to see how ill he was upon his return home. Perhaps, they hoped, Philip would now acknowledge that his constitution was simply not up to the rigors of touring. Perhaps he would finally take their advice and go to college. But Philip's mind was made up; he declared that as soon as he was well enough, he would go back on the road. Philip was not his parents' only concern, however. They also tried to persuade Dard to complete his schooling and go to college; these arguments also fell on deaf ears. Unlike Philip, however, Dard had no idea what career he would pursue. He did know one thing for certain; he would not choose a career that required more academic schooling.

During this respite, in October 1902, Dard and Philip produced a multi-page circular for the magic act. The circular gave Dard his first opportunity to develop more sophisticated designs in color. (plate 5) Philip wrote the text and probably set the type; the colophon announced that the printing was done at the family newspaper's job press, the Yoctangee Press. The cover and matching envelope were either a dark brown or maroon paper, while the loose sheets were printed on a coated white paper. The circular would have been an expensive item to produce, however, which may account for the relatively few extant copies.

By November, after less than two months' rest, The Wizard was well enough to go back on the road, and The Phil Hunter Company set out for Michigan and nearby states. Besides Philip, the lyceum bureau signed up a violinist and a cartoonist who took Dard's place in the company. Exactly why Dard was left behind is not known, but the most likely explanation is that his help was needed in the remodeling of his parents' home, which had been an ongoing project for a year. While Philip was away, Dard received almost daily letters from him similar to this one written from Bad Axe, Michigan.

Dear Bill: . . . Had five gold fish stolen other day—four left. Eight to meet me tomorrow. Feeling all right but not getting much sleep. Short jump tomorrow and will get a few hours in the afternoon. Business big every place, do all the business. Other fellows couldn't do it any more than fly. Hurriedly, Phil.

And later the next week, Philip wrote to his father,

Am feeling good—in fact getting used to getting along with little sleep. Am eating chocolate, which is said to be good for people who work when they ought to be sleeping . . . Figuring out time, taking care of the baggage and running the show generally in addition to the financial responsibilities makes pretty hard work, but I'm getting used to it. . . . Would get along better with Dard along, but things are all right. Then, too, I would rather have somebody who would keep up appearances as he would, for Anderson [the violinist] and Cox [the cartoonist] do not, and seem to have had very little experience traveling.

By Christmas 1902, Philip was home for the holidays, and, notwithstanding the rigors of the tour, he not only seemed fine, but he had actually gained weight. A few days after the New Year's celebration, the company departed again without Dard, but he did join it a few weeks later. The brothers were delighted to be together again; finally, Philip had someone reliable to help him. But when the brothers returned to Chillicothe in April, Philip was ill. A benefit had already been scheduled, which was to be Dard's

hometown debut, and, not wishing to spoil the event, Philip got up from his
sick bed to perform. The *News-Advertiser* reported,

> Mr. Dard Hunter . . . drew a dog and kennel, Sitting Bull's portrait,
> a full length poster of a woman, and a night scene in Holland, all in 10
> minutes . . . Phil Hunter, the Wizard, of this city, closed the show. It has
> been nearly a year since Mr. Hunter appeared before a home audience,
> but as before he mystified all completely and sent the audience away
> wondering how it was all done. Despite the handicap of a very bad cold,
> he presented one trick after another in rapid succession, and while
> Old Glory, which he seemed to produce from nothing, was being waved
> to the breezes, the curtain was lowered, and the show ended.

The brothers spent much of April 1903 designing a second circular that
was printed up in large numbers by the Interstate Lecture Bureau. (plate 6)
This one included photographs of Phil and Dard who also drew numerous
sketches underlying the text. One depicts a tablet of paper on an easel with
an Indian head drawn in chalk. Nearby is a rack with the inscription, "DARD
HUNTER HYS RACK." A cut-out heart adds decoration, and this motif became
one of Dard's favorites. Close examination of the stool nearby reveals it to
be "Mission" in style, complete with exposed tenons. Dard signed and dated
this drawing: H 1903.

In mid-May 1903, The Phil Hunter Company packed up and left for a
tour that took the brothers as far south as Louisiana and as far west as
Colorado. In August, they returned home, exhausted. This time, Philip was
so ill that he had to cancel the last few venues, and there was concern that
the company's next tour would have to be called off. Everyone's worst fears
were confirmed when a specialist diagnosed the early stages of tuberculosis;
he was also suffering from heart strain. Although there had been advances in
the treatment of tuberculosis since his grandmother's death, it was still
a deadly disease. The most common treatment was to provide the patient
with plenty of bed rest, good food, and fresh air. After a few weeks' rest,
Philip began to improve, but even he realized that he would have to forgo
the 1903–1904 tour.

DARD BRIEFLY ATTENDS UNIVERSITY

In August 1903, Harness Mound, a Native American mound near Chillicothe, was being excavated. Not having much else to do, Dard, and Philip
when he was well enough, visited the site and became friends with Dr. W.C.
Mills, supervisor of the dig and curator of the Ohio Archaeological and

Historical Society Museum. On many of these visits, Dard made drawings of mound artifacts, which were published in the *News-Advertiser*. It is quite possible that Dr. Mills convinced Dard to give Ohio State University a try. Although not entirely convinced he would find this any more interesting than previous educational experiences, Dard did enroll as a special student in the College of Engineering in September 1903. He signed up for architectural drawing, taught by Thomas E. French.

It is also possible that he took ceramics from Edward Orton Jr. This supposition is based on an announcement in the *News-Advertiser*, which appeared a month after classes began, that Dard was to teach a course in clay modeling and cartoon work the following March. Coincidentally, it was at this same time that Rudolf Lorber was artistic director of the Florentine Pottery Company. During early October, Dard was home from school due to an illness, and it is possible that he visited Lorber then. Perhaps, along with discussions about modern design and ceramic technology, the two talked about the hands-on training available in Vienna. In any event, Dard soon returned to classes, but on November 5th, after only two months, he officially withdrew from the university. The reason for his decision is clear. Four days later, The Phil Hunter Company left for a tour that would take it to the west coast, and Dard was contractually obliged to lead it in Philip's absence. He did not relish this, however; he hated being on the road as much as Philip loved it.

ON THE ROAD AGAIN

Almost daily, Philip received letters from "Bill" that often included a sketch of places where Dard performed or the hotels where he stayed when not sleeping on the train. He also wrote about the chronic problem the company encountered because the bureau continued to send out circulars announcing the imminent arrival of Phil Hunter. When it was clear that Philip was not in the troupe, managers of the opera houses, Masonic temples, etc., "raised hell." Exasperated by the repetition of this unpleasant scene at every stop, Dard wrote Philip, "I don't think that the show will finish the season because they all want *you*. Every place we have been you are boomed to 'beat the band.'" Fortunately, Dard learned how to mollify the managers long enough to get the curtain up. Once the company took the stage, even the most outraged audience soon appreciated the talents of Nicoli, the replacement magician, and, of course, Dard. "Mr. Hunter . . . is different in every way from the ordinary chalk talker. He transforms the platform into a veritable artist's studio and on easels of various shapes and sizes with tinted paper and chalk of many colors makes pictures of all kinds; Indian Heads, Golf Girls, Poster Pictures, anything, everything."

The company slowly made its way westward across the plains and over the Rocky Mountains. Finally, in late November 1903, after a few exasperating weeks, Dard had a few days' rest in Los Angeles, California. He unpacked his suitcase and took in the sights. Immediately, Philip was barraged with letters about the exciting things Dard was seeing. Using the letterhead of the New Glenwood Hotel in Riverside, he wrote:

> This hotel is positively the finest thing I ever saw. It is exactly as I would have made it. You can't imagine how it makes me feel to look at it. It almost drives me crazy. It is "Old Mission" until you can't rest. I have gotten more ideas in this one building than I have gotten from any thing I ever saw. It is great. Positively grand . . . I'm going to make a few of these things I have seen when I get home. There is a mantel in one room very much like mine only made of very rough bricks. Fire bricks that have been melted until they have run all out of shape. It is the grandest thing I've seen since I have been in existence. Every room in the place is fitted with Mission furniture, the rooms are all beamed and have hinge plates and double doors . . . Will make our hall up great when I return.

At last, Dard had found something that truly inspired him. However, the Mission furniture in the New Glenwood Hotel were not the first examples of this style he had seen. In 1901, he and Philip visited the Pan-American Exposition in Buffalo, New York where Mission furniture, usually in oak of simple, unadorned construction, was first seen by large sections of the American public. There was also the Mission-style stool he drew for the 1903 circular.

Since he was already familiar with this style, why did he have this epiphany now? At this point in his life, the twenty-year-old Dard realized that what he had was a peripatetic existence full of frustration; what he yearned for was a career that would challenge him, preferably one that would allow him to use his manual skills. Given his father and grandfather's interest in woodworking, it seemed the ideal choice. Having made this decision, Dard wanted to return home immediately, but he could not abandon the company. However, he did have some funny experiences on the way back home. For example, from South Dakota, he wrote Philip,

> Came to Deadwood on the stage, great trip. There were two old cattle men in the stage with us and they kept us amused so we did not mind the trip. One of them had not heard about the Chicago fire *yet* [32 years

earlier, in 1871] and we had to explain all about that to him. He wore a big overcoat made of mountain goat hair and the other had one made of buffalo skin. The other one was a little ahead in knowledge, he had heard of the Johnstown flood [1889]. The stage which Buffalo Bill now uses used to run over the same road that we came over, running from Deadwood to Sehyenne [Cheyenne]. The one we rode in is nearly 50 years old and is almost the last one in the state . . . I wouldn't like to live in these parts although I like to look at them . . . No Indians near here. If there were I wouldn't be writing to you.

Dard arrived home in March 1904, and he lost no time trying to convince his parents that the hall needed modernizing. After all, he argued, the Hunters, noted for their forward thinking and interest in arts & crafts, could not be behind the times. His parents deemed the hall too public an area for Dard's "Mission" experiment, but they did allow him to transform the informal dining room. During that spring and early summer, he set about making replicas of the things he had seen in California. Out of sheet copper, he formed hinges for a cupboard and escutcheons for the dining room door decorated with a punched shield and crossed sword and scepter. These fittings also feature a dark patina and cone-shaped studs. Dard also made two footstools, a short table, and a very large chair. (plate 7) All appear to be in oak (some are painted) and have plain members, as well as exposed tenons. Possibly during this period, Dard made another oak chair, decorated with a carved mahogany panel, "Sit down & rest thy weary bones." (plate 8)

The pleasure he took in making these furnishings prompted him to seek a job where he would receive a salary as well as training. To this end and with his parents' support, he sent a letter to Elbert Hubbard, head of the Roycrofters in East Aurora, New York inquiring about a job in the Furniture Shop.

Chapter 3

If you . . . remember the pre-horseless-carriage days of soft dirt roads and shady lanes uncluttered with billboards, filling stations, road stands, and antique shops, when the fresh, redolent aroma of horses permeated the air and the smell of warm gasoline fumes, burning oil, and hot rubber had yet to be introduced into our civilization, then it is probable that you will recall Elbert Hubbard and the heyday of his Roycroft Shop in the village of East Aurora, Erie County, New York State.
Dard Hunter

In the early 1890s, Elbert Green Hubbard was a successful salesman and partner in the Larkin Company (soap manufacturers) in Buffalo, New York, but he really wanted to be an author. To expedite this goal, he sold his interest in the Larkin company, studied at Harvard for a brief period, traveled to England, and finally, in November 1895, became the proprietor of the Roycroft Printing Shop in East Aurora, New York. One of the press's first publications was *The Philistine: A Periodical of Protest*. The small magazine, whose cover was cheap brown butcher paper, slowly garnered an audience, chiefly because of Hubbard's rather unorthodox views and humor. By 1900, the circulation of the magazine was around 100,000.

By early 1904, Philip was reading *The Philistine*, but his father thought Hubbard was a hypocrite, and he said so in a biting editorial.

> The Philistine, a magazine whose chief mission is to protest, also objects to what it calls the ostentatious waste of the vulgar rich, as if the consumption of the products of labor were a crime . . . The Philistine insists that the rich make display of fine houses, fine jewelry, fine raiment and many servants to attract attention to themselves. Why not? Does not the editor of the Philistine wear long hair and persistently kick down the idols and the ideals of others for that very purpose? And why should not Mr. Hubbard do that? He has wonderful talent along certain lines of effort. If he had not advertised himself by his idiosyncrasies, manifest

in his "kicking" propensity and long hair, he might just as well have been dead for all the wide public would know of him, and if he were not known his efforts at reform would be futile, for they would not have attracted attention. If he has a right to make brutal display of his eccentricities, certainly another man has the right to make vulgar display of means if he can afford to do so. Certainly there is no excuse for a man being a miser, whether it be of talent or money; if he have either one, it is his duty to give others the benefit, but it is expected that there shall be a fair exchange.

Notwithstanding his father's dim view of Hubbard, Dard badly wanted a job at the Roycroft, which by then included an Arts & Crafts community that manufactured, among other things, a line of Mission furniture. He wrote to Hubbard in June 1904 asking for a job. Hubbard replied:

Dear Mr. Hunter: Your kind favor received, and contents carefully noted. If you lived in our vicinity, I have no doubt but that you would be working here in the Roycroft Shop with us, but as it is I will have to explain that we only employ people who live right around here in our immediate vicinity, and as it is just now we have more workers in our shop than we can well make room for with our limited facilities. With all kind wishes, ever, Your sincere, Elbert Hubbard.

Many would have been put off by such a discouraging letter, but not Dard. He was confident he had the skill to make good furniture, but how could he convince Hubbard? He had an idea. Earlier that year, he had seen advertisments in *The Philistine* for the Roycroft Summer School where students learned by practice. The diverse subjects taught at the school included bookbinding, drawing, illuminating, cabinet-making, gardening, typesetting, foreign languages, vocal and instrumental music, physical culture, English literature, history, expression, and dramatic art. "Daily concerts and lectures on Art, Literature and Right Living through the exercise of the three H's, HEAD, HEART and HAND" wrapped up the curriculum.

While Dard saw the summer school as an opportunity to learn a skill and bring his talents to Hubbard's notice, his parents must have hoped that while in the school, where as much attention was given to the fine arts as to craft, Dard *might* become interested in the former. If that did not happen, however, at least he would learn a trade. So with his family's encouragement, on 12 July 1904, Dard left on the train for East Aurora via Buffalo, New York.

When he first walked onto the Roycroft Campus, Dard thought he had arrived in heaven. The buildings, inside and out, featured those Mission and "old world" details that he so admired: hand-wrought furniture and metal fixtures and fittings, exposed beams and vaulted ceilings, and ivy-covered fieldstone walls. There were even broad expanses of green lawns kept neat by grazing sheep. He immediately dropped a note to his family telling them about the campus and his classes. He also let it be known that from now on his "official" name was Dard. (As far as could be determined, William Joseph Hunter never legally changed his name to Dard Hunter.) Obviously, Philip considered himself an exception and continued to send letters to "Blossom," "Bud," "Button," or "Flower," although the envelopes were addressed to "Dard Hunter."* (Documenting Dard's activities while he was in East Aurora has been difficult. Although the letters he wrote while on tour to California are in the archives, for some reason only a few written between 1904 to 1910, except for his letters from Vienna, were saved. However, some of the family's letters to Dard were kept, and references in them indicate that the quantity and quality of Dard's correspondence left much to be desired. "If you would make your letters shorter, I wouldn't have to spend so long reading them," Philip wrote, sarcastically. Therefore, the best sources of information from this period were occasional notices in the Chillicothe *News-Advertiser* and the East Aurora *Advertiser*, as well as the few extant letters written to Dard.)

In the 2 August 1904 issue of the *News-Advertiser*, Dard wrote a long description of the Roycrofters, after being coaxed to do so by his father. Although only a small portion of the article is quoted below, it is clear that he was captivated by the spirit of the place and by Hubbard.

[The Roycrofters] are a settlement of peculiar thinking people who make useful and beautiful things as well as they can. They are called cranks by outsiders and perhaps they are cranks, for they are all original thinkers and work out original ideas. And these are the factors, as I understand, of the crank . . . Mr. Hubbard not only thinks differently, but dresses differently, from others. He wears his curly black hair very long and a huge necktie adorns his neck. Most of the time he wears overalls, but he himself is not an artisan, which is to say he does not work in the shop with his hands, but his brain does a great deal of the hardest work that is done here . . . Nearly all the Roycrofters allow their hair to grow and wear ties like the Fra. I have a big tie and I go bareheaded like all the others here.

Upon reading this, William worried that his son was becoming too "Roy-croftie." (colorplate 1) He wrote Dard of his concerns and included lots of fatherly advice.

> I was fearful that you might get the long hair and big neck-tie habit, and maybe wear a red carnation and sing alto. If you can resist all this and learn to draw and such like things, stay as long as you desire. Drawing is the basis of all the things you like and it would be a great advantage to you to learn all you can of this factor of art . . . When you come home the thing to do is to make some furniture and get a demand for it. If it seems to sell well, then build a factory; if not you will have the money the factory would cost in your pocket. It is always best to crawl before you walk. Have a basis for a business; the rest will come naturally.

The acquisition of drawing skills was very important to William Hunter, as was technical training in schools, and he had been tireless in his advocacy of the latter from the early 1880s. Only two weeks before Dard was born, he had written, "Drawing is the basis of all industrial arts. One who can draw can use tools . . . All mechanical work is simply drawing with other tools than the pencil."

As we know little of Dard's daily activities at the summer school, we can only guess about the number and types of objects he made (there are no indications that he took any "academic" classes). From his father's letter, however, it would appear that he did take drawing. Based on a particular form of his monogram, it is possible to date a few graphic designs made during the second half of 1904. These include a bookplate for Beulah Rudd Hood and an advertisement for Hubbard's *Essay on Silence*—a blank book.* (plate 9) Each of these was signed with his monogram encircled by a flourish, almost identical to the one he used for a 5 July 1904 *News-Advertiser* illustration. (Through photography, Hunter's drawings were turned into printing blocks, known by a variety of names: zinc, cut, zinc cut, line block, and line etching, the term used in this book.†)

While at school, Dard may have made an unsigned, undated earthenware vase, the so-called Iris Vase.‡ (plate 10) The vase's shape and decorations are elegantly modeled, and the glaze is similar to the Grueby Faience Company's matte green glaze, very popular at the turn of the century. The only piece of furniture safely attributable to Dard's summer school experience is a fumed oak bookcase. (plate 11) It exhibits the usual Mission characteristics of exposed tenons and simple, straight members, but compared with the "Sit down and rest thy weary bones" chair, this bookcase shows improved design and execution. On the apron of the top shelf is carved "Dard Hunter." The *D* and *H* are "cameo," and the lettering is similar to that used for "Ohio History Notes and Comment." Rounding out the design are the ubiquitous hearts. Even though he went to the Roycroft Summer School to learn cabinetry, once this bookcase was completed, Hunter decided that he had learned as much as he wanted about that craft. Apart from some lamp bases, he never again made any furniture.

By early September, Dard wrote Philip that he was keen on going to Europe, having been inspired by the modern designs in the periodicals *Deutsche Kunst und Dekoration, Dekorative Kunst,* and *International Studio,* which he discovered in the Roycroft library.* The urge to see the architecture and decorative arts of Germany and Vienna greatly appealed to him, but a number of considerations, the lack of money, for one, caused him to postpone these plans. One reason for staying was prompted by a conversation he had with Hubbard regarding stained glass. Dard was interested in learning this craft, which was neither taught nor performed at the Roycroft. Hubbard thought this was a splendid idea, as he planned to enlarge the Roycroft Inn and stained glass windows would greatly enhance the building. He arranged an apprenticeship for Dard with the J. & R. Lamb Company, a New York City firm well known for its ecclesiastical stained glass work. Dard was delighted. He would learn a new trade, one unique to the Roycroft, and on the successful completion of the apprenticeship, he would finally attain his goal to be on Hubbard's payroll.

"ROYCRAFTER" DARD HUNTER

Dard studied at the Lamb Studios from mid-September to mid-October 1904, after which he was back in East Aurora. That his apprenticeship was only a month long attests to the fact that he was a fast learner. All thoughts of going to Europe were forgotten as he eagerly put what he had learned at Lamb's into practice. Now an official Roycrofter, Dard Hunter celebrated by having formal photographic portraits taken by Clara Ragna Johnson, an attractive young woman who worked in the Roycroft office. (plate 12) (Although several poses were made, the one reproduced here was later used in advertising, as well as a watermark for his personal stationary.) Whether or not Clara was a love-interest of Hunter's is open to speculation, there are indications that he was wooing several unidentified Roycroft "girls."

In mid-November, the *News-Advertiser* announced Hunter's new status.

A Roycrafter

Dard Hunter . . . went [to East Aurora] to spend a few weeks at the
Roycroft summer school, but his own art ideas were so highly appreciated by the head masters that he was induced to stay and become a
Roycrofter, with the result that he has been made the head of the
stained-glass designing and making department. . . . The Roycroft shops
are model in every particular; the buildings are artistic and surrounded
by lawns, trees and flowers, and all the workmen are artists who earn
higher wages than is possible elsewhere, for the Roycroft publications
command three times the prices that the products of ordinary factories
command. Everything about the place is ideal for the artist-workman,
and the atmosphere is like that of an art center of Europe. Mr. Hunter
has been requested by the head man of East Aurora to start a Roycroft
pottery, and as he has good ideas along this line it is likely that he will
do so.

From the dearth of dated ceramics from this period, it would appear that the
plan to establish a pottery was short-lived. (In 1906, Hunter made another
effort to establish a Roycroft pottery, and this is described later in the
chapter.) However, there is one extant ceramic made by Hunter, which is
similar to his earlier Iris Vase; it is called the Papyrus Vase.* (plate 10) While
the former was neither signed nor dated, the Papyrus Vase is marked with
the Roycroft trademark, Hunter's monogram, and "3" [the mold number].
This number implies the existence of at least three molds, although no other
ceramics from this period have been identified. Although the vase is not
dated, Hunter's flourished monogram is identical to that found in the July
1904 newspaper drawing, the Hood bookplate, and the Hubbard advertisement mentioned above. These four are the only known instances of that particular style of monogram. Therefore, it is safe to assume that they all date
within the second half of 1904.

While working on the stained glass windows for the Inn's dining room,
Hunter made his first design for the Roycroft Press: the title page of Hubbard's second edition of *The Man of Sorrows*, copyrighted January 1905.
(colorplate 2) The unsigned design was printed in black on Japan vellum, a
high quality, cream-color paper with a satin finish. The color was hand-
applied by the press's illuminators, who may have included Hunter himself.
Although the letter style is similar to his earlier designs, the maturity and
restraint of the composition were undoubtedly the result of the training and
constructive criticism he received at the Summer School and at Lamb's.

Hunter's next graphic design project was for the press's February 1905 edition of Washington Irving's *Rip Van Winkle*. (plate 13) This book carried Hunter's design concept beyond the title page to include large chapter initials and embossed suede leather cover. (plate 14) Hunter's landscapes were loosely based on the work of popular graphic designers Will H. Bradley and Louis Rhead, and most are drawn in a style reminiscent of wood engravings.

These graphic designs proved to be quite popular with Hubbard, and Hunter's work on the Inn's windows was again interrupted so that he could draw "A Roycroft Dining Room" for the *Aurora Colonial Furniture* catalogue published that spring. Hunter's normal monogram, without any flourish, appears here for the first time in a Roycroft publication. Shortly after the publication of this catalogue, his designs in Ralph Waldo Emerson's [*Essay on*] *Nature* appeared. (plate 15) Hunter's designs for *Nature* display a consistency of motif and a maturing drawing style compared with *Rip Van Winkle*. The mixture of letter styles on the title page represents a transitional stage between the display type Hunter knew from his newspaper days and the classic typefaces used in Roycroft books. In addition to the title page and initials, Hunter designed a tailpiece and colophon, as well as the cover. Thus *Nature* represents the first book fully integrated with Hunter's designs. The color scheme of *Nature*, like that of *Rip Van Winkle*, is basically black and red, although a light yellow background was used for *Nature*'s chapter initials. Hunter recalled, "In regard to books [Hubbard] would always say, 'give us something with fireworks in it and make it any colour, just so it's red.'"

In late June 1905, Hubbard received a commission to have his best Roycrofters create a souvenir book for philanthropist Thomas W. Lawson, to be presented to him less than a month later at the Albert Lea [Minnesota] Chautauqua. Hunter was instructed to shelve his other projects and pen the title page and seven text pages in black ink. He also illumined the decorative borders of plants in jardinieres and garlands in green, orange, and gold watercolor. (colorplate 3) In addition, painter Alex Fournier made five monoprints and five watercolors, one of each to a page, of scenes around Albert Lea. Master binder Louis Kinder created the special leather binding with onlays. The mahogany box with copper hinges and clasp was designed (and executed?) by Theo. Neuhuys. Even though the project was not completed in time, it was sent anyway. In the local newspaper accounts of the presentation, the unique book received appreciative comment, "It is a costly and rare book and would be considered a treasure by any art connoisseur or collector in this or any other country." Although Hubbard asked to have the book returned so that it could be completed, Lawson declined to do so, as he was pleased with it as it was. Overall, this is a remarkable object, not the least because Hunter, a Roycrofter for less than a year, was allowed to carry out the most exacting part. It is thought to be only one of two calligraphed books ever executed by him.*

STAINED GLASS PROJECTS

At the end of March 1905, construction on the renovation of the Inn commenced. The first items Hunter designed for it were copper light fixtures that featured cut-out hearts; these were made in the blacksmith shop. The windows Hunter had been working on for months were installed in Hubbard Hall, the Inn's dining room. Although the date of installation is unknown, indications are the work was completed by that summer. In his autobiography, Hunter described these windows.

> . . . there were eight windows, each about nine feet in height and about three and one-half feet wide. I drew a full-scale design for the windows— clusters of tulips in many colors, with a blue-sky background—and laid the "masterpiece" before [Alice and Elbert Hubbard]. They were overjoyed, or at least they said they were, and gave me permission to order material and construct the windows . . .

Miriam Hubbard Roelofs, the only child of Elbert and Alice Hubbard, recalled the windows' demise, a remarkable event that occurred several months later.

> When [Hunter's windows] were finished and installed, they were much admired not only by the Roycroft colony, but by many visitors. But Hunter was unhappy. He heard the windows called "pretty" which to him was a nasty word. Red tulips and a bright blue sky! Cheery, but art! And Dard had a reverence for "art." This went on all summer until Dard grew desperate.
>
> So one morning after a bad night in which visions of those wretched red tulips had polluted his sleep, he rose early, found a ladder and a hammer—and smashed his windows. He was still on his ladder, hammer in hand, when in walked Mr. and Mrs. Hubbard on their way to breakfast.
>
> Knowing Dard and his temperament as an artist, it is not surprising that between his anger at the tulips and his agony at destroying what he had made, he was weeping. (My guess.) At any rate he blurted out, "I could not stand those horrible flowers."

Then (and this my vivid memory), Father did not blow his top, as the current saying is, but remarked, "Another time, wait for warm weather."

Now the BUT. A Big BUT. Who cleaned up the mess? Dard. Who helped put up the temporary windows? Dard. Who went to work that same day to design new windows? Dard.

Again he worked hard. The new windows were really beautiful— "not pretty." Dard's judgment had profited by his first effort. And I think, costly as the experiment had been, Father was satisfied with the result.

The new windows also featured flowers, but instead of tulips, these were "conventionalized roses in subdued white and green glass." (plate 16) The rose was an international design motif made popular by the Scottish architect and designer Charles Rennie Mackintosh and his wife, artist Margaret Macdonald. Their work regularly appeared in the foreign periodicals that Hunter read, and it is obvious that he drew inspiration from their designs. These windows were Hunter's first foray into modern art on a large scale. The typical Roycroft style, however, was still a mixture of English Arts & Crafts and American Mission. Nevertheless, the Hubbards allowed Hunter to make his artistically modern statement in this very public space. By bestowing their blessings on these and subsequent designs, they sent Hunter a message: Continue giving us fireworks!

Hunter's next window project were those for the Roycroft library, also located in the Inn. This elegant design also features the rose, but Hunter distilled the flowers, leaves, and stems down to simple shapes constructed of clear glass and lead came. (plate 17) Hunter's signature appears in the center of each rose, an *H* conjoined on both sides by a *D*.

In December 1905 and again in March 1906, Hunter wrote to the Opalescent Glass Works in Kokomo, Indiana inquiring about glass for lamp shades. During this period, he designed several lamps, depicting in one, windmills, and in another, a ship in full sail. The wood bases are Mission in style. A more interesting project was the Piano Floor Lamp. (plate 18) While the oak base was Mission, the thin metal rods that supported the shade reflect a more modern style. The stained glass background of the domed shade was made in a variety of colors on which was superimposed a row of encircling dragonflies, a popular design motif. In 1917, Felix Shay, a Roycrofter, wrote a description of Hunter's reaction to this lamp. Although Shay's reminiscences are not to be wholly relied on—he was quite prone to exaggeration—the account may suggest the fate of this lamp, now known only through contemporary postcards and photographs.

[Hunter's] pet aversion was loose-lipped critics. Once a perfect forty-eight lady passed judgment on a huge-domed piano-lamp, made of a thousand bits of stained glass, wondrously blended, by Dard.

"This is very pretty, Mr. Hunter," she praised him tartly. "You surely seem to know your business!" Whether it was the word "pretty" or the word "business" or the way up in G voice, that nettled him, is not for us to say!

"Oh, I do know my 'business,'" he replied evenly. "That the lamp is 'pretty' is only one of its faults. There are others!" And he picked that Lamp to pieces figuratively and literally; bending and twisting it, striking at its vulnerable points, leaving it a wreck! The while passing out one of his rare, sarcastic "Lectures on Art." This time on Stained Glass and its influence on the Centuries and Civilization. "You see," he said finally, "this lamp is just junk."—And it was! He knew what he wanted to do. He did it. He worked constructively, unselfishly, toward a definite accomplishment; nor cheap compliments, nor flashy rewards could dazzle him, or turn him aside!

It is not clear how much of the physical work Hunter actually did in making the stained glass lamps or windows. Undoubtedly, he fashioned the wooden bases and metal fittings for the earliest lamps, but eventually he passed designs to the furniture and blacksmith shops. He probably did most of the stained glass work himself, however, although it is known that he trained at least one woman to help him.*

THE DEATH OF WILLIAM HENRY HUNTER

At the same time that Dard was making great strides at the Roycroft, his father was awarded an honorary master of arts degree from Marietta [Ohio] College. Even though he was suffering from a slight indisposition, he received his degree on 14 June 1906. His condition grew worse, however, and acute appendicitis was finally diagnosed. Dard received a telegram to come home immediately. Following an operation, the doctors thought William's chances of a complete recovery were good, but shortly after midnight on 20 June, at the age of 54, he died. Of course, a long obituary appeared in the

News-Advertiser, but his standing in the community was such that even his bitter rival, the Republican editor of the *Scioto Gazette*, devoted over two columns to William Hunter in praise of his tireless efforts on behalf of Chillicothe.

After his debts were settled, Hunter's estate was valued at over $28,000, not including real estate. His half-interest in the paper was divided between Harriet, Philip, and Dard, and this provided each with a steady income.

DARD RETURNS TO WORK

The sudden death of husband and father shook the family to the core, but soon they were back at work. Harriet started writing articles under a new nom-de-plume, "Rosabel Rosemond," similar to the one she had used in Steubenville. Philip also took up his pen to write editorials. Dard returned to East Aurora and continued working on designs for another set of windows for the Inn.

Another activity that occupied him during this period was pottery. In plate 19, five different pieces of Hunter's ceramic work are illustrated.* (Note: The tall tree vase is not by Hunter; it is marked with the monogram TM or KM.) The tree motif is featured in many of these pieces. The angular trees decorating the mug first appeared in "A Roycroft Dining Room" from the 1905 catalogue, *Aurora Colonial Furniture*. The organic trees and mushrooms appeared in both *Rip Van Winkle* and *Nature*, also from 1905. The dragonfly appeared in the Piano Floor Lamp. Only the candlestick is devoid of decoration.

Like the earlier Iris and Papyrus Vases, these ceramics were made in two-part molds. Unlike them, the 1906 pieces are porcelain, and the glaze, white. However, many pieces were left unglazed, and these have a translucent, satin quality that is more handsome than the glazed versions. The Roman numerals VII and IX, incised into two of the bases, are mold numbers. Hunter's monogram and the Roycroft trademark appear on the bottom of each of these pieces (except for the tall vase), and most of them are dated 1906. Were these ceramics to be a Roycroft product line? It is assumed that they were made with the idea of setting up a pottery shop, but for some reason, the plan was abandoned.

Hunter also made a ceramic lamp base during this period, evidenced by the Roman numeral III incised on the bottom. While his monogram appears, the Roycroft trademark does not, indicating that this may have been intended as a unique piece for his use. The base is in the form of a tree up which wiggle two salamanders (another popular design motif). (plate 20) The shade is made of green and yellow glass representing leaves and fruit; it is called the Salamander Lamp. He also made a ceiling shade to match, which originally hung from six projecting tabs. At some point, Hunter gave both of these pieces to the Hubbards, and they remain in the family.*

The most important graphic design Hunter did that year was for Alice and Elbert Hubbard's *Justinian and Theodora. A Drama Being a Chapter of History and the One Gleam of Light During the Dark Ages.* (colorplate 4) The title page for *Justinian and Theodora* was a double page, the second time he used this format—the slightly earlier *Love Life and Work* was the first. Not coincidentally, the striking black and orange daffodil design has the look of stained glass. The letter forms are more unified and restrained compared with those used in earlier title pages; specifically, the over-slanted letters have disappeared. The title page design, with slight variations, appears throughout the book in the running heads, tailpieces, initials, and the colophon.† With *Justinian and Theodora*, Hunter successfully transferred his modern design ideas to the printed page.

A TRIP TO MEXICO

In the three years that had passed since Philip was diagnosed with tuberculosis, his health had steadily improved. However, the cold, damp Chillicothe winters were particularly hard on him. To avoid this, Harriet and her two sons left Chillicothe in October 1906 to spend the winter in Mexico. They stayed in Cuernavaca where the dry, warm climate was a welcome relief to Philip. Dard kept himself busy visiting the local potteries, and it is more than likely that in one of these he made a hand-built, terra-cotta vase. (plate 21) Based on a native Indian pottery shape, the unmarked vase has three applied salamanders very similar to the ones on the lamp base made a few months earlier. He also visited an Otomi Indian village and witnessed the manufacture of "paper" made from bark beaten flat into sheets, called *amatl*. (Two decades later, he wrote about this experience in his 1927 book *Primitive Papermaking*.)

In January 1907, when Dard learned that he would be named head of the art department upon his return to the Roycroft, he immediately left for East Aurora. His mother and brother remained behind, returning to Chillicothe several months later. Philip's health greatly benefited from the sojourn, so much so that he allowed himself to think seriously about the future, including the possibility of marriage.

HEAD OF THE ART DEPARTMENT

After an absence of three months, Hunter found a number of improvements at the Roycroft. The Print Shop had electric lights and new printing equipment. Subscriptions and production were on the increase, and many departments had been relocated to better accommodate this increase in orders.

Befitting his new status, Hunter was given his own studio located on the third floor of the Print Shop tower. He threw himself back into work. "Dard Hunter—you know Darderino the Swede—well he is making some new Art windows in the Inn. They are the best yet. Take a look. Free with meals, 50 [cents]." Hunter made a number of preliminary designs for the windows to be located in the Inn's Reception Room (colorplate 5), the small office off that room, the vestibule, and the basement. The design the Hubbards approved was not the most avant-garde of the group, but it was modern enough. The proportions, which vary slightly for the differing window shapes and sizes, are harmonious and elegant.

Clearly, by this time, the Hubbards were comfortable with Hunter's modern designs, and their confidence encouraged him to continue in this vein. But there were other problems in their relationship. In November 1907, he wrote Philip,

> I now think of quitting here after Christmas. I must go where I will become something. Maybe to Europe. Can get a good salary if I should go and come back here. I need to get away and see a few things.

He had saved enough money to finance the trip, but he needed a traveling companion, someone who could speak German. Philip was an obvious choice, but he was not strong enough to make the trip. Perhaps his new friend, Roycroft pianist Edith Cornell, who was fluent in German, Italian, and French, would join him—as his wife.

Chapter 4

I think it's up to me to do from the U.S. what these fellows have done from Europe or Vienna rather as only Vienna is much influenced. . . . We can surely get some ideas from these fellows. Dard Hunter

Following his sojourn in Mexico, Philip Hunter was well enough to spend July and August 1907 in East Aurora where he spent most of his time with Clara Ragna Johnson (Dard's portrait photographer). Harriet, who had accompanied Philip, liked her, too, and in September, Clara went to Chillicothe for a long visit. Romance was in the air, but Philip was not the only Hunter smitten. Dard discovered that he was more than just interested in the new Roycroft pianist by the name of Edith Cornell.

Helen Edyth Cornell, her given name, was born in Williamsport, Pennsylvania on 24 March 1879 to Emma and Edward A. Cornell, a pharmacist. Like most young ladies from middle-class families, Edith received a good education. In 1898, she graduated from Miss Bennett's School in Irvington-on-Hudson, New York. There, in addition to piano lessons and other subjects, she studied French, German, and Italian. After graduation, Edith moved to New York City both to play the piano and to hear others play. She soon found a teacher, and as her skills and repertoire grew, she became known in musical circles and was often invited to play at the gatherings of the social elite. Within a few years, Edith was playing recitals and, on a number of occasions, received top billing. As often as she could, Edith took advantage of the city's numerous concerts. She particularly admired the great Polish pianist Ignace Paderewski, and whenever he was in town, she went to see him. It became her greatest wish to take lessons from his teacher, the renowned Polish pianist and composer Theodor Leschetizky, who lived in Vienna. As much as she wanted to go, however, she simply did not have enough money, nor could she go unescorted.

In mid-1907, she visited East Aurora at the invitation of one of the Roycroft vocalists, Jean B. Kerr. Although she had no intention of staying, Edith played for Alice and Elbert Hubbard, and she so delighted them that they offered her a summer engagement. Her decision to remain in the sleepy village, rather than return to New York, was undoubtedly influenced by the presence of a tall, handsome young man with strikingly blue eyes, an engaging personality, and an odd first name: Dard Hunter. It appears that Dard and Edith were immediately attracted to each other, although he was somewhat intimated by her considerable education and her desire to be an independent, professional woman. She liked him not only for his good looks, but because he, too, had a burning desire to make more of himself. She was also four years older than he was, a fact she managed to keep from him for years.

DESIGN PROJECTS

While Dard and Edith were courting, from the end of 1907 through February 1908, he worked on a number of Roycroft projects, the most important of which was Hubbard's new magazine *The Fra, a Journal of Affirmation*. This magazine was not only philosophically the opposite of *The Philistine: A Periodical of Protest*, it was printed on better paper in a larger format. For the cover of *The Fra*, Hunter designed a geometric rose border. (plate 22) This square rose quickly became his "signature" design motif. Not only is his monogram included within the design, but an *H* appears in the center of all of the roses, conjoined with backward and forward *D*s. Except for a short abandonment of this design when he left the Roycrofters in late 1910, *The Fra* cover design remained virtually unchanged until June 1915, following the deaths of Elbert and Alice Hubbard. The popularity of this design was such that variations of his rose and thorny stem motif appeared in numerous Roycroft brochures and pamphlets from 1908 until the demise of the business thirty years later.

In the latter half of 1907, Hunter also made designs for a number of important books, one of which was Alice Hubbard's *Woman's Work: Being an Inquiry and an Assumption*. (plate 23) Her first solo venture into print, Alice wrote about feminist issues for which she had the complete support of her husband. Hunter designed a deceptively simple title page with two sheaves of wheat fanning out at the top. Some of the letters intertwine, others overlap; the tail of the *Q* is bent back and looped over the wrong way. These oddities do not make the text any less readable, however. By condensing letters in the longer words, he organized the whole into a balanced block. While the typeface of the text is rather ordinary, it is printed in a grey-blue ink, which creates a very modern look when contrasted with the yellow ochre of the chapter headpieces and tailpieces, the running heads, and the initials. This color scheme is repeated on the title page.

But the designs that heralded Hunter as a unique artist within the American Arts & Crafts Movement were done for *The Complete Writings of Elbert Hubbard*. (plates 24 and 25) The twenty-volume publication was issued from 1908 through 1915.* While the title page design is wonderful, the letter forms used in the initials represent the apogee of Hunter's style. The solid letters are set against and partially embraced by diaphanous forms. Each letter is held in bounds by a simple border with a square to punctuate each corner. The inspiration for this letter treatment came from an alphabet published in *Petzendorfer Schriftenatlas Neue Folge*. Borrowing from this work, Hunter improved it by enlarging the space each letter occupied and adding the border.

A FUNERAL AND A WEDDING

Although not recorded either in letters or the *News-Advertiser*, it is likely that Dard and Edith announced their engagement around New Year's Day 1908. Jules Maurice "Gus" Gaspard, a Roycroft artist and a close friend of both, drew formal portraits of Dard and Edith, which are dated January 1908; these were probably engagement presents. (plate 26)

Philip was making plans, too. He and Clara Johnson were on the verge of announcing their engagement when, without warning, tragedy struck on 21 February 1908.

Philip Courtney Hunter Passes to His Maker

Philip Hunter, the well known young magician of this city, died suddenly at the home of his mother, Mrs. Harriet Hunter on North High street at four o'clock Friday morning. Although he had been an invalid for a long time his death was entirely unexpected. He retired on Thursday night apparently as well as ever, but was taken with a hemorrhage that brought on the end.

The young man had been making a most heroic fight for health, and several times it seemed as if he must certainly succeed. Stricken with a fatal malady when very young he had more patience than the ordinary man possesses, and for nearly six years he fought against the inevitable. . . . But his Christian fortitude was in vain and he was taken to his Maker at last.

Edith happened to be visiting Harriet and Philip at the time, but Dard and Clara had to travel from East Aurora to attend the funeral. Philip was interred in Grandview Cemetery alongside his father. The grief-stricken Harriet was greatly consoled when she accepted Clara's offer to be her live-in companion.

Dard was deeply affected by the death of his brother, his best friend. At some point, Dard and Philip had made a pact that whoever died first would try to communicate with the living brother. Dard recalled, "Phil drew up an elaborate code involving mystic symbols and devices so that no practicing spiritualists could possibly deceive. After my brother's death, spiritualistic mediums were given every opportunity to act as mediators between us . . . [but] the secret symbols devised by him for direct communication between us never appeared."

Less than a month after Philip's death, Dard and Edith were married on 24 March, her twenty-ninth birthday; the groom was twenty-four. It was a quiet family ceremony in the Cornell home in Williamsport. Harriet and Clara did not attend. The newlyweds left immediately for New York City, where they sailed for Italy.

Alone together for the first time, Dard began to notice one annoying thing about his wife, which he had been able to ignore: her religion. Edith had been brought up a Baptist but, like many of her school friends and fellow Roycrofters, had converted to Christian Science, a burgeoning religion at the turn of the century. Dard had been brought up in the Methodist church, and although he had no strong religious allegiances, he despised the teachings of Mary Baker Eddy, the founder of Christian Science. Fortunately, apart from this, Dard was very pleased with his partner. He wrote home, "Bunny is a great girl and we get along most beautifully. She's the best that ever happened."

After several weeks on board ship, the couple arrived in Naples in mid-April. They took a side trip to Mount Vesuvius and Pompeii, where he was most impressed with the lettering carved into the public buildings, "the most graceful stuff I have ever seen." Before taking the train north, they went on a short excursion to Egypt where Edith, who was far more adventurous than Dard, rode a camel. On their way back to Naples, the ship stopped at Messina, Sicily, and it was here that Dard first saw the preparation of papyrus as a writing support.

ARRIVAL IN VIENNA

As the Hunters traveled north, they spent a few days in Rome, Florence, and Venice. In each city, the couple visited art galleries and churches. They were both overwhelmed by the beauty of the original works of art each had previously known only through reproductions. From Venice, they took the train into Austria. The sleeping car was too expensive, so they sat in the second-class carriage. On 12 May, they arrived in Vienna following an interesting night.

[The train compartment had] only one seat but we both managed to sleep a little. . . . The conductor told me that I could not stay in the same apartment [*sic*] with Bunny as she was a lady. Said I'd have to go to another as men & women could not occupy the same one. I told him I would. After he left I put on Bunny's hat & veil and raincoat so when he came back he did not know but what I was a woman so I stayed all night.

In the same letter home, Dard added:

The Viennese style which is a distinct style of modern art is apparent everywhere even in the butchers shops and places one would never dream of looking for it. They are surely advanced in regard to modern decoration. Nearly all the art manufactured for all Europe is done here and at Munich. . . . I am going out to find work to do as soon as we get settled but I am doubtful if the pay would be very good. Bunny says she is going to try to do some accompanying. She speaks German quite well & is a fine manager. I let her make all arrangements . . . as she is very good & not backward about it in the least. Fine child. . . . Will let you know about my success in getting something to do, if not will need some money in five or six weeks but I'll let you know. I hate to spend money most awfully.

After several days searching for accommodations, the Hunters found rooms at Chimanistraße 15 in the Ober Döbling district of Vienna. Their rooms were part of a small house occupied by the Otto Hertz family. (plate 27) In a letter home, Dard gave a detailed description of their first days.

We get breakfast & the rooms, light & services of maids for about 7.50 per week. The maid is very fine, she comes in the evening and turns down the bed, opens the windows, puts a glass of water at each bed, lights the lights, puts out one's night clothes and locks the door. In the morning she comes in and gets all the shoes and clothes & polishes them & washes the clothes. . . . Both the Herr and Frau of the house are fine, regular and gracious people & make things very nice for us. . . . We went to a restaurant out in a park not far from here last night for supper. It is this regular German cafe with vines on all sides. We ordered beefsteak and almost had a fit when it comes. The steak was in the center of an immense plate, very large & thick & exceptionally good. It was surrounded by the following articles. This is true & not exaggerated in the least. A little dab of each; an egg, water-cress, pickle, butter, horse-radish, mustard, beets, tomatoes, prunes, potatoes, lemon, sardine, roast-beef, cold boiled ham, bologna, spinach, beans, mayonnaise, pork, cucumber, radish, cabbage and lettuce. I took it all down so as not to forget. The cost .40 apiece. What do you think of that. You will say I stretched it but it is the actual truth. . . . They are all very busy now with the festival, it is the 60th anniversary of the Emperor's [Francis Josef I] Ruling. It is to be the first thus ever held in Austria. . . . I am hoping a lot as this town is full of art. Bunny wants to take some lessons, the best teacher charges about 3.20 a lesson and a piano can be rented for 5.00 a month as I understand. . . . Love, D.

Dear Folkes, Dard has not left much room for me but as he has told everything I shall have to wait until later. We are in clover here. It really seems too good to be true. We wish you would come over and join us. We have room for you. Love. B[unny].

As soon as he could, Hunter went to see the exhibitions of the Vienna Secessionists. He also planned a visit to the Wiener Werkstätte (Viennese Workshops), which produced the most important of the Viennese decorative arts.

Tomorrow we go to the "Wiener Werkstätte" and also this week to the model city [Sanatorium Purkersdorf] built by Otto Wagner who originated the modern art movement. There is a church there, the only one in the world built on modern lines [Kirche am Steinhof]. Has windows by Kolo Moser which are the only ones in existence of Biblical figures drawn in the black style which is entirely modern. I have seen pictures of them in the German art magazines before I left the U.S. and thought them the greatest thing I ever saw. I hope I will not be disappointed in the real. . . . I am getting a better idea of the new styles every day as I see so much of it here.

After his first visit to the Wiener Werkstätte, Hunter wrote that he was somewhat disappointed in the work he saw there, but on a subsequent visit, he owned that the objects made there by hand were marvelous. His visits to the workshop and exhibitions not only gave him the opportunity to see the work of the artists and designers he had admired from afar, but more importantly, it initiated in him a resolution:

I think it's up to me to do from the U.S. what these fellows have done from Europe or Vienna rather as only Vienna is much influenced. . . .

Here an artist is not considered a half-witted fool as in many places in the United States. We can surely get some ideas from these fellows.

Finally, Hunter felt able to define his role in the development and popularization of modern art for the American market, but he also must have realized that any attempt he might make on his own would be destined to fail. The only way he could accomplish his goal was to return to the Roycroft, where his designs would reach a very large market. However, it seems that at this point, Hunter was reluctant to do that. (Some have theorized that Hubbard financed Hunter's trip to Vienna so that he could develop a modern style for the Roycroft Shop merchandise. However, because there are no references to such a relationship in Dard's many letters home and because of his requests to his mother to send money from his savings, this theory seems without foundation.)

Hunter's hopes of finding design work in Vienna were dashed when he learned that it was difficult, if not impossible, for foreigners to be employed. He decided instead to try working on a freelance basis, and his landlord's son Fritz Hertz suggested that he approach the publishing house, K. Heller und Sohn. Hunter took a portfolio of some of his drawings and a few Roycroft books including *Justinian and Theodora* to the interview, but even though he returned to Heller's in July, no commissions resulted. Discouraged about the failure of his graphic designs to excite interest, Hunter visited the workshop of Carl Geylings Erben (Carl Geyling's Heirs), the firm that made Koloman Moser's stained glass windows for the Kirche am Steinhof. Inspired by work he saw in progress at Geyling's, Hunter turned to drawing designs for stained glass and glass mosaic. Uncharacteristically, he decided to incorporate the human figure into these designs.

The first of two extant drawings for stained glass is a triptych for a Viennese café. (plate 28) The rather amusing design depicts four waiters (or stout waitresses!) carrying steins of foaming beer. A popular German drinking proverb is delineated in rather cryptic letters at the top and bottom. Hunter later stated that Geyling executed this window, but its whereabouts is unknown. The second design was also reputed to have been made by Geyling for a mausoleum in south Vienna. However, on a slide of the drawing, Hunter inscribed "Höhe Warte," a district in north Vienna. (This author made several visits to cemeteries in these and other locations in Vienna and environs but was not able to locate these windows.) Like the café design, this second work is also a triptych. (plate 29) The mirrored images on the outer panels are highly stylized female figures, each holding a jardiniere from which cascade three branches.* Inspiration for this work and the next was from the poster designs of the Secession exhibitions, particularly the one for the XIV *Ausstellung* of 1902 by Alfred Roller.

Perhaps, the most complex design in Hunter's entire oeuvre was for a large glass mosaic panel. (colorplate 6) Like the funereal window, two female figures face each other, each holding a vase from which branches overflow and terminate in square roses and spirals. The only three-dimensional aspects of the figures are the exposed faces, arms, and hands; otherwise, the design is two-dimensional and geometrical. The whole and various components of the design are bordered by checkerboards that Hunter made more interesting by adding staggered squares of orange, black, and sparkling gold. On the verso of the drawing are two rough sketches of the panel, either as free-standing or mounted to a wall. In front of these, a table and chairs sit. An inscription in Hunter's hand reads, "Used behind a fountain in a Vienna restaurant . . . a panel about eight feet in height." (The Geyling firm's registers were searched to discover if the aforementioned designs were executed, but there is too little information in them to identify any projects except by clients' names. In addition, experts in Viennese art were consulted to find out if any had seen or knew of these designs, but no one recognized them.)

When the prospect of steady employment seemed hopeless, Hunter wrote that he was excited about the possibility of attending the K.K. Graphische Lehr- und Versuchsanstalt (roughly translated, the Royal-Imperial Graphic Teaching and Research Institute). "I find that a foreigner can enter and will look further into it. Everything is there, all printing & lithography, making of plates, designing of every kind." But because the semester ended in early July and he planned to leave before the next began, Hunter had to put aside plans to enroll. To his mother, he explained away his disappointment, ". . . people in school I have found don't know much." (His desire to attend the institute lingered, however, and in 1910, he did become a student; these events are discussed in Chapter 6.)

THE TRIP HOME

As he could understand only a few German words and he had no job, Dard felt increasingly isolated and depressed the longer he stayed; he was looking forward to leaving Vienna in mid-August. Edith, on the other hand, was having a wonderful time. Her piano teacher was Frau Marie Prentner, who, like Paderewski, was a pupil of the renowned Leschetizky. Although the master had a reputation for cruelly dismissing students who did not play to his satisfaction, this did not dissuade Edith from her goal to play for him. However, as the Hunters' departure date neared, Edith knew she was not yet ready for an audience. Prentner, realizing that her pupil had great potential, tried to persuade Edith to stay to gain more experience. Ambivalent about her feelings in this matter, Edith asked Dard what she should do. He turned to his mother for advice.

> I would go back and work at the Shop in order to keep her going. She has a very brilliant future before her and maybe after a year over here she could be able to support me which would be a God send. . . . I would like her to stay. She seems to think that it is a wife's duty to be by her husband's side. My side has gotten along 24 years without her and I guess I can a little longer. As it is now I am only a little dog running along behind and if she gets any more independent I won't even be the dog.

Although Harriet's reply is unknown, Dard's subsequent letters suggest that she fully supported Edith's ambitious plans. To be able to send Edith money, Dard wrote to the Hubbards to find out if they wanted him back. Alice Hubbard immediately replied that she and the other Roycrofters were eagerly looking forward to his return. An exuberant Dard wrote home, "I think now I can get a pretty good salary there. I will have more confidence in myself and they will have more in me." Everything was set for Edith to stay. However, as the day of her separation from Dard drew closer, she had second thoughts. This dilemma resolved itself when two visiting friends of Edith's talked her and Dard into accompanying them to France. And with that, the party left Vienna in mid-August 1908 and traveled by train west toward Salzburg. After an hour or so, they got off in the Wachau valley and walked along the Donau (Danube). They stopped in Gmunden on Traunsee (Lake Traun), a small village that Frau Prentner had suggested as a stopping-off point. The Americans ended up staying for three weeks in Gmunden at Schloss Ort, a quaint castle comprising two buildings: one located on the shore of the lake and connected by a bridge to the other on an island.

When the weather permitted, Dard donned his hiking boots and *lederhosen* and walked to nearby villages. On one of these trips, he visited a Catholic church, which he vividly described to his mother in less than complimentary terms. Having been brought up a Protestant, he found the rituals, images, and relics foreign and uncomfortable. But whatever he thought of the prevailing religion of Austria, he described the people as kind and generous.

In mid-September, Dard, Edith, and their friends set out on foot for Munich, arriving a few days later. From there, they took the train to

Darmstadt, where he and Edith visited the house of Albrecht Dürer. Finally, the party arrived in Paris, and after a tour of the great museums, they left for home. On 11 October, the Hunters were back in America.

BACK AT THE ROYCROFT

After accompanying Edith to her parents' home where she remained for a short visit, Dard went directly to East Aurora. He was eager to translate the many examples of modern decorative art he had seen in Vienna into acceptable forms for the domestic market. An excellent example of this resolve is reflected in changes to the cover of Hubbard's periodical *Little Journeys*. (plate 30) The title on the January 1908 cover, which Hunter designed just before his trip to Vienna, is enclosed in a simple architectural border. The distinctive lettering gives the design a unified look compared to the odd combination of Old English and classic fonts used for the older cover designed by Samuel Warner.

Revitalized by his Vienna experience, Hunter rejected his early 1908 design and less than a year later, completely redrew the cover. He not only used a simpler version of his Viennese alphabet, but also introduced one of the rejected stained glass window designs made for the Inn in 1907. Although these design motifs predate his trip abroad, his bolstered confidence and enthusiasm convinced him, and the Hubbards, that fully modern design was a natural progression in bringing the Roycroft into the twentieth-century and making its products unique in America. The first appearance of the new Hunter design for *Little Journeys* was the January 1909 issue.

Chapter 5

Hand-made things are prized above everything: that is, things of an artistic or decorative purpose. All esthetic articles made by hand are constantly in demand. The machine-made thing is no longer appreciated. Dard Hunter

Inspired by the beautiful silver teapots, cutlery, jewelry, etc., that he saw at the Wiener Werkstätte, Hunter started working in metal as soon as he returned to East Aurora in late 1908. He attempted both hammering and repoussé work on a pair of copper bookends and a letter holder, none of which he finished. (plate 31) Obviously such large pieces were not to his liking for he soon switched to jewelry. Indeed, his easy success in this medium may have prompted him to consider starting a correspondence school. If this school was to succeed, however, Hunter needed to coalesce his artistic thoughts and experiences into a personal philosophy that *must* be rooted in the manufacture of objects by hand; a philosophy that could be easily understood by prospective students. This reverence for the hand-crafted object had been taught to him and nurtured by his father, who had in turn learned it from his father. The Wiener Werkstätte proved to Hunter that this philosophy could form the basis of a successful business. And so early in 1909, he started the Dard Hunter School of Handicraft. He was not prepared, however, to quit the Roycroft. He asked the Hubbards if they minded if he operated this business while still working for them. No doubt fearing that he would leave if they voiced any objection, they agreed to the plan as long as it did not interfere with his other duties.

The first ad for the Dard Hunter School of Handicraft ran in the April 1909 issue of *The Philistine* and included his profile, which he drew after his portrait photograph taken by Clara in late 1904. Before running the ad, Hunter put together a small pamphlet titled, *Make Arts-and-Crafts Things at Your Home*, which was printed by the Roycroft Press. Oddly, the pamphlet and the two hand-illumined initial *M*s were in the traditional Roycroft style perhaps because Hubbard persuaded him that modern design might scare away prospective students.* As it gives a complete description of Hunter's philosophy, as well as being rare, the entire text is quoted.

MOST everybody is becoming more and more particular about the things they wear and place in their homes. Hand-made things are prized above everything: that is, things of an artistic or decorative purpose. All esthetic articles made by hand are constantly in demand. The machine-made thing is no longer appreciated.

Of the things made by hand, metal-work and leaded art-glass are perhaps the most desired. Metal-working includes jewelry and all things made in metal with an art intent. Wonderful effects can be produced by the use of metals and semi-precious stones. What is more beautiful than a hand-made buckle or watch-fob executed in silver and copper, set with a malachite or azurite! Or a jewel-box in copper with silver hinges tipped with corals! Then, too, larger things are made by hand in metal that are most effective and useful. Lamp-bases, nut bowls, paper-knives, trays and dozens of other articles combining the practical and artistic.

Working in leaded and stained glass is also most fascinating. This craft includes, mainly, the making of windows and lamp-shades. The use of opalescent glass of delicate coloring for shades, and lamp-bases made of copper, make, indeed, a handsome lighting fixture. Windows of any size, either in landscape or conventional designs can be used in any home. The same sash that held the old pane of glass can be used for the leaded panel.

Perhaps of all the crafts, these two—metal-work and leaded glass— are the most interesting. The reason these things have not been taken up by lovers of the arts and crafts, is because they have been unable to get the right kind of instruction.

MR. DARD HUNTER is devoting his life to arts and crafts. He has worked in the leading art shops of Europe, and is now foreman of the mechanical art department of The Roycroft Shop. Mr. Hunter's work includes these two most interesting crafts, metal-work and leaded glass. His work is entirely done by hand. He uses no machines. Mr. Hunter, with his experience, can enable you to make in your own home the things that he makes. He will give you instructions, all the tools needed, and materials too, if you desire. You can become a craftsman or craftswoman, without difficulty, with his help. His instructions are simple and easily understood.

Mr. Hunter has two branches of instruction, the jewelry and metal-working craft, and the making of art-glass windows and lamp-shades.

The metal-work instructions include the making of the most simple thing, up to difficult and skillful work. In the first lesson you are given something to do—perhaps a buckle or watch-fob to make in silver and copper. There is no tedious working before you begin to make something; you will be interested from the very start. The instructions are all plain and practical. There is nothing left for you to wonder about. All kinds of soldering, setting of stones, and in fact, everything pertaining to the making of modern hand-made jewelry and metal-work is clearly taught. If you at any time have difficulty you are at liberty to send your work to Mr. Hunter for advice. He will tell you just what is needed. Perhaps he will fix it himself and return it to you.

The leaded art-glass instructions include everything connected with the making of windows and lamp-shades. In this work, as in the metal course, the worker is given something to do from the beginning. The first lesson is making a leaded glass window in a conventional design. One that can be used in your home, as it can be made any size.

Pattern-making, the cutting of glass, leading, soldering, cementing and everything needful in the work is thoroughly treated.

The making of these things can be accomplished in your own home during your spare time. You will be surprised how quickly you "take hold."

The materials used are very inexpensive. The metal required for a piece of jewelry would amount to only a few cents. Glass and lead for window and shade mats sell at fifteen cents a pound. All designs needed are furnished with instructions.

This arts-and-crafts work is entirely suited to ladies and can be taken up by them as readily as by men.

The course in either craft extends over an indefinite period, owing to the length of time the worker has at disposal. The price for either the metal-work course or the leaded art-glass course is $15.00, or $25.00 for both. This includes all tools needed. Don't you think you'd like to make arts-and-crafts things?

DARD HUNTER
CRAFTSMAN
EAST AURORA, N.Y.

                                        CH..

One curious statement that appeared in the pamphlet and the ad is, "In Vienna, Munich and Darmstadt I have worked in the leading Art Shops." It is clear from his letters home, articles in the papers, etc., that this is untrue. What was the purpose of this exaggeration? It made good business sense. A prospective student would feel better sending money to someone who, by virtue of an impressive European background, could teach all that was promised. Hunter had no doubt whatsoever that he could teach his students all they needed to know, and he knew that what he had to offer was of extremely good value. Unquestionably, Hubbard encouraged Hunter to inflate his experience, but this exaggeration did not end there; it was enlarged upon for decades. After a few years, Hunter probably believed it, too.

The instructions Hunter mentioned in the pamphlet were *First Instructions for the Making of Hand-made Jewelry* and *First Instructions for the Making of Leaded-glass Windows and Lampshades.* These were both copyrighted with the Library of Congress on 16 March 1909. While the copies Hunter supplied to the Library could not be found, a copy of the instructions for the jewelry course was recently discovered. In them Hunter explained and illustrated the various steps in making buckles, pendants, rings, stick pins, and brooches. On the last page of the instructions, Hunter included two photographs of objects he had made. (plate 32) Unfortunately, no description of the leaded glass course has been found.

As students enrolled, Hunter kept a notebook of their names, courses, and progress. Students were from all over the United States, representing the geographical diversity of the readers of *The Philistine.* In the first year, 149 people signed up, but only 22 names remain in the notebook; the other pages were ripped out. Of these 22, 10 were women. The amazing success of Hunter's school greatly bolstered his confidence as well as swelled his coffers. The income was not all profit, however, as he supplied each student with a copy of the instructions and the necessary tools to make either jewelry or leaded glass. He also supplied a small amount of copper and silver. He sent each student information about obtaining other materials such as semi-precious stones, stained glass, lamp fixtures, sash bars, etc.* A conservative estimate of $10 per person times 149 would have netted Hunter a profit of about $1500—a considerable sum of money; the average Roycrofter's annual salary was a tenth of that.

COLLABORATION WITH KARL KIPP

At some point in early 1909, Karl Kipp, who worked in the bindery, showed an interest and considerable talent in metalworking. Hunter was glad to have someone whom he could train to take over the art metal work that seemed destined to become an important Roycroft product line. This idea to remove Kipp from the bindery was supported by Hubbard because, later in 1909, a full (and presumably, second) set of metalworking equipment was purchased.* By the end of 1909, Kipp and Hunter, as craftsman and designer respectively, were collaborating on simple copper objects: nut sets, serving-trays, belt buckles, paper-cutters, ash-receivers, etc., which were sold through the Roycroft Shop.†

During 1909 and 1910, Hunter and Kipp collaborated on several projects that married their skills in crafting stained glass and copper. The first was a unique lantern, known as the Chandelier. (plate 33) The Chandelier has four stained glass panels, three of which depict men engaged in making a book; the odd panel is a checkerboard of light and dark green glass. The first panel is The Designer, who holds a roll of paper in one hand and a compass in the other. The Designer was responsible for the book's decoration, typography, and format.

The next panel is The Printer. The printing press was modeled after the wooden one used by Gutenberg in the mid-fifteenth century. In the fore-ground is the ink table, upon which sits a leather-covered dauber used to transfer the ink to the surface of the moveable metal type. The watercolor Hunter made for this panel is strikingly similar to an image entitled "Printer at Press," which appeared on the inside cover of "The Art-Revival in Austria," the 1906 Special Summer Number of *The Studio*. (colorplate 7) Although Hunter signed and dated the watercolor 1904, stylistically that year is too early. Near the end of his life, Hunter wrote that he made the stained glass panels between 1905 and 1908 and that they were later put into the copper framework by Kipp. The most likely date for the watercolor is 1908, and it may have been drawn in Vienna. The Printer's sinewy arms are identical to those of the figures in the glass mosaic design (compare color-plates 6 and 7).

The letter style of the scroll words "The Printer.." in the watercolor is completely appropriate. It is Hunter's version of Gothic *textura*, the style of type used to print Gutenberg's masterpiece, the 42-line Bible of 1454–55. The letters are followed by two diamond-shaped periods. While these are appro-priate to *textura*, Hunter had used x-shaped manuscript periods for many years before this. (Not coincidentally, these periods and dots are identical to those he later used for his typeface.) Although the words "The Printer.." are in the watercolor, they do not appear on the Chandelier panel, nor do titles appear in either of the other two panel scrolls. (Interestingly, Hunter's mon-ogram, cut from sheet copper, appears in the lower right corner of this panel and not on The Designer, which in 1909–10 would have been more appropriate. It is possible that the monogram was added some years later after which time Hunter had become a printer.)

Moving to the right, the next panel depicts The Bookbinder. The piece of furniture in the foreground is a backing press, or vice, into which a sewn, text block has been inserted, spine up. The hammer used to round the spine is in The Bookbinder's left hand. The whereabouts of the drawings for The Designer and Bookbinder panels are unknown. Lastly comes the hinged door made up of squares of two colors of green glass.

The four panels form the sides of a "building" made entirely of copper. While the surfaces of the copper are not hammered, rods ending in spirals with knobs in the center decorate the corners, the roof, and the "eyebrow" mullion windows. Four spiral rod and knob "feet" were soldered to the base of the lamp.

Two early photographs of the Chandelier, one of which is plate 33, show it hanging from long-link chains. It was not electrified, and instead, interior candles may have provided light to illuminate the glass. At some point, the Chandelier was electrified, and eventually, it was hung in the Roycroft Inn surrounded by an incongruous wrought-iron, four-shaded fixture whose stained glass bodies are similar to the checkerboard panel of the Chandelier. Recently conserved, the Chandelier has been returned to its original state.

After the Chandelier, Hunter and Kipp made a number of other lighting fixtures, including the so-called Chapel Lanterns that hung from beams in the Roycroft Chapel and the cylindrical, hanging "Electroliers" with matching wall sconces for the Inn. All of these fixtures have in common most of the following details: spiral-ended rods, stained glass in greens and purples, unhammered copper surfaces, on-lay squares in German silver, and cut-out squares. (In the 1995 restoration of the Roycroft Inn, the "Electroliers" and sconces were replicated to a wonderful effect.)

The apex of the collaboration between Hunter and Kipp was a lamp presented to the Hubbards, probably in 1910. In fact, this lamp is, arguably, the most handsome of all of the objects made at the Roycroft. (colorplate 8) It is called the Salon Lamp because it sat on a table next to Hubbard's dais in the Roycroft Inn's Salon. The shade, in greens and rose pink, was made by Hunter. His signature motif, the square rose, encircles the shade, and his monogram is found in the center of each with an additional *D* conjoined onto the right side of the *H*. Flanked on either side of this are two inward-facing *K*s.* (Kipp later used a monogram of two back-to-back *K*s as his Tookay Shop trademark.) Eight copper rods, each ending in a spiral and knob, form the stem of the lamp. The delicacy of the hammering on the base and shade cap is a testament to Kipp's skills.

By mid-1910, the objects being made by Hunter and Kipp were so good that the Roycroft Corporation's board of directors decided to form the Art Copper Shop to specialize in a product line of metal objects of modern design, as well as take in commissions. As Hunter was no longer making jewelry, Hubbard hired another craftsman by the name of Winche, "Fra Winchewonder," who specialized in this medium until he left in October 1910; nothing more about him is known.*

When Hunter left the Roycroft in August 1910, Kipp was put in charge of the Copper Shop. His reputation as craftsman and designer was quickly established. "He . . . could make anything that would come out of copper sheets by dint of careful thought and good muscle, and . . . he'd rather make special designs than anything he knew." Thus was the bald Karl Kipp, "Fra Baldini," described in the 1910 *Roycroft Catalog: Books, Leather, Copper, Mottos.*† As the popularity of the copperware grew, so did the number of craftsmen employed to produce it. In its heyday, the Copper Shop, excluding the women who worked in the finishing section, had about two dozen workmen.

Things You Can Make

The last student of the Dard Hunter School of Handicraft signed up in February 1910. As Hunter was busy getting all of his assigned design work done before he left for Vienna in August, he did not think about running ads for another round of the school until that summer. Knowing that he would not be around when students enrolled, he entered into a partnership with Kipp. Hunter put together an updated booklet entitled *Things You Can Make.* (plate 34) This time the cover left no doubt that the jewelry and stained glass illustrated in the instructions (presumably the same as those used in 1909) were modern in style. In addition to the fourteen pages of text, there were tipped-in halftones of jewelry, the Dutch Lamp, the Piano Floor Lamp, as well as three of the rejected window designs for the Inn's Reception Room windows. Also illustrated was Edith's red leather jewelry box with hammered silver hinges and escutcheon inset with repoussé copper hearts and turquoise stones. (plate 35)

The tools included in each course were also described and pictured. The costs were increased to $25 for the jewelry course, $20 for the leaded glass, or $40 for both. Once the promotional material was ready, advertisements went out to several magazines. The earliest known appeared in the August 1910 issue of *The Caxton Magazine,* and it is very similar to the one published in *The Philistine* in 1909. In the November issue of *The Craftsman*, a different ad appeared; Hunter's portrait is replaced by two pieces of jewelry. The last sentence of *The Craftsman* ad reads, "Let us send you a description of our plan of teaching and pictures of the things made by our pupils." While this implies that some of the objects pictured in *Things You Can Make* were made by others, it is more likely that all were made by Hunter.

By the time *The Caxton Magazine* ad came out, Hunter had put together additional copies of the instructions and a number of tool sets. All Kipp had to do, while Hunter was away, was ensure that these were sent to the students as they enrolled. As Hunter's notebook contains no listing of students after February 1910, it is likely that Kipp kept the records. It is also possible that the second year of the school was a failure. The Dard Hunter School of Handicraft had plenty of competition from established institutions, and as its prices were comparatively high, it may have priced itself out of the market. In any case, after October 1910, Hunter made no reference to it.*

LAST ROYCROFT DESIGNS

During his last year at the Roycroft, Hunter developed two new design motifs for the Roycroft Press which were significant departures from his established style. The first motif was based on the garland, and its earliest appearance was on the cover of *The Roycroft Leather Book* (1909). (plate 36) The garland was composed of the by-now-ubiquitous square rose and stylized leaves swathed in ribbon.

The second motif might be called the bluebell design, a component of which included the spiral. This design appeared first on the title page, initials, tailpiece, and cover decoration of Hubbard's *The Mintage* (1910). (plate 37) Done in black and white, this design had its origins in *Life Lessons* (1909). Both use the spiraling leaf and stem forms, but the bluebells and cartwheel flowers of *The Mintage* give needed relief to the dense design of *Life Lessons*. The bluebell design was later produced in vivid colors for a Colgate Company box cover.

Hunter's only design that was also a social statement was for Hubbard's brochure, *The Standard Oil Company* (1910). (plate 38) At first glance, the cover appears to be a pleasing arrangement of squares, triangular shapes, and panels, but in his autobiography, Hunter explained the design's significance.

> We did considerable work for one of the large oil companies, a corporation in bad repute at the time because it was regarded as a "trust." Hostile newspapers in editorial comment called the rich company an

"octopus," implying that the corporation reached out and grasped smaller and weaker organizations, to the detriment of the common people. . . . I could not restrain myself, and when I made the design for the cover of the brochure I used a conventionalized octopus as the motif. After the lettering had been added I submitted the drawing to Mr. Hubbard, not fully realizing the gravity of the situation in which a big, well-paying order was at stake. Mr. Hubbard studied the design for fully a minute, and then he looked up at me with a dim suggestion of a smile. I thought I detected a slight twinkle in his brown eyes. I expected to be sent back to my studio to make another, and less pointed, design. But, instead, his only comment was: "That's great, the officials of the oil company are so imbued with their own righteousness they'll never recognize themselves."

One of the last design projects Hunter carried out before he left for Europe was an advertising brochure promoting the Roycroft Inn. This brochure was designed in its entirety by Hunter and consisted of a mailing and an inner envelope that contained a six-page booklet describing the Inn. Accompanying the booklet was a series of six colorful cards of exterior and interior views of the Inn and other campus buildings, printed from wood blocks cut by Hunter.* Of the six cards, there are four views of the Inn: the entrance, the Peristyle, the Reception Room, and the Music Room; and exterior views of the Roycroft [Print] Shop and the Chapel. (colorplate 9) Everything depicted in the cards—furniture, plants, buildings—were stylized and reduced to bare essentials. Clearly, the inspiration for the strong colors was based on Wiener Werkstätte postcards, while the simplistic landscapes bear a strong resemblance to drawings done by Josef Hoffmann's students illustrated in a February 1907 article in *The International Studio* about Viennese arts and crafts schools.† While the text of the booklet creates a feeling of warmth and coziness about the Inn, Hunter wanted the cards to portray the Roycroft campus as *the* place in America to find the latest in modern decorative design.

FAME SPREADS INTERNATIONALLY

Hunter's reputation as an innovative American designer was such that in late 1909 his instructor at the Ohio State University, Thomas E. French, invited him to include his Roycroft/Viennese alphabet in the second edition of his book, *The Essentials of Lettering. A Manual for Students and Designers.* Hunter was thrilled, and he immediately set to work producing his alphabet, in uppercase only, along with the Arabic numerals except zero. In addition to the alphabet, he also submitted a German-language title design for Oscar Wilde's play *Salome*. A number of national and international letter designers were represented in this book, including Rudolf von Larisch. Perhaps it was seeing von Larisch's designs that convinced Hunter that he *had* to study at Vienna's K.K. Graphische Lehr- und Versuchsanstalt where the Herr Professor taught.

Perhaps to impress school officials or prospective Viennese clients, Hunter prepared his portfolio in advance. He drew several title pages for German-language books. One was for a two-part work by Carl [Karl] Larsen (1860–1931). Part one is *Poetische Reisen in deutschen Landen und im [großen] heiligen Russland* (Poetic Travels in Germany and in [Great] Holy Russia); part two is *Im Land[e] des Weins und der Gesänge und im schönen Portugal* (In the Land of Wine and Song and in Beautiful Portugal).* The title page for *Poetische Reisen* is a white-line design emerging from a solid black background, a style reminiscent of wood engraving. (plate 39) It is interesting that here Hunter relied heavily on his old Roycroft designs, such as seen in the 1905 *Nature*, when he could have easily experimented with more geometrical ones, although the borders do show movement in this direction. This title page, drawn in India ink, was made into a line etching and proofed by the Roycroft Press, but no published examples have been discovered.

For the title page and initials in *Im Land des Weins*, Hunter used similar motifs seen in *Rip Van Winkle* and *Nature*. (plate 40) However, this work displays a much more mature sense of line and composition compared to *Poetische Reisen*. The border is very striking, and Hunter used it in two other works from this period: the title page for an unpublished edition of Emerson's *The Essay on Nature* and a bookplate for William Jordan Howard. (plate 41) In the latter, the arrangement of stems, sprouting from alternate sides of the branch, give the border an undulating rhythm, repeated in the roots of the tree, which, like squirming worms, attract two crows.

Two other designs made during 1910 were for works by the then popular German author, Ernst Hardt. One design was for Hardt's play, *Der Kampf ums Rosen rote* (The Struggle for the Red of Roses); the other for *Aus den Tagen des Knaben* (Of Boyhood Days). For this latter work, however, Hunter was confused; he credited the work not to Hardt, but to Gustave Flaubert. Both designs were drawn in black India ink with red and green watercolor added; the central theme is the rose. For *Der Kampf*, the letter style was classical with Hunter's signature overlaps and flourishes. On the verso of the drawing is the notation "in zinc," which implies that the design was made into a line etching and printed, but again, no evidence that it was published has been found.† For *Aus den Tagen*, Hunter used his Viennese-style letters to create forms that are bold and well proportioned. (plate 42)

He incorporated the same rose, leaf, and pot motifs as in *Der Kampf*, but this time turned the flowers upside down. Whether this withering of the roses has any connection with the title is unknown (perhaps signifying the loss of innocence?), but the design is nonetheless an interesting variation on this motif.

A few months before he was to leave for Vienna, Hunter wrote to national and international trade journals with a short biography, original drawings of the German-language title pages (including the incorrectly-credited Flaubert title page), *The Essay on Nature*, the Howard bookplate, and Roycroft title pages for *Manhattan*, *The Mintage*, *Woman's Work*, and *The Roycroft Leather Book*. Those that subsequently published articles about Hunter and illustrated his work included *The American Printer*, *The Pacific Printer*, and *The British and Colonial Printer and Stationer*. (The latter was particularly generous in the amount of space it devoted to Hunter; illustrated articles appeared in the 3 November 1910, 29 December 1910, and 9 March 1911 issues.)

The earliest article appeared in *The American Printer* in October 1910, and it was based on information supplied by Hunter and someone at the Roycroft, probably Felix Shay. With a little rewording here and there, similar descriptions appeared in the other magazines.

> Dard Hunter has been at the head of the art department in the Roycroft shops for seven years, during which time he designed more than half a hundred books, cover plates from several of which are here presented as representative of his work—his style, we may say, tho this is a broad one owing to his very wide experience in the art fields of both this country and of Europe. He is, perhaps, the first in America to introduce here the Austrian and German styles.
>
> Mr. Hunter began, as so many before him have, in a newspaper office, doing the coarse kind of work there required for cheap paper surfaces. He attended many art schools, designed pottery and tile and mosaics in stained glass work in South America; studied in Munich and Vienna, and has now gone to Europe, locating there in a village in the Tyrol in Austria, from which place he will continue work for publishers both in this country and Europe, but with artistic surroundings, and the quiet beauty of environment that makes for good product to sensitive souls.

But even before this article was published, Dard and Edith were on their way to Vienna where each would fulfill a goal begun in 1908.

Chapter 6

"In my portfolios of old work there are many specimens of printing . . . that would pass today as the very essence of the most modernistic. No, I cannot enthuse about the 'moderinistic new note,' as I have been through it long since. This style will not last a great while because it is too easily done, and nothing that is easy ever lasts; it is the difficult that endures." Dard Hunter

On 26 August 1910, the Chillicothe *News-Advertiser* reported the departure two days earlier of the Hunters and their friend, Roycroft binder Sterling Lord. "Mr. and Mrs. Dard Hunter of East Aurora, N.Y., sailed . . . [for] Vienna, where Mr. Hunter will pursue a special course of study." Arriving in September, they eventually found affordable lodging suitable for three at Gymnasiumstraße 16 in the district of Wahninger, a little south of their previous residence. Dard sent home this amusing description of the noisy and malodorous environs.

> One could never imagine anything beautiful or romantic happening on Gymnasiumstrasse anyway. Across the street are the following stores on the first floor: a vegetable shop which displays some fresh things every morning and wakens us up at about 2:30 getting these things in to display. This is the only bit of green we see and is called "an outlook on a garden" in the for rent ads. . . . A Gasthaus [guest house] is next and they have a phonograph that keeps us awake until the vegetable wagon comes. Under, we have a bakery and the sweet smells of baking come up through the air shaft on which our dungeon opens. That is the window opens on this shaft. By dungeon is meant the library, sometimes called toiletten. Also an umbrella store is under us and a delicatessen store where they have much cheese and much stink. Is also a glass shop next door and a bookbinder on the second floor. Right across the corner is a grocery where I go to get molasses to make ginger bread which always burns. One night they gave me crude oil (by mistake) but it was

discovered [in time]. . . . This we have to look upon save for a tree up about a block which relieves a little. The sky is some time seen but never the sun or his sister. Thus we live from day to day.

Almost as soon as they arrived, Dard and Sterling went to the K.K. Graphische Lehr- und Versuchsanstalt. The institute was government-sponsored with about 50 men and women students enrolled each year. Students had to be 18 or older, and after graduating from the two-year program, they were expected to go into the graphic arts or photography.* After observing a few classes, Dard wrote his mother, "I'm not much of a believer in schools but I'm going to try this out a little while." On 20 October, Dard and Sterling enrolled as special students, and each signed up for the same three courses: Lithography, Drawing Composition, and Book Decoration.† Dard foresaw only one old problem, "Nobody down there speaks any English so it is hard to get all. German comes slow but am getting a little gradually."

In both of Hunter's autobiographies, he described the difficulty he encountered gaining entry to the institute, even though his letters home gave no such hint. The following excerpts are taken from his first autobiography, *Before Life Began*, written in 1941.

> For years it had been my ambition to enter the Royal Austrian printing school. . . . I was told that it would be impossible for an American to become a student in this renowned institute as it was under the direct sponsorship of Emperor Franz Joseph, and the rule of the school was that only students who had previously earned diplomas from industrial schools operated by their own governments were eligible. Inasmuch as the United States government operated no schools of art or industry it was almost certain that I could not be admitted. . . . Not to be dismayed, however, [in 1908] I went to the school and had an interview with the Herr Direktor, Dr. [Josef Maria] Eder, K.K. Hofrat. The austere Direktor explained to me the requirements of the Institute and told me emphatically that my entrance was out of the question as I did not possess a diploma from a school under the direct jurisdiction of my own government. While it was not at that time my privilege to enter the famous Austrian school of printing I did learn considerable through observation and self-study during my residence in Vienna.

This implies that Hunter had heard of this institute, or one like it, *before* he went to Vienna in 1908. Although Rudolf Lorber of the Florentine Pottery

Company in Chillicothe could have given him some information, it also
could have come from the 1907 *The International Studio* article on the arts and
crafts schools, the *Kunstgewerbeschulen*, mentioned in the previous chapter.
This article described enrollment requirements, and even though the
Graphische was not an art school, per se, the prerequisites were similar. Men
and women were accepted on an equal basis; foreigners were admitted only
as extraordinary students who paid ten times the fees paid by ordinary students; previous education was required for all including at least four classes
of a *Realschule* (high school); and lastly, the criterion that may have caused
Hunter all of the confusion, no foreigner was admitted without special permission from the Austrian government.

What actually happened when Dard went to the institute in June 1908?
At that time, Dard wrote that the reason he did not enroll was because
classes were nearly over, and he could not start the next term as he planned
to leave Vienna in August. Of the necessary diploma, Hunter made no mention. A few pages later in *Before Life Began*, the story continued.

> . . . [on my return] I was determined to enter the Austrian school, even
> if there were no industrial schools under the United States government.
> There is a way to overcome almost all obstacles and this I proceeded to
> find—I would create an imaginary school and fabricate my own diplo-
> ma! With a large sheet of genuine parchment, an engraved copper plate
> which I had made, and some gold seals and ribbons, I made a diploma
> purporting to be from an American-sponsored institution. The diploma
> was a fairly creditable piece of work and I felt that when I eventually
> unrolled this counterfeit masterpiece in the office of the Vienna school
> even the gloomy old Herr Direktor would have to give in and permit
> me to become a student in his inaccessible school. . . .
>
> [When I returned to Vienna in 1910] I could hardly restrain myself
> until I could go to the Graphische Lehr- und Versuchsanstalt and present
> my forged diploma from a school that did not exist and from a country
> whose government had never operated an art or trade school. I was
> rather hoping that the severe and unapproachable Herr Direktor,
> Dr. Eder, had either died or been retired in the interim, but my hopes
> were not fulfilled. As I entered the dismal office in Bahnhofstrasse there
> sat the same Herr Direktor with the same flowing red beard, ponderous
> mustaches, and heavy eyebrows. I could not detect whether or not he
> remembered me; of this he gave no intimation. I unrolled the parch-
> ment diploma before him; I knew he could not decipher the wording,
> for I had learned in my previous interview that the pompous K.K. Hofrat
> was untutored in English, but I was well aware that to an Austrian the

gold seals and ribbons would be impressive. Dr. Eder evidently wished to convince me that he understood the contents of the document, so he studied it for several minutes; then he reached for his pen and filled out a blank qualifying me for entrance. I was at last to be a student in the most famous school of graphic arts in the world.

As there is no mention of this forged diploma in any of the extant letters Dard wrote home during 1910, perhaps he was reluctant to admit this deception to his mother. Given Dard's penchant for hyperbole, it would be easy to dismiss this diploma as pure fiction, but a few facts have come to light that confirm its existence. First, in January 1909, he wrote to E.W. Turner, a printer in Buffalo, and inquired about buying a used etching press. Eight months later, Dard asked Turner to explain how to prepare an etching plate.* In *Before Life Began*, Hunter stated that he engraved a plate for the diploma, but it would have been much easier to have etched it—engraving was a term often applied to any intaglio process. (It should be noted that the description of the diploma varies subtly but importantly from the same story Hunter tells in his 1958 autobiography, *My Life with Paper*. For example, the phrase about the engraved copper plate was omitted in the later book.)

A more direct piece of evidence for the diploma came up during a conversation this author had with Paul McKenna. He recalled that while researching his book on the Roycroft Print Shop, one of the Roycroft "girls" he interviewed said she remembered donating a piece of metal foil from a candy wrapper to Dard for the diploma's "seal."

On the institute's registration forms, which Dard and Sterling filled in themselves, the applicants were asked to note any practical training or secondary education; both wrote "Roycroft Shop." Nowhere on the form did either list the fictitious school that had awarded the bogus diplomas (presumably, Sterling needed one, too). Perhaps the diplomas indicated that the two men had graduated from the Roycroft. If that was the case, Elbert Hubbard must have enjoyed sharing in the deception as he penned his signature at the bottom of the parchment documents!

DESIGN WORK IN VIENNA

Despite the language barrier, Dard did very well at the institute. After making a few sheets of marbled and paste papers with Sterling, he dropped out of the book decoration course to spend more time making lithographs under his teacher V. Mader. His two extant lithographs, arrangements of stylized plants and fruits, are chromolithographs; that is, they were printed in many colors, each requiring a separate stone. He continued with the drawing composition course taught by E. Puchinger. It is possible that Puchinger's classes were taught at the Kunstgewerbeschule (Vienna's School of Applied Arts) as Dard later stated that he graduated from that institution as well as the Graphische.

At some point in the term, Dard joined Rudolf von Larisch's class in letter design. This was a great relief to Dard as the Herr Professor spoke English. Perhaps because the communication between student and teacher was on a deeper level, Hunter made his most intriguing design under von Larisch's tutelage. It was a title page for *Salome, Tochter der Herodias. Eine Tragoedie in einem Akt* by Oscar Wilde. (plate 42) Although similar to the earlier design drawn for French's *Essentials of Lettering*, to which von Larisch had also contributed, this *Salome* is sensational and erotic. What makes this bold work so unique to Hunter's oeuvre is the depiction of the female figure —the most anatomically explicit he drew. In this drawing, for the first and only time, he portrayed emotion. St. John's countenance, even in death, exudes a strength that conquers the depravity of his voluptuous tormentor. One can almost sense the greed, lust, and blood of the biblical story. *Salome* is Hunter's only work that approaches art; the viewer becomes more than an observer. Unfortunately, *Salome* had no successors.

During Dard's short stay in Vienna, he received only one commission and that was for the January 1911 cover of the American journal, *The Pacific Printer*. (plate 43) This design was printed in two shades of brown on a background of dark cream. The fanciful trees in the jardinieres are loosely based on those found in the title page of *The Mintage* (see plate 37), while the Christmas tree ornament-like blooms echo those found on the Roycroft Inn promotional cards (see colorplate 9). The spiral is a recurring theme in this design as it was in others done earlier in 1910, including the lamps and lighting fixtures made with Karl Kipp.

The Pacific Printer cover was signed: DARD HUNTER •• VIENNA. By electing not to use his monogram, Hunter ensured that the reader knew exactly who the designer was. In addition, the journal proudly announced, with only a few errors:

Another Step Forward

The *Pacific Printer and Publisher* begins the New Year with a striking new cover, designed and drawn especially for it by Dard Hunter, famous as an artist and designer. Mr. Hunter has spent the winter working and studying in Paris, Munich, Berlin and Vienna and it is from the latter city that he sent the drawing.

The *Pacific Printer and Publisher* does not believe in "tooting your own horn" too much, but with all modesty believes that it can call attention to its "new dress" with pardonable pride. It is one of the hand-somest, most striking and effective covers of any printing journal published.

When Dard finally received a copy, he wrote his mother, "Am much pleased with a cover I made for them."

EDITH

Almost as soon as she arrived in Vienna, Edith began taking piano lessons from her old teacher, Frau Prentner. As the Hunters' departure date loomed nearer, Prentner again begged Edith to stay so that she could play for Leschetizky. To his mother, Dard confessed that he did not think it was right for Edith to pursue a career, "I think she plays plenty good enough now but she has ambition to be great which is in the end piffle." As usual, though, he had a change of heart.

> Monk [Edith] will go see Leschetizky soon about a lesson as she is anx-ious to get one as it will be of great assistance to her. Of course she will not learn much from the old squeeze but be of benefit if she teaches in London which same I may have her do. . . . I want to give her all the advantages I can as I would like her to be self-supporting in case I would be took down. It is always nice to have one's wife able to supply the family needs in this age of automobiles and street-cars. She seems much elated at her being able to study and this gives me pleasant thoughts as she tries to do her best in every way. As for her being here alone, would say she is capable of self preservation. Vienna is a mild city and much safer than would be New York, Chicago or Chillicothe.

Fortunately, Edith's scheduled lesson with Leschetizky was moved up. Just as Prentner had known, Edith performed very well, and she was invited to return for a second lesson. However, her most fervent wish having been granted, Edith saw no reason to stay any longer, and she prepared to leave for London with Dard and Sterling.

On 10 February, Dard and Sterling went to the institute for the last time. "To-day at school we got Diplomas with Stamps, seals and signatures. They are very fine, I guess they gave them for an honor to us more than for attending the school as we were not in any special course and weren't really entitled to them." The *Zeugnis* (term report) certified that Dard Hunter, *außerordentlicher Schüle* (special student), took courses from Puchinger and Mader; both graded his performance *vorzülich* (first-rate). Presumably be-cause he joined von Larisch's class in mid-term, he did not receive a grade in that course. Today, Hunter's first *real* diploma hangs prominently in Mountain House in Chillicothe; unfortunately, the whereabouts of the "forged" one is unknown.

LONDON

On 12 February 1911, Dard, Edith, and Sterling left Vienna by train for Hamburg, where Sterling remained to study bookbinding and renew his acquaintance with ex-Roycroft binder, German-born Peter Franck. When Dard and Edith arrived in London, they settled in a residential hotel at 32 Lexham Gardens in Kensington. While Edith unpacked, Dard went looking for a job. Much to his relief, he immediately secured a position at the Carlton Studio. Unhappy about the ordinary kind of advertising work performed there, however, he soon left it for another position.

> This one is at the Norfolk Studio, 3 Arundel Street, Strand. . . . They are going to advertise me which is what I want. Are getting out a circular now advertising my work (CH) will be out in a few days. . . . They seem to like my junk. . . . It's easy for me to get jobs, the hard part is for me to be satisfied with same. I guess I'll never be satisfied until I get a place of my own. . . . I forgot to say that they serve tea in this studio and not in the other so that also is an inducement. I guess I wouldn't have any trouble in getting jobs anywhere but I want to get over the job idea before long. I hate to be bought by the week. I hope some day to do the buying myself.

Within the month, the Norfolk Studio issued a four-page leaflet announcing the availability of its new designer, Dard Hunter. "Two Hundred Million Times" the cover announced with Hunter's monogram prominently displayed. The inside text read:

> Two hundred million times. Think of it! Imagine 200,000,000 booklets or circulars! At a conservative estimate CH has appeared on over two hundred million printed things, such as booklets and circulars, magazines and newspapers. This speaks well for the quality of the Ideas and Designs of CH—the man who from his studio in Vienna has directed the Art Department of one of the largest printing and magazine and book publishing houses in America. CH has a style that is absolutely unlike that of any other artist we know of. That is one reason why his designs get orders. Before returning to America, Mr. Dard Hunter has agreed to work in our Studio. We can therefore offer you—for a limited time— the opportunity of securing some of Mr. Hunter's work. If you are at all

interested, write or 'phone us, when we will arrange to keep any appointment you may make. Norfolk Studio . . . Designers and Illustrators.*

Hunter's many Norfolk Studio designs for brochures, letterheads, and
commercial advertising were based primarily on the garland, the bluebell,
and the spiral. The commission that brought him the most attention was for
Penrose's Pictorial Annual, 1911–1912. This yearbook for the advertising trade
was decorated entirely with his designs: title page, greeting page cartouche,
chapter heads, initials, tailpiece, dust jacket, cover, and endpapers. (plate 44)

When Sterling arrived in London from Hamburg in early May, he had
no trouble finding a job as a bookbinder. Even though his salary was one-
twelfth what Dard earned, it was enough to pay his portion of the rent for
the room he shared with his friend at Lexham Gardens. By the time Sterling
arrived, Edith had already left for Williamsport as both her parents were ill.
Less than a day after her departure, Dard wrote to his mother, "Monk is
always so cheerful that one misses her greatly."

Sterling spent his evenings at the Technical College in Finsbury, and
after much cajoling, he convinced Dard to take enameling and cloisonné
classes taught by Alexander Fisher, who had had work illustrated in *The
Studio.* When classes ended in June, Dard won second prize for a small cloisonné plaque. Not surprisingly, the decoration is made up of elements found
in his graphic work: green heart-shaped leaves on curving stems and yellow
berries against a blue background.

ANOTHER EPIPHANY

Dard worked for the Norfolk Studio only in the mornings, and he initially
spent his spare time at the South Kensington Museum (now the Victoria &
Albert Museum) where he copied patterns found on textiles, which he
intended as designs for book endpapers. One day he ventured across Exhibition Road to the Natural History Museum (now the Science Museum). While
wandering through the exhibits, he came upon a model of a papermaking
machine. As he was familiar with the paper machine—he had lived across
from a papermill in Steubenville—he did not pay it much attention, but he
was drawn to the simple equipment used to make paper by hand.

The mould and deckle upon which paper was formed particularly held
his interest. He was also fascinated by the designs in wire sewn onto the
metal "cloth" that covered the wooden mould. Determined to find out
more about these designs, called watermarks, he spent many afternoons in
the British Museum Reading Room perusing books on that subject and on
the history of papermaking (see Appendix A. Papermaking by Hand: A
Brief Description of Materials, Tools, Personnel, and Techniques). In a

notebook, he wrote synopses of those books; later, ones on lithography, typography, and letterpress printing were added. He also noted the books he wanted to buy, and when he was not working or reading, he was browsing the bookstores around the British Museum and along Charing Cross Road. Thus the seeds for Dard Hunter's library and collection were sown.

As technical questions came up in his readings, Dard went back to the museum to look at the artifacts. He knew, however, that he would never understand paper unless he made it. In his autobiography, he briefly described this important phase in his life.

> . . . from the labels on the exhibits I was able to ascertain the names of the firms responsible for the presentations of this material to the Museum. The papermaking moulds had been made by T.J. Marshall and Company, Stoke Newington, North London, a firm established in 1792. . . . I visited the shop . . . [where] I found Mr. Dudley Marshall, the grandson of the original founder of the firm . . . a portly old gentleman, [he] had no end of interest in my desire to learn about the making of handmade paper and did everything in his power to assist me in my quest. . . . A small paper-making vat, a beater, and other utensils for testing hand-moulds were fixtures in the basement of the building and it was in this dark, damp cellar that I first made paper by hand.

This first experience was also mentioned on a fragment of a tongue-in-cheek letter Dard wrote in early July.

> . . . I am quite great over here. I get about as much pay as any designer in England. However I have quit to take effect to-morrow. We will be off [on a walking tour] about Wednesday or Thursday as I have to go to the British Museum & make drawings of watermarks from 1390 to 1700. At the Mill to-day I got along nicely. I can make paper as well as anybody and will put in a plant when I get settled if it ever happens. I am quite a genius and all should be very proud to know me as I am far beyond any of you. . . .*

At the Science Museum, Dard also examined the materials and equipment used to make type for letterpress printing. Of course he had done this type of printing from an early age, but it was probably not until he took von Larisch's course that he first learned the traditional steps in making type. This peaked his interest enough so that even before he left Vienna, he was collecting type specimen books.

In the same way that Dard learned about the Marshall company, he discovered that much of the museum's typography materials had been donated by the H.W. Caslon Company. He wrote the firm asking if they had any out-of-date equipment he could have. They replied, "[We] have much pleasure in presenting you with an old Hand Mould which was used in our Foundry upwards of a hundred years ago. . . . There are very few of these old Hand Moulds now left and in time they will become very valuable." This two-part mold, made of wood and metal, was used for casting 20-point type. (Although never used by Hunter, it later served as a model for a mold he fabricated to cast his 18-point type. In 1921, he donated both molds to the Smithsonian Institution.)

In their spare time, Dard and Sterling talked about what they would do when they returned to America. One recurring plan was to go into business together. Sterling would be the bookbinder, but Dard's role changed constantly: farmer, bookseller, book printer and publisher, lithographer, papermaker, or a combination of some, or all, of these. Perhaps the long walk in the country, which he and Sterling planned, would provoke a decision. But the primary reason for the walking tour was to avoid London during the celebrations and large crowds expected for King George V's coronation in July. When Dard asked his bosses for a week or two off, they refused, and he promptly quit.

As the grandstands went up along the parade route, Dard and Sterling left town with their luggage slung over their backs. They headed west toward Wales with plans to stop in Bath and Chester. There is only one letter and a postcard extant from this trip, and they indicate Dard's dramatic shift in interest from Secessionist Vienna to Tudor England. In the same epiphanic way, they are reminiscent of his letters about Old Mission furniture written eight years earlier.

> We passed through Newent where we had a cold joint & some stout in a very quaint inn. All of these places with beamed ceiling & large fire places with settles all around . . . [the Red Lion Inn] was one of those places that I only thought existed in pictures. . . . At Fown Hope in front of the church are the old stocks & whipping post, it is a very old town & all the houses are thatched & half-timbered. . . . The country is beautiful, the finest I have ever seen, everything is such a vivid green & the flowers are abundant, especially roses which grow all over the houses and are every color.

The post card pictured a half-timbered and thatched schoolhouse in Woebley in the Cotswolds. On the verso, he wrote: "This is a fine old place, will build something on these lines. I have learnt how to make a thatched roof." And indeed, less than a year later, Dard built a small paper mill complete with a thatched roof and a water-driven wheel.

Once back in London, Sterling decided to return to America while Dard was welcomed back at the Norfolk Studio. But soon impatience set in. He wrote Edith, "I am beastly tired of it here. I want to get the farm found so it can be in the making this winter. . . . This is not my life work here & it is simply floating so what's the use in going on with it here. I have all the experience I can get here." An idea was forming to establish a paper mill and a type foundry, and to print lithographs while running a farm. But he could not leave as his mother, Clara, and an aunt had arrived for a several-months visit to the British Isles. Finally, in late October, Dard left for home in their company.

Dard went straight to Williamsport to be with Edith, eager to discuss his plans with her. In the months they were separated, she had decided to set aside all thoughts of having her own career and to concentrate on her marriage. She and Dard now had to find a place where he could build his paper mill, and she could establish a home for their future family.

EVALUATION OF HUNTER'S DESIGN CAREER

When he arrived on the Roycroft campus in mid-1904, Hunter's goal was a simple one: learn to make good furniture by hand. Almost as soon as he arrived, however, the Roycrofters realized that he was special. During an interview with Patricia Scott, the daughter of a Roycrofter recalled,

> [The] respect for Hunter's abilities was shared by everyone at Roycroft. . . . Hunter was in a hurry to learn everything possible. He methodically worked himself from workshop to workshop, beginning with the printing shop all the way through to the illuminating shop that was usually occupied by women only. He impressed everyone with how quickly he absorbed the materiel he was presented with and with the facility and skill of his craftsmanship. They were also impressed with the very high standard of perfection that he set for himself.

Within a year of his arrival on campus, visitors to the Roycroft Inn and other campus buildings saw Hunter's designs in the stained glass windows, lamps, and lighting fixtures.* His designs were not limited to East Aurora, however. They were familiar to the millions of readers of the books and periodicals published by the Roycroft Press. In addition to being available on the campus and through the mail, Roycroft products were sold in large department stores all over the United States.

According to the Norfolk Studio leaflet, Hunter's monogram appeared two hundred million times. But did the public know who was responsible for those designs? Unless paying a great deal of attention, readers could easily overlook the designer's tiny monogram on the cover of, for example, *Women's Work* (1908). Only if a reader took the trouble to read the colophon at the end of the book would she have learned that the "Title page, initials and ornaments designed by Dard Hunter, the typography by Charles [Cy] Rosen, and the whole done into a book by the Roycrofters at their Shop." Occasionally, Hunter's name was mentioned in advertising that appeared in Roycroft periodicals and catalogues, but generally the buying public was unaware of the names of the Roycroft artisans. The situation was not helped by Hubbard, who often publicized his Roycrofters with their fraternal names, e.g., Fra Baldini and Fra Winchewonder. (Interestingly, Hunter seems not to have been given this particular appellation, although he was not without nicknames, "Darderino" being the most common.)

While it would be very gratifying to say that Hunter influenced modern American graphic design, it would be incorrect. Modern letter forms such as his did not commonly appear in American trade journals and magazines until many years after he left the Roycroft, as perusal of *The American Printer* over the years 1909–17 confirmed. In 1909, Edmund G. Gress in *The American Printer* commented:

> The secession style is worthy of study, as are any new or old ideas in typography, for the typographer who advances is he who keeps up to date and allows no cobweb or other evidences of inaction to find dwelling place in his brain-pan.

But no one except Hunter seems to have taken this advice to heart. The following note appeared in the same periodical two years later, "Dard Hunter . . . used to puzzle readers of the *Fra* and the *Philistine* by some of the "secession" or "insurgent" designs he got up for those publications. . . . His style of lettering and design is unique and popular. . . ." While Hunter's design successes were substantial while he was a Roycrofter, they faded on his departure. Some of his graphic designs continued to be used by the Roycroft Press after he left, but only a few successfully survived the transition; *Pig Pen Pete* (1914), based on *White Hyacinths* (1907), is one example. Karl Kipp was the one major artisan at the Roycroft who continued to base his designs on Hunter's.

In 1908, Hunter had determined "I think it's up to me to do from the U.S. what these fellows have done in Europe." By 1910, he realized that this goal was a futile one: Secession-style lettering was not going to appear on American butcher shops through *his* efforts. Hunter, along with every other American artist working in the decorative arts was hampered with the fact that, traditionally, only artists working in painting, sculpture, or architecture influenced aesthetic taste. This taste was the domain of the rich, and because the vast majority of Roycroft products were purchased by people who lacked wealth, they had no power to change aesthetic taste. Even the Wiener Werkstätte, which made very costly decorative arts, considered the American market inadequate until 1922, when it opened a store in New York City.

In London in the summer of 1911, Hunter was trying to decide which path to travel down: the well-trodden modern design one, or the uncharted but challenging traditional book arts one. That September, he wrote to the publishers of *Il Risorgimento Grafico* in Milan, Italy, sending them the blocks (line etchings?) of *Salome* and a drawing (also of *Salome*?) for reproduction. They acknowledged the receipt of these items and also included some mild criticism and a suggestion.

> The drawing for cover you have sent us is very notable for distinction and we are very pleased to reproduce it, but we have noted this drawing be of german style and we should have desired for the number of our Review, in which we will write of your work, a drawing for the cover in which result greater your personality, your artistic and original style. Can you make a drawing with these characteristics? We use the drawing you have sent us for a cover of another number.*

These last comments must have caused Hunter to reflect that, for years, he had been earning a living as a designer, but how much of this work could truly be called original? It was in the sense that few in America were employing the same motifs, but otherwise much of his work was inspired by others. Until he discovered watermarks and hand papermaking, he assumed he would continue earning his living as a designer. Once he made paper by hand, he realized that he wanted to pursue a line of work that would be done primarily for his personal satisfaction. If this work happened to be influential or profitable, it would be a bonus only. However, the knowledge that he could earn money as a freelance designer gave him the courage to strike out into the economic uncertainty of experimenting with hand paper-making, typography, and printing. He assigned only one criterion to this work: it had to be done by hand, by his own labor.

Chapter 7

Even these books did not please me. . . . Perhaps it is better that I did not reach my ideal, for had this been accomplished life would have ceased to be interesting. When we cease struggling we cease growing. Dard Hunter

After their reunion in Williamsport, Dard and Edith returned to Chillicothe in late 1911. From his mother's home, Hunter began the process of finding a suitable property where he could farm and experiment with hand paper-making, typefounding, and printing. To fulfill every aspect of his dream, the property had to include not only a house and arable land but also, most important of all, a plentiful source of pure, running water. Advertisements were placed in newspapers such as *The Christian Science Monitor* and *The New York Times*. At this point, Hunter also began cutting punches for his type.

That winter, while they waited for responses to their ads, the Hunters returned to East Aurora for a few months. This return is somewhat surprising as just a year before, from Vienna, he wrote his mother this scathing indictment of the Roycroft.

> My mind however does not run East Aurora way as I believe I have fully recovered from that disease. Poetically speaking I have been vaccinated by the virus of something better, something nearer the ideal. My time there is spent I believe as my mind seldom reaches back to that beautiful little village with its surface of good cheer and its gizzard of strife, jealousy and hate.

But Hunter was not a man who held negative thoughts of people for long (and it is not at all clear to whom he was referring in this quote). Bolstered by the exciting, challenging career that lay before him, he probably enjoyed his stay in East Aurora in early 1912 more than any other period except those halcyon days eight years before. Although he rarely wrote of the Roycroft once his reputation as a printer and author was established, he occasionally recalled Elbert and Alice Hubbard, "[They] were both remarkable individuals—sincere, kindly, generous, understanding. I shall always remember them with the deepest affection."

In addition to designing several commercial booklet covers for Hubbard during this visit, Hunter probably designed business stationery for The Oakwood Binders and had it printed up by the Roycroft job press. The Oakwood Binders were his friends Sterling Lord and German émigré Peter Franck, also an ex-Roycroft binder. By March 1912, the two men had set up shop in Pittsfield, Massachusetts. (Oakwood was the street Lord and Franck had lived on in East Aurora.)

While among the Roycrofters, Hunter may have re-read an article by Natalie Curtis, "An Historic House on the Hudson," published in *The Craftsman* in 1909.* The article described an eighteenth-century house with a farm located near the western bank of the Hudson River in Marlborough-on-Hudson, New York. Perhaps Dard and Edith took the train down to Wolfert's Roost, as the house was then called, and discovered that it was for sale, but no matter how he found out about the property, once Hunter saw it, he knew it was the perfect place to set up his enterprise. By May 1912, he was the proud owner.

Where did Hunter get the money to buy the house? Certainly the property was not purchased with savings from his Roycroft and London salaries—all of that had gone toward the Hunters' living expenses abroad. It is more likely that his share of his father's and brother's inheritances, which were considerable, was finally put to use. Harriet Hunter may also have contributed some money toward the purchase just to see Dard and Edith settled.

The following description of the house and land is from a brochure Hunter put together when the property went up for sale in 1917. (plate 45)

During the reign of Queen Anne (or in 1714 to be exact) Gomez, a Spanish Jew, was given a grant of land comprising six thousand, nine hundred acres along the Hudson. He selected the most picturesque spot in this vast tract and built a one-story stone house. He used the native stone and built to last. He made the walls three feet thick and at either end of his house he built a great stone fireplace. . . . In his stone house he had one large trading room and two smaller rooms—one used for furs, the other for beads. Gomez lived and traded at this stone fortress for a great many years. He became rich and at the time of his death he was one of the wealthiest and most respected of New York merchants.

The trading post of Gomez subsequently changed owners, and in 1772, four years before the Revolutionary War, it was bought by a

patriotic Dutch-American named Wolfert Acker . . . [who] built upon
the stone one-story house a second story of brick, laid English-bond.
These bricks and tiles were made by Acker's negro slaves, in homemade
moulds from clay gathered along the banks of the Hudson.

Wolfert Acker's house was the meeting-place of the Whigs in all
that part of the country and stood for the great principle of political
independence . . . [Acker] lived in this house until about 1830, when he
died, and he now lies in the quaint village graveyard in Marlborough.

The next purchaser of the Gomez-Acker house was Henry Armstrong, a gentleman of the South. He came with his bride for their
honeymoon and remained sixty years! During his occupancy the novel
of the Civil War, "Rutledge," was written. Many scenes of this old book
are laid in this historic house.

The next two owners are unimportant, but they both appreciated
the charm of the place and did not disturb the old-time atmosphere.

In 1912 Dard Hunter purchased the property, making but six owners in the 203 years of its existence. . . .

This property is in Orange County, N.Y., about 58 miles north of
New York City. It is 5 miles north of Newburgh, a city of 30,000, one
mile south of Marlborough, a village of 2,000. . . . The property contains
27 acres with some 15 acres in woodland. The property is in the heart of
the Hudson Valley fruit belt and about eight acres are set out in paying
fruit—young apples, bearing pears, grapes, currants and some 2000
raspberry bushes. A large garden, with asparagus, rhubarb, currants,
gooseberries and peaches; garden and farm tools, etc.

. . . The lower floor contains living-room, dining-room and library
all thrown together by large arches . . . [and] is completely furnished
with Craftsman furniture in oak, some of which was designed especially
for this house.

For many years, it was thought that Hunter had bought the Craftsman furniture, but it almost certainly was purchased by John A. Staples, who owned
the house from 1904 to 1911. Gustave Stickley, whose company made the
furniture, was a good friend of Staples's and a frequent visitor to Wolfert's
Roost.* Staples sold the Craftsman furniture with the house to John Ballard
(1911–12), who in turn sold it to Hunter. (It was customary then to sell
houses furnished.) The upstairs bedrooms were in the colonial style, and
Edith was responsible for adding a few antiques including a chair that was
covered with a Wiener Werkstätte fabric purchased in Vienna.†

Not surprisingly, Hunter made some stained glass windows during the
early months of 1913. For the library, he made two panels, each with a

landscape in a cartouche surrounded by plain, leaded glass. These panels were set a few inches into the deep window well in the east wall and appear to have had hinges allowing access to the outside window. A striking room divider was set into the upper part of an arch between the dining room and the library. This five-section panel was made of leaded glass squares into which were set colorful ships in two cartouches. Again, sections were hinged to allow ventilation.

A year after Hunter bought Wolfert's Roost, he decided to drastically change the facade of the house. He wanted to add Greek columns and other classic architectural details to the porch off the kitchen, as well as the front entrance. Fortunately, this plan was never carried out, possibly because of the cost, and thus the historic facade of the house was preserved.

As for farming, Hunter selected a five-acre meadow on land west of the house and set out raspberries, gooseberries, and grapes. The first crop came in in 1914, but for a variety of reasons, the farm was not a success.

THE PAPERMILL

In summer 1912, construction began on the papermill. Hunter chose to build it on the site of an earlier grist mill located just below the dam on Jew's Creek, also called Acker's Creek, just across the Huckleberry Turnpike from Wolfert's Roost (see plate 45). Wishing to forego all modern conveniences in the making of his paper, Hunter planned to use a waterwheel to provide power to the mill; this power would run a beater used to macerate rags into pulp for papermaking.

The architectural style of the quaint mill was based on the half-timbered, thatched buildings Hunter had seen during his walk in the Cotswolds the previous summer. The mill was a very modest building, about 14 x 16 feet, which fit unobtrusively on the site; indeed, rather than cut down obstructive trees, Hunter incorporated one into the porch. (plate 46) The foundation and fireplace were made with fieldstone and the walls of "oak beams from the former grist mill that had been stored in the barns and the hand-moulded bricks left over when the second storey of the house was built by Acker's slaves. The roof . . . was thatched with rye straw grown for the purpose in a five-acre meadow above the old house." The windows complemented the English character of the building: simple leaded glass quarrels, or diamond-shaped panes. In summer, window boxes filled with flowers added color. The only hints of Hunter's past designs could be seen in the front windows' bottom saddle bars, or supporting rods, which ended in spirals, and in the two small, otherwise plain, windows which flanked the chimney. These were each decorated with a leaded CH.

A narrow porch ran the length of the front and along the east side of the mill. Access was via a rather rickety-looking footbridge, although it was also possible to walk along the top of the dam to reach the porch. Hunter had the stone dam heightened to make the level in the pond higher so that water could be diverted via the race to the wheel. He hired a local wheel-wright to make the overshot wheel of cypress and pine; he purchased the gearing mechanism, shafts, and bearing boxes. The mill and waterwheel were nearly completed by the time winter set in at the end of 1912.

PAPERMAKING BEGINS

Even though the mill was unfinished and he had no beater, Hunter could not wait to make paper. In August 1912, he received his first pair of paper-making moulds—one wove, one modern laid—from the T.J. Marshall Company, the English firm where he had first made paper. (For a detailed description of the papermaking moulds and watermarks associated with Dard Hunter, see Appendix B.) That November, Marshall's shipped Hunter sixteen pounds of beaten pulp from linen cuttings. Although the length of time it would have taken for the pulp to reach Hunter can only be surmised, it must have been quite smelly by the time he received it. Working some-where in the house, which he now referred to as Mill House, he formed a sheet or two of paper with the well-rinsed pulp on the small moulds. In the Hunter archives, there is a partial sheet with the pencil notation: "First sheet of paper made by Dard Hunter at his mill in America. From pulp brought from the Batchelor Mill in Kent. 1912." The contradiction in this inscription can be clarified by the fact that Marshall's only made hand moulds and dandy rolls. Therefore, it had purchased the beaten pulp from the Joseph Batchelor mill in Little Chart, Kent. (Incidentally, this was the same mill that made paper for William Morris's Kelmscott Press.)

During the long winter, Hunter continued cutting punches, and he organized his library. (plate 47) Instead of designing a personal bookplate, he used a stamp, one advantage being that it could be applied to samples of paper and drawings as well as books.* (plate 48) He also had time to set his priorities for the coming year. Because no one in America was making paper by hand on a commercial basis, artists and printers had to buy expensive, imported papers. Hunter was sure that a market existed for American-made paper, and he decided to cater to this market. But while a successful business would give him an income and a reputation, its main purpose was to provide him with the experience and expertise he so keenly wanted. Realizing that he was not ready to make paper for professionals, he decided to make stationery: small sheets, note cards, and envelopes. He ordered a second pair of slightly larger moulds from Marshall's in early 1913. Hunter also wanted to offer custom watermarking, and he began experimenting with both simple wire and the more complicated, so-called light-and-shade, shadow, or *chiaroscuro*, watermarks (see Appendix B).

While Hunter could experiment with papermaking without using a beater, to make large quantities of paper of uniform quality, the machine was essential. After writing to many firms, Hunter finally ordered a small beater from the Mills Machine Company in April 1913.* By the middle of that year, he had either purchased or made the following pieces of equipment, which were installed in the papermill: an oak and iron screw press; a copper-lined, cypress vat; a rag cutter and duster; a boiler for processing linen and cotton cuttings; and papermaking felts. He inquired about buying a used plater, which imparts a smooth surface to paper, but no evidence has been found that one was purchased. His supplies included soda ash to soften and remove any sizing from the rags, bleach to lighten them, animal glue for sizing the sheets, and gum for sealing envelopes. After a few false starts, the beater was soon processing the half-stuff purchased from American mills.

By June 1913, he had made a variety of note cards and papers with matching envelopes, which were packaged up and sent out to prospective clients. Convinced he now knew enough about papermaking to make book papers, Hunter purchased a pair of large, modern laid moulds from the English mouldmakers, W. Green, Son & Waite. Paper made on these moulds could be folded to make a variety of book sizes including: a folio (full sheet folded once = two leaves = four pages); a quarto, abbreviated 4to (full sheet folded twice = four leaves = eight pages); an octavo, 8vo (full sheet folded three times = eight leaves = sixteen pages); etc.

In addition to plain sheets made on the new moulds, Hunter made decorative endpapers using aniline dyes to color the pulp green, gray, blue, brown, or rose. First, he formed a sheet in a base color. Then into the still wet sheet, he carefully swirled pulp of a different color, almost as if marbling. He also seems to have made several partial dips in different colored pulps to create patterns.† (plate 49)

An early design for his letterhead included a post of paper in a screw press flanked by his initials with the words, PAPER MADE BY HAND AT THE HUNNY SUCKLE MILL, alongside.‡ Actually, this might have been a joke as it could be a pun on Edith's nickname, Bunny, but in any case, he decided on the simple and direct DARD HUNTER MILL. By 1914, he had cast enough type to print the letterhead, but as he did not have a press, he probably set the type and prepared the art work for line etchings for the large letters and the press device, and sent them to the Roycroft job press. (plate 50)

Throughout 1914, he received orders for paper, but he could only fill the small ones because the wooden press did not function properly, and there never seemed to be enough water in the millpond. In early 1915, he strengthened the press, and the situation improved somewhat, but he could not do anything about the water level. Generally, his business was not a success, although he had many inquiries. While people were interested in unique, handmade paper with custom watermarks, only a few were willing to pay for the luxury.

While Hunter was busy working in his mill, war was brewing in Europe. It was during the first week in August 1914 that the fragile peace was broken. President Woodrow Wilson wanted America to maintain neutrality and most citizens agreed. Although interested in the events taking place across the ocean, Americans were not significantly touched by them until 7 May 1915, the day a German U-boat sank the British liner *Lusitania* off the coast of Ireland. Among the 1,198 dead were 128 Americans, including Alice and Elbert Hubbard. On Independence Day, Hunter attended the impressive memorial service arranged by Elbert "Bert" Hubbard II, who took over the Roycroft upon his father and stepmother's death.

THE BOOK HARMONIOUS

During the latter part of 1914, Hunter tried to locate a second-hand proof press, but he could not find one at the right price; what printing projects he had in mind are unknown. Once winter set in, he retreated to Mill House to continue working on his type and to catch up on his reading. At this time, he was also compiling a bibliography of the papermaking and watermarking titles in his library. That December he almost certainly read "Europe and Good Printing in the Days of Peace" in that month's issue of *The American Printer*, which included comments about his mentor Rudolf von Larisch.

Austria and Its Influence

". . . [Professor Rudolf von Larisch] has expounded his tenets in his 'Unterricht in ornamentaler Schrift,' [*Teaching Ornamental Writing*] a work of great value to all interested in this subject.

"What he aims at is form, configuration and spacing, to add rhythm to the letters themselves, and to harmonize one with another in the building up of the word; for even the simplest of words rightly rendered should be decorative. He does not consider the creating of new forms of paramount importance, but sets much store on the relation of the letter to the word, the word to the sentence. These should fit into one another in the same manner as the component parts of a perfect piece of architecture; for, as in architecture we see the foundation of all art, so in lettering the basis of all book decoration is to be sought. This theory is supported by the study of early printed works, and more particularly so in those printed towards the end of the sixteenth century. Here we see the aim was to achieve harmony in type, ornament and illustration. This, too, is the aim of those who produce artistic books other than those issued by the ordinary publisher."

After reading this, perhaps Hunter realized that the next logical step was to form a personal philosophy about the manufacture of the artistic book by combining what he had learned about making paper and type with von Larisch's ideas about printing and typography. To that end, Hunter began drafting a series of articles on the book arts. In January 1915, he wrote H. Alfred Fowler, editor and publisher of the book lovers' quarterly *The Miscellany* asking if Fowler was interested buying his handmade papers and in publishing an article about his work.* Fowler replied,

> I have long been an admirer of various handmade papers, having printed several books on the various stock papers, but it has never been my pleasure to make the acquaintance of your paper before.
>
> I did not know that such work was being done in America! Your watermarks are quite wonderful and I did not know that that sort of thing was being done in America either. Do you make the white stationery with the head (of Byron, is it not?) [Hunter's Large Portrait] watermark for sale? If so, I should be interested in receiving information concerning the price of it.
>
> Your remarks in re an article in The Miscellany about your work are also of much interest to me. . . . Would it be possible for you to prepare the article and send it to me? You would be far more conversant with the finer points of the work than I would be and so the article would be far more satisfactory, generally, if you would prepare it.

As the deadline for the next issue was less than a month away, Hunter immediately sent Fowler a draft of "The Lost Art of Making Books." The article was less a description of Hunter's mill activities, than a condemnation of both American and English private presses. Generally, Fowler liked the article but suggested that the author tone down his more caustic comments. Hunter took his advice and in the final version, his criticisms were quite mild. The article, which appeared in the March 1915 issue of *The Miscellany*, presented Hunter's view of the "book harmonious."

The Lost Art of Making Books

It has always seemed to me that the printer did not penetrate deeply enough into his art. Of course it is understood that in speaking of the printer the private press book producer is implied. In examining the specimens of books of this kind it would appear that printing is a lost art, in the truer sense. In the ancient times a printer was something more than a man who simply brought types and paper together and formed a book: he was a typefounder and ofttimes a paper maker as well. Nowa-days our printers, even the best of them, are content to buy their paper and types, which of course are good but are not their work. The type has perhaps been designed by an artist who did not even know of the existence of the press proposing to use it and has been made in one of the great foundries entirely by machine.

The paper probably comes from a foreign country from mills that are unacquainted with the book of which their paper is to form such an important part. The type and paper were never made to be used together, they were not made for each other. The printer combines the type and paper, the least part of the work, and then his name goes in the colophon as the maker of the book! The printer therefore has done little: he sets the type (in the making of which he has had no part), arranges the margins, and attends to the several details. Then with the paper that has been made by men who have no interest in his book and in whom he has no interest, he makes the printed page.

I have designed and seen through the press over a hundred books, from duodecimo to folio, made in this same way. I never felt that I was doing very much, and I was not, for I was simply *printing* books, not *making* them.

The man that produces consistent books in the future must be a typefounder and paper maker as well as a printer. By a typefounder is not meant simply a man who designs the letter but he must also cut the punches, strike them into the copper bars that go to form the matrices, and then justify these shapeless units to the hand mould from which he can cast his fount. The paper-making-printer must need know how to fashion the paper-moulds from brass and mahogany: he must be able to produce the watery fibrous pulp from the linen rags; and he must be able to form the sheet, give the "shake," couch the water leaf, and see the wet, tender sheet through the pressure press to the drying loft.

The paper should suit the type in regard to colour, size, laid and chain lines and thickness: also, the water-mark should conform to the title of the book in which the paper is to be used. The type and paper should combine, and this is not possible if each is made by distinctly different men without this unity in view. In the private press books too many individuals are represented. Perhaps twenty men, or more, have to do in the making of the type and as many more carry out the different stages of the paper making. Then the printer, in combining the type and paper, adds more personalities until the finished book becomes a conglomeration of ideas and workmanship.

The consistent book will be a personality because it will be made by few men; that is, few hands and minds will construct the volume, all working together with but one aim. But, better still, the book should be the work of one man alone. In this way, and only this, will the volume be truly his. There must be a better understanding between the three arts and when this better understanding exists we will produce the much talked of, but seldom seen, book harmonious.
Dard Hunter.

(*This is the first of a series of articles by Mr. Hunter dealing with the making of books. Our first illustration presents a drawing of the author's historic home in which is located the typefoundry and print shop: the second depicts "The Mill" after an etching by [Ralph M.] Pearson where the only paper mill on the American continent making handmade paper is found. At these places the author is working out his ideas for "the Book Harmonious."—Ed.*)

In this pivotal article, Hunter was able to synthesize what he had learned from von Larisch, what he had gleaned from the books read at the British Museum and in his own library, and most importantly, what he had experienced in papermaking and typefounding. (However, it has to be said that his statement about the ancient printer being "ofttimes a paper maker as well" is far fetched.) In "The Lost Art," he defined the book in its purest form, and in a few words demoted to less than ideal those "revivalist" books published by such presses as William Morris's Kelmscott Press and its American equivalent, D.B. Updike's Merrymount Press.

Quickly following the appearance of "The Lost Art of Making Books," an article with the same title was published in the 24 June issue of the *British and Colonial Printer and Stationer*. Before the year was out, Hunter had a few related articles published in other trade magazines.* As a result, he quickly made a name for himself on both sides of the Atlantic as an outspoken proponent of the traditional hand book crafts, especially papermaking. The unique quality of his articles was that much of what he wrote about papermaking was based on personal experience, which gave his statements an authority missing from other treatises on the subject.

But the most important outcome of "The Lost Art" was the opportunity for Hunter to make the world's first one-man book, the "book harmonious." For the previous three years, the Chicago Society of Etchers had issued keepsakes for its members. In March 1915, Ralph M. Pearson, the Society's vice president, approached Hunter about printing the fourth in the series: *The*

Etching of Figures by William Aspenwall Bradley.* Although he may have wanted to author his first book, Hunter reasoned that the commission would give him an immediate opportunity to put his ideas into practice, not to mention a little income. The Society's secretary, Bertha E. Jaques informed Hunter that 250 copies of the book had to be delivered by December 1915, for which he would be paid $3.25 each, which included the cost of the binding. Hunter had nine months to make the paper, finish his type, print the book, and have it bound by his friends, The Oakwood Binders. This was ample time, he thought, as long as everything went according to plan.

Considering his exacting standards for the "book harmonious," it seems contradictory that Hunter did not include binding as one of the labors. In this respect, however, he was following the practice of the early printers/ publishers who sold books in sheets to booksellers who, in turn, arranged to temporarily bind them. It was up to owners to have their books permanently bound. But the real reason why Hunter did not bind books? There were a number of people who were binding books in the traditional manner; he was only interested in exploring crafts that no one else was doing.

MAKING PAPER FOR THE BOOK

As Hunter wanted his paper to resemble that used in sixteenth-century books, he ordered a second pair of large moulds from W. Green, Son & Waite in March 1915 with antique laid covers. His first pair of moulds of the same size had modern laid covers, which did not come into common use until the late 1700s.

While waiting for the new moulds, Hunter decided to experiment with rag preparation, beating, and sheet formation. It seems that up until this point he had been buying half-stuff, but for this special paper, he ordered 100 pounds of new unbleached cuttings. The resulting paper did not come out as he had anticipated, however. Realizing that the books he had read about the preparation of the raw material were woefully inadequate, he sought professional advice from the owner of the Drury Paper Company, Charles Drury Jacobs, with whom he had done some book dealing. Jacobs was glad to help out his ardent colleague, "[You] boiled the new rags in chloride of lime [calcium hypochlorite] . . . [but first] you should have attempted to dissolve the original soluble oils by the use of weak caustic soda [sodium hydroxide], then, later boiling in chloride of lime. By the use of the chloride of lime alone you will always parchmentize your stock." When this and other niggling technical problems were resolved, Hunter formed a number of sheets on one of the modern laid moulds onto which he had attached his DH-in-a-heart watermarks in two diagonal corners. At the end of April, Hunter was pleased to show Pearson a few decent sheets.

Although the antique laid moulds were expected any day, they did not arrive. Fearing that they were lost, Hunter decided to make as much paper as he could using one of the modern laid moulds. Just in case he might have to use this paper in the book, he replaced one of his DH-in-a-heart watermarks with one of the Society's seal—an etching press set in a circle with the words: CHICAGO SOCIETY OF ETCHERS. (plates 51 and 52)

That summer, he spent many long hours in the mill.

During the warm months I ran the mill . . . but with the limited amount of water in the millpond it was difficult to beat the tough new linen and cotton rags sufficiently to assure evenly-felted sheets of paper. After a summer rain storm I would take advantage of the abundant water, rising in Williams Falls a mile or more distant, flowing down the brook through the pasture lands of our neighbours, each little spring and tributary adding its trickle to the stream, and at last over my wooden water-wheel turning the small beater and macerating the rags for the paper. When there was a goodly fall of water the capacity of the mill was about one hundred and fifty sheets of paper a day . . . I had no helpers in the paper mill; the cutting, dusting, and boiling of the new white linen and cotton cloth was all my work; the beating, or macerating, of the cut and boiled rags also fell to me, and when the stock was finally ready, after days and days of beating, I formed the individual sheets of paper in the moulds. I couched each moist sheet upon the woolen felting and lastly pressed the "post" of waterleaf paper in the huge wood and iron press I had myself built. This press was actuated by a heavy iron bar reaching half way across the mill. The expelling of the water from the newly-formed paper was trying labour and oftentimes I would have to call upon Jim Gallagher, the farmer who cultivated the small fruit, to assist me in turning down the press. After considerable water had been pressed from the paper and the felts removed, I would again press the sheets placed in a pile, one upon the other, and finally hang the paper to dry in the attic of the house across the road.

By September, Hunter was desperate: the moulds had still not shown up. He wrote Pearson advising him that the book could not be completed by December as promised and asked for an extension. Pearson passed the letter to Jaques who wrote Hunter in mid-October: "It did not seem at first that our publication could be delayed until March first [1916], in justice to our associate members. But we are led to believe that the high artistic merit of the book will compensate for its late appearance, and we therefore accept your letter with the earnest hope that it will be possible for you to carry out your ideas without modification or delay." Fortunately, by the time Hunter received Jaques's letter, the moulds had been found and delivered. To one of them, he applied the two watermarks taken from the modern laid mould. Papermaking began in earnest.

The Etching of Figures was to be published in a quarto format, which meant that eight pages would result from one sheet of paper. As there were seven pages of text, the title page, a two-page foreword, and a colophon, at least two sheets of paper were required for each book. Taking endpapers, pastedowns, and spoilage into consideration, Hunter probably figured on making four sheets of paper per book. Multiplying four times 250 copies meant that one thousand sheets, or two reams, had to be made. Under optimum conditions, Hunter estimated he could make 150 sheets a day, and at that rate, it would take him only seven days to make the paper, but things did not go well. In mid-October, a friend wrote: "[I heard] you had started on a new batch of paper after rejecting the first and that you would not take up the printing until November."

Examination of blank sheets of paper in the Hunter archives reveal that many have a "cloudy" appearance when examined in transmitted light, denoting uneven formation; many also contain knots—small clumps of fiber (see plates 51 and 52). Knots are not only visual defects, but they are often hard enough to break type. These faults are mentioned because, in fact, they exist in some of the sheets that did pass muster. There were also problems not apparent to Hunter at the time. For example, the paper in most of the copies of *The Etching of Figures* examined by this author is now badly stained. There are two types of staining: small brown spots, usually called "foxing," and a wavy, brown discoloration. Foxing is usually associated with minute iron deposits in the paper that become sites for fungal attack and localized cellulose breakdown. This results in small, red-brown spots with lighter colored halos. The wavy staining was probably caused by uneven evaporation of water or animal size from the sheet. This could have occurred at several points during the manufacture of the paper, as well as during the drying of the damp, printed sheets.

DARD HUNTER'S TYPEFACE

Besides the paper, another task that Hunter had to complete in a hurry was the type. He had started this task even before moving to Marlborough in 1912, by which time he had finished cutting about ten punches following the steps described in Joseph Moxon's *Mechanick Exercises, or the Doctrine of Handy-Works* (1683). While this book provided much of the technical infor-mation that enabled Hunter to cut and cast his font of type, other references were used to determine the basic shape and size of the letters. In Hunter's

handwriting, "My old friend" appears on the endpaper of Theodore Low
De Vinne's *The Practice of Typography* (1902), along with many other pencil
notations as well as smoke proofs.* One section was highlighted by Hunter:

> The modern punch-cutter is not fettered by arbitrary rules: he does not
> conform to the models devised by Albert Dürer. . . . He is at liberty to
> design characters that may be taller or broader, thicker or thinner, than
> any heretofore made, but he is required to make all the characters of a
> full font system as to style, so as to show perfect correlation.

But Hunter greatly admired Albrecht Dürer's work and knew his model
alphabet from von Larisch's class. He also found it illustrated in his copy of
Edward Strange's *Alphabets. A Manual of Lettering*, purchased in London.
(plate 53) Heeding De Vinne's advice to make some changes, for example,
Hunter made his final *A* quite distinct from Dürer's: a slab serif intersects the
apex. (plate 54) Generally, Dürer's models and Hunter's uppercase letters
have a lot in common; both exhibit a certain flourish in the concave serifs, as
well as a slight curve in the arms of the uppercase letters, *L* and *E*. Hunter's
uppercase letters also were inspired by the Venetian roman typefaces of late
fifteenth-century typographers such as Nicolas Jenson and Erhard Ratdolt,
but the lowercase models were found in *Della Historia Vinitiana de M. Pietro
Bembo Card. volgarmente* printed in 1552 in Venice. According to an inscription,
this book was purchased by Hunter in 1914. Because of the presence of
smoke proofs of the lowercase *r*, the numbers *1, 2,* and *3,* and a sketch of the
lowercase *a* in the margins of this book, it seems likely that he began work
on the lowercase letters that year.

Hunter made his type size 18-point, which according to Hunter II was
selected because it "was the smallest size that could be conveniently cut and
still remain in a pleasing proportion for a folio page of text." However, it
appears that Hunter originally intended to cut and cast just enough type to
use for his letterhead. Although he later said he preferred his typeface on
the folio page, Hunter printed all of the projects done at Marlborough and
the first book issued by his Chillicothe-based press in a quarto format.

Once the shape and size of the letters were determined, the steps in
type-making could begin.† The first step was to sculpt each letter, numeral,
or punctuation mark, wrong-reading, on the end of a steel bar called a
punch. Periodically, Hunter made smoke proofs to see how the letter was
taking shape. These proofs were made by holding the punch in the flame of
a candle. Soot accumulated on the face of the punch, and when pressed on
paper, the image of the letter, right-reading, was evaluated. In many cases,
Hunter impressed these proofs in the margins of books he was consulting.

Once the punch was completed, hardened, and tempered, it was driven into a copper bar, called a matrix, making an impression of the letter, right-reading. After justification, each matrix was placed in a hand-held, two-part mold, and using a molten metal alloy, Hunter cast his font of type by hand.

As mentioned earlier, the first use of Hunter's type was for his letterhead, printed sometime in 1914 (see plate 50). The largest letters were printed from a line etching, as was the press device. (An earlier ream label was printed with a similar typeface called Ivanhoe, in a smaller point size, made by the Keystone Type Foundry. Some pieces of this type were altered by Hunter with gravers to make them appear more like his typeface.)

By late 1915 or early 1916, Hunter had cut sixty-three punches: all of the lower- and uppercase letters including two Rs. Perhaps thinking he would not need them, or that if he did, he could always alter letters from the 18-point Ivanhoe font, he did not cut punches for the Q, X, and Z. He also cut no ligatures, e.g., fi, ffl; or accented letters, e.g., ü. Punches for all of the numbers were cut except 6 and zero. The 6 was printed using the cast 9, upside down. The zero was the cast lowercase o with the inside of the bowl reamed out with a graver to create an even thinness of line. Although a punch for 1 was cut, it was never cast; the cast i served after the dot was filed off.

When viewed as a whole (see plate 54), Hunter's typeface displays irregularities in both the size and shape of some letters, but he did not want his type to emulate the "perfect" modern foundry types made by machine. Rather, he wanted to capture the essence of the early typefaces that he said possessed "a freedom of stroke unknown to-day." Printed on handmade paper, Hunter's typeface is lively, rhythmic, and sculptural, and it reminds us of those early printed pages where the hand of the punch-cutter can be seen, as well as felt.

The Etching of Figures

Once the paper and type were ready, Hunter printed a proof of the book on the large, used R. Hoe & Company Washington hand press that was purchased a few months before.* Not surprisingly, Hunter based the open book, double-page format on that of early printed books (see plates 57 and 66). The tail (bottom) margin is the largest, followed in decreasing width by the foredge, the head, and the gutter. While these proportions are aesthetically pleasing, in older books the wide margins also served as places for notes, corrections, etc. They also provided a "margin of error" against the bookbinder's plough, which was used to trim the text block after sewing.

Once the pages were proofed and corrected, printing began. Hunter needed an uppercase X to print the date of publication in Roman numerals on the title page and in the colophon. Using gravers, he altered Ivanhoe Xs by making the straight serifs concave and narrowing the stems. He used the Ivanhoe parentheses unaltered. There was also no *ü* in Hunter's typeface, which was required if he was to print "Dürer" correctly. This was solved by filing down his cast colon until just the two dots remained on a sliver of metal. He then fitted this into a filed-out gap at the top of a cast *u*. In years to follow, he made other accented letters and ligatures as required by altering either his type or Ivanhoe.

After printing the text, Hunter worked on the decorations for the title page and cover label. (plate 55) For these, he made detailed drawings that were converted into line etchings. The label and title page decorations bear no relation to any of Hunter's previous design styles, and the enduring motif, the branch and leaf, makes its first appearance in this book. In February 1916, he finished printing *The Etching of Figures*. As there was little time before the extension deadline, he quickly collated the folios and sent the signatures to the binders. The books were half-bound in vellum with a commercial dark grey, laid paper cover. (For more details, see Appendix C. Descriptive Bibliography of Dard Hunter's Private Press Books.)

In each copy, The Oakwood Binders placed a leaflet.

This book entitled "The Etching of Figures" is probably the most unique book that has ever been printed, and will in time become of inestimable value.

You as a possessor of a copy of this book will undoubtedly deserve to preserve it in a more permanent binding.

We are doing all of Dard Hunter's binding as well as this temporary binding on this book and we have designed a [full] vellum binding at the suggestion of Mr. Hunter which is especially appropriate for this book and which we offer you for $10.00.

We will be pleased to send you the descriptionof the binding or to bind the book according to your idea. The Oakwood Binders. Pittsfield, Mass.

Once he had a copy of the bound book in his hands, Hunter could finally look back over his achievement, already summed up in the Foreword.

In an exhaustive study of papermaking and typography, Mr. Hunter has never seen mention of a book produced in which paper, type and printing were the work of one man as they are in the present volume. Printing as an art reached its highest development between the years 1470 and 1590. Most modern book printing produced by the revivalists tries to imitate this old work by using the most modern methods. Mr. Hunter's idea, during many years of research and experiment, which has culminated in the production of this book, has been to work as the sixteenth-century printers did, using, so far as possible, the same tools, materials and methods. By this means, it is hoped, the same general characteristics that are so pleasing in many of the early volumes, will, at least in a measure, be found in this book.

The board of the Chicago Society of Etchers was so pleased with *The Etching of Figures* that Hunter was immediately commissioned to print another book to be ready by the end of 1916. Although this left a mere eight months to make the paper, print the book, and have the copies bound, Hunter had no trouble meeting the deadline. This second book was *The Etching of Contemporary Life* by Frank Weitenkampf, director of the art department at the New York Public Library. The paper and type of this quarto volume were the same used for the previous one. Again, Hunter found that he needed a few more pieces of type—the uppercase *Z*, the question mark, and exclamation point—and these were made by altering Ivanhoe type.

The *manière criblée* decorations—white dots on a black background—drawn for the title page, headpiece, and initial *A*, give this book a rich look compared with *The Etching of Figures*. (plate 56) The branch and leaf motif is repeated in the decorations, and there is a new addition: a hanging shield with a cut-out heart and the initials, DH. Eventually this motif became as commonly associated with Hunter as papermaker and printer as the square rose had been when he was a designer.

The paper quality in *The Etching of Contemporary Life* is a vast improvement over the earlier book. The paper appears to have been made entirely on the antique laid mould with the same watermarks. Minor foxing is only occasionally found, and the wavy lines of brown discoloration are, by and large, gone. The knots are still present as is the somewhat cloudy formation, but the overall look and feel of the paper, although still somewhat thick, are more reminiscent of incunabula papers.

Bound copies of *The Etching of Contemporary Life* were distributed to Society members in early 1917. Again, a leaflet from The Oakwood Binders was included that described an alternative binding designed by Hunter of "full pigskin, of beautiful brown color; stamped in blind on front and back cover with ornament designed by Mr. Hunter and finishing with hand tooling." Upon returning from a lecture trip in April, Bertha Jaques found a copy of the book in this deluxe binding amongst her mail. She wrote to Hunter, "I do not suppose that any description I could write would quite convey the sense of surprise and delight as I opened that perfect box to look upon a perfect and harmonious book—everything a unit in color and treatment, just as if it had flowered from one bud." *The Etching of Contemporary Life* is the paragon of Hunter's one-man books; unfortunately, it was the last book for which he personally made all of the paper.

The last commission Hunter did for the Chicago Society of Etchers was not a book, but a folded, two-page keepsake devoted to the work of J.C. Vondrous, a member of the Society. After a visit by Jaques to Hunter's mill in the summer of 1917, she wrote a letter describing the project.

> This year we plan to give our associate members an etching by one of our best men. It is to be matted, enclosed in a heavy paper folder stamped with the seal of our Society, and enclosed with the etching will be a very brief account of the etcher and his work. It just occurs to me that you may have, say 250 sheets of the hand-made paper with our seal, and I would like some sort of an idea of what it would cost to have one sheet for each package printed in your type, with initial letter—say perhaps the size of one of our pages you printed in the book. And could you do this as late as the last of November in order that the pages could go out December 15th?

This letter suggests that by summer Hunter had stopped making paper, probably because there was insufficient water to power the beater. The next opportunity for papermaking would not be until spring 1918, well past the December deadline. After sorting through the paper left over from the previous books, Hunter found he did not have enough with just the Society's watermark to use it exclusively, and Jaques agreed that paper with the DH-in-a-heart watermark could make up the difference.

Vondrous executed an etching titled *The Old Town Bridge Tower*, a scene in Prague, and Jaques wrote the text. Two hundred and fifty copies of the folio were quickly printed on pages measuring 11.75 x 8.25 inches and sent out in November 1917 as promised. For the decorations, Hunter again incorporated the branch and leaf motif with his initials enclosed in a shield; the cutout heart was omitted. This motif is seen not only in the initial *T*, but it follows "ETCHERS" and forms the tailpiece. (plate 57) These decorations were printed in red ink from line etchings. More ephemeral than the two previous books, which is why it is very rare, this folio is an important transition between Hunter's Renaissance style and his original style reflected in the books he later authored and printed.

Chapter 8

For myself, I have reached a point where I must get a paying business regardless of the so-called artistic side of it and I cannot see anything else half so sure as the paper mill. Dard Hunter

On 15 May 1917, Dard and Edith Hunter became the proud parents of a son. Dard immediately wrote to his mother to give her the good news.

Dear Mother (Grandmuz) and the little ones:—Have been very pushed as you may know so have not written sooner . . . the doctor came about eleven and the little fellow was born almost immediately. He is quite a big chap long with large feet and broad hands like his pa. Head is large and has a bit of light curly hair. Eyes so far kind of blue and large like his ma's. He has turned out to be just as we had all hoped and longed for—like his father. His nose was quite flat at first but now it is developing into a large massive affair. There is a goodly lot of meat for a big nose when it starts to take on some shape. Forehead like mine. Ears very close to head, large and like mine. Broad shoulders and straight. Is very reddish like an Indian and really a cute little face for one just 24 hours old. I saw him just after he was bathed and I thought he would be messy but he was a good looking kid even so early as that. Is fond of eating and although the milk wagon is not ready for a day or so yet he likes to hang on and think he is getting something. Sleeps pretty well off and on but has a voice too and as he is hungry, the first few days without any restaurant it is hard for him to keep quiet. . . . I am sure you will all be pleased with Dard as he is a fine piece of manhood. Have only time to write a hurried note so must close now, little Daddy and his mamma send love to you all. Lovingly, Father
[in pencil] B[unny] is very well and has just got through reading my proof on the Bibliography I prepared for the U.S. Forest Service. The nurse is very good & gets along finely with all. Jim is hauling the dung

we did not haul last year. I buy no more as it is high this year. Is a beautiful day. You should see the new one.   VERY FINE.

The "little ones" were Clara Ragna Johnson and Dard's cousin Junius K. Hunter. Together with Harriet, they had been regular visitors to Marlborough and were married there in October 1916. By this time, Junius owned half of the Chillicothe *News-Advertiser* and was the paper's manager; Dard owned the other half, and he served as vice president. The steady income from the paper helped the Hunters over periods when he was not making any income from the mill. Perhaps because they had no children of their own, Clara and Junius remained close to the Hunter family until their deaths in the 1950s.

As to the young mill hand's name, Hunter later wrote, "His mother insisted that he be named Dard, although I was desirous that he bear the name Cornell, after his mother's family. He was called Dard." To celebrate the arrival, Hunter printed a birth announcement. (plate 58)

The bibliography referred to in the letter came about when, in early 1916, Hunter wrote to the members of the Committee on Bibliography of the Technical Association of the Pulp and Paper Industry (TAPPI) asking if they were interested in publishing an annotated bibliography of the handmade paper and watermark materials in his library. They were, and at the end of 1916, Hunter submitted his manuscript. Little more than a week after Dard Jr. was born, it appeared as an official publication of the committee under the title, *Handmade Paper and its Water-Marks: A Bibliography*. In its introduction, Hunter announced his intention to continue writing about papermaking, "This bibliography was originally made as a working list for forming a library on ancient papermaking and watermarking to be used in writing a book on these subjects which I expect to be able to have ready in two years' time."

PLANS TO EXPAND THE MILL

After finishing *The Etching of Contemporary Life*, Hunter was busy filling orders for a small group of discerning people who wanted quality, handmade papers. These included fine printmakers such as Gustave Baumann, Ralph M. Pearson, Bertha Jaques, and C.E. Maud, and private press printers such as Porter Garrett and Taylor & Taylor. But his frustration about his inability to fill large orders and to price his papers more competitively grew. By the summer of 1917, he knew that if his papermaking business and printing activities were to continue, he needed dedicated buildings; he was not at all happy about living and working in Mill House. He also needed better equipment, an assistant (in particular, someone who could sell the product), and greater water power. The first three problems would have been relatively easy to solve. For example, in an undated sketch, he flanked the papermill with two small buildings in complementary styles: one for drying and finishing the paper; the another for printing and typefounding. But all of these improvements would be for naught if he could not make paper all year long. Although he could have used other sources of energy, such as electricity, Hunter was determined to use only water power. If he stayed at Marlborough, he either had to increase the diameter of the wheel or replace it with a more efficient steel one. Either option would have been costly, but could be done. The real problem, over which he had no control, was that the water supply in Jew's Creek was neither plentiful nor regular.

Thus, finding another site for the Dard Hunter Mill became a priority, and in the autumn of 1917, the Hunters decided to put their property on the market. They immediately moved into a cozy apartment in Newburgh, New York, a few miles to the south, primarily so that Edith and the new baby would not have to spend another cold winter in Mill House. During November 1917, Hunter drove back and forth to the Mill House to print the Vondrous folio.

As mentioned in the previous chapter, in preparation for the sale, Hunter put together a small leaflet describing the house and land. Charles H. Kingsbury, a Boston photographer he had met in East Aurora and who had already taken photographs of the Marlborough property, was hired to take more photographs of the house's interior. When received from the Roycroft job press, the leaflets were sent to real estate agents and people who inquired about ads seen in *The New Country Life* and *The Christian Science Monitor*. The reason stated for leaving the property was: "Owing to the necessity of getting a place with great water-power this exceptionally unique and historical property is offered for sale at a price much below its actual cost and value."* Although not mentioned in the leaflet, Hunter verified to a real estate agent that although the property had cost him over $17,000 (that included the original purchase price and cost of renovations), he was asking a mere $15,000.

He also sent out letters to real estate agents informing them of his intent to find a country property.

The acreage is not important as I do not care to farm. There may be few or many acres.

I desire an old stone or brick house on the property, of fine architecture and one that will take to remodelling. There need be no improvements in the house. A house built eighty or a hundred years ago would suit me best as buildings were built better then and were more pleasing in design than houses of a later period.

There must be a fine large brook running through the property. This stream need be pure and never-failing—even in the driest weather. An old mill or the foundations of a former mill would be acceptable as I wish to use the stream for developing water power.

The house should set well back from a good road. There should be fine, old trees and views from the house. Not too far from a beautiful village and within easy motoring distance from a larger town . . . will pay immediate cash. Address Dard Hunter, 146 Montgomery St., Newburgh, N.Y.

Real estate activity during the winter was slow, but finally, in April 1918, a buyer for Mill House was found: Martha Gruening of New York City. On 1 May, she signed the deed to the property, having paid Hunter's asking price. Interestingly, Hunter added a clause to the sale agreement, which stipulated that if Gruening wanted to sell the property within five years she was to "permit [Hunter] to purchase the said premises at the same price as may be offered by the proposed purchaser. . . ."*

THE BIRTH OF CORNELL CHOATE HUNTER

On 6 April 1917, the United States entered into World War I on the side of the Allies. Although he had wanted to enlist then, Hunter put this idea aside after the birth of Dard Jr. Throughout June and July 1918, the Allies were gaining the upper hand in France, and Hunter finally decided that if he was going to "down the Kaiser," he had better sign up soon. It was a hard decision, however, because he and Edith were expecting their second child in early 1919. Much to Edith's relief, Dard decided to join the engineering corps; this would keep him out of harm's way while still allowing him to "do his bit." On 4 September 1918, Dard signed over his power of attorney to Edith, but as it turned out, he never had to leave Newburgh. Kaiser Wilhelm II abdicated on 9 November, and the armistice was signed two days later on the 11th hour of the 11th day of the 11th month, 1918. The fighting was over.

When Mill House was sold in May 1918, Dard wanted Edith and Dard Jr. to return to Chillicothe, but they could not because the town was under quarantine; the deadly Spanish Flu had gripped the town. Confined at first to the large eastern cities, the influenza eventually spread throughout the United States. The third largest army training center in the United States,

Camp Sherman, was in Chillicothe, and the camp became a breeding ground for the disease; thousands of soldiers died there. By the time the epidemic finally ran its course in 1919, more than half a million Americans had died— about 10 times the number of battle casualties.

Thus confined to Newburgh, the Hunters' second son was born in their apartment on 3 February 1919. As Edith's father had died a few months earlier, there was no question this time as to how the boy would be named: Cornell Choate. As soon as Edith was able to travel, the Hunter family moved back to Chillicothe to live with Harriet and her tenants, Clara and Junius Hunter.

MOUNTAIN HOUSE

Almost as soon as he arrived back in Chillicothe, Hunter learned that Mountain House was for sale. Situated on the brow of Carlisle Hill, the house was visible from nearly all points in the town situated below the hill. Perhaps Hunter had always harbored a desire to own that impressive house, and now that he had the money to do so, it seemed foolish to pass up the opportunity. Although there was no stream on the property, he reasoned that he could find suitable mill property elsewhere in the vicinity.

On 6 March 1919, he signed the deed for the property, which included the house, a dance pavilion (now called the summer house), a garage (now the barn), and five acres of land on which was an orchard.* He wrote to his best friend, Sterling Lord, about the house,

> [It] is not large and it is not just the style of house I would build but the location is unique and I got it very cheap. The entire place could not be duplicated for fifty thousand. There are five acres, much fruit, a garage and very pleasing shade trees . . . we have electric lights, natural gas, city water and hot water furnace. I feed and attend to the bowels of the latter. . . . Much grass to mow, a honey suckle hedge and Jinko tree, the only one of its species extinct except one on Mrs. Eddy's grave and one in the British Museum on Shaftsbury Avenue.†

Mountain House had been built in the early 1850s by Dr. Louis Meggenhofen for Oscar Janssen and his family.‡ Together with thousands of other Germans, Meggenhofen and the Janssens had fled their homeland during the uprising of 1848. Many settled in southern Ohio, which provided a safe and prosperous haven. One of the distinguishing features of the house is the bottle-shaped windows—a feature entirely in keeping with its original function as a winery and a tavern, as well as a residence. Originally, the roof line was castellated, but this feature had been removed by the 1890s, and classical moldings and a cast iron railing topped the house. (plate 59)

According to an elevation made by a Chicago architectural firm, Hunter's original plan was to completely classicize the exterior, just as he had wanted to do with Mill House. The bottle-shaped windows were to be removed and all other architectural details squared. Two-story ionic columns were to be situated at the front and pilasters were to flank the two towers. Whether it was because these renovations were too costly or Hunter had second thoughts about altering the unique architecture of the house, only the gothic windows and door from the original entrance that overlooked the town were removed. These were replaced with a five-section window for the new library. (colorplate 10) In November, Hunter wrote Lord,

> The library is hardly started as I am going to make it quite a room. The windows I am working on now and that is the first move toward the decoration of this room. There are five mullioned windows, each six by three feet so you see there is a lot of leading to do. I put in the fourth window just now and will finish the fifth in a couple of days. In three of the windows are panels of stained glass, the first the paper-maker, then the typefounder and the printer. The paper-maker is the only one of the panels that is finished but I am putting in the windows with the idea of fixing the panels to them when the colored glass is completed. There will be an elaborate ceiling and the walls panelled. I have an old stone mantel to go in—a copy of an Italian fireplace. There will be built-in shelves on two sides of the room to hold about 3000 books. I expect to get the room done in the next four months. Then the interior will be finished save for a few minor finishings.

The library windows remain just as Hunter described them in 1919; he never completed the two panels of the typefounder and the printer. Later, much larger stained glass panels of those subjects were made that now hang in front of each of the four undecorated windows.

Hunter spent seven months making the house habitable, and although the work was far from complete, Edith and the two boys moved in in October 1919. Today the library, as well as many of the other rooms downstairs, appear much as Hunter finished them in 1920. The most impressive room in the house, the library, is decorated with dark wood paneling of neo-Jacobean design. The three interior doors are covered with now-faded tapestries very much in the style of William Morris. Escutcheons for these same doors were made by Hunter. Each was cut from silver-plated sheet brass in the shape of an ax blade within which is a rose in a circle; a silver-plated knob accompanies each plate. Charles Filson's posthumous portrait of William Henry Hunter hangs over the "Cretan" stone mantel, set diagonally across one corner. The other rooms—dining, music, and hallway—still retain their classical décor although general refurbishing has been carried out over the past seventy-odd years.

While he was working on the renovations, Hunter and Morris Schlosser of M. & F. Schlosser, paper dealers, discussed setting up a papermill in Chillicothe, utilizing the Marlborough papermaking equipment. By the latter part of 1919, however, Hunter decided that setting up his mill near Chillicothe was not realistic because the water was hard, and the expense to soften it was prohibitive. Instead, he had another idea that he conveyed to Lord.

I have just about abandoned the idea of making paper except for my own amusement but I have a new scheme on now that I think will work out. I expect to get in with an English mill and import paper here from there. This idea is in progress of development and I feel sure it will come to a successful business.

The only problem was that Hunter had little interest or aptitude for business matters. He especially disliked being a salesman, and so he constantly asked Lord to go into business with him. He even offered his old friend a building site on the Mountain House property. Although sorely tempted, Lord ultimately declined. A newly married man with a child on the way, Lord wrote that he needed a secure job; Hunter's "scheme" was simply too vague. Lord, in fact, was no longer working as a binder; the Oakwood Binders having closed several years before. Peter Franck had returned to Germany. Lord and his wife, Ruth, had moved to Burlington, Iowa where he was bookkeeper for the Leopold Desk Company.*

HUNTER TRAVELS TO ENGLAND

In January 1920, Hunter applied for a passport and a visa, a new requirement following the war, to visit England. The passport gives the first accurate description of the 36-year old Hunter: height: 5 feet 11.75 inches; forehead: high; eyes: blue; nose: prominent; mouth: straight; chin: dimpled; hair: blond; complexion: fair; face: oval; distinguishing marks: none; occupation: book designer. The object of his visit was given as "Professional work." Hunter listed his occupation as "book designer" rather than "papermaker" in case there was any suspicion that he was going to England to acquire information or equipment, which would enable him to set up a handmade paper mill in America. Of course, the real purpose of the trip was to arrange with one or more of the English mills to make paper after his specifications, which he would sell in the United States under his name.

Arriving in late April, he settled into a bed and breakfast in London. After a day or so, he wrote Edith a long letter from the site of his first day trip, the papermaking town of Maidstone, Kent.

To-night I sit in me room in the Nag's Head at nine and it is almost light enough to see without a light. I have been on the go since I last wrote you & have learned much. It seems many weeks since I got to England but only four days.

Yesterday I went out to see J. Waite of the mould making firm of W. Green, Son & Waite at 134 Albany Road. It is in a Dickens' part of London off of Old Kent Road and one of the quaintest streets I have seen in the city. J. Waite's place looks very queer and even of a more ancient aspect than Marshall's place at Stoke Newington . . . [Waite's brother] said neither of them had ever been permitted to go in a hand-made paper mill & they doubted if I could see inside of one. When I told him I was going to Maidstone he wanted to go with me to get in on my face. However, I thought this would queer my game so I sneaked off this A.M. alone. I will go & see Waite again of course as he can tell me more. Last night I went to the London office of the Whatman Paper Co. at 9 Bridewell Place, E.C. They have an immense office & after much talk & explanation about how I was writing a book on the history of hand-made paper I was given a letter of introduction to the mill owners. This is the largest & oldest of the hand-made mills & make the original J. Whatman papers, so much noted. I had already a letter from J. Bar-cham Green Mill saying they would show me through. I left London at 8 this morning & got to Maidstone at 10. Went off to the [18 vat] Whatman Mill & Mr. Barston [Balston], the owner took me over entirely. It was most interesting, as you may know, but I will not now go into detail. The mill setting is beautiful, being along a stream and many flowers & well kept lawns & gardens, as only the English climate & skill can make. They treated me wonderfully well & I had a real time & learnt *much*.

I then went over to the Green mill on the tram to Tovil which is a rather small quaint village. After walking through a mile of lanes, stone walls on either side covered with ivy, I came to the mill laying down in a beautiful valley surrounded with hedges, apple trees & many, many flowers in full bloom. They were very glad to see me & had lunch ready for me but I arrived too late. After going over the mill Mr. Green & his son took me to the house to have tea, where I met the family of Greens. The house is a large spacious place with much old furniture & splendor & the garden and grounds are equal to Hampton Court. They have many gardens, green houses, automobiles & altogether a wonderful estate, such as I have never seen before. All from a 5 vat mill which they have had for 110 years. Both mills are over booked with orders & will accept no new business. The Greens wanted me to stay for Sunday at the house but I did not feel like it . . .

I have found out much about hand-made paper. I think it is practical to make it in America. The most startling thing that I did find out, however, is that hard water is what they want. The more lime the better. They use spring water & it is hard & let the brook water (soft) float away. Neither mill uses water power. The stream the Green mill is on is smaller than the Marlborough one but they do not use the water. The water through here seems to all be soft. Mr. R. Green says the soft water idea is all bosch & that the hard, limey water makes the most desired quality to hand-made. This is good knowledge for me. The things I saw to-day have repaid me for the trip many times.

During the first week in May, Hunter visited two more mills. First was the W.S. Hodgkinson Company's Wookey Hole Mill, near Wells, Somerset, where he made a sheet of paper. Two weeks later, a Mr. Lunnon sent sent Hunter that sheet with a note: "I told the men they had sent me along the wrong sheet. My congratulations on your shake." The other mill visited was the George Wilmott Mill in Shoreham, Kent. With every tour, Hunter increasingly liked the idea of switching from importing paper to establishing his own mill. The revelation about the benefits of hard water meant he could start up a mill near Chillicothe without too much expense. There were other problems, however. He needed better equipment and skilled personnel, as he did not intend to make paper himself. In an effort to solve these problems, Hunter placed an anonymous advertisement for used hand paper-making equipment and an experienced vatman in the *World's Paper Trade Preview*. Mr. F.H. Palmer, associated with a defunct hand papermill in Downton, Wiltshire, answered the ad, listing much of the equipment Hunter needed. After visiting the Palmer Mill, Hunter decided to buy a vat, a knotter (used to remove clumps of fibers from the stock), and moulds of "various sizes from large post to foolscap . . . £3 per pair." Palmer arranged to have these crated and shipped to Chillicothe.

In a letter home, Hunter noted that he had also received a reply from "a vatman wanting a job but will take this up later. I have no fear about labor as I think I can train it myself. All I want now is equipment." In fact, this vatman was Robert Parry Robertson, a man who would eventually be linked with Hunter's papermaking enterprise.

THE HUNTER MILLS

Hunter arrived back in Chillicothe in June 1920. Immediately, he wrote to American paper equipment manufacturers inquiring about a large beater, a press, a tank that could be used as a stock chest, a plater, rag duster, and felts, as well as flax and hemp waste, linen pulp, and new cotton rags. Of these, according to Hunter II, he purchased a large Emerson beater and two hydraulic presses from a used equipment dealer. These went into the barn.

In July, he was delighted to receive a request from the Coy, Hunt & Company for a quote for 72,000 sheets of paper. Although he could not fill it, the order convinced him that a market for handmade paper existed if he could make it cheaply enough. Nationally, business was booming. Employment was high, and people had money to spend. The time to start a new business was ripe, especially if it was one like personalized stationery that would appeal to a growing middle class.

But the nagging problem remained: finding someone who would be responsible for handling the business side of the enterprise. When it was clear, once and for all, that Lord would not join him, Hunter began corresponding with the Butler Paper Corporation in Chicago, the American Writing Paper Company in Holyoke, Massachusetts, and Douglas C. McMurtrie of The Arbor Press, Inc. of New York City. In the end, it was the Butler Corporation that made formal arrangements to go ahead with the hand papermaking and watermarking business, to be called The Hunter Mills. The company was to have controlling interest in the business, with Paul Butler as president and Dard Hunter as vice president and general manager.

Hunter's lawyer, John A. Poland, looked over the proposed agreement and wrote his client a cautionary note: "You will pardon me in saying that, among your characteristics, as I have estimated them, is your tendency to submerge your personal interests, rather than to obtrude them; and as this is a matter of the most vital importance to yourself and your small, but very interesting family, you should now protect yourself and them as well." An old colleague from the Norfolk Studios, Eric Warne, also warned, "making your own stuff gives the biggest chunk of kudos . . . whereas working for another man or concern means that he or it takes a good rake-off and you collar the residue. And, after all, if you are your own boss, you can go to it when and wherever you feel like it."* Notwithstanding this advice, Hunter agreed with the plans the Butler Corporation drew up. After all, his primary goal was to establish the only hand papermaking mill in the United States, not to make a lot of money. As far as "kudos" was concerned, he was sure that, ultimately, the name Dard Hunter would become synonymous with the best handmade paper and custom watermarks available anywhere in the world.

Finding a place to establish the mill was the next hurdle. A suitable property in Old Lyme, Connecticut was found, and following a site inspection by Hunter, Butler started negotiations to purchase it. At one point, a group of concerned Old Lyme citizens wrote Hunter that they were very eager to have him develop the property into a mill, and even offered to throw in some money to clinch the deal. By the middle of 1921, however, a business depression began, and the cautious Butler representatives decided to lease rather than buy the property.

The Hunter Mills was to have a number of vats each requiring at least three workmen, plus extra hands who would be in charge of beating, sizing, drying, sorting, and finishing the paper. Hiring experienced English hand papermakers would get the mill up and running quickly, with the added advantage that foreigners would expect less pay than American workers (assuming any could be found). One of the vatmen being considered was Robert Parry Robertson, the Englishman who had answered Hunter's earlier ad. Butler arranged for Robertson to be interviewed by a London firm of paper agents. From his home in Maidstone, Robertson wrote to his prospective employers, Butler and Hunter,

> I understand you desire to establish the manufacture of paper by hand and require a man who understands the process of such production and is able to make and couch paper . . . .
>
> It must be understood that the manufacture of paper by hand is an Art and this, in England, has attained a high degree by reason that it is somewhat inherent, son following father, in the learning of the Art, to a degree practically unknown in any other industry.
>
> What salary are you prepared to pay for a suitable man?
>
> In the event of our agreeing to terms would you be prepared to pay the necessary expense for the removal of my wife and three children? Your reply, informing me just what you require, will be welcomed and, if the terms are satisfactory, I can arrange to come practically at once.

Following the London interview, the paper agent's representative confirmed that Robertson was a first-class papermaker, but he doubted that he would be "suitable for taking entire charge of your Mill. . . . Personally he seems a very decent reliable sort of man." Regarding Robertson's managerial skills, Hunter was not concerned as he was to be mill superintendent. Robertson was informed of the conditions under which he would be hired, but when the Butler Corporation asked Hunter if they should make an offer to Robertson, he replied no. Frustrated with Hunter's inability to commit to the project, Butler decided to pull the plug on The Hunter Mills. Hunter did not protest too loudly, as he had developed serious doubts about linking his name, expertise, and energy with the large corporation. Worldwide, business was suffering a major decline, and Hunter did not want to be dependent on a corporation that might cut its less profitable divisions at a moment's notice. While cordial letters between Hunter and Butler regarding the project continued to be exchanged over the next five years, The Hunter Mills never materialized. Robertson was not out of the picture, however, although it would be another six years before he again heard from Dard Hunter.

THE HUNTER FAMILY

The primary sources of information concerning the private lives of Dard, Edith, and the boys are his letters written home during trips, and to Sterling Lord. Perhaps the most shocking revelation in one letter to Lord occurred in late 1919, when Hunter wrote that he was prepared to leave his family for five or six years to work abroad. It is hard to imagine how this affected Edith, but she knew that Dard would never leave her and the boys for long, if ever. She also knew that he needed to use his friends and family as sounding boards to bounce off ideas. In the same letters in which Hunter wrote about some remote corner of the world where he would seek his dream, his affection for home life, with all its trials, also appeared.

> We had a Christmas tree and many toys [some of which Hunter carved from wood] so that it is quite impossible to step without falling over a B. and O. railroad train or a mail cart. Children bring many new experiences into the lives of their parents and I am learning something new every day. Our kids are now at the nose blowing stage so that when one is not attending to ones own drippings he or she is mopping up one of the children. We have all had colds in spite of good Muz Eddy and I hope it will soon be over as I detest such things, especially when very productive.

and,

> By the by I am growing a fine pair of side-burns which would delight
> your tonsorial heart. They were originally an inch in length but I am
> letting them creep down so that now they are well nigh near my chin.
> I am carving them in nice designs and to date I have had them repre-
> senting a square rose, basket of fruit and lolly-pop. My next try will be
> an elongated D on one side and H on the other. They are red with a
> touch of henna. . . . Little Dard Jr. goes to kindergarten every day, his
> mother taking him. She also takes Cornell Choate with her and brings
> him back so that I have a little time each morning, however, the rest of
> the time I am nurse. C.C. is now 2½ and in many ways is the best of the
> two. Dard Jr. is smarter and more delicate but the other one is more
> robust, duller and of rather weighty disposition like Dada. Dard Jr. is
> the image of his mother and all his traits and dispositions he gets from
> either the Cornells or Choates.

Edith seems to have been quite content with her life. She took and gave
piano lessons, and whenever possible played in public. Her friends were
numerous, and card playing was an almost daily event. Dard, on the other
hand, had few close friends in Chillicothe; this made him an excellent cor-
respondent.

EXHIBITS AT THE SMITHSONIAN INSTITUTION

In September 1921, Hunter had a shock when a newspaper notice concerning
him appeared in over 200 newspapers. He sent a clipping with the errors
underlined (here in italics) in a letter to Lord.

> Books Made by One Man Unique Capital Exhibit
> What are believed to be the only books ever produced—from the con-
> tents to the printing and binding—by one man working alone have just
> been placed on exhibition at the Smithsonian Institution.
> They are the product of *the late* Dard Hunter of Chillicothe, Ohio,
> *who wrote* two books, designed the type with which they were to be
> printed, cast the type, set it, printed the production with a hand press
> and then *did the binding*. Hunter also manufactured the paper that was
> used.
> This is part of the general exhibition in the division of graphic arts
> in the institution.

His accompanying letter explained,

> The N.Y. Herald had a long obituary which was copied in other papers so that Edith had a deluge of letters, telegrams from friends, grave-diggers, tomb-stone carvers and second husbands. I fooled them all and while I am ready to pass out I feel that I would like to do a little more in life before I leave. You see I went out of this world [during an operation on his throat] when I took the ether and I distinctly remember having a long earnest talk with Saint Peter about paper making and he told me he wanted me to help him with his work of inspection. Heaven is not a bad sort of a place from the little look I had but while it must be comfortable I imagine it would get very tiresome seeing the same faces all the time with an occasional new one from time to time. I did not get to see even a glimpse of the other place as we drove by so rapidly and the man only pointed it out.

The misunderstanding about Hunter's "death" resulted from a misinterpretation of some public relations material for an exhibit. The person responsible for that material was Ruel P. Tolman, Assistant Curator of the Division of Graphic Arts for the Smithsonian Institution's United States National Museum. Hunter and Tolman began their association in August 1920. Tolman, an amateur etcher, was having difficulty finding suitable paper for printing intaglio plates. After asking Hunter to send him samples of paper and prices, Tolman proposed that Hunter prepare "an exhibit showing the process of making paper, illustrated with the materials used, molds and photographs of the actual working conditions under which fine paper is made." Hunter, remembering those fateful days in the Science Museum in London when he was so taken by the appliances of papermaking and typefounding, was thrilled by the prospect of inspiring other young people. The more Hunter thought about the import of the exhibit, the more artifacts he wanted included in the 8 x 2 feet display case. "Beside the moulds, there will be wire watermarks, wax casts of dies, felts, papers, size [animal gelatin], rags in different stages, photographs of operations and perhaps some drawings showing the construction of moulds." To make the exhibition quite unique, Hunter sent letters to colleagues in England and Europe asking for donations of old moulds, watermarking paraphernalia, papers, etc. The mouldmakers W. Green, Son & Waite and the mills of J. Barcham Green, W. & R. Balston, and Van Gelder Zonen in Amsterdam, Netherlands all sent items.

In March 1921, he packed everything into cases, including his type-
written labels on Marlborough paper, and shipped them to Washington,
D.C. As soon as he had unpacked the exhibit, Tolman wrote, "it certainly is
a most excellent collection of material, and I feel that the Museum is to be
very highly congratulated upon receiving this gift from you." The accession
memorandum listed 90 specimens in all. Tolman arranged the material into
the case, although he wrote that he was having some difficulty getting it all
in. He took photographs of the exhibit and sent copies to Hunter with the
comment, "I would be very glad to have any criticisms which you may give
in regard to its installation and any suggestions for its improvement. The
exhibit attracts a great deal of attention and is very much appreciated."
Hunter was delighted with Tolman's organization of the material.

A few days later, he asked Tolman if the museum would like unbound
copies of *The Etching of Figures* and *The Etching of Contemporary Life*, and mentioned in passing, "All of the material and appliances I used in their making
is stored away as it will never be used again. It includes all the punches,
type, matrices, moulds, etc. etc." After reading the books and thinking over
Hunter's comments regarding his type, Tolman asked if he would consider
designing a second exhibit on typefounding. Hunter responded that the
type appliances were to be exhibited in the Graphic Arts Show in Chicago in
July, but after that, he would be happy to send them to the museum. He
also explained,

> I well realize that the whole outfit is crude and extremely primitive but
> my one idea was to imitate the old typefounders as nearly as I could and
> try, to at least a slight degree, to arrive at some of the pleasing charac-
> teristics of the ancient typographers. Some critics have said that I have
> done this, others that I have gone a long way from it. However, it was
> an attempt and it involved a number of years work with no remunera-
> tion so the endeavor will have to be accepted for what it is worth.

The loan, rather than gift, of the typefounding artifacts consisted of 884
specimens that included the punches, the matrices, the old Caslon mould
and Hunter's handmade one, assorted files and gravers, and nearly seven
hundred pieces of type. Tolman quickly put together the exhibit, which
included examples of fine printing by Norman T.A. Munder of Baltimore.
The American Type Founders Company promised to assemble a companion
exhibit showing the modern methods of typefounding. Tolman wrote a
press release about this new exhibit, but he later explained to Hunter, the
papers "got it some balled up, even to placing you in heaven."

A few months later, Hunter sent two moulds to Tolman for the museum collection: "One is a bamboo mould, such as was used by the Persians as early as 700 A.D. and [the second] was this type of mould that was used in Europe at the introduction of paper-making about the eleventh century." Examination of the 12 x 22 inch bamboo mould indicates that it was probably constructed by Hunter. The laid lines are of a crudely split bamboo, about 6 splints per inch, and these are laced together with cords and attached to the ribs running under each chain line. The wooden ribs are doweled into the bamboo frame held together at the corners by thongs. There is no deckle. The second was an oak and brass mould from the Van Gelder Zonen Mill received by Hunter in late 1920. Apart from some of his later limited editions books, these moulds were the last significant gifts Hunter made to the Smithsonian.

Chapter 9

In a venture of this kind one must not consider expense or labor, for if these things were considered beforehand, the paper would remain rags, the type crude metal, and the ink would stay in the ink-pot. Dard Hunter

Throughout his later years at Marlborough and during the early ones in Mountain House, Hunter continued to research and write about papermaking and watermarks. Editors of journals such as *Paper Trade Journal*, *Paper*, *The Printing Art*, *The Inland Printer*, *The American Printer*, and the *Scientific American* regularly wrote asking for articles.* For the most part, Hunter gladly accommodated them. He had a facility for quickly writing concise, informative articles on technical subjects that were easily understood by people in a variety of fields. For example, he often wrote about paper for typographers and printers. If material for these articles could not be gleaned from his collection, he wrote to libraries in America and Europe requesting information. His association with TAPPI's Committee on Bibliography did not cease in 1917, and he soon became a member of the committee. In 1920, he was asked to translate a French papermaking bibliography compiled by Charles Dumercy, which was published by TAPPI and appeared in the *Paper Trade Journal* the following year. (As he did not read French, Hunter hired A. Papineau-Couture of Ottawa, Canada to do the translation.)

One result of these articles was that collectors of art on paper, books, stamps, and currency wrote asking him for historical information, authentication, and valuation. While he offered what information he could regarding the first two, he avoided making valuations. As reliable technical information on papermaking was scarce, these collectors were excited to learn from Hunter that he was preparing to write a book on papermaking and watermarks. From past references, it is clear that he had wanted to do this for more than a decade. In the early 1920s, the opportunity to fulfill this goal was ripe, and in preparation, Hunter stepped up his book purchases to increase his already substantial library.

While corresponding with Ruel Tolman about the typefounding exhibit for the Smithsonian Institution, Hunter mentioned that he would not use his type again to print a book. Tolman was disappointed to hear this, and in late June 1921, he wrote Hunter, "It seems to me there is but one more thing for you to do, and that is to write a book, set it up and print it on your paper. Then you would truly have a book all yours from start to finish, in thought, expression, design and everything else." In the same letter, Tolman suggested that Hunter lend his type-making appliances rather than give them to the museum just in case he needed to borrow them to make more type. Hunter replied, "It has always been my idea to print a book on paper and watermarking but it had not occurred to me to use my own type." A few months later, he was enthusiastic enough about the idea to write that he wanted to cut another, "better" font of type.

By December, however, he had lost interest in either printing his book or cutting a new typeface. That month, Charles "Cy" Rosen, the Roycroft printing superintendent, told Hunter that it would cost about $750 to print 500 copies of his new book. Hunter considered this far too expensive, but he thought of a way to offset some of the cost. The previous month, he had received a proposal from Bert Hubbard to design Christmas cards for the 1922 season. After receiving Rosen's estimate, Hunter suggested a scheme to Bert.

> You ask about the business end of [the Christmas card] proposition and I will try and give you a little idea of what has occurred to me. . . . For some ten years I have been working on a book dealing with Ancient Paper-making and Watermarking. This book is to be issued in an edition of five hundred copies and there will be more than one hundred quarto pages. It has always been my idea to print this book myself but I fear it is rather a large undertaking single handed. I wrote to Mr. Rosen about printing the books and he has already given me an approximate figure on the work. . . . I am wondering if you would care to have me design the cards at East Aurora and see my book through the press at the same time. There are also several other jobs that I might be able to turn your way.
>
> If this would be agreeable to you to have me make the cards at the Shop I could do it for about three hundred dollars a month and I would say that I would be able to produce about four cards a week besides assisting with any other work that was to be done. With the three hundred I would like to have my own personal living expenses. I think you will agree with me that this wage is not out of reason for one of my experience.

But Bert saw no profit for the Roycroft in this scheme, and he politely turned Hunter down.

It is clear from this letter that Hunter had a good idea of his book, and in fact, he had been sending information about it to correspondents, including Sterling Lord.

> Thank you for the information regarding the paste paper. I have done nothing with it yet but want to make the binding papers for my book when it is done. The text is almost completed and then I have the illustrations, that is the full-page ones. There will be something over 170 pages all told so you see it is almost a real book. They keep selling right along—two this week—and when they bring $25.00 each it amounts up. I have had a good many fine write-ups of late and those have helped. In the March number of *Ben Franklin Monthly*, Chicago, I have a three page (5 ills.) story about myself. It may seem very egotistical but one must do this to get along, I find. . . . I am hoping that the day will sometime come about when we can have a neat little business together. I well realize how lacking I am in many ways in running a business as the manufacturing is all that appeals to me.

The title of the book underwent a number of changes from *Ancient Paper-making and Watermarking* to the final one, *Old Papermaking*. The edition also diminished from an initial 500 to 300, and finally to 200 copies. Hunter was troubled about limiting the edition to 200, as relatively few people would be able to own and read the book. With that in mind, he wrote to the English booksellers and publishers B.J. Batsford, Ltd. (as well as to an unidentified New York publisher) inquiring about a commercial edition, perhaps numbering a thousand. Batsford was quite enthusiastic about the prospect but suggested that the availability of both editions be known as soon as possible as "some of the subscribers for the 'de luxe' edition may feel aggrieved when they find that a cheaper edition is to be available." Although Hunter soon dropped this idea, in 1930, *Papermaking Through Eighteen Centuries*, an enlarged version of *Old Papermaking*, was published by William Edwin Rudge.

Once he had decided to print the book himself, Hunter thought that he had enough Marlborough paper, but after a careful cull, this turned out not to be the case. Having no means of making quantities of paper himself, he decided to have it made in England.

In February 1922, W. Green, Son & Waite confirmed that Hunter's pair of large antique laid moulds had been received, and the work to sew on the new watermark was "well in hand." This watermark consists of a branch from which hangs a shield with his initials enclosed. Snuggled between the broken end of the branch and to the left of the shield is "1922." (plate 60) Of course, the origin of this watermark can be traced back to the projects printed for the Chicago Society of Etchers.

The watermark's branch sports two simply drawn trifoliate leaves. Although these leaves, or rather the number of them, would have significance in later books, it is unlikely that they had any particular meaning in this watermark. Two of the 1922 Branch watermarks were sewn to each of the two moulds in diagonally opposite corners. Each was positioned so that once the sheet was folded twice into a quarto format, the watermark appeared on every other page in the lower right corner, parallel to the bottom edge.

Once the moulds were ready, they were sent to J. Barcham Green's Hayle Mill, and soon samples with differing surface treatments were sent to Hunter for his approval. After test printing the samples with a rebuilt Paul Shniedewend No. 2 Printers Proof Press he had purchased in early 1922, Hunter preferred the HP, or hot pressed, paper. In July, Hunter received slightly over 25 reams of white, first quality sheets, and over 3 reams of seconds. Including shipping and duty, the cost to Hunter for 14,668 sheets of paper was about $645, or 4.4 cents per sheet.

While waiting for the paper to arrive, Hunter worked on getting the studio ready. He described this room to publisher and bibliophile, Elmer Adler, on the occasion of the publication of his last limited edition book in 1950.

> The studio where the books are printed is attached to the house and is reached through the hallway of the main house. The name "Mountain House" is one that has clung to this property for a hundred years and it is not of my origin; in fact, I have never liked the name, but after so many years a change was not advisable. . . . The studio is two stories in height, open to the roof, with a narrow balcony around the second floor level; there is a large sky-light in the roof. . . . The printing shop below is about twenty feet square.

Decorating the walls were woodcuts Hunter had made of the Marlborough Mill, as well as watercolors of European cityscapes. Because the studio was not linked to the house's furnace, a stove provided heat. However, for much of the winter, it was simply too cold to print. The skylight provided most of the light by which Hunter printed, but after he lost the sight in his left eye, he could only work in the studio on sunny days. There were two small rooms off the studio that were later made into a fire-proof vault and a darkroom. On the balcony level, the damp, printed sheets were hung to dry. (Eventually, the overhang and a small room beyond became Dard II's wood-, metal-, and gem-working area.)

Once the studio was organized, Hunter began printing the illustrations, of which there were two types: those printed within the text and those appearing as plates interspersed throughout the book. For the latter, he decided to use a variety of papers, including the Marlborough paper water-marked with the DH-in-a-heart. Because a very smooth paper was required for some of the plates, he ordered several types of Japan vellum. He also used paper that he had had made in England for Vojtech Preissig (see Appendix B). For years, Hunter had been buying lots of old, blank paper from book dealers and collectors, which he, in turn, sold to artists and printers. This activity ceased, however, when he decided to use most of his remaining collection as specimens for his book.

Most of the illustrations for *Old Papermaking* were scenes in papermills from different countries and centuries, showing, for the most part, the vatman, coucher, and layman at work. Most of these illustrations were taken from books and prints in his collection. When he did not own the book, he purchased photographs of plates from other libraries and collectors. Some of these illustrations were of poor quality, and Hunter spent many hours retouching or completely redrawing them. If a particular point was not illustrated, Hunter drew a new plate. Whereas the beginning chapters of the book covered the history of papermaking, the last part covered the history of watermarking. Consulting such authorities as Charles-Moise Briquet and Harold Bayley, Hunter made many delightful drawings of watermarks, most as the image appeared on the mould showing the laid and chain lines. The line etchings required to print the illustrations were made by the Bucher Engraving Company in nearby Columbus, Ohio. As soon as he received these, Hunter printed the illustrations that did not appear within the text.

In mid-May 1922, Hunter received word from Hayle Mill that his paper had been shipped, and he prepared to start printing the text. Soon he realized that he needed more of his type to complete the job, and just as Tolman had predicted, Hunter had to borrow some of his appliances and type from the Smithsonian exhibit.

Having finished the colored plates for my book on Papermaking and Watermarking, I am about ready to proceed with the text. It was my original idea to cut another font of type for this book but owing to the shortness of a life time, I have decided it would not be wise for me to commence another font. As it is I have spent nearly ten years in getting the material together for the book so I feel I will have to let the new type go.

I am wondering if you could send me the matrices for my old type, with the NEW mould? Also I would like the thirteen lines of type you have and the ladle. It is a big task to cast type by hand and every letter counts. You might retain a couple lines of type if you like. However, I will send it all back to you within a month or so (perhaps two weeks) and when the book is done I will give all of the type to the Museum as well as the other things. This, I am sure, will be my last book and I will be honored to give everything connected with this outfit to the Smithsonian outright. . . . I would like if you would send the junk by express so it would not be lost.

Over the next few weeks, Hunter cast another font of his type and returned the materials to Tolman in June.

After much sweating I have finally finished what characters I will need for the new book. This is not the kind of weather to stand over a metal pot all day. . . . I think you may now enter the material as a *gift* as I do not see how I will ever need it again. I am sending two lines of type composed which will take the place of the thirteen lines sent me and which I am using. I *am adding an* additional piece of junk in the way of an old composing stick which (if we are to believe the date) is from the early seventeenth century. While I cannot vouch for the authenticity of this stick I see no reason why it is not an ancient one. At any rate it will act as a holder for the two lines of type.*

Throughout June and July, Hunter continued to prepare the illustrations and the captions. For the smaller illustrations, he printed captions in his 18-point type, had them reduced by 40 percent, and made into line etchings. Examination of these captions gives a clue as to the order in which Hunter printed the illustrations. In several two-color plates bound between pages 26 and 27, one of the captions utilizes the uppercase *A* with the serif at its apex. This serifed *A* appears in three other captions, including two text illustrations used at the end of the book. In all other instances the *A* is without a serif. Apparently, just after the commencement of printing, Hunter decided that he did not like the serif, and rather than cut another punch, he simply filed it off every *A* he cast.

After the paper arrived in late July, the first trial printing on it was an announcement, "A SUNDAY NIGHT MUSICAL AT THE MOUNTAIN HOUSE AUGUST twentieth mcmxxii." Inside, the program announced that Edith Cornell Hunter would play Rachmaninoff's *Prelude in C sharp minor*, as well as accompany two soloists. Also printed at the top of the program is a small 1854 wood engraving of Mountain House.

Hunter set the type for *Old Papermaking* directly from his notes. Proofs had to be made each time the type for new pages was locked in the press, because the text lines on the front and back of each page had to be in perfect alignment. If not, both impressions would be seen—a sign of careless printing. In addition, he had to find the right ink, the proper degree of paper dampness, and the perfect amount of packing in the tympan. The ink Hunter used was not of his own manufacture, as was often assumed by others, but was Engravers Proof Black made by the Sinclair and Valentine Company. Dampening the paper was necessary for a number of reasons: first, the paper had a rather compact and hard finish; second, less ink was used when printing damp; and third, Hunter's type was so irregular that a soft, pliable paper was required to print from it. Hunter experimented with a number of different techniques before he arrived at a satisfactory method. (plate 61) In November, he wrote to Lord about progress.

> It is running more smoothly now too that I have gotten on to the use of the press, paper, and ink, a combination that always has to be broken in, no matter what the skill, as handmade paper takes different treatments in the way of wetting, rollers, impression, and ink. I can only do about sixteen pages a month as I set the type, feed the press and ink all myself. It is tedious work and when it is all done I will be glad. Should I count my time at the rate of a grave digger I would come out far behind with the 200 copies at $25.00 each.*

When he finished printing, Hunter turned his attention to the nine specimens of paper and watermarking to be tipped in at the end of the book. The first four were antique laid papers dated 1480, 1580, 1654, and 1725. These were followed by an undated, modern laid paper; the first wove paper, dated 1757 pulled from Baskerville's *Virgil*; and three examples of modern light-and-shade watermark portraits closely connected with Hunter —his Small and Large Portraits as well as the Lord Byron watermark (see Appendix B).

Old Papermaking

In the last few months of 1922, impatient customers wrote asking why the book had not appeared in September as promised. Hunter apologized, adding that it would be several more months before the book would be finished. He also suggested that if an inquirer had not already done so, it would be wise to send $25 to guarantee a copy as the edition was going fast. Book dealers asked for a discount, and at first Hunter refused, but later he allowed a 10 percent discount on orders of two or more books. By May 1923, printing was nearly finished. He was unsuccessful in coaxing Sterling Lord into binding the book (Peter Franck was still in Germany), and so he made arrangements with Charles Youngers of the Roycroft bindery. With little notice, Youngers bound one copy of the book so that it could be included in the American Institute of Graphic Arts' "Exhibition of Current American Printing—Fifty Books Selected by the A.I.G.A." Two weeks after the exhibit opened in New York, AIGA's committee chair wrote Hunter,

> Your book on old paper making in the present Institute exhibition is creating unusual and favorable comment. I have heard of one or two people who wish to buy the book and I would like to buy a copy for myself—or at least I would like to ask you what the price is. I saw Mr. Goudy Saturday and I told him that I was going to write you. He told me to say that he would also like to buy a copy unless the price prohibits him. . . . It is a most interesting and beautiful piece of bookmaking and I would like to congratulate you both on its authorship and its mechanical production. With best wishes, Yours very truly, Burton Emmett.

In fact, by the time Hunter received Emmett's letter, he had decided to issue a prospectus describing the contents and the price. He arranged with Norman T.A. Munder of Baltimore to print 900 copies on the 1922 Branch watermarked paper. Although the arrangement of point sizes of the typeface is a little peculiar, Hunter was pleased enough with the result. In June 1923, he sent a prospectus with a letter to each person who had shown interest, as well as to potential customers.

Once the AIGA exhibition and prospectus business was out of the way, Hunter concentrated on getting the rest of the edition together for binding. Edith helped tip in the photographs, facsimiles, and specimens. Unfortunately, Hunter chose rubber cement as the adhesive, and within a few years, the papers were badly stained. Eventually, the tipped-in illustrations and specimens came loose, causing no end of complaint among Hunter's customers. (Years later, Peter Franck tried to reduce the staining by bleaching and soaking in milk with varying results.)

Old Papermaking is in an attractive case binding, a combination of text paper on the spine and paste paper over boards; the blue, green, red, or purple cover papers were made by Hunter. On the spine, the title and author's name were printed, and below this was printed the watermark found in paper Gutenberg used—a bunch of grapes. Additionally, a box covered with text paper was made for each book. A printed label on Japan vellum was pasted onto the front of the box. As a gift, Youngers bound the author's personal copy in full vellum.

Old Papermaking was a critical and financial success, measured by the fact that the entire edition was sold within nine months of its publication. Well-earned praise for its content and production came from owners and disappointed potential owners alike. One admirer wrote, "I envy you for making the opportunity to do an entire work yourself. This is a feat which William Morris himself never accomplished." Hunter reveled in this praise, and many articles about him and the book appeared in the paper and printing trade magazines in this country and abroad. One reviewer, *most* of whose comments must have pleased Hunter, wrote:

> [*Old Papermaking*] is, moreover, the only thorough and accurate treatise on the subject. . . . [while it] is somewhat awkwardly written. . . .
>
> This is much the most elaborate of Mr. Hunter's books [including the Chicago Society of Etchers books]. All of them, however, possess a quality not unlike that of the Fifteenth Century Italian volumes. His type has strength, individuality, and genuinely significant form. A page by him is beautiful purely as design. The paper is remarkably satisfying, and the type forms an integral part of the page. Printing and paper do not seem separate, as they do in the work of some of the best presses of the last half century. Mr. Hunter's success in eliminating this impression of separateness is due partly, I believe, to his employment of wet-printing, which is uncommon in contemporary work, but which is essential to the best results on handmade paper. Each volume, considered as a whole, possesses marked aesthetic unity. The chief reason is obviously the fact that it is the work of one man, who has made the paper, cast the type, and devised the page design to fit what he conceives to be the essence of the volume.

While many of these articles and reviews relied on previously published material about Hunter, it has to be said that some misleading, or at least ambiguous, information came directly from him. For example, people assumed that Hunter had made the paper for *Old Papermaking* just as he had done for the Marlborough books. In an article Hunter wrote well after he ordered the paper from England, he stated: "This book also will be unique in its way, for not only will I have made paper and type for it, but I shall be the author as well." The prospectus for the book proclaimed, "'Old Paper-making' is printed upon Dard Hunter watermarked hand-made paper with the type made originally by him for this book." While these statements are accurate—most of the plates were printed on his Marlborough Mill paper and the moulds used to make the text paper for the book were Dard Hunter's watermarked moulds—the juxtaposition of the words makes it seem as if Hunter made all the paper himself. Although he could have easily clarified these points, he did not do so, and in fact he repeated them in future prospectuses and articles.

PRINTER'S MARK

It is interesting to note that nowhere in the prospectus nor anywhere in *Old Papermaking* do the words "Mountain House Press" appear. In fact, Hunter did not so designate his press until 1927, when *Primitive Papermaking* was published. However, on the title page of *Old Papermaking* there does appear the so-called printer's mark—a device, or trademark, used to identify a particular printer, press, or publisher. (plate 62) Hunter's mark, not surprisingly, was based on the branch-with-leaf motif that appeared in his Marlborough books and the Vondrous folio. To this motif, which also incorporated the shield with his initials, he added three symbols derived from old watermarks: the bull's head, the Pommée cross, and a clover leaf. From the top of the bull's head grows a staff at the end of which is a clover leaf—an old symbol of the Trinity. But in this instance, the clover leaf paid homage to the first American papermaker, William Rittenhouse, who used this symbol in his watermarked paper. The Pommée cross is one with arms of equal length and circles at the ends, and Hunter cleverly incorporated one end of the cross into the bull's nostril.

This first appearance of Hunter's printer's mark with its two leaves and the clover leaf probably did not have any other meaning. However, in his next book, *The Literature of Papermaking*, Hunter added another leaf for a total of four, signifying the number of books from the private press of Dard Hunter, including the Chicago Society of Etchers books. This continued during Hunter's lifetime and with every book published printed with the Hunter typeface, either Senior's or Junior's, another leaf was added.

ANOTHER SOURCE OF INCOME

Closely following the publication of *Old Papermaking*, Hunter became involved in a non-book-related project, a new building for the Chillicothe *News-Advertiser*. With Junius Hunter, Dard was co-owner of the paper and as such received a weekly income, which allowed him the freedom to pursue his printing, publishing, and collecting activities. In September 1923, Dard and Junius decided to move the paper into new premises and purchase the latest printing equipment. As usual, Hunter wrote Lord about the project, ". . . after this plant is up I will be free to go away as I have no active part in the running of the sheet, simply a minor stock holder." It was typical of Hunter to give everyone, even his best friend, the impression that he was not well off, although in fact he was.

Hunter's contributions to the new building included three stained glass roundels, each 14 inches in diameter, made to decorate the office windows. One of the roundels depicts the founding of Chillicothe in 1796, with a rendition of the state house and the inscription "The First Capitol of Ohio 1800–1816 AD." The second depicts the founding of the newspaper on 11 June 1831. The third is the Great Seal of the State of Ohio, with the accompanying shaft of wheat and bundle of arrows. The roundels now hang in the entrance of the newer Chillicothe *Gazette* building.

The Literature of Papermaking 1390–1800

Not entirely satisfied with *Old Papermaking*, Hunter wrote to Lord,

> The book looks fair but like all other attempts it looks like it might have been much better. However, it is an attempt and will have to go at that. My next book (if ever there is a next one) will be much better as experience is the greatest teacher. . . . We are growing old and each year adds greater difficulties and robs us of the desire to move and become pioneers once more. I think with my work I should be near [New York City] and perhaps it will come to pass. My next birthday says 40 years and you know when one reaches that advanced age it is best to prepare for the next world rather than the present one. They told me in [East Aurora] that I looked younger than ever, but they were always kind there. The great Beyond gets nearer and nearer and the few remaining years that we have ought to be made the most of. I only hope old-age will not creep upon me too strong that I may get to do some real decent work before the grim-reaper reaps. . . . While in N.Y. I saw the Public Library binder and printer. They spoke of you and Peter Franck and admired your work so much; were sorry to learn of your demise from

the bookbinding craft and your entering upon a work in which one eats. They thought it noble of you to run the Oakwood [Binders] as long as you did and said you all deserved great credit. Both said it was not possible to do fine work in books and live at the same time. They are no doubt right for I find it quite true; I would starve on books alone. Too bad but the world is such.

A year later, in a March 1924 letter to Lord, Hunter mentioned that he was starting on his next book, the second part of his *magnum opus* on paper-making and watermarks: a bibliography, *The Literature of Papermaking 1390–1800*. Actually, this book was an update of the 1917 TAPPI bibliography.

While there are many similarities between *Literature* and *Old Papermaking*, there are also major differences. While the paper and type are the same, the format of the book was enlarged from a quarto to a folio. Although this meant that only half the number of pages would result from the same sheet of paper, Hunter preferred the look of his 18-point type on the larger page. The cost of paper was not a primary concern, however, as it could be purchased from England relatively inexpensively; the largest outlay was in the binding. After careful consideration, Hunter decided to bring out *Literature* in a portfolio. He assumed that this would cut down the cost of the book, making his profit greater. Not entirely happy with the Roycroft binding for *Old Papermaking*, Hunter was pleased to receive a letter in November 1923 from his old friend Peter Franck.

> [I was recently told that] you had published another of your hand printed books on Papermaking. . . . Perhaps you will sometime have some of these books bound by Hand and I would like to call your attention to my aim of opening up a bindery, where books will be done the genuine old way from the sewing up. If you have some work please communicate with me and give me a chance. . . . I came back from Europe only 4 weeks ago with my wife [Cornelia], who is here for the first time.

In July 1924, Hunter and Franck settled on a cost of $2.35 for each portfolio: an unadorned, three-quarter linen binding with grey laid paper—and occasionally, paste paper—covers and linen tape ties. While the cost was more expensive than that for *Old Papermaking*, Hunter felt that Franck would do a much better job. The primary advantage was that portfolios could be made well ahead of the publication of the book. This meant that Hunter would not have to wait on the binder before the finished book could be sold.

However, Franck, as consummate a craftsman as Hunter, was anxious to do some serious binding. "With the right advertising I believe the best bindings could be sold with your book, but I am not in [a] position to suggest this to you." In fact, the only known fine bindings that Franck did on *The Literature of Papermaking* were for his and Hunter's personal copies. Hunter's copy is beautifully bound in full vellum with the title, author, and date of issue on the spine, as well as the title and printer's mark in the front cover, all hand-lettered by Cornelia Franck.

As usual, the printing of *The Literature of Papermaking* began with the illustrations. Hunter had decided to include a facsimile of the title page of each of the annotated books, whenever possible. For the most part, Hunter owned the books listed, but for missing titles, he wrote to libraries in this country and abroad to gather information and photographs. To make the facsimiles, he again sent photographs and drawings to the Bucher Company to have line etchings made. He selected the paper for the facsimiles from his dwindling collection of old papers, matching the original as closely as possible; he also used Marlborough paper in a few instances.

Hunter planned to use his type again, and this time there was no need to borrow from the Smithsonian. In a letter to Frank J. Lankes of the Apple Tree Press in Gardenville, New York, Hunter mentioned,

I hope to cut another face someday as I feel that I can now do so much better. I am working on some ornaments to go with the type and they will be cast in a new mould I have just had made. . . . When printing from hard type (such as mine) and with damp paper the type lasts a long time, especially on small editions. My only reason for cutting a new face would be to get a better one.

While in N.Y. I had a very nice visit with [Frederic W.] Goudy and met most of the notable typographers of the city. I have here-to-fore been rather alone with but little communication with the Great American printers.

I am now working on the text for two books, first my Bibliography and next the work on Primitive Decorative Papers. I think this book will take me to the South Sea Islands, Japan, China, Java, etc. etc. I plan to make it my best effort.*

Using a March 1924 letter as scrap, Hunter made a few pencil sketches for type ornaments: a bell with a clapper; two Cs conjoined, one inverted which also forms an H (for Cornell Choate Hunter?); and a shape that resembles Ohio. Although he ordered steel bars for punches and inquired

about copper for matrices within a month of writing Lankes, no type ornaments have been found that might date from this period. Hunter was also
thinking about making new matrices from his old font of type. Using a pre-
cise hand mould and new matrices, his font would have been more uniform
and easier to print, but he did not follow up on this idea.

In preparation for printing the text, he purchased leading and metal
furniture, and another font of 18-point Ivanhoe (whereabouts unknown).
The reader may recall that a set of 18-point Ivanhoe was purchased by
Hunter for use in the Chicago Society of Etchers books. Assuming that he
would never again print anything substantial, he gave that font of Ivanhoe
to Ralph Pearson, along with the Washington hand press. For *Old Papermaking*, he had to use the Ivanhoe Z, and either he had retained a few pieces or
borrowed it from Pearson. As *The Literature of Papermaking* contained many
foreign words, he had to buy a new font of Ivanhoe, as well as alter his type
to produce accented letters such as *ü* and *é*.

In October 1924, Hunter had the copy for the prospectus ready, and he
asked Will Ransom, a book designer and printer, to print it. The two had
been communicating for over a year. In May 1923, Ransom had purchased two
reams of Hunter's 1922 Branch watermarked paper for a book by C. Stansfield
Jones, *XXXI Hymns to the Star Goddess Who is Not by XIII: Which is ACHAD.**
Unfortunately, the book proved a financial disaster (as did many private
press books during this period), and Ransom was chagrined about not being
able to pay Hunter for the paper. Therefore, when Hunter asked him to
print the prospectus, Ransom was happy to do so to offset part of his debt.
He wrote Hunter that he was also "proud to be associated, in however minor
a way, with one of your productions." Ransom hand-printed the prospectus
in Caslon type on Hunter's Large Portrait stationery. There was only one
problem: this heavily sized paper was meant for manuscript ink rather than
printing ink, and so the paper had to be dampened before printing. Ransom
wrote hoping that Hunter would not mind the resulting cockling, "I like it,
but some people do not."

Chapter 10

I want to turn out something good as I feel I have the power for something really fine. If my work had to stop now I would feel that my life had been a complete failure & be greatly despondent. I think I have the ability for good stuff if I can do it—physically. Dard Hunter

During the autumn of 1924, Hunter began having problems with his left eye. While this was annoying, he could still type long, humorous letters that expounded on a variety of topics—politics, the past, the children, Edith, the maid, and pets. As an important insight into Hunter's personality, one such letter to Lord is quoted in its entirety.

Dear Teddy:—Your good letter just here and as it is a very dark, rainy day I will write as I cannot see to work. I have had so much trouble lately in a physical way that I really only do about an hour's work each day. It is, as you know, my eyes. No I am not going to vote for Kool Kal the Klu Kluxer [Calvin Coolidge]. I don't know what he ever did except hold a political job from the time he became of age. I have never heard of anything that he did in any office except keep his silly little puppet mouth shut. All of his pictures look as if he was smelling a dead rat. I must confess I don't think much of Charlie Bryan but I do think a great deal of J.W. Davis. Here is a chap that has really done something and pays $84,000 a year income tax which shows he is smart. In Ohio there is not the slightest question but what the Democrat governor will be elected and I look for the state to go to Davis. Kool Kal simply gets me, I can't abide him for a moment, he is such a weak insignificant little runt without the slightest qualifications for the presidential cushion of these great states of our red, white and blue republic. The whole dam thing is an outrage and I hope some one gets hung as we need more decent men and fewer politicians in office. Some times I think I will run for dog catcher myself and show the public just what a real dog catcher should be. For the past seven months I have been working on my new book which is now drawing to a clothes [*sic*]. It is a folio and Peter made the portfolios in which each copy will go forth. The price is thirty dollars but you need not remit as I will send you a gratis copy in remembrance of times past. A good many are sold but not all. My next book is to be on Primitive Papermaking and I will have to go around [the] world to gather material for same. Have a lot of specimens already but no first-foot information. If you can arrange your affairs I would like to have you go along. It is not an expensive trip but a long hard one. I leave S.F. and go at once to Tahiti and from there journey to the other points in the remote parts of the world. Come go along and get a new outlook on life. This country is too full of Rotary, Kewanee, Lions, Owls, Bats, Rats, Fords, Bathtubs, piffle and politics. Let's get away and get a new look-out on the thing for the U.S.A. does not hold it all by any means. The whole trip can be made for about one thousand dollars and maybe not that if you should die down in Fiji. My work has been really very successful in an artistic way and things are moving along in good shape. After twenty years of struggle to keep the old wolf from the gate I am at last getting to a place where I can not only make enough money to support the canary but have a place in the realm of arts and grafts that is at once enviable and free from taint. My trouble now rests with my great physical weakness which I am trying hard to surmount both by the help of Mother Eddie and Material Medica. My left eye has entirely gone back on me, that is it has refused to function, which is the proper word used by all Rotary speakers. Should left [*sic*] eye take a notion to do the same as left eye has already done I will be left in the cold as then I would have to give up my work and take to a wheeled chair. I have been treating with our local osteopathic Dr. Still and he has given me upwards of 50 worth of treatments but to no avail. I have tried everything but Lydia E. Pinkham [a popular, efficacious tonic]. The oculists say it is nerves and the medicos say they don't know what it is. All I know is I can't see. That is strange about you meeting Wil Nikoli, for such did he spell his name when I knew him upwards of 25 (¼ century) years ago. This was before I went up to the lately Elbert Hubbard's art pavilion even which was a long time ago as you know. I don't recall much about Wil but as I remember him he was a sort of a chump. There was a kid with him who acted as assistant named, as I remember, "Bobby" [Dobski] and he came also from that famous town in Illinois called Monmouth. Did you know that Mrs. Gaspard came from there? Anyway I was with Nicol (his right name) for several months and I believe we went to California together and the north-west, in fact I believe we toured your noble state of Iowa. I have forgotten all about that trip as so much has happened since. If you see the little squirt remember me to him and tell him he is a dam fool. After I went with him, or he with me rather, I was with four or five other magicians and toured many remote, unheard of places so I just can't locate him or where we went exactly. All I remember was he was hot for money and had a glass diamond that he was continually polishing with a piece of toilet paper. It is well that our memories are not overly long as if they were our minds would become a sort of garbage can. Just as well to forget the past, or parts of it, the same as a swill pail is emptied occasionally. Now I have given you a long earnest letter sit right down to a Leopold desk and give me an old fashioned ringer, one that is not tainted with big business, income tax, Kewanee or Klue Klux. All of these things give me a pain in the spinalgogetus. The boys are doing well in school, reading Hamlet and adding figures like a burrows [Boroughs]. I fear if they keep on so well and go clear through high school and clean through college they won't be worth a cuss to anybody. I count on the stupid boy every time for I was one myself and I know. Dard, Jr. had his first suit of clothings today—pants, coat and vest—and he is very proud. Cornell goes to the first grade although only 5-½ but he wanted to go and his mother wanted to get rid of him around the house all day. Now I am here all the time but when I go to Fiji she will be able to play bridge every day all day. We have a little Fijian here who washes the dishes and looks at her African face in the mirror to see if she is turning white. She has bobbed her kinky wool and has it ironed every day to extract the springs. She has got it to the point where it resembles that on the head of Rudolph Vaselino. Mother, Kitty and June are all the same. We have a German police dog (Duetschespolitzipantsgrabberhund) which Edith imported from Fortsheim, Germany. He is full-blooded policeman and cost more money than either of the children. His name is "Kola" spelled "Coula" named after Mr. Wil Nikoli. Today he (the dog) is rather indisposed as he swallowed a green paint brush and he is being treated by our C.S. practitioner for worms. Every little while I slip him a dose of castor oil which keeps him in condition unknown to Mother Eddie. He is a nice dog and will grow in to a right manly fellow but too much C.S. will get under the most delicate skin. We also have a yellow canary which Edith raised from seed, she got him to sing and the dog to house watch. However, the dog does the singing and the canary is turning out to be a fine night watchman. I am still the check signer as heretofore.

With kindest regards to your family of wives and growing children, I am, very faithfully yours, DARD.

Two months later, in November, Hunter was admitted to Grant Hospital in Columbus suffering from a serious hemorrhage in his left eye. Doctors performed an operation, but they could not save his sight. They also could not agree on the cause, but it was generally attributed to stress. In later years, Hunter wrote, ". . . when I was building the small paper mill in Marlborough, I had been struck in the left eye by a flying spike, but little was thought of the incident at the time. The shock had apparently been more severe than I realized. . . ." It now appears that the real cause for the hemorrhage and loss of sight was due to Hunter's having the disease histo-plasmosis.*

Thus, Hunter spent his forty-first birthday, Christmas, and New Year's Day in the hospital. Word about his condition rapidly spread, and he received many letters filled with hopes for a speedy and complete recovery. It fell to Edith to answer all of the letters and deal with the phone calls. Accounts of his progress were even reported in the personal sections of several trade papers. While he was despondent about his future, it pleased him to think that if his work did cease, at least it would be missed.

The end of 1924 was an already emotional time for the entire family, when a second tragedy struck: Harriet Hunter suffered a fatal heart attack and died on 25 January 1925. She was sixty-nine years old. It is impossible to estimate how much Dard was affected by the death of his mother. Perhaps his grief can be measured in what he could not bring himself to say to Lord in a handwritten letter the day after she died, "Dear Sterling:—Just a note to say that Mother passed away last night after only a few days illness. Sincerely, Dard."

He decided to dedicate *The Literature of Papermaking* to her. On the back of a letter of condolence, he worked on the dedication: "This book is dedicated to the memory of my Mother, H.R.H. 1859–1925. The only person who understood my exertions." Over this inscription appears the simple: "To H.R.H. and E.C.H." In the end, he chose, "Dedicated to the Memory of My Mother Harriett [sic] Rosemond Hunter, 1858–1925." (She was actually born in April 1855.)

Fortunately, most of *The Literature of Papermaking* had been printed by the time Hunter was hospitalized. Only a few of the introductory pages needed completion. In spite of the fact that Hunter's doctors had prescribed complete rest for several months, by early February, he was back at the type-case where he set the Prefatory Note just as his mother had copied it out—the last thing she wrote before she died. The page is decorated with a large initial *D* printed in red, in the center of which is a Jester or Fool (for foolscap, an old designation for a paper size similar to the modern legal size). The frontispiece is a sepia photogravure of the Marlborough Mill, which led to all kinds of confusion as readers assumed that Hunter was still located in that quaint setting.

By March, Hunter had received the prospectus from Ransom and copyrighted *The Literature of Papermaking* at the Library of Congress. As was the case with *Old Papermaking*, this new book was also displayed in the AIGA's annual juried exhibit, "Fifty Books of 1925," held that year at the Grolier Club in New York City.

A YEAR OF REST AND INDECISION

In February 1925, Edith, who maintained her husband's correspondence and then helped him through his mother's death, succumbed to an illness. Because she would not allow herself to be administered to by doctors, she sought complete rest at the Christian Scientist home in Boston, where she remained for several weeks. Recent events had left Hunter feeling despondent and drained, as can be seen in a letter he wrote to Charles Brigham at the American Antiquarian Society:

> In one of your letters to me you asked about my library. I do not know whether or not you have heard about my misfortune but I have had considerable trouble with my eyes during the past six months. . . . It now looks as if I would never be able to do any more close work and I am leaving May 23d for a several years' stay in Europe. So my books may be for sale.

Although he had been planning to go to the Orient to collect material for his next book, *Primitive Papermaking*, it is clear from the above letter and others written at this time that Hunter was seriously considering giving up printing and publishing altogether. In England, he hoped to relax in the company of old friends, as well as travel in Ireland and Scotland, the birthplaces of his ancestors. But by the end of April, the dark cloud that had enveloped him began to dissipate, and he felt an increasing desire to get back to *Primitive Papermaking*. He canceled plans to go abroad; however, he did recognize a psychological need to get away from home. Upon Edith's return in May, he traveled to New York City, where he attended the opening of the AIGA exhibit. While in the city, he stayed with Quinby Duble-Schelle, a family friend from Marlborough days and a relative of the Dubles, old friends of Edith's. They went on a long trip through the eastern states and ended their sojourn at the Duble Camp on Mount Riga, near the village of Lime Rock, Connecticut during the months of July, August, and September. Harrison Elliott joined them at the camp as he was between jobs, having worked for the International Paper Company in Philadelphia until that summer. Elliott and Hunter went on to East Aurora and arrived back in Chillicothe in October. That trip cemented their relationship, and over the next few years, they were almost daily correspondents. Completely rejuvenated, Hunter wrote to Lord about his future plans.

> Elliott and I are planning to go into papermaking and printing of books down east and are now looking for a suitable acreage on which to build a small shop. Will be in the vicinity of [New York City,] Ridgefield, Conn. perhaps. . . . Don't feel that I care to live in Chillicothe again. May sell out here, at least the houses. Feeling better. . . . Expect to go abroad this winter and start in the spring on our new venture.

"Harry," "Hairs," "Hal," or "thy harold," as Elliott signed his letters, was more pragmatic than Hunter about these grandiose plans. He had been poor and knew that dreams did not put food on the table or pay the rent. Although Hunter continued to write about one scheme and then another, Elliott had to bow out when he finally secured a position in the advertising department of the Japan Paper Company in New York City in early 1926.

Hunter kept busy during the last months of 1925 by making stained glass panels. On the verso of a letter dated 7 October, there are two designs for a panel of the Willcox Ivy Mill, complete with the dove and branch and ivy leaf watermarks used by this early American paper mill. Although it is not known if this panel was executed, it bears a striking resemblance to an extant set of three panels Hunter did make. These small panels commemorate the papermills of the first English papermaker, John Tate; the first American papermaker, William Rittenhouse; and the reviver of hand papermaking in America, Dard Hunter.* Work on a larger panel, intended for a window in the mill Hunter still hoped would come to fruition, began in November.

> I am making a leaded glass window for my new mill and between cutting glass I will drop a line to you. With only one eye one grows tired easily and then there is always the thought that a piece of glass may fly up and put the other optic in its grave. This window is rather a large affair depicting the vatman in the act of making a sheet of paper, the

man at the press, and stampers, paper hung to dry, etc. I am making it to fill in a gap of time between the period I came here and when I will go [abroad].

This panel, measuring 46 x 25.75 inches, is titled in the glass, "PAPY-ROMYLOS 1662."* (colorplate 10) Inspiration for this panel came from G.A. Böckler's *Theatrum Machinarum*, published in Nürnberg in 1662. Papy-romylos translates from the Latin as papyrus + mill, or papermill. Apart from their aesthetic qualities, these windows show an astonishing technical ability for someone recently blinded in one eye.

Primitive Papermaking

In December 1925, Hunter traveled again to New York City, this time to find a building where he and Elliott could set up their small papermill and print shop. The search was fruitless, but in the heady atmosphere of the big city, Hunter was again inspired to return to *Primitive Papermaking*. Eager to tell Lord about it but without his typewriter, Hunter wrote in longhand. The writing is as legible (or illegible) as usual, but the lines have a distinct slant from the lower left to the upper right, an indication of his impaired sight.

> I do have a couple of books in mind that *must* be done for the sake of the great gasping public, waiting for every word that drops from my pen. From this bit of sarcasm you might think I was peeved at the reception given my dribblings in book production—but not so at all for my work has been given far more attention than it has deserved or expected from me. I really am surprised at times the way some do regard my ama-teurish attempts at book-writing & book-making but I have enough sense to know just how little my junk does amount to. The public may be fooled but I am not. If my right eye holds out (& I think it will—is getting stronger) I want to turn out something good as I feel I have the power for something really fine. If my work had to stop now I would feel that my life had been a complete failure & be greatly despondent. I *think* I have the ability for good stuff if I can do it—physically.

When he returned home, Hunter immediately made plans to travel to the South Sea Islands.

The idea to write a book on the primitive "papers," or more accurately, the beaten bark material, of the Polynesian islands and Central America actually began in late 1923. From that point on, Hunter read everything he could get his hands on pertaining to the subject. He wrote to consuls, major collectors, libraries, and museums asking for references, photographs, and specimens, as well as tools. Over a two-year period, he amassed an enviable collection of *tapa* from the South Seas and *amatl* from Central America, primarily Mexico. He could have written his book without going abroad, but as he mentioned to Lord, he needed to see the manufacture of this material "first foot." He did not, however, feel it necessary to revisit Mexico, as he had seen the making of *amatl* during his sojourn in Cuernavaca in 1906.

In mid-February 1926, Hunter left by train for San Francisco; Edith agreed to serve as "secretary" while he was away. To save money on telegrams, the Hunters decided on short coded messages, although Dard reassured Edith that if there was an emergency, she should not spare words to make the situation clear to him. Just before he sailed for the South Pacific, Hunter sent her a letter in longhand, having packed away his typewriter.

> Dear Edith:—.... The trip now seems long & I fear it will be rather lonesome but it must be undertaken. I do not think I will start out again alone as it is depressing, especially with my sight as it is. I notice it so much more in the city where there are large crowds & so much traffic. In the S.S. Isles & N.Z. I will not be bothered as there the cars are not so numerous or is there so much hustling. . . . Do take care of the boys & yourself as I will worry about you all. Never neglect the children *for any cause whatever*. If they are sick—get doctors—this is my wish. Please respect my wishes!! I think they will be all right. Take care of them no matter how much else you have to give up. They are the important part of your life—far more than religion, music or card play. . . . Lovingly, Daddy.

Listed as Dr. Dard Hunter on the ship's passenger list, he shared a first-class cabin with another man, and while the ship was cramped, the passengers proved good company. Normally a shy and reticent man, Hunter wrote, "I find my smoking habit has a tendency to make more of a 'mixer' of me."*

The ship sailed in a south-southwest direction toward the French Polynesian Islands. After twenty days at sea, the first port of call was at Papeete on the island of Tahiti. From there, the ship's next landing was at Avarua on Rarotonga Island. While at these two ports, Hunter collected newspapers, broadsides, and postcards that he mailed home with notations to "Please save this," but no *tapa* was made on either island.

He then sailed to New Zealand, landing in Wellington on 15 March 1926. After a brief visit, he traveled by train to Auckland, where he was to meet the next ship. Hunter very much enjoyed the New Zealanders, describing them to Edith as charming, hospitable, and admirable people. It was cooler there—a welcome relief from Tahiti, where temperatures hovered around 110 degrees F. From the few extant letters written during this journey, it is clear that Hunter was homesick and tired, but he was glad he had come. While he complained a bit that he was having problems with his eye, his letters were mostly filled with descriptions of people who invited him to their homes and took him to the theater. In fact, his social life was so busy that he had no opportunity to revisit Wellington and other cities. Although he wanted to stay longer in Auckland, he was most anxious to get back to work.

On 27 March, he sailed from Auckland to the Fiji Islands and the capital, Suva, the first port of call. To see *tapa* being made, Hunter traveled on to the island of Taviuni. Here the natives, women primarily, prepared the bark "cloth" in the traditional manner. Differing from paper in formation, not raw material, *tapa* is made by removing the white inner bark from the stalks of shrubs related to mulberry. First, the long, relatively thick strands are moistened and then beaten with intricately carved sticks over a prone log until flattened into a small sheet. To make larger pieces, sheets are over-lapped, and the joints beaten until the separate pieces become one. Con-tinued beating renders increasingly wider and thinner sheets and by joining these, very large pieces can be made. Stamped or stenciled decorations, usu-ally in geometric patterns, are applied in primarily reddish browns and black. The *tapa*, which can be as soft and supple as textile, can be used as clothing, floor mats, or wall coverings. By the time Hunter arrived on the islands, very little genuine, good-quality *tapa* was made; most pieces were inferior *tapa* made as souvenirs.

After collecting bark, *tapa*, tools, and whatever else he could from the Fijian craftspeople, Hunter proceeded to the Tongan Islands. The ship landed at Nuku'alofa, now the capital of the island group. The sound of the beaters against the log led him to a group making a ceremonial piece. As not many Westerners were interested in this traditional way of manufacturing *tapa*, the natives were delighted by Hunter's enthusiasm for their art and craft. Again presents were given him. Some days later, he traveled to Lifuka of the Hapai Islands, but found no *tapa* being made. At the Vavau group, he found a woman beating bark. He wrote about trying to emulate her rhyth-mic pounding, but found it surprisingly difficult and fatiguing. As before, he was presented with *tapa* and with a number of the tools he had seen in use. Hunter's last fact-finding stop was at Apia on the island of Upolu in the Samoan Island group, where he also saw *tapa* manufactured. Packing up his treasured possessions, Hunter embarked for the trip back home via

Honolulu. He finally arrived on the mainland on 5 May and took the train east, arriving in Chillicothe around the 12th. He had been away for nearly three months.

His first priorities were to catch up on his correspondence and to write the last of two articles about his trip, to be printed in the *News-Advertiser*.* Throughout the summer of 1926, Hunter collected together his notes from the trip and started work on *Primitive Papermaking*. In this endeavor, he had help from his friend Martha Trimble Bennett, who became his copy editor, the role his mother had played.

He examined each piece of *tapa* in his collection. (plate 63) He planned to include samples of these materials, as well as the unprocessed bark, as tipped-in specimens in the book. He spent considerable time drawing many illustrations of *tapa* beaters and facsimiles of bark cloth that he could not include as specimens. Hunter devoted more time and effort over this book than any of his previous ones. He wanted this book to be his best effort, as he felt it could possibly be his last.

In October 1926, he received the text paper: over 8 reams of light cream color, antique laid paper, again made at Hayle Mill. Hunter preferred this slightly toned color to the earlier white sheet, and the paper was also 6 pounds per ream heavier. The moulds used were the same ones upon which the 1922 Branch watermarked paper had been made, but as was noted in the prospectus, Hunter changed the watermark to match his printer's mark as it appeared on the title page of *The Literature of Papermaking*. This water-mark, called the Bull's Head and Branch, also included DARD HUNTER. (plate 64) (It is puzzling, though, why Hunter chose the printer's mark from the previous book with four leaves as the basis for the watermark to be used for his fifth book.)

Peter Franck was again commissioned to make portfolios of the same basic design and materials as those made for *The Literature of Papermaking*. During their correspondence, Franck mentioned that Bruce Rogers was selling a special edition of his book on Geoffroy Tory, the sixteenth-century type designer, for $75. This inspired Hunter to raise his price for *Primitive Papermaking* to that amount from the original $60.

By February 1927, Hunter prepared to begin printing the text, but he found that he was low on a few letters in his font. He wrote Tolman asking for a loan of the matrices for the lowercase *a*, *k*, *r*, and *e*; he confirmed that he did not need the mould as he had purchased one from Germany a few years before. However, when Hunter cast the letters in this new mould and tried printing with them, he realized there were problems. To Tolman, he explained, "I now find the mould I have here is not the proper height for my type." Indeed Hunter's hand-cast type made in his hand-fashioned mould was not uniform. On the press bed, this caused much frustration. Dard Hunter II later explained,

> During the process of pulling impressions on his Washington hand-press, the type had an inclination to be forced slightly up in the middle of the form because of the inaccuracy of the type body formed by the hand-made mould. More than once I have seen him become so exasperated and irritated by this deplorable situation that, with hammer in hand, he attempted to smash as many letters as he could. Another time Mother was in the studio print-shop when this aggravating condition was about to reoccur. I saw her place her hands over the type in the bed of the press, thereby preventing him from smashing it.
>
> Because of fewer words in a line for a quarto format, this inaccuracy would not be so evident as it would be in a folio. In measuring a line of type the width of a folio, (in this instance, about seven and five-eighths inches long), there is a variation of almost one-sixteenth of an inch difference from the head to the foot of the line of type. In addition to this difference, there is also a deviation from height-to-paper of about five to six thousandths of an inch throughout the font, but this is not critical because the handmade paper, softened by dampening, tends to absorb this inaccuracy. Considering these imperfections, it is not too difficult to sympathize with his vexation and annoyance.

From this description, it is no wonder that at the conclusion of printing each of his books, Hunter declared he would never print another. *Old Papermaking* had not caused too much trouble, and *The Literature of Papermaking* had relatively little text, but *Primitive Papermaking* was much longer and was a folio. In August 1927, printing of the text was finally complete, and as before, Hunter vowed never to use his type again.

The prospectus for *Primitive Papermaking* was, for the first time, printed by Hunter. Using half of a sheet of his Bull's Head and Branch paper (and some sheets of the 1922 Branch watermarked paper) folded once, he printed the prospectus in Caslon Oldstyle No. 471. It is clear from the prospectus that Hunter still thought of his press as the Dard Hunter Press. Soon after the prospectus was printed, however, he decided to change the name. On the title page of *Primitive Papermaking*, the imprint MOUNTAIN HOUSE PRESS appears for the first time. Also on this page appears the printer's mark with the requisite number of leaves on the branch: five. (plate 65)

Two colors of ink were used to print the title page; the title and printer's mark were in what Hunter called "Tonga brown," while the remainder was printed in black. This rich, organic brown, which Hunter mixed himself, is echoed in the sepia photogravure frontispiece, a reproduction of a 1852 chromolithograph of Chillicothe showing Mountain House soon after its completion. In addition, the brown ink was used throughout the book at the beginning of each of the four parts, as well as for the large initials.

Hunter expressed doubt that *Primitive Papermaking* would sell well at the unheard-of price of $75. But, he reasoned, if the cost of the trip was included in the normal expense of producing an edition, he had no choice. He need not have worried, however; orders started pouring in soon after the prospectus went out. Once the owner received his or her copy, a congratulatory letter was invariably sent to Hunter. Compliments were well received, but perhaps none as welcome as that sent by Peter Franck, "What a work of beauty. I think it the most marvelous book I laid my hands on in all my career as a binder." (plate 66) But the most critical, fair, and meaningful assessment of the book came from his old friend Ralph Pearson.

Have been waiting to read the book before acknowledging to see if the first thrill of seeing and touching it was maintained thruout.

Dard, you have made a precious book. It reeks with distinction. Lawrence Gomme was here when I opened it and I asked if there was still a market for the special extra fine editions. He said yes for the job of distinguished craftsmanship, no for the ordinary de luxe editions. The recognition you are getting for what you are doing proves this of course and my private guess is that your work has been a potent influence in creating respect for the craftsman and waking book people up to the limitations of the pseudo.

The title page is sheer joy to look upon. The dark red ink goes perfectly with the black. Paper and type belong together—with the same roughness and hand made quality. The binding is a suitable housing, the wrapping tape a suitable restraining influence. The enclosures of original specimens make the book invaluable on the subject side and fit in with your creation of their setting. The drawings in text are bold enough to go with type and paper—as on pages 26 and 32 and prove the richness of that combination. In contrast the drawing on page 11 is too weak.

Two items that I don't like and that hurt the harmony so consistently maintained elsewhere in my opinion are the *old* print frontispiece and the photostats. Neither belong. I realize the illustrative value of the latter but wish you could have translated the material into line drawings. The former is inexcusable and I feel like calling you down roundly for doing it. That *old* plays into the hands of our ancestor worshippers and my picture of you is of you doing just the reverse—forcing attention and respect to the living producer. You have evolved from the past in all this work and I shall never be satisfied till you definitely put that phase all behind you where it belongs and turn thoroughly to creation as you have in this book (with this exception).

So bunches of thanks for my copy. It pleases me that you want to give me one even after you have so thoroughly arrived and when the books are in such demand.

Following the success of *Primitive Papermaking*—it sold out in less than six months—it was obvious to Hunter that his books had gained an enviable and well-deserved reputation for the quality of the information, clarity of writing, and beauty of production, not to mention value, particularly investment value. However, he did receive a number of complaints from dealers who were given little or no discount. Katherine White of Dawson's Book Shop in Los Angeles offered a remedy.

"Primitive Papermaking" . . . is so very good that it would have sold equally well at $100.00 and had you given the dealers a 25% discount at that figure your expenses of shipping would have been materially decreased and the turnover of your initial expenditure increased. That is only a suggestion, but after all people who will pay $75.00 for a unique publication will pay $100.00 quite as readily and the work undoubtedly merits the price.

Hunter had five years to consider this suggestion before the next Mountain House Press book, *Old Papermaking in China and Japan*, was published, but he did not take Ms White's suggestion. In that five-year interim, he became totally immersed in fulfilling his dream of starting up an American mill to produce handmade paper.

Chapter 11

After Primitive Papermaking *was printed in 1927, my enthusiasm for making paper by hand took a dubious turning: the establishment of a commercial handmade-paper mill, the only one in the Western Hemisphere.* Dard Hunter

Following the failure of the Hunter Mills to materialize in the early 1920s, Horace Mann of the Bucks County Historical Society (now the Mercer Museum in Doylestown, Pennsylvania) tried to prevail upon Hunter to sell all of his papermaking equipment to the society. Hunter agreed, but never got around to shipping it. After several years, Mann finally gave up, and the equipment remained crated up in the barn at Mountain House.

Plans to set up a paper mill came and went. At one point, Hunter even had the idea of starting an artists' colony where all aspects of the book arts would take place. He wrote several like-minded souls, Will Ransom and Frank Lankes included, asking their opinion of this idea, but no one felt that such an esoteric enterprise made fiscal sense in those unpredictable times. Following this disappointing response, Hunter joined up with Harrison Elliott to try to establish a paper mill and print shop in New York City. Elliott, who worked for the Japan Paper Company, was very interested in making paper by hand, but unlike Hunter, he was a pragmatist. While he wanted to be a part of this exciting plan, he also knew Hunter well enough to understand that his friend had great difficulty committing to projects, i.e., spending money. Elliott's response to one of Hunter's grand plans was preceded by a note at the top of a letter, "SCHEME NO. 352,896. When replying, please refer to above number." Hunter rarely allowed himself to be upset over Elliott's gibes, but eventually he realized that Elliott was not "something like myself," as he had described the ideal business partner in a letter to his mother in 1917.

As he prepared to go on his South Sea Islands trip in early 1926, Hunter contemplated that his dream to establish a papermill might remain just that. And one could argue that it might have gone unfulfilled had it not been for Harry A. Beach, who first came to Hunter's attention in May after his return from the Pacific islands. Their association was initiated by Elliott. While Hunter was halfway around the world searching for *tapa* makers, Elliott was trying to arrange a hand papermaking demonstration to be held as part of the 150th year celebration of America's independence. Elliott had arranged for Hunter to do the demonstration, as he was thought to be the only person in the country capable of such a thing. It was much to Elliott's surprise, then, when another hand papermaker came to his notice. He could not wait until his friend's return to write this letter.

> You will be interested in the telegram which I received yesterday . . .
>
> Kalamazoo, Mich.,
> May [April] 5, 1926
>
> "If you have not completed arrangements for the equipment to be used in hand-made paper section of Sesqui-Centennial Exhibit, I am in position to furnish you two men with years of experience in all branches of hand-made trade in England. We have complete equipment of vats, moulds, press, etc. We can make unusual and artistic water marks. Harry A. Beach."*

Within a day of returning from his trip, Hunter read Elliott's letter and wrote to Beach. He received an immediate reply from Mrs. Isabella King Beach, as her husband was away on business.

> Some time ago, Mr. Beach organized, after three years of effort, a small group of hand paper makers, principal among whom is a man of wide and varied experience in the English hand made trade. This group is known as The Guild of Handcraft Paper Makers. They have a complete equipment and are manufacturing.
>
> I am reasonably sure that Mr. Beach would not care to dispose of any of the equipment, because I know that he was months in getting it together.
>
> If present plans carry, he will make a business trip to Cincinnati the last week of this month or the first of next. He will have with him then samples of his paper and watermarks. I feel sure that he will be only too glad to call on you in Chillicothe.

This small group actually just consisted of Beach and J.H. "Jim" Armstrong. According to the Guild of Handcraft Papermakers' Articles of Agreement dated 9 April 1926, Armstrong already had considerable experience in the manufacture of hand made paper in America and "foreign countries." According to Armstrong's son, Richard, his father was an expert mould maker who had been in charge of the T.H. Saunders Mill in England and whose great-grandfather worked in the mill in Dartford, Kent. Beach, on the other hand, had no practical papermaking experience; he was a salesman for Garrison's News Agency, distributors of stationery, greeting cards, and high-grade novelties. His primary function in the guild was to find a market and sell the product: watermarked stationery. Beach particularly hoped to cater to Hollywood stars, and indeed, the Guild's first two customers were Mary Pickford and Douglas Fairbanks, although it is not known exactly when this paper was made.*

Hunter was intrigued, and he invited Beach to visit Mountain House in late May or early June 1926. Inspired by Beach's enthusiasm for establishing a proper mill, Hunter renewed his search for a suitable site, preferably in New England. Because his name was well known by certain agents, he signed some letters "Mrs. Helen Edith Cornell" and "Cornell Choate Hunter." With a few leads in hand, he and Elliott traveled to New England in June and July, but their search was fruitless. Upon his return, the frustrated Hunter immersed himself into printing *Primitive Papermaking*; at least this was something over which he had complete control!

At the end of November 1926, Beach, who was now working for the Renard Company, manufacturers of fine toilet soaps, made another visit to Mountain House, and this time he brought along Armstrong. After the meeting, Beach wrote to Hunter,

> Although I realize that there are many obstacles to be overcome, I am sure, that with your co-operation and guidance, it will not be many months before we will be located in the east, and doing the thing we want to do.
>
> Jim is really enthusiastic. His coming in contact with you and your work brought back to him the thoughts of his old trade very strongly, and I feel certain that within a short time after we have received the beater we will send you some very satisfactory specimens. . . . My contact with you has been a great source of inspiration to me, and I want you to know that I appreciate your trust and help.

As a measure of his confidence and interest in the Guild of Handcraft Papermakers, Hunter sent his small beater used at Marlborough to Kalamazoo. Beach promised to send samples of paper as soon as the beater was set up. However, it was months before myriad problems were worked out; it seems that the technical expertise of the Guild members was somewhat lacking. Although Hunter neglected to write Elliott about these new developments, he kept Lord up to date, "We are still thinking of a hand-made paper mill and there is now a chap interested in the scheme that may push it to some termination. I always lacked the business ability and the knack of organization so let the thing slide along, although I believe there is a future for a mill of this kind."

In April 1927, plans for another trip east took shape. A letter from F. Clark of the East Hartford Manufacturing Company in Burnside, Connecticut—a mill that made high-grade papers—confirmed that Hunter and Beach visited there in early May. Part of the Burnside property included a stone building dating back over 150 years that had been used for loft drying and finishing paper. Clark assured the men that the building had possibilities as a papermill, and although Beach and Hunter saw other properties, none seemed as satisfactory as the mill site at Burnside. Before any further action was taken, however, Beach had to hurry home, as his wife was well along in another pregnancy. Finally, in early July, after a few anxious weeks, Mrs. Beach gave birth to their second daughter (their seventh child). A very relieved Beach wrote Hunter that mother and baby were fine. He also wrote that Armstrong had also "given birth" to some paper, which, although fairly dirty, would do for envelopes.

Beach kept in touch with Clark at Burnside, but Hunter was not terribly enthusiastic about the stone building, as it was not large enough to house a working mill, his library, and, most importantly, his collection of papermaking and printing artifacts—his future museum. While he preferred to leave the arrangements to Beach, he also avoided giving him the go-ahead, a tactic previously used in his dealings with the Butler Paper Corporation. Indeed, the indefatigable Beach renewed negotiations with that company to act as sole distributors for the Hunter/Beach mill paper. Beach also wrote Hunter that Paul Butler was very interested in personally investing in the mill, but just between them, neither wanted Butler to become an equal partner.

While these negotiations were taking place, Hunter was also planning another trip to the Orient. It is obvious that Hunter saw his role in the mill venture as "spiritual" rather than practical, once paper production commenced. The question remained, however, where would the mill be established?

THE PROPOSITION

In January 1928, Beach wrote that because of a flood, the paper company in Burnside had ceased operations, and that the stone building was no longer available. A potential property in Lime Rock, Connecticut came under consideration. Beach wrote:

> Even if the present Lyme Rock mill buildings are not satisfactory, no doubt they could be remodeled, or some other building in the community put to use. If the location is what you want, let's by all means decide to go there. The letters that you sent me show that they want you, and I feel sure that we could lease the buildings and later on remodel them or build to suit ourselves. . . . I am very much in earnest about the mill and I have my heart set on joining with you on this project at the earliest possible moment, for I believe that it is foreordained to be both pleasant and successful.

Unfortunately, less true words were ever spoken.

The northeast corner of Connecticut, in which Lime Rock is located, had historically provided the country with wood and iron. One of the numerous abandoned foundries nestled in the foothills of the Taconic Range was the Barnum-Richardson Company, which manufactured pig-iron and general castings. Many of the larger of the B-R buildings were located in Lime Rock on either side of a creek, the Salmon Fell Kill, just below a dam. It was these disused buildings in which Hunter and Beach were interested.

In the 1920s, Lime Rock, a village located in the town of Salisbury, was a curious place. After the foundry closed, the workers had moved away, and Lime Rock became a virtual ghost town. Local residents Albert and Edith Stone felt, however, that the village had potential, and they bought up most of the empty houses and company buildings. Within a few years, the Stones' vision became reality, as their property was purchased and buildings remodeled; gradually, the village turned into an artists' colony.

Perhaps it was during Hunter's long stay at the Duble Camp with Harrison Elliott in 1926 that the pair inspected the nearby abandoned foundry. Although the property did not seem very promising then, Hunter did remember that the buildings were large and that there was a turbine used to gather power from the dammed stream already in place. Attached to the north end of a large frame building, situated on the west side of the creek, was a small cottage and an old grist mill, and to the south end, a fine brick building, which Hunter envisioned as a home for his museum.

In his January letter, Beach also mentioned that he was looking for alternative investment sources that would not expect to have any control in return for their money. The rarely pragmatic Hunter thought this highly unlikely and wrote Beach that he was not opposed to giving up some control as long as he and Beach were the major stockholders. Beach agreed and added, "won't you get some plans formulated for the rebuilding of the Lyme Rock Mill if that is going to be necessary. How about designing a watermark for the use of the Dard Hunter Mill? Then too we will need artistic shipping labels."

In fact, Hunter had already written Stone about the property. In May 1928, after months of negotiations, Hunter bought all of the B-R buildings on both sides of the creek for $3,000. (plate 67) The sale of the foundry, which was an eyesore, was welcomed by the residents of Lime Rock. The fact that it was to be turned into a papermill was received with enthusiasm, especially when it became known that the famous author and printer Dard Hunter was to be its artistic director. Bernhardt Wall, an etcher and publisher, lived across the way, and his was the first welcoming letter Hunter received. Wall, like many etchers in the country, was eager to make use of the handmade paper that would be produced in Hunter's mill.

A few days before the property was legally Hunter's, Beach proposed the next steps.

the attorney . . . [should] draw up the papers of the incorporation for, say, a $50,000.00 capitalization and we can take out $30,000.00 of this, the balance to be left in the treasury. I believe that this will be a reasonable amount and will be the better way to handle it, rather than capitalize just for the exact amount that we put in. My suggestion as to the name, would be The Dard Hunter Paper Mill, Incorporated. I am sure that he can have all of this accomplished and send the papers on to you and then you can come [to Kalamazoo], if you will, or I will make a trip to Chillicothe and we can hold our first regular business meeting, which will be necessary in order to make it all legal.

It should not take more than two weeks to do this and as soon as it is accomplished, I believe the thing for us to do is to move Jim and his family down to Lime Rock. He will be there then with his car, so that if you will go down there too, all the setting up of vats and equipment can be arranged and completed . . . it is my idea, that in order to save money, we should not begin paying salaries to ourselves until it is absolutely necessary. As soon as the place is running and we can turn out paper for sale, then it will be time enough, I believe, for me to devote all of my time to it. I will plan on working for month or so selling the cosmetics in New York so that I can run up to Lime Rock every few days and be of help. . . . I want to make it clear that I am willing to devote all of my energy and every penny available to make the mill a success.

I not only have great respect for your ability as an artist, but also my limited association with you has given me a very high regard for your personal qualities and integrity. Your accomplishments in the unusual work you have been doing surely prove that when you start a thing, you see it through to a finish, surmounting things that to the average person would appear unsurmountable. I am banking on you and looking forward to a long and pleasant association. As soon as school is over, I will move my family . . . we must get the proposition started as soon as possible. Believe me it can't be too soon to suit me.

An undated memorandum was duly drawn up, which bears the signatures of both men. The main points were:
- the corporation was to be known as The Dard Hunter Mill Company;
- the purpose was to manufacture and sell handmade paper for stationery and book-printing;
- Dard Hunter was to purchase the property and arrange renovations;
- once the buildings were repaired, all would be conveyed to the corporation on terms to be agreed upon;
- Hunter and Beach were to provide such papermaking equipment as they had and were to be credited for same in their ownership of stock of the company;
- the stock was to be owned in equal interests, and the payment for same could be cash;
- the property real or personal was to be brought into the corporation;
- Hunter was to be general manager and supervisor of the mill;
- Beach was to secure orders, sell the product, and hire competent labor;
- in the event of dissolution or liquidation of the corporation, certain equipment and machinery would be returned to the parties furnishing same;
- the parties agreed to complete the general scheme and agreements of the corporation and its proposed activities before purchase of the property by Hunter.

Once the memorandum was signed, the attorney was directed to have stock certificates printed up, but this was never done. In the meantime, Armstrong crated up the Kalamazoo papermaking equipment, which included a vat and press, as well as the Marlborough beater. Beach also suggested that his wife, Isabella, receive a few shares of stock as Edith already had hers. This was fine with Hunter, and each wife was given the same number of shares.

On 18 July 1928, all parties met in Chillicothe at the office of Hunter's attorney, John Poland. The name of the organization was shortened to Dard

Hunter, Incorporated, and the requisite documents were signed and notarized. Hunter arranged to transport the English papermaking equipment—purchased in 1920—from Chillicothe to Lime Rock. Before leaving for Lime Rock in early August 1928, Hunter conveyed the mill property from his ownership to the corporation's for $1 (this turned out to be an illegal transaction).

The local *Lakeville Journal* noted the arrival of Hunter and Beach a few days later.

> Dard Hunter, maker of one-man books has come to stay for a few weeks, stopping at Lime Rock Lodge. For a week a box car has been standing on the side track of Lime Rock R.R. Station, containing apparatus for the making of hand made paper. Peculiarly, Mr. Hunter bought this lot of machinery in Salisbury, England, some nine years ago. . . . And so it comes, that the shipment came to Salisbury, Connecticut, where it will be put up and operated as it did 120 years ago in the Merrie England. The curiosity of the hamlet's residents is at last satisfied, knowing that there is actually such a person as Dard Hunter. . . . Harry A. Beach, President of Dard Hunter, Inc., has reached the field for operations in respect to the paper mill. He is a brisk individual, and something is going to happen. With the outfit is Mr. Elliott, a paper man from New York City.

"Brisk" ended up being Elliott's favorite adjective for Beach, the man who had replaced him in Hunter's "Great Work." The Lime Rockers found Hunter a shy and modest man; by comparison, Beach was a charming extrovert. Great things were expected of the mill, and Beach had every intention of satisfying everyone's expectations. Hunter was more circumspect; "the whole thing [is] an experiment of course and no one knows how it will turn out," he wrote to Peter Franck.

WORK BEGINS ON THE LIME ROCK MILL

Hunter went to Lime Rock to oversee and help set up the equipment in the large, three-story frame building on the west side of the creek. However, when he got there, he realized that he had grossly underestimated the amount of work needed to accomplish that task. First, two local men were hired to remove all of the old wooden casting patterns and clean the filthy building. Plumbers were called in to install water heaters for the mill and a bath and kitchen sink for the brick building. All of this took the better part of two months. Hunter and Beach decided to tear down the large foundry building on the east side of the creek, and reusable building materials were utilized in refurbishing the primary buildings. Hunter concentrated his personal efforts and a large proportion of his spending on the brick building, as it was to be his residence, studio, and museum. Indeed, he neglected the renovation of the mill building in favor of it.

Some of the equipment also needed refurbishing. Clark, from the defunct Burnside mill, volunteered to be the consulting engineer, and he arranged for the large beater, purchased in 1920, to be refitted at a reduced cost.* Other pieces of mill equipment had to be purchased, including a stuff chest (from which the pulp was gravity-fed to the vat) and a plater (which imparted a smooth surface to dry paper). Later, when Clark's old Burnside mill was dismantled, Beach obtained another plater, loft poles, and drying frames.

FINDING PAPERMAKERS

Curiously, there was no mention of Armstrong in the *Lakeville Journal* article, and he had been left out of the memorandum forming the mill. Perhaps he felt that his position in the Lime Rock mill would be a subordinate one and decided to abandon the scheme, or perhaps he returned to Kalamazoo after seeing the poor state of the buildings. But even if Armstrong had joined the enterprise as papermaker, additional skilled help would have been required. Certainly, at this point in his career, Hunter had no desire to make sheets of paper, ream after ream, day after day.

When the proposition was first conceived by Hunter and Beach, they envisioned a two-vat mill. The workmen required for each vat were the vatman, coucher, and layman. Additional laborers included a beater man, sizer, boilerman, plater-man, and felt washer. Women could sort and cut rags, help in sizing and parting sheets, and inspect finished paper. Some of these people could perform more than one task, but even so, the minimum number of workers required per vat was about five. Where in the world were there such workers? It was not long before Hunter remembered the English vatman Robert Parry Robertson, first contacted in 1921. As Beach was responsible for hiring the mill workers, he sent off the first letter to Robertson. This was followed by one from Hunter, to which Robertson replied in October 1928.

> I am very pleased to hear from you once again and to know you are determined to place on the market a paper which will be second to none.
> I agree with your intentions to use only the best materials in its manufacture as this is only what a craftsman has the right to expect. It's

an old saying, but very true, that you can't make bricks without straw, and you can't make paper with inferior materials. . . . The mistake, in this country, has been in the lowering of the materials used, even common woodpulp has been used in some English hand made papers and I know who uses that today; some of the Antiques used by the Japan Paper Co. of New York, etc. are made at Little Chart mills. I have couched some of them. Hammer and Anvil; Crown & Sceptre; Crown & Bible, etc., and a lot of other antiques. They were not all they seemed to be, you know.

I shall only be too pleased to come to your country and stay there. As things begin to develop I can get other men to come also; men who I know and what they are capable of doing. . . . Both my son and myself are looking forward to the day we come to you when we shall be prepared to put our full experience into turning out our best work, and by so doing, make the trade name prominent in the history of papermaking.

Even before receiving Robertson's eager letter, Hunter knew he had to convince the United States immigration department that the English papermakers had unique skills. To prove this fact, he placed advertisements in the trade papers for vatmen and couchers, but received no responses.* In mid-October, immigration inspectors visited the mill, and after speaking at length with Hunter, went away convinced that the Englishmen would put no Americans out of work. However, it was not true that experienced American hand papermakers were extinct. In 1917, when Hunter considered expanding the Marlborough Mill, he had contacted James Walter Norman, who, with his father William, had worked in the hand papermaking mill operated by the L.L. Brown Company of Adams, Massachusetts until 1907. In 1917, it was Lord who learned that Norman was living in Pittsfield, Massachusetts and working for the Eaton, Crane Paper Mill in nearby Dalton. As Hunter did not follow through with the expansion at Marlborough, no further action was taken, but in 1928, Hunter spread the word that he was interested in contacting Norman. Hunter wrote Lord that he and Norman were to meet in late November 1928, but it is not known whether they ever met. Suffice it to say, Norman never worked in the Lime Rock mill.

Hunter spent little, if any, time in Lime Rock over the winter of 1928–29, but by May, both he and Beach were again working full-time in the mill. That summer, Mrs. Beach's mother, Mrs. Peter King, and her sons, Hugh, Peter, and John Rogers-King, moved to Lime Rock to help install the equipment. While Hugh and Peter worked only occasionally in the mill, John became foreman and, eventually, the only person associated with the mill in whom Hunter had complete trust.

EARLY PROBLEMS AT THE MILL

Hunter returned to Chillicothe in late August 1929 discouraged because building renovations were proceeding slowly and costing more and more money. He felt that Beach, who was supposed to invest equally in the project, expected him to pay all of the bills. Permission for the Robertsons to enter the country had also not arrived, although, as Beach pointed out, there was little reason for them to be in Lime Rock when paper could not be made. Beach was also pressuring Hunter to pay the expense of bringing them over.

To raise cash to pay the accumulating debts, Beach contacted Julius W. Butler of the Butler Paper Corporation. At the end of September 1929, a draft agreement was drawn up between Beach, Hunter, and Butler in which the latter was to purchase a one-third interest in Dard Hunter, Inc. for a total of $20,000. The Butler corporation was to have sole distribution rights for the paper. In this document, it was stated that Hunter and Beach had each invested $20,000 in the company: property ($8,000), equipment ($15,000), labor, materials, and improvements ($7,000), as well as "good will" valued at $10,000. Unfortunately, this partnership never materialized because Butler wanted to see a financial statement verifying that the business had a sound financial and organizational base. Such a statement, unless falsified, would have shown that Beach and Hunter had actually put much less than $15,000 each in the proposition, that the debts were substantial, and that the company was in disarray. Beach's frustration with the situation was obvious in a long letter he sent to Hunter in early December 1929. From this letter, a number of things were clarified:

• The corporation had never been organized in a way that protected the financial interests of the partners. Beach explained that each partner should have put equal amounts of cash into a corporate account, minus the cost of any equipment, etc. The treasurer of the corporation should have paid bills authorized by the partners and kept a record of moneys received and expended.

• The firms that were supplying the company with materials and labor constantly confused the person Dard Hunter with the company Dard Hunter, Inc. Hunter initially paid company bills from his personal account, but at a certain point, he decided to stop. Beach did not have a clear idea what moneys Hunter had expended, and the converse was also true. As a result, distrust slowly welled up between the partners.

• It is clear that Beach was sincere in his affection and regard for Hunter even though, at the same time, he was exasperated by Hunter's seemingly arbitrary decisions regarding the welfare of the mill.

• Beach lived in Lime Rock while Hunter spent comparatively little time there. Beach was upset that he had to face irate creditors alone. He had given up a lucrative job, moved his large family east, and for months had not only received no salary but had spent considerable amounts of money.

• Finally, there was the nagging issue about the brick building that had captured most of Hunter's attention from the beginning. Tensions were later eased when Hunter conveyed the property, legally this time, to the corporation; a conciliatory Beach agreed that Hunter should retain ownership of the brick building.

On 10 January 1930, Hunter received an alarming letter from Beach stating that creditors wanted their money in five days. An account sheet gave the total indebtedness of the corporation at over $2,300. Beach wrote, "I'm glad you feel the debts should be paid as you mentioned in your last letter. However that doesn't pay them." Amazingly, throughout this crisis, Hunter never wrote anything derogatory about Beach, even to his confidant, Sterling Lord. He did not blame Beach for the difficulties the two men were having, as he realized that they were both in over their heads. Hunter had relied on Beach to take care of business matters; although Beach thought he was capable of doing this, he was not. Things took a positive turn, however, when on 6 March 1930, Robert and Thomas Robertson entered the United States. Hunter and Beach met them at Ellis Island and drove them to their new home in Lime Rock. A few days later, Hunter wrote, "The two Englishmen have arrived and we will probably be making paper within three or four weeks. It is a long, tedious task and I would not go through it again. I can see why there will be very few handmade paper mills in America."

Chapter 12

It is a white elephant with red and green stripes, BUT it is my *white elephant and always will be.* Dard Hunter

On 5 May 1930, nearly two years after the property was purchased by Hunter, the first sheet of paper was made in the Lime Rock mill.* (plate 68) Robert Robertson was the vatman and his son, Tom, was the coucher. John Rogers-King may have acted as layman until the rest of the Robertsons arrived from England. In addition to his other responsibilities, Rogers-King was in charge of the beater. (A variety of moulds were used in the mill, and in many instances, different watermarks were used on the same mould, see Appendix B.)

At first, everyone's spirits were high as the first posts of paper were made and dried, but within a week, Hunter was despondent. He wrote about his frustrations to Dard Jr. a few days before his thirteenth birthday.

> The mill has been, as you know, a very discouraging thing and I cannot yet see the way clear for the making of salable paper. Our stock thus far has been quite dirty and it seems difficult to determine the cause. The first beater was a combination of about half linen and half cotton and it required about 30 hours to beat this hard material. This beater made about five reams, every sheet of which is quite spotted and dirty. The second beater was made up of all cotton and today the Robertsons are forming sheets from it. This too seems to be spotted with minute particles of dirt and we have been at a loss to find the source. I hope that the next lot will be better after the pipes and equipment are cleaned from the constant flow of pulp. The whole project, from start to the present, has been a task that at times I would have given up had I not had the intense interest in the development of a handmade paper mill in America. There are always things to discourage one and you will find as the years come that each little difficulty must be surmounted with

calmness and determination. It never does to let any hardship get the better of you. I want to see good paper turned out of the mill and after that is accomplished I fear my interest may be relinquished as I care more for surmounting difficulties than I do for the every day humdrum after a thing has once been placed upon a firm and commonplace footing. Perhaps this is not the right attitude, but your father is a peculiar person and I hope you will not have the artistic traits that I possess which make one's life rather difficult.

Mr. Beach is quite the opposite and although he is supposed to be a business man and salesman I would not trade my ability in either of these things for his knowledge of them. While he has a certain amount of force and a great deal of enthusiasm he lacks something vital and I very much doubt if he and I ever go on together for long.

I hope that your mother will bring you and your dear brother Cornell here this summer for at least a little while. It is a quiet place and you might have a good time for a little while. The Beach children would play with you, but they are all younger than both of you boys. . . . Everybody asks about you children and your mother as she is a great favorite here among all who met her last summer.

A week later, Dard wrote Edith, "The paper is looking better. . . . This is the third beater full and it is the best we have had as to absence of dirt and the like." In this same letter, Hunter's first observations of the Robertsons were made.

Last night I gave an inscribed copy [of *Papermaking Through Eighteen Centuries*] to the Robertsons and I have never seen such reverence as they showed. They are both so simple and to see their much-loved craft treated in a book was too much for them. They went through it, page at a time, and every illustration called forth much comment and praise. They are very refreshing in this modern world and I only hope they can be kept so. . . . "Old Bob," as he calls himself, does not have much use for B. [Beach] and I don't know how things will come out. He feels that his craft should be reverenced and held in high regard and B. being a product of modern America does not always act just as R. thinks he should. He calls B. the showman. R. resents any display being made of the work and I think rightly. It may be that I will sell my interest after the thing gets going as I feel that I would far rather work alone as I have always done.

It is unfortunate that Hunter did not sell his interest in the mill then. He could have settled into the brick building, worked on writing and printing books, and organized his museum. Being in close proximity to the mill would have allowed him to act as artistic advisor and designer of fine watermarks to earn a small, but steady income. He would have enjoyed meeting the many notable artists who visited Lime Rock, including his friends Ralph Pearson and Julius J. Lankes, as well as John Taylor Arms, Childe Hassam, James McBey, and Troy Kinney. The fact remains, however, that Hunter did not sell out.

Hunter remained in Lime Rock for much of 1930, and for the most part it was an exciting, productive year. On 15 June the *Waterbury Republican* ran a half-page article, "English Craftsmen to Apply Skill in Lime Rock Mill." Photographs of Robert and Tom Robertson appeared, and it was reported that the remaining family would soon be leaving England. In August, Robertson's wife, Emily; youngest son, Reginald, and his wife, Carolyn; and daughter, Gladys, with her fiancé, Leonard Godding, arrived in Lime Rock.* (plate 69)

The best description of the mill and the brick building appears in this article.

The rambling old foundry on the banks of the river is undergoing all sorts of changes while Lime Rock looks on and marvels. The building, with its huge hand hewn beams held together with hand made pegs, is so big that Mr. Hunter can house his paper mill there and still have a large portion left. This he is putting to good use. He is restoring the end nearest the bridge which leads from Lime Rock to Salisbury and here will be the library where are to be housed his priceless collection of books on the subject of paper making, to which he has recently added another of which he is the author, "Papermaking Through Eighteen Centuries," published by William Edwin Rudge. The name of Dard Hunter is familiar to everyone interested in hand made paper and beautiful books. He has spent 20 years in gathering what is the most remarkable collection on the subject of paper making now in existence, and it is for this collection that he is building the library, most of the work of which he has done with his own hands.

Stained Glass of His Own Manufacture
He tore down the extreme end of the old wooden foundry and in the space where it stood, he will lay out a formal garden [called locally, the Dard Hunter Park]. This will be surrounded by the original brick

wall and will border the mill pond. After he tore down the section, Mr. Hunter himself plastered up the old brick wall retaining all the original bricks and hand hewn beams and pegs and built an enormous stone fireplace himself. This is at one end of the library, which will be lighted by stained glass windows which he made himself, for this master craftsman works in glass too. Back of the library will be his studio and on an upper floor to the left of his studio, will be his apartments, consisting of a long living room from which the other rooms open. The whole effect is spacious, artistic and individual. George More [*sic*], a young sculptor who works in a barn across the road and does interesting carvings in wood, is making a panel of Mr. Hunter's water mark design to go over the library door. He is also making carvings of a paper maker and a coucher to go on either side of the fireplace. Mr. More is making the preliminary sketches for a model, to be carved entirely in oak, of a medieval paper mill. This is for Mr. Hunter, too. The machinery and figures of all the workmen will be shown in detail, each figure to be about 18 inches high. It is expected that the library and Mr. Hunter's apartments will be ready by the month of July. . . .

Dard Hunter himself moves in and out of the buildings and around Lime Rock, an aloof and reticent man who prefers to be let alone rather than to be talked to. He does not encourage idle visitors although those genuinely interested are welcome and he is constantly receiving requests from schools and colleges to allow their students to go through. Graduates from Yale and Columbia universities are to be received there during the next few weeks. A number of prominent people who are having him make water marked paper for them have also requested to be allowed to watch him as he models his design intaglio in wax, casts the male and female dies of copper, and continues with the process which produces fine, clear portraits in light and shade.*

The stained glass windows were the end windows of the brick building, which Hunter eventually made of dark yellow diamond-shape panes, complementing the building's Old English look. From Hunter's rendering of the mill, it is clear that the large panel, "PAPYROMYLOS 1662," was to be placed in the window next to the door on the road side. (plate 70)

THE PAPERMAKING MODEL AND THE BUST OF HUNTER
George Moore, a freelance artist, lived in Lime Rock in the summer. He and his wife, Carmelita Gomez, who was in the cosmetic business, spent the rest of the year in New York City. Moore, as mentioned in the newspaper article,

was working on the wood figures for Hunter's library, but soon these became part of a commission from the Crane Paper Mill for a scale model for their proposed company museum in Dalton, Massachusetts. The model was to include the vatman, coucher, layman, vat, stuff chest, two moulds, couching stand, and press, all for $3,000. (plate 71) Moore was in charge of carving the figures while Hunter made the press and vat. Edith and the "Boyz" drove over to Lime Rock in August 1930 and were put to work weaving the covers for the miniature papermaking moulds, as well as the watermark: Z. Crane 1801. A local artisan, Michele Zacchio, made other parts for the model, including the moulds, stuff chest, mould washing tank, and couching stand.* To give authenticity to the model, the Robertsons formed sheets of paper on the small moulds, which measure about 5.5 x 6.25 inches. The opening of the Crane Museum was in late October, and the model, supported by a table measuring about 7.5 x 2 feet, is still on display.

Moore also carved a large oak panel for Hunter's library at Lime Rock, depicting his printer's mark used for *Primitive Papermaking*, the last book Hunter had printed to date. The low relief carving measures approximately 25 x 42 inches. The artist signed it with a simple M in the lower right-hand corner; it now hangs in the studio at Mountain House. Moore also fashioned the wire watermarks for the mill's papermaking moulds.

During Edith's visit in August 1930, she became close friends with George and Carmelita. But a few months after she left, Dard wrote her, "[George and I] get on very well although some of the villagers think a duel should be fought out by us. . . . They are a queer lot, these Lime Rockites and one gets one's fill during the summer." The couples laughed over the preposterous linking of Dard and Carmelita, little dreaming that Beach would later make an issue of it. But something was wrong between Carmelita and George, and soon afterwards, she left him to pursue her own career in New York City. During 1931, the lonely Moore led a pitiful existence in Lime Rock, relying for the most part on what little work Hunter could throw his way. To repay his patron, Moore sculpted a bust, which was cast in bronze by Bauer & Co. in Munich, Germany. Moore received the finished sculpture in early 1932 and submitted it for admission to that year's National Academy of Design exhibition. Unfortunately, the 26-year-old Moore was killed in a car accident in late March. Six days later, Carmelita received word that the bust had been rejected by the Academy; at least George had been spared another bitter disappointment. (The bust is now on display at the Robert C. Williams American Museum of Papermaking.)

DARD HUNTER ASSOCIATES, INC.

A few months after papermaking commenced in May 1930, Beach was obliged to sell a few of his shares to Royal Kellogg to raise money to pay salaries and his mounting debts. As a consequence, the name of the company was changed to the Dard Hunter Associates, Inc. On the new letterhead, Hunter was principal; Beach, business manager, and John Rogers-King, mill director. Kellogg was a silent partner. W.D. Harper, owner of a paper company of the same name and a friend of Kellogg's, took a keen and active interest in the running of the mill. Kellogg recommended to Hunter and Beach that they give Harper sole distribution rights to the mills' paper, taking a 25 percent commission on all orders. They reluctantly agreed.

Following a visit to Lime Rock in August 1930, Harper wrote Hunter that if the mill were to survive it must be better managed. He even offered to eliminate anyone connected with the mill whose "personality is going to grate against yours," by whom he meant Beach. To his credit, Hunter did not take advantage of this offer. Harper sympathized with Hunter's feelings and saw him as the mill's artistic director, but not as the day-to-day manager. To keep the mill's operations under control, Harper instructed Rogers-King to keep a record of all transactions and to send a copy of the report to him every day. (Unfortunately, few of these records exist, as they give details of mill operations.) Harper hoped that this daily report would finally put the mill on a sound management basis. Hunter hated this imposition of efficiency, but he did see some improvement. He wrote Edith,

> The mill has been laid down so far as paper goes for a week, so that the turbine might be mended. It was not giving off the power that we expected of it. The men have been sizing as we have 10 reams ordered and they must go out this next week. They go to Rudge, one size [for] an edition of some unpublished works of Thoreau and the other lot for a year book of the Quarto Club. Also we have orders for some special stationery and a few small lots. . . . We decided, or rather it was decided by [Harper], that we should draw out some kind of salaries from the co. Next week they will start I hope, but this week I let the co. pay my board bill which had got to $83.00. I will not use my own money hereafter as I will do as Beach does. I think things will work out in time.*

The relative calm did not last.

> Our great trouble has been the lack of selling and no one is to blame for this save Beach and Harper. They both seem to lay down on the job and

I really feel that I am the only one who can sell our paper as the printers know me and will buy simply to please. Just at present the mill looks like a financial flop, but no one can tell yet. The trouble started when our original agreement was broken by Beach giving over the selling to Harper in order to sell some of his stock. . . . But Harper coming into the cromo [?] threw Beach out of what he is best suited for and in order to have a job he took the management of the mill and made a botch of it. Last night Mr. Robertson stopped in the Lodge to see me [the apartment in the brick building was too cold] and told me about "hold 'arry" being a nuisance around the mill with his fool ideas about efficiency and the like. He really has no business in the mill at all, but I have been so busy on the [Crane] model that I have not been there at all. So all in all, the thing is in a mess and I feel that it may be better for it to fail than to go on in this way. This is my last partnership! ! ! ! ! ! ! !

As a precaution, Hunter deeded the brick building over to Edith so that the Associates could not lay claim to it if the corporation went bankrupt.

The publishing house of William Edwin Rudge had ordered ten reams of paper, and the Associates knew that the mill's future could very well hinge on the success of that order. Before Hunter could inspect it, five reams were shipped and promptly returned because the paper was "dirty." A replacement batch was made, but this time Hunter rejected it before it left the mill. In a letter home, he remarked that making paper in the old, dirty building was discouraging for everyone as only one sheet in five was acceptable. Eventually, the dirt problem was resolved long enough to complete Rudge's order, which was used in the yearbook of the Quarto Club published in late 1930.* Elmer Adler, publisher of *The Colophon*, also received paper that was used for a short description of the Lime Rock mill written by Hunter, "A Revival of Handmade Paper in America" (Part 4, 1930).

Feeling that the Rudge fiasco might give the mill a bad name, Hunter took the unprecedented step of accompanying Beach to New York City on a selling trip. They assembled a number of samples and packaged them in a portfolio with an attractive label on the front identifying the contents as "Handmade All Rag Paper" (see plate 71). By the end of the trip, Hunter resigned himself to the fact that while the samples appealed to men in the paper trade, they were aware that the supply was unreliable. The tired and discouraged Hunter went back to Chillicothe just in time for Thanksgiving; unfortunately, there was little for which he could be thankful.

By the middle of December 1930, Beach's strategy changed. Without Hunter, it was useless for him to try to sell printing paper, and so he aimed his sights at a market he knew, the upscale stationery market. With one of his daily progress reports, Rogers-King added a note to Hunter about this new venture.

> Things look better. We are sizing a lot and sending it along to be turned into stationery. It seems the logical outlet to me at present. Selling book [paper] means a supply on the shelves of many sorts from which to ship. A couple of reams is useless as book, but will make a sizable and salable lot of stationery.
>
> I am convinced that a month will see us well on the right path to make the mill take care of itself financially. The reception accorded to the stationery in New York is encouraging, and I find that a sheet absolutely a flop as a book sheet will make a good looking stationery when cut up. At least 90% is good for that product. We can slowly work into the other as we go along.

Not only was paper cut up for stationery, it was also dyed in the sheet making it possible to convert unsalable white, dirty printing paper to attractive red and blue note paper.

It was at this point that Hunter finally gave up hope that the mill would ever be what he had envisioned. He had nothing against the production of stationery with or without special watermarks, but his primary goal had been to supply printers with a choice of high quality handmade papers. By the end of 1930, it was clear to him that the mill could not exist much longer, and his interest turned from the quality of the paper the mill could produce to the quantity of money he would ultimately lose. He was pleased that, through Edith, he had retained the brick building, and no matter what happened to the mill, he planned to make it the place where he would have his museum.

By mid-February 1931, the mill proposition seemed close to an end. From Chillicothe, Hunter ordered 15 reams of his Bull's Head and Branch watermarked paper to use in what he thought would be his last limited edition book—a history of papermaking in China and Japan. As soon as the order was completed, the moulds were shipped to Chillicothe. When he received the paper and the bill, he complained bitterly that the paper was of uneven quality, and that he was prepared to pay only a fraction of the invoiced cost. Wrangling about this issue went on for years until Hunter finally got his way.

At the end of March 1931, Hunter had to go to New York City. He had received a telegram from Kellogg imploring him to bring the Lime Rock deeds and corporation papers, as both Rudge and Robertson were threatening to sue the corporation. Into the fray entered Kellogg's lawyer, Ten Eyck Remsen Beardsley. He reviewed the corporation's history and came to the conclusion that certain things had not been done, such as filing the corporation's name change. An interim agreement was finally reached that at least satisfied the Robertson suit; the family was given four weeks of back pay, with a promise to pay the remaining debt soon. Hunter and Beach each contributed $500 to help pay for this and to settle other immediate debts.

Tensions at the mill eased for a few days, but soon everyone was in a tizzy again. Letters, telegrams, and telephone calls, sometimes threatening, sometimes conciliatory, kept Hunter and the other interested parties busy until 15 May. On that day, Dard Hunter Associates, Inc. went into receivership. Hunter was stunned to learn that the receivers were the lawyer Beardsley *and Beach*. Unfortunately, the receivership did nothing to ameliorate the situation and work in the mill came to a virtual standstill. Robertson threatened to return to England, and he wrote Hunter pleading letters asking for money still owed to him by the company. While he was very sympathetic to the family's plight, Hunter could only reply that he was no longer responsible for any company debts. A number of bitter letters were exchanged between the two, and it is significant that from this point on, Hunter was careful to make carbon copies of all letters regarding the mill.

Amid this chaos, Hunter did receive some good news. First, the American Institute of Graphic Arts conferred upon him the Medal of the Institute in recognition for his role in ensuring "American understanding of paper making, type design, and bookmaking." Hunter was grateful, but he carefully pointed out that he would accept the medal only if it was to honor his research work, "but if it is given for any of my book-making activities I must decline." Second, Lawrence College in Appleton, Wisconsin conferred on him the honorary degree of doctor of letters, Litt.D., in June. Interestingly, it was Bertha Jaques, who had received the same degree the previous year, who brought Hunter's work to the college's attention. Her recommendation was reinforced by the officers of the Institute of Paper Chemistry, which was affiliated with Lawrence College.

While Hunter was in Appleton receiving his honorary degree, Beach moved his family into the brick building; the neighbors could hardly wait to tell Hunter. Very upset about the invasion of Edith's property, Hunter entreated Beach to leave, but his pleas fell on deaf ears. Wrongly assuming that his presence would get Beach out, Hunter arrived in Lime Rock at the beginning of August 1931 and moved into The Lodge, where he could keep an eye on the activities across the bridge. In a letter to Edith, he reported,

Beach had gotten himself beautifully disliked by the village in talking so freely about my character. He started one story which has come to me from several sources. I am supposed to be defending myself at the present time in a suit of a woman in Canaan, also Geo. Moore is suing me for alienation of affections. I is a bad, bad man. The Canaan woman is suing for assault, I understand. . . . Beach was greatly surprised to see me here and I have been told by many that I could not have arrived at a more opportune time. . . . The report was in circulation that I went abroad with Carmelita, Geo. tells me. Of course, you and the boys know that I did not, but don't be too sure as I am an elusive little fawn. I am a terrible guy with the womens. What with all my suits for brick-buildings, breach-of-promises, assaults on females, and alienation of affections, I am kept pretty busy and I get but little sleep.

He was also happy to report that he and Robertson were back on friendly terms. By 19 August 1931, Hunter was back in Chillicothe not having set foot inside the mill or the brick building. He could hardly believe it when he learned that the receivers hired a new foreman, Albert Stettner, a papermaker from the Zerkall mill in Cologne, Germany. Although there were no orders, paper continued to be made, only to be stacked up in the mill, unsold. In October, Rogers-King reported that there were over 70 reams of paper in the loft.

THE SALE

On 11 December 1931, Hunter was legally released from any liabilities of the Dard Hunter Associates, Inc. While this came as a great relief, he despaired that he had been forced to hand over the deed to the brick building to the receivers. In January 1932, Rogers-King and his mother left for Los Angeles, California to join Peter and Hugh. Stettner went to New York City where he eventually found a job with the Japan Paper Company. With Rogers-King and Stettner gone, everyone assumed that the mill would be sold immediately. Earlier, in anticipation of a sale, Hunter had complied a list of personal claims against the company. The total came to $12,377 and that sum did not include the money he had paid for the property or any improvements made to the brick building. He doubted, however, that enough money could ever be realized from a sale to pay his claims.

Months went by, but no effort was made by the receivers to sell the property. In April, Harrison Elliott reported to Hunter that the "brisk Mr. Beach" had landed a huge order of 50 reams from George Macy, director of the Limited Editions Club. One of Hunter's Lime Rock friends wrote that the mill was running day and night. In an attempt to protect his name and reputation, Hunter wrote to Macy, "I do want you to know that I am personally not in accord with the present methods of making or selling the paper."* Hunter must have felt a certain ambivalence when he learned that Macy rejected the paper. When Macy's order had been placed, the receivers had valued the mill at $16,000, but after the paper was returned, rumors flew around Lime Rock that the value was down to $4,000. Following the Macy debacle, the Robertsons finally conceded that the mill would never provide a living wage, and most of the family got jobs at the Hotchkiss School in nearby Lakeville.

From November 1932 for nearly a year, the mill remained idle. Finally on 5 October 1933, a notice of sale appeared in the *Lakeville Journal*: on 4 November, all assets of Dard Hunter Associates, Inc. were scheduled to be sold at a public auction. The property included three parcels: the land and buildings; all machinery, furniture, and equipment in the mill; and all paper located in the mill. The parcels were to be offered separately, but if unsold, as an entirety. The court reserved the right to refuse any offer it considered too low.

Hunter arranged with Elliott to accompany him to the sale, although he expressed no interest in bidding on either the property or the paper. However, he was interested in purchasing the equipment if he could get it at a reasonable price. His plan was to sell it to one of several museums who wanted to set up papermaking exhibits.

Several months after the auction, Hunter described the event to Rogers-King.

> I had planned to stay a week or so, but after getting to the village everything seemed so sad that I gave it up and returned with Elliott. I had not been there in over two and a half years and naturally I noticed many changes, the most pronounced being the absence of George Moore. While Lime Rock has improved physically . . . I felt more or less lonesome and strange without the Kings and others whom I knew. . . . Mr. Beach was there, rosy and fat; also Mr. Beardsley (who seems to be a right nice chap), and Mr. Kellogg. The sale was pathetic, with about fifty of the curious there. The equipment was offered first with no bidders, the paper came next with one bid from Mr. [Melbert B.] Cary [Jr.], a friend of mine, for fifty dollars! Mr. Beach said the paper amounted to $4,000, but you know how generous he is with ciphers. At last the whole place, equipment, paper, and all was put up and Mr. William J. Weber made one bid of $2,500 and paid down his ten per cent.

I was amused, but did not make a bid on anything as I was totally uninterested. I did, however, approach Mr. Weber about the equipment, inasmuch as the Science Museum, Chicago, had asked me to try to get it for them. They offered to pay $250 for the vat, lifting box, knotter and chest, also small beater. When I left New York I was under the impression that the sale would be approved by the court and Mr. Weber would come into possession of the property. He told me he wanted it for a sort of "Roycroft Shop" and I knew at once that if this was the case there would be another sale very soon. Mr. Weber did not impress me as being artistic in any way, he operates a small commercial printing shop in the city and is vice-president of the N.Y. City school board, a great Tammany man.

I see I have written quite a long paragraph so I will start another. Several weeks ago I was written that Mr. Weber had neglected to come forward with the balance of cash and had defaulted three or four times. Then I had another letter stating that the good gentleman had had a stroke or something, and was clear out of the picture. Also that another sale would be held some time. Thus the poor old mill's death is prolonged for another spell. What will happen next I do not know, but the old wreck may linger in its misery for many years to come. Sometimes I think I should buy it just so it can have a respectable funeral, and put an end to the misery.

The flour mill roof has collapsed completely making a rather sad approach from Lakeville way. I was informed that the boiler had been allowed to freeze up and burst. That fine red boiler you put in place with so much energy! ! ! ! The bright red paint is all gone and it now looks like a display at the junk yard, covered with rust and scale. Old, dry pulp was over everything, just like the mill had been operated and stopped without cleaning up. . . . In any event Litchfield County is still one of the prettiest places in New England and I will always think of the years most pleasantly, and without any animosity toward any one. It was all good experience, but I fear you were the one person who fared worst as all of the work fell upon your shoulders, and you had the blunt of the whole trying situation. I have never figured my financial loss and never intend to do so, but it was considerably more than anyone realizes. I will always believe that Mr. Beach was the one person who came out best, not entirely in the mill, perhaps, but it was a good move for the family, and especially for Mrs. Beach.*

In fact, Weber finally did purchase the mill for his original bid. In April 1934, together with Albert Stettner, lured away from the Japan Paper Company, Weber restored the buildings and refurbished the equipment. However, it was another two years before rumors had Weber ready to start making paper, but the mill continued to lie idle.

HUNTER REPURCHASES THE LIME ROCK MILL

Perhaps because neither Dard Jr. nor Cornell was interested in the newspaper business, Hunter and his cousin, Junius, sold the Chillicothe *News-Advertiser* in November 1938. As a result, Hunter suddenly had a lot of cash. He decided to buy back the Lime Rock mill. Working secretly through various agents, his chance came in the summer of 1939. From Boston, he sent a special delivery letter to Dard Jr.

> Now, what I want to know is this: Do you want the property? That is, do you think we could use it and after I am gone will you want it? You must remember (all joking aside) that I will not live as long as you will, in all probability. Therefore, the mill, if bought, would be your baby and you would have to look after it. I don't think Joe [Cornell] has much interest in handmade paper so you will have to decide. I am willing to get it and have always regretted that I did not have it before, but as I was fearful (as I always am) that I should not buy it when I could have had the place for around $4,000, in 1933, at the sale. I will say that I have always regretted I did not buy and even now I am inclined toward the purchase, but I will not do anything unless you say so, for you are the one to be consulted, you and your mother. Please let me know by telegram upon receiving this letter. In the meantime I will make an offer of $6,500 on the property, but I do not think this will buy it, but I will not pay the full price unless you say so. I offered $6,000 last fall, but was refused. The place is worth $7,500, I suppose, but beyond this price I would not be able to say as property Lime Rock way is in good demand. It is a white elephant with red and green stripes, BUT it is *my* white elephant and always will be. Someway I am glad that I like white elephants as I would hate to be too prosaic.

Dard Jr. and Edith telegraphed Hunter that he should go ahead. Weber, not knowing who made the offer, accepted. After several anxious days wondering whether the old man would change his mind, Hunter became the owner of the Lime Rock mill for the second time at the end of August 1939. After a quick inventory, Hunter estimated that there were 75 reams of sized papers of all types and colors plus another 4,000 pounds of unsized, unfinished paper. Most of the sized paper was moved to MIT where Hunter had set up his museum, and eventually, some of that to Mountain House; years later, the unsized paper was shipped to Chillicothe.

In September 1939, Hunter wrote George Mead of the Mead Paper Corporation to see if he was interested in starting up a hand papermaking mill. Mead declined because of the uncertain market: England and France had declared war on Germany earlier that month. Although he had many offers to lease or sell the mill buildings, Hunter simply could not give up the idea of making paper there again. Finally, in 1943, John J. Cunningham, a retired papermaker, was allowed to rent the mill after persuading Hunter that together they could get the mill running. World War II interfered with those plans, however. Although Cunningham paid rent for seven years, he hardly set foot inside the mill and never lived there.

After the war, Dard Jr. and Cornell expressed an interest in running the mill, and after all the pros and cons were discussed, Hunter transferred the Lime Rock property into their names in September 1948. Except for some repairs that were made over the next two years, nothing else happened. By 1950, Hunter had to concede that the mill would never again operate under the Hunter name. He contacted his friend D. Clark Everest, president of the Marathon Paper Company in Neenah, Wisconsin, to see if he was interested in buying the mill. Hunter's telegram caught Everest at just the right moment, and he wired Hunter to name his price. Hunter hesitated, still reluctant to let his dream go, but eventually he was persuaded to sell when Everest promised to employ both Dard Jr. and Cornell to help run the mill. The sale took place in September 1950. Everest paid $12,500 for the mill, and the proceeds were divided between Dard Jr. and Cornell.

Perhaps paper would have been made in the mill again, but within a few months of the purchase, Everest found himself caught up in the Korean War. By the time that conflict was over, Everest was no longer interested in making paper by hand. His friend Westbrook Steele, president of the Institute of Paper Chemistry, spoke to him about opening a paper museum, and in late 1953, Everest donated all of the papermaking equipment in the Lime Rock mill to this new venture. He gave the mill buildings and land to the village.

The mill sat abandoned until a flood in 1955 all but washed it away. For several years, the ruined buildings lay in the Salmon Fell Kill until they were finally removed and a new bridge was constructed over the site. No vestige of the noble experiment, or as Hunter called it, "the white elephant with red and green stripes," exists today.

Chapter 13

It is my desire . . . to gain a first-hand knowledge of the way the people live and something of their daily habits and the like. In other words, I wish to ascertain something beyond the mere technical aspect of their papermaking. Dard Hunter

At the beginning of 1929, the country's economic situation was anything but good. Wild speculation in the stock market eventually led to Black Tuesday, 29 October 1929, when huge blocks of stock were sold for what they could bring. Although President Herbert Hoover tried to convince the public that the underlying economic structure of the country was sound, many felt that there was serious trouble ahead. Indeed, the end of 1929 spelled the beginning of the Great Depression. The Hunter family, however, was little affected by these dire events, and it would be several years before any real change in their lives could be measured. Happiest when involved in more than one project at a time—the Lime Rock mill was still under renovation—Hunter began two books in 1929, both commercially printed titles.

The first was published in 1930 by William Edwin Rudge under the title *Papermaking Through Eighteen Centuries*. In the preface, Hunter made it quite clear that *Eighteen Centuries* was not a reprint of any of his previous work; rather, he explained, some material originally intended for *Old Papermaking* had been omitted because of the physical limitations of producing that book. Compared to *Old Papermaking*, with its 104 text pages and 26 illustrations, *Papermaking Through Eighteen Centuries* consisted of over 300 pages of text and 214 illustrations, including the facsimile reproduction of many early watermarks. The edition numbered 2,500 copies and each book sold for the rather high price of $17.50. Surprisingly, given the country's financial crisis, sales were brisk; those who could not afford Hunter's limited editions were delighted to finally own a book by him. But after 1931, sales slowed appreciably, and Rudge dropped the price to $15.00. By late October 1933, it was again reduced to $7.50, which temporarily increased sales. In 1936, the Rudge publishing firm went out of business, and Hunter took that opportunity

to purchase the remaining 476 unsold copies of the book.* Wanting to
ensure the widest possible distribution of the remaining copies, Hunter sent
announcements about its availability at $4.50 to trade journals, and as a con-
sequence, the book quickly sold out. This turned out to be a shrewd business
maneuver, as Hunter had purchased the books and had them bound for
about $2.00 each. The profit netted him more than his royalties would have
been on the original price.

The second commercial book, begun in 1929, was prompted by letters
from schoolteachers and children asking how to make paper by hand.
Hunter proposed to the editor of the *Industrial Education Magazine,* published
by the Manual Arts Press in Peoria, Illinois, that they publish a book aimed
specifically at schoolchildren. Initially, the editor was skeptical about the
potential sales for such a book, but within a month of receiving the outline,
he agreed to publish it under the title, *Paper-Making in the Classroom.* It
appeared in 1931 at $1.50.

In the preface, Hunter stated, "Several years ago my two young sons
developed a great liking for paper and paper-making and it has been their
interest and devotion to the craft that has prompted me to compile this
book." The paper formation steps are charmingly illustrated by photographs
of the Hunter brothers, Dard Jr., the 13-year-old "vatman," and Cornell, the
11-year-old "coucher," as they made paper in the summer house, a gazebo-
like structure on the grounds of Mountain House. (plate 72)

Upon the publication of *Paper-Making in the Classroom,* Hunter was not
surprised to receive Harrison Elliott's typically caustic comments, question-
ing the efficacy of the common household meat grinder to reduce boiled rags
to pulp. While Hunter's reply to this criticism is unknown—indeed, it is not
likely he ever made one—he had anticipated Elliott by publishing a "dis-
claimer" in the preface: "While the paper fabricated will naturally not be of
the finest, the mere act of carrying out the entire process will give the
worker a far better comprehension of the formation and construction of
paper than by any other means." Unfortunately, this book did not sell well,
even given its broad appeal and low price. Hunter felt that the primary
reason for this was that the publisher did not market it to the right audience.

"PEREGRINATIONS & PROSPECTS"

During September 1931, Hunter answered the many congratulatory letters
he received concerning an autobiographical article, "Peregrinations & Prospects," which had appeared in *The Colophon.* For this issue of the quarterly
journal, the Lime Rock mill had made 10 reams of "Salisbury," a white,
modern laid sheet measuring 24.5 x 19.5 inches. It is a great testament that

over sixty years later, "Salisbury" is still white while all of the other papers in the issue have turned varying shades of brown. Interestingly, Hunter commented rather negatively on this paper to Rogers-King.

> By the way, I have a proof of the "Colophon" article printed on the Lime Rock paper. While the paper prints well (all paper prints well when skillfully handled), the colour is rather displeasing and the feel of the paper does not satisfy exactly. It is not "a skin you love to touch." However, it is not at all bad and is equal to any of the European make. I'll do my best to get you a copy of the "Colophon" with this signature. Of course, as you know, both the feel and colour of the paper are due to the half-stock and not to any of the processes in actual making. I have been doing some experimenting in water-colour printing on the unsized white paper and it prints very well; it is a good colour and has a proper "feel."*

"Peregrinations & Prospects" deals primarily with Hunter's career as a printer. The only illustration is a photogravure of one of Kingsbury's "portraits" of the Marlborough Mill taken in 1913. (It is not known on which wove paper this was printed as there is no watermark; in the author's copy, this paper, like the other text papers except "Salisbury," has turned brown.) Taking the opportunity to make a small jab at W.D. Harper's efforts to make the Lime Rock mill "efficient," Hunter wrote,

> I do not now think of myself as a typographer, or yet as a papermaker. I like to be known as an amateur research worker in the field of oriental and occidental papermaking by hand. I must confess that I am not particularly interested in machine-made paper and I know of no greater bore than a journey through an efficient machine mill. In fact, I am not overly interested in efficient handmade paper fabrication or anything else that embodies efficiency, service or co-operation.

He also told the story about the diploma he made to enter the Graphische in Vienna, but by far the most intriguing and humorous tale is the one involving a most unusual book.

> One of my earliest [Roycroft] commissions was the hand lettering of a book. . . . The job must be done in my most flourishing style on Japanese vellum. The client, a widow of tender years, was staying at the Roycroft Inn, and the book was a memorial to the good lady's late

husband who had died shortly before, leaving a tidy sum to our customer. . . . I had the pages all lettered ready for binding and had con-
fected a mournful title-page covered with urns and black draperies. As
I was to design the cover as well, I went to the bindery and procured a
full assortment of all the materials in the shop—pigskin, calf, morocco,
and several other kinds of leather. With these specimens and the hand-
illuminated text under my arm I went to the young widow's room at
the Inn so that she might choose the leather she liked best. She looked
over the samples but appeared uninterested in them. I was much gratified, however, that she thought well of my lettering and complimented
me highly. She then told me she would supply the binding materials
herself, and going to her trunk, took from it a rolled parcel. The book,
she announced, was to be bound in the leather contained in the parcel. I
unrolled it but could not determine the kind of leather. I hated to show
my ignorance, but finally mustered sufficient courage to ask what sort
of an animal had produced it. It was from the back of her late husband,
she said—she wanted the book to be a true memorial to him. We bound
the book according to specifications and the widow left the shop a satisfied customer. Years later I learned she had married again, and I have
often thought what a strange feeling the second husband must have had
when he saw the memorial book on the drawing room table, perhaps
thinking of himself as Volume Two. Let us hope that this was a strictly
limited edition.

One outcome of "Peregrinations & Prospects" was a request from a
feature writer for information of a personal nature that would form the
basis of an article for *The New Yorker* magazine. Hunter disliked this sort of
thing, and in the hope that he would bore the writer into giving up this
idea, he wrote about his daily routine in minute detail.

You ask for some material regarding my "life from day to day, etc."
While this is a new angle, I will try to set down some information which
may be of help to you in your articles.

   There is one question that I am constantly being asked and perhaps
if I will answer it for you it will give you a little idea of my own feelings.
The question is this: "why do you live in Chillicothe instead of one of the
great art centres, like New York?" I will say that I live in Chillicothe because I was raised here and I have always disliked the large centres of
population, especially American cities. Chillicothe is rather a picturesque
little town and people live very much as they did fifty years ago. I am

not known at all here and when I am introduced to anyone it is usually with the reference that I am the son of the late William H. Hunter, who, during his day, was the forceful editor of the local newspaper. Hardly anyone knows of my work and in the city directory I am listed as having "no occupation." I continue to live in Chillicothe because it is quiet and I can work undisturbed. I have no ambition to be "a big toad in a little puddle," in fact, I have no ambition to be a toad at all.

It will be difficult for me to tell of my "life from day to day" as I have no set routine. Usually I arise about 8:30 and always retire at 10, no matter if I have to leave a visitor to do so. I work until three every afternoon in the winter, when the light grows dim, and in the summer somewhat longer. Each afternoon I take a walk in the woods arranging my route so that I can spend a half hour or so at the News-Advertiser office, a daily newspaper that has been in the Hunter family many years. I do not take any active part in the management of this paper as I am not fitted for this work. I am not a good "mixer" and I dislike to discuss politics and the affairs of the day as those subjects interest me but little. I never talk about my own work and I very much doubt if there are a dozen people in town who know what I am trying to do.

You ask about the things that I eat. I am not particularly interested in food, but one of my favorite things is cold, thick toast, fairly well charred on both sides. I find it difficult to get properly made toast in New York as it is always served with a cover and therefore it retains its heat; also the cooks in the city restaurants and hotels do not seem to be able to burn the toast just as I want it and I have no end of trouble over this apparently simple accomplishment in cuisine. I am also very fond of baked apples and I find the New York cooks do these very well, only I wish they would be more particular about taking out all of the core. My one aversion is to find a bit of egg shell in my food as this breaks down my morale quicker than anything else. In New York they seem to delight in having egg shell in various kinds of victuals as in the public eating places I have found it in almost everything, even in things that I never thought were made with eggs. I presume this is done intentionally so that the patrons will be convinced that real eggs are used instead of something synthetic. I go to New York about twice a year and I always do so with reluctance as I know that I will be tortured by noise and the great crowds, as well as by egg shell in my food and hot, unburned toast.

There is one custom that I have carried on for many years and I believe it is a good one and has had a great deal to do with preserving my splendid health. During the life of Thomas Bewick (1753–1828), the great

English wood-engraver, he always ate two figs before retiring for the night and he attributed his fine constitution and longevity to this practice. In my early youth I became much interested in the life and work of Bewick and I was so impressed by his method of keeping well that I long ago adopted his idea. Only in my case I use two, uncooked, dry prunes instead of the Bewickian figs and all through these years the plan has been most successful. Even when I go to New York I take sufficient prunes with me so that I may have the accustomed two each night before retiring. For instance, if I am to be gone two weeks I take 28 prunes, three weeks 42 prunes, etc. Also on my long trips I manage to take the kind of prunes that I like best as they should be hard, well wrinkled and of a very dark, black tone.

You ask about the kind of people I like and dislike. I have no aversion to people as I feel that they all have a certain place in the world and certainly none of them asked to be placed on this earth. I like simplicity and loathe egotism in people. I have found that the greatest egotists are those that have accomplished the least. I am not socially inclined and try to avoid this sort of thing as much as possible.

Just at present I am working on a book dealing with old Oriental papermaking and it will probably be a year before the edition of 200 copies is ready. About half of each edition goes to libraries and the balance are taken by collectors. My books are sent to almost every country on earth and the subscription list varies but little from one edition to another. I have always made it a point never to hold books for the heavy premium that follows their publication.

I hope that I have given you about what you desire, but if there is any additional information, either serious or otherwise, that you may wish, please let me know.

When the article did not appear, Hunter assumed his strategy had worked. To his complete surprise, five years later, on 23 April 1936, a watered down version appeared in *The New Yorker*'s "The Talk of the Town" section.

Hunter's ability to laugh at himself, ably demonstrated in this letter, was one of his greatest assets. His closest friends were also blessed with good senses of humor. One was Julius J. Lankes, the wood engraver, who made a print for Harrison Elliott titled, *The Critic*. Apparently Elliott told Lankes that he wanted to write a history of toilet paper, and the print was to be the book's "frontispiece." (plate 73) In October 1931, the block and a copy of *The Critic* was sent by Lankes for Hunter's collection. Long assumed to have been made for Hunter, the print, which hangs next to the commode at

Mountain House, bears Lankes's inscription: "To Dard Hunter—the artist."
Harrison Elliott was The Critic.

Old Papermaking in China and Japan AND OTHER PROJECTS

After the publication of *Primitive Papermaking* in 1927, Hunter vowed never
again to publish a limited edition using his own type or doing the presswork.
Assuming that he would make arrangements for another fine press to
publish the book for him, he spent most of 1928 through early 1930 gathering material for a book on Japanese and Chinese papermaking. In May 1930,
when the Lime Rock mill was finally producing paper, this activity was
shelved, but when the mill went into receivership in 1931, Hunter was free
to focus his attention on *Old Papermaking in China and Japan*. Once the book
was published, he planned to travel to India and Asia.

As nearly four years had passed since Hunter had last been at the press,
the frustrations experienced in printing *Primitive Papermaking* were dim
memories, and he decided to print *Old Papermaking in China and Japan* himself. He did have one major concern about doing the presswork—his poor
eyesight. This problem was overcome by working only when plenty of
natural light came through the studio skylight. His decision to issue the book
under the Mountain House Press imprint was also based on financial considerations. He had serious doubts that the book would sell well given the
Depression, and the less money he invested in it, the less he had to lose. It is
to his credit that he never wavered from his commitment to publish the
information he had spent years gathering, no matter what it might cost him
financially or physically.

During the autumn of 1931, Hunter prepared and printed the illustrations. He asked J.J. Lankes to make woodcuts of two plants, *kozo* and *mitsumata*, which yield fiber for traditional Japanese paper. Lankes also cut
blocks for the title, printer's mark, large initials, and some Chinese characters. Hunter also had line etchings made from his drawings or from illustrations from books, and many of these were later hand-colored by Edith.

By May 1932, Hunter finished printing *Old Papermaking in China and
Japan* and sent Franck the dimensions for a portfolio. However, Hunter
changed his mind about the portfolio after reading Berthold Laufer's *Paper
and Printing in Ancient China*, published in 1931 by the Caxton Club and
bound by Franck. He asked Franck to give him an estimate for a similar
binding for his book: "I [want] a simple canvas back and [side papers] suitable in some Chinese design which I would make." Franck was delighted.

Despite the bleak financial times, Hunter decided to sell *Old Papermaking in China and Japan* for the same price as his previous book, $75. He

did not expect, however, that the book would sell as well as previous volumes. Only after he received sufficient orders to cover the cost of binding, $8.50 per book including a slipcase, would he send Franck sets of sheets for binding.

While he was reasonably pleased with this book, he did not consider it his best work; he reserved that honor for *Primitive Papermaking*. The edition was 200 copies, limited primarily by the number of specimens of tipped-in papers and bark. Within a few months, Hunter discovered that the bark specimens were staining adjacent pages. The worst copies were set aside and designated "not for sale." After Hunter's death, some of these copies were sold in portfolios at a discount.

As with the previous Mountain House Press books, *Old Papermaking in China and Japan* was printed with Hunter's type, but this was the last time it was used for a book. Except for some of the illustrations, the paper, bearing the Bull's Head and Branch watermark, was made in the Lime Rock mill. Will Ransom, then at the Printing House of Leo Hart in Rochester, New York, also printed the prospectus on Lime Rock paper. In it, Hunter announced that the next book in production was to be *Modern Handmade Papermaking in the Orient*, rather than one on hand papermaking in India as had been previously announced.

Hunter was right about *Old Papermaking in China and Japan*; it sold very slowly. It was also the first of his Mountain House Press books *not* included in the AIGA's list of "The Fifty Books of the Year."

LIFE WITH TEENAGE BOYS

In July 1932, many banks failed, including one in which the Hunter family had accounts. In addition, companies in which the Hunters held stock suspended dividend payments. They were more fortunate than most, however, for the family could rely on income from the *News-Advertiser*, although goods and services were often bartered for advertising. Thus the Hunters managed reasonably well during the Depression. In fact, their financial situation was healthy enough to enroll Dard Jr. in a private school, the Western Reserve Academy in Hudson, Ohio, later that year. "[Dard Jr.'s] marks are not so good. . . . He is more mechanically and artistically inclined and his school work goes to blazes," Hunter wrote to Lord. Hoping that more personal attention and directed studies would improve the fifteen-year-old's chances of getting into college, Dard Jr. started at the Academy in September. By the end of his first year, he had made noticeable improvements in all subjects. His teachers noted that he had more confidence and was more self-reliant. Overall, his best subjects were manual and physical training; his best academic subjects, math and Latin.

Back in Chillicothe, Edith kept busy with church and social activities. Unfortunately, not much is known about her, as there are few letters from or to her in the archives dating from the 1930s. During this decade, she is known primarily from Dard's letters, such as this one to Frank Lankes.

> While I am not of the [Christian Science] cult, Mrs. Hunter is a strong adherent and has always wanted me to suggest to you the many possibilities of the religion. She fully believes in it and in the twenty-five years that I have been married I have never known her to have the slightest sickness, or even the slightest minor ailment. As I said before, I am not of the cult, but I think there are many good things to be said about this particular religion. I have never taken *any* religion seriously myself, in fact, I think they all have many, many faults.

Unlike many of her contemporaries, Edith had a rich and fulfilling life extending far beyond Chillicothe. She was not afraid to travel by herself; on the contrary, she loved the independence a car gave her. Dard, on the other hand, could not drive and on the whole preferred the quiet solitude of home where he could work. The exception, of course, was when he traveled abroad.

Papermaking Pilgrimage to Japan, Korea and China

In 1933, a political change occurred that ultimately led to the end of the Depression. On 4 March, Franklin Delano Roosevelt was inaugurated President of the United States. He promised an aggressive policy to deliver the country from financial chaos, and over the next few years, a number of projects that provided work for the unemployed were initiated. While the so-called New Deal had its opponents, the general public began to feel positive effects from it, and the program gathered popular support. Implementing the New Deal, however, was all consuming, and consequently America's interest in world affairs waned. Little could people have guessed that, as a result of Hitler and Japan's aggression in China, America would be embroiled in a world war in less than a decade.

While the situation in the Orient impacted little on America, it had implications for Hunter's plans. At the beginning of 1933, he finalized arrangements to travel to Japan with side trips to Korea and China. However, he had ambivalent feelings about the journey, "I rather dread the trip as it will be a hard, tedious one. It is necessary though as I am getting in a rut which is a bad thing and only a decided change and a certain amount of hardship will pull me out." In fact, the trip was likely to be more than simply hard and tedious, it was potentially dangerous. Two years before, Japan had set up a puppet government in Manchuria, an area of China that bordered northern Korea. Although the United States government advised against visiting the area, Hunter was determined to go. Harrison Elliott, who was working for the Japan Paper Company, also warned Hunter that the Japanese had a reputation for not divulging "trade secrets," however gracious and amiable they might be socially.

Thus forewarned, Hunter sailed on 1 March 1933 for the land of "cherry blossoms and bullets." Twenty days later in Yokohama, he was met by Mr. Fukukita of the Oji Paper Company, which was headquartered in Tokyo. (The two men had first met during Fukukita's visit to the Lime Rock mill in 1928.) They traveled by train to Tokyo, where Hunter checked into the Imperial Hotel, which was built by Frank Lloyd Wright in 1915. (Interestingly, Hunter makes no mention of this in his letters.) Finally having access to a typewriter, Hunter wrote a long letter home.

Yesterday we had to lie in the harbour all night as we arrived too late for the doctors to come on board. The two towns, Yokohama and Tokyo looked quite romantic with the low lights and Fuji in the background covered with snow. . . . One of [the examiners] was asking if I was connected in any way with newspapers and thoughtfully I answered no. At the customs it was quite simple as the examiner seems to be looking only for rhinoceros horns, dried liver and cow mature. These things are actually listed in the forbidden objects, but after proving that I was not entering the country with my bags filled with cow dung I was allowed to proceed. Mr. Fukukita came to the ship, as well as Mr. Seki, the head of the Paper Association of Japan, and Mr. Nakane of the U.S. Department of Commerce. Had I not been met I fear the confusion of getting from Yokohama to Tokyo would have overtaxed my skill as a traveler. . . . [After lunch] I was met here at the hotel by a reporter from the large Daily "Hochi" and he interviewed me and took my picture for the issue tomorrow. . . . All day I have been in conferences with various Japanese gentlemen who are extremely polite and bow and bow to one another and to me.

Just when I will leave here I cannot say, but not until I have finished the plan laid down by my friends. . . . Tomorrow starts the long journey into the country side where things will be vastly different and interesting. I think I will get all that I need here in two weeks, or even less as the "plan" seems to be quite comprehensive and takes in much within the next week. . . . One sees or hears nothing of war and everybody is extremely kind and polite, although it is trying to listen intently all the time to the English, although my guide, Mr. Yamada speaks quite well having been to Oberlin [College] 3 years and Yale one.

Must close now before I am called down for another interview or conference. It seems strange to come to a city 8,000 miles away from home and be known well enough so the telephone is ringing almost constantly and I am being called down stairs every few minutes.

From Tokyo, Hunter and Yamada went to Gifu, Osaka, Kochi, Nara, Kyoto and Nagoya, and at each stop, they visited hand and machine paper-mills. Hunter did not write about these mill visits to his family, and instead wrote about the sights, the theater, and the bizarre Japanese food and commodes. (plate 74) By the time he arrived back in Tokyo, the exhausted Hunter was eager to have a day or two to himself, but the needed respite was not to be. As soon as he settled into the hotel, he was wined, dined, and interviewed as before.

Yamada made the arrangements for Hunter's trip to Korea, which he made unescorted. From Seoul, he toured hand papermaking mills, and in curio shops, he purchased printing blocks, inks, and a variety of papers. Within ten days, he was back in Tokyo making plans for his return trip. He was looking forward to the relative peace and quiet of the sea journey. Tongue-in-cheek, he described his ideas about a new career to Lord, "it is possible that I will return to Japan as several gentlemen are most anxious that I become a Buddhist priest and . . . I would have something to do with book printing and decoration along with the study of the Zen religion." This "aspiration" was also relayed to Harrison Elliott, along with a description of the business aspects of the trip.

Yesterday completed our round of the hand-made paper mills of Japan as we went to the only paper village left, Ogawa-machi, Saitama-Ken . . . there are about 300 mills in the county[prefecture], none of which have above two vats. . . . I have estimated that there are in operation at present between 1500 and 1800 small mills making hand-made paper. Most of this is, of course, used locally where it is manufactured. I am told by Mr. Shigeo Nakane of the research department of the Commercial Department at the U.S. Consulate, that no other person, either Japanese or foreigner, has made such a complete tour of the mills in this country. I have traveled over 7,000 miles in Japan and Korea and thoroughly inspected about 160 mills and visited about 500 mills but did not go into the details. So many are alike, making the same kinds of paper, that it would be impossible to go in every one . . . the trip has done me a great deal of good—mentally, morally, spiritually, physically.

Hunter decided to sail directly to San Francisco, rather than make any side trips. After three months abroad, he arrived home in mid-June. As Dard and Edith agreed that if he went on an extended trip, she could travel upon his return, she and the boys were soon off for Chicago to see the Century of Progress exposition. After she saw Dard Jr. and Cornell safely on the train back to Chillicothe, Edith went on to California for a month.

After attending to the usual backlog of correspondence, Hunter began preparing the text for *Papermaking Pilgrimage to Japan, Korea and China*. He was eager to tell exactly how the Japanese made paper by hand—a technique quite different from western papermaking (see Appendix A). Having decided not to print the book himself, Hunter arranged with Elmer Adler of the Pynson Printers to publish it.

When he was not working on the manuscript, Hunter made a stained glass panel, his last, depicting a Japanese woman sitting in front of a vat making sheets of paper. Although hampered by poor eyesight, Hunter managed the work because the design was fairly simple and the pieces of glass were large. The panel, measuring 37 x 22 inches, hangs in the library at Mountain House (see colorplate 10).

While Hunter had the manuscript and illustrations ready by the beginning of 1934, it took Pynson Printers over two years to publish the book. In some ways, this was advantageous to Hunter because it gave *Old Papermaking in China and Japan* no competition. Adler sent out announcements in mid-1934, and as the country's economic situation improved, orders began to accumulate. In January 1936, Adler organized an exhibition "showing details in the planning and in the making of Dard Hunter's book," and by May, the book was available.

In *Papermaking Pilgrimage*, Hunter described the technical similarities and differences in Korean, Chinese, and Japanese papermaking and compared these to Western practices. He emphasized that the primary difference in the craft as practiced in Japan versus in any other country was that papermaking by hand was considered an art. Everywhere in the world, he wrote, paper was a ubiquitous commodity. In Japan, Korea, and China, however, its use was carried far beyond what would be considered normal in Western culture. For centuries, these countries used paper as ceremonial objects such as "spirit paper," clothing, umbrellas, building materials such as windows, doors, and lanterns, all kinds of packaging, personal hygiene products, not to mention as a support for printing, painting, and writing. Hunter was as fascinated with this cultural aspect of oriental, particularly Japanese, paper as with its manufacture.

Three hundred and seventy copies were printed, each numbered and signed by the author and the publisher. Hunter would have liked to print a larger edition, but he was limited by the number of specimens. Much to Peter Franck's disappointment, Adler decided to have Gerhard Gerlach, a teacher at Columbia University, do the binding because he underbid Franck by half. Franck assumed that Gerlach could afford to bind the book for so little because he used student labor. The final half-binding was black leather with black side papers, onto which was printed an oriental design in gold and red. The most complicated aspect of the binding was the insertion of many paper specimens of differing sizes. *Papermaking Pilgrimage to Japan, Korea and China* sold for $37.50—much lower than Hunter's last two Mountain House Press books. It was an immediate success, and the edition was practically sold out in a year.*

While the financial success of the book was gratifying, Hunter was more pleased by the excellent reviews he received for his scholarly work and writing abilities. As in previous books, he had provided his readers with heretofore unavailable information, but it was not simply the technical details that were appreciated; the story Hunter told of his experiences and the people he met was compelling reading.

Years later, Hunter included details about his trip to Japan in both the 1943 and 1947 editions of his most popular book, *Papermaking: The History and Technique of an Ancient Craft.* Interestingly, a part of a story told in the later edition does not appear either in the earlier edition or in any of the letters he wrote during his visit. The scene was his last night in Japan in 1933.

I learned that my companions were considering the purchase of an elaborate gift that was to be presented to me on the night of the final dinner. . . . I suggested that they give me something readily procurable and inexpensive—for instance, some seeds of the mitsumata and gampi plants. This they cheerfully agreed to do. When the rather tiring banquet was at last over and the guests were about to depart, I was ceremoniously presented with a finely made box fitted with two compartments: one side held a number of ounces of the coveted mitsumata seeds and the opposite space was filled with the seeds of the gampi. In all innocence I accepted the token of friendship and told my hosts that I would plant the seeds in my own garden in America. Little did I suspect on that last evening of my visit in beautiful Japan that my kind and obliging

Japanese friends had caused every seed that had been given to me to be boiled until all possibility of germination had been destroyed!

The fact is that Hunter did receive seeds of the *mitsumata* plant from Mr. Seki in June 1934, complete with directions for successful cultivation. (Hunter was well aware that the *gampi* plant could not be cultivated under any circumstance.) He immediately planted some seeds in his garden and sent a few to Harrison Elliott. In an October 1937 letter, Hunter mentioned that the *mitsumata* trees were still doing well. So what was the reason for this deception? In 1947, the war crimes perpetrated by Japan against her enemies, including American prisoners of war, were strongly denounced. Doubtless, Hunter felt it necessary to make up the incident and include it as a negative —but not awful—note in his otherwise positive view of the Japanese people.

Chapter 14

I traveled second class because I have the feeling that more can be learned about a strange country and its people by associating with the natives themselves.
Dard Hunter

Almost as soon as Hunter returned from Japan in June 1933, he made plans to travel to India, having postponed that trip for several years. Setting aside the early part of 1935 for the voyage, he planned to make his first trip around the world by stopping again in Japan, then on to Indo-China, Siam, and India, returning to America via the Suez Canal. While he made arrangements with a Mr. T. Venkajee for the visit to India, he had no contacts in Indo-China or Siam although he was assured by the American consuls that guides and translators would be available on his arrival.

Once his affairs were in order, Hunter took the train to New York City, where on 13 January 1935 he boarded a ship bound for Manila and Hong Kong via the Panama Canal. At Hong Kong, he joined a smaller ship for the port of Haiphong in Tonkin (then a province of French Indo-China, now Vietnam).

Hunter left Haiphong for Hanoi traveling "first class" on a Renault omnibus. In *Papermaking in Indo-China*, published in 1947, he recalled a horrific accident when the bus driver hit and killed a woman. Hunter left his seat and helped move the mangled body to the side of the road. This incident affected him deeply, and later he wrote, "I consoled myself in the thought that this sadly neglected girl had at last found peace, the first real rest she had ever known. . . . A lovely Anamese girl had been slain, but there were millions more! Life means so little in the Orient." With no other formalities, the bus continued on its way to Hanoi. With his locally acquired guide, Hunter traveled by ricksha to the papermaking villages of Yen-Thai and Lang-Buoi, where paper was made from plant fibers of the *Daphne* family, similar to Japanese *gampi*. When there was enough light, he typed long letters to his family detailing his adventures; these were reprinted in the *News-Advertiser*.

Upon his return to Haiphong, Hunter traveled through the Gulf of Siam to Singapore at the tip of the Malay Peninsula. From Singapore he joined the northbound train to Siam on 7 April 1935. So began another long, hard, but rewarding journey.

> The normal person in making the journey from Singapore to Bangkok would travel by steamship through the China Sea, into the Gulf of Siam, and, after a week's comfortable voyage, would land in Paknam, the entrance port for the Siamese capital. Not being a normal person, however, I chose to journey to Bangkok by the winding railway that penetrates through the rubber plantations and jungles of the long and narrow Malay Peninsula, a distance of eleven hundred and eighty-eight miles, requiring about sixty hours of travel. . . . Again, not being a normal person, I preferred to travel second class rather than in the long grey first class carriage in which were seated two of the perspiring white passengers. These two gentlemen were the usual British tourists with their khaki shorts, tropical cork helmets, and superior swagger which the British seem to cultivate while traveling in their outlying possessions. I traveled second class because I have the feeling that more can be learned about a strange country and its people by associating with the natives themselves.

Once Hunter reached Bangkok, he acquired another guide. They took a small boat up the canals until they reached Bangsom, the site of the remote papermaking mill owned by the Niltongkum family. (plate 75) Hunter took many notes, but only a few of his photographs turned out. After his return home, he arranged to have a photographer from Bangkok retrace his steps and photograph the papermakers again.

At some point during the trip, Hunter decided not to go on to India. He wrote to Venkajee to advise him of the change of plans. Venkajee was understandably upset as he had already made many arrangements, but he ended his letter with another invitation to Hunter for a future visit. On the trip back home, the ship stopped in Sumatra, Ceylon, Arabia, Port Said, and, finally, New York. On 25 May 1935, he was back home, where the proofs for *Papermaking Pilgrimage to Japan, Korea and China* were waiting for him. As soon as he and Edith finished going through them, he began work on three manuscripts for books based on the recently completed trip: *Papermaking in Southern Siam* (published in 1936), *Chinese Ceremonial Paper* (1937), and *Papermaking in Indo-China* (1947). By then, Hunter had also decided to print these three books himself. He had had no real problems with Elmer Adler over

Papermaking Pilgrimage but disliked having so little control over his books. He also wanted all of the profits.

Papermaking in Southern Siam

Having vowed never to use his type again, Hunter chose a complementary face, Caslon Oldstyle No. 471 in 18-point, for these books. The paper chosen for the text of *Southern Siam* was left over from *Old Papermaking in China and Japan.*

Papermaking in Southern Siam is a short book with only 30 pages of text, three specimens of paper, one piece of bark, and a sample of the mould cloth used. The frontispiece is a lovely hand-colored wood block print by J.J. Lankes of the *khoi* plant, (*Streblus asper*, Lour.), the primary source of fiber in Siamese papers. Franck made a one-quarter black leather binding with side papers of a seated Buddha, printed by Hunter. Because the word "Southern" could not be aesthetically hyphenated on the spine, it was left out.

To avoid undue competition with *Papermaking Pilgrimage to Japan, Korea and China,* issued in May 1936, Hunter withheld the announcement of *Southern Siam* until late July. Immediately, he was inundated with orders for the slim book, and Franck barely kept up with the binding. Just a month after the book was announced, Hunter wrote Adler that *Southern Siam* had nearly sold out; he regretted printing so few.

In *Papermaking in Southern Siam,* it is clear that detailing the devotion of the Niltongkum family to papermaking was as important to Hunter as detailing the materials and techniques of the craft. He was in particular awe of the eighty-year-old Mrs. Piung Niltongkum, who did all of the arduous tasks associated with beating the bark and forming the sheets. A good photograph of her does not appear in the book, however. Hunter explained to a friend that she was camera-shy, and with her betel-stained, black teeth not very photogenic. *Papermaking in Southern Siam,* because of its small edition, remains the most elusive of the Mountain House Press books.

Chinese Ceremonial Paper

As soon as *Papermaking in Southern Siam* was at Franck's bindery, Hunter started work on his next book, *Chinese Ceremonial Paper,* "a monograph relating to the fabrication of paper and tin foil and the use of paper in Chinese rites and religious ceremonies." In addition to information gleaned from his trips, much was also supplied to him by Dr. F.A. McClure, Mr. Y.F. Woo, and Mrs. Wang Yintai, who were credited in the book. As usual, Hunter included specimens of papers, many of which were "spirit papers," symbolizing money the deceased person needed in the afterlife. These papers were ceremoniously burned at the funeral. Much of this "money" was a coarse bamboo paper, onto which was pasted a smaller piece of extremely thin tin foil. Further treatments included a coating of seaweed, which turned the silver-color of the foil to gold, and sometimes a woodcut design was over-printed. Hunter even included an ⅛ inch thick Pekinese funeral "coin," made of laminated paper covered with metal foil. Rather than limit the specimens to small sheets, he included several full-sized prints, the largest measuring 22 x 13 inches.

While Caslon type was to be used again, Hunter decided not to use Lime Rock paper for the text, although it was used for the illustrations. It is possible that he did not have enough of it, but from his numerous com-plaints to Franck, it is clear that he found printing on that particular batch of paper extremely trying because of irregularities in surface texture, sizing, and thickness. Instead, he chose a Japanese paper, similar to that used for *Papermaking Pilgrimage to Japan, Korea and China.*

By June 1937, Hunter decided to sell *Chinese Ceremonial Paper* for $37.50, a price based on his estimate of the binding costs. Although he and Franck had corresponded regularly during the summer, Hunter never received an actual quote for the complicated binding. As soon as Hunter collated the 79 numbered pages, the photogravures, the colored prints, and the numer-ous and bulky specimens, he shipped the edition of 125 to Franck. *After* the prospectus quoting the price was printed, Hunter received Franck's bill for the first 50 copies, and he was astounded at the price of $9.88 per book! He wrote to Franck immediately with instructions to bind another 25 copies and send the remaining 50 books back. By the next day, however, Hunter had calmed down; he wrote Franck to bind all of the remaining copies. No doubt he was happy to receive a letter from Franck with an offer to reduce the cost to $8.50, and even more pleased when he eventually reduced it by another dollar.

Franck was put out, however, at having to lower his price to below the actual cost of the binding. The fact that he, wife Cornelia, and daughters Yanna and Helen did all of the work meant that the money stayed in the family, but it was barely enough to pay bills. In September 1937, a desperate Franck wrote Hunter,

> It worries me that you say in one of your letters that you can not pay me for the work until you get the money [for the book]. If I had known be-fore of this uncertainty I would not have dared to bind the books. For about 4 to 5 months I was able the first time in the seven business years to keep my bank balance above the required $100.00 but alas now I am down again to $10.00.

I would appreciate very much if you do what you can to help me maintain my credit so laboriously built up lately. As the president of a bank it ought not be difficult to do me this favor.

With his reply that corrected Franck's impression that he was a bank president, Hunter sent a check. Edith was due to return from her several months' visit to Austria, and Hunter wanted this situation cleared up before she arrived home.

Without her, the three Hunter men had been fending for themselves. Cornell, then 18, remembered her absence.

During the summer, my mother . . . traveled to Austria to continue her piano studies under [Frau Prentner,] the same teacher she had some twenty-five years before.

This left my father in charge of my brother and me. My father was far from a gourmet cook; in fact, he knew nothing whatsoever about cooking. His favorite food was raisin bran, so with lots of this cereal and whatever came in a can we seemed to get by. However, my brother and I couldn't quite see ourselves with this type of menu for the whole summer, so we suggested that it would be nice to take a trip to the East Coast.

At first my father flatly refused, but after much coaxing he finally consented to go with one condition. It was that he could go in his easy chair, which I think he had in his own mind would eliminate any thought of travel. We had earlier purchased a new four-door automobile which was quite boxy, blue in color, a trunk in the back, and wooden spokes in the wheels. My brother and I proceeded to remove the rear seat of the car, and with much twisting and turning we got his easy chair in the back of the car. There were curtains on rollers on all of the windows in the back of the car so it was quite private. After my father saw this arrangement he could only consent reluctantly to go on the trip.

With our bags packed and the supplies placed in the car we set off at 6:00 AM for Erie, Pennsylvania, which was to be our first destination. At that time all of the roads were two lanes and went through every village and city. Another stipulation was that we were not to drive over 35 miles per hour, but my brother and I fudged a little on that when he wasn't looking. He always said that he never wanted to go any faster than a horse could trot. . . . [After visits to East Aurora, Williamsport, Mt. Riga and Lime Rock, and southern Maine, we headed home] on the

Pennsylvania Turnpike which I thought was one of the wonders of the world, going across the state without having to stop for a traffic light.

We arrived back in Chillicothe without further incident and looked forward to my mother's return and her marvelous meals.

When he was not "vacationing" with his sons, Hunter was preparing most of the manuscript for the fourth book in his modern oriental paper-making series, *Papermaking in Indo-China*. However, he was in no hurry to publish it as he had published three books in the previous eighteen months. He thought it wiser to wait until *Chinese Ceremonial Paper* was sold out before putting another book on the market. Besides there was another book on the horizon, one based on his upcoming trip to India.

THE TRIP TO GANDHI'S INDIA

Soon after Edith's return home, Hunter embarked on his oft-postponed trip to India on 11 October 1937. Always eager to travel to foreign lands, Hunter was particularly excited about this trip as Venkajee had included in the itinerary a visit to Wardha, where Mahatma Gandhi was conducting a series of experiments in manufacturing paper by hand. Hunter had been warned, however, that Gandhi rarely met foreigners, or even high Indian officials, if he could avoid it.

The freighter was very slow, and it was not until 13 November that Hunter finally landed in Karachi, the westernmost port of India (now in Pakistan). There he met up with his guide, Mr. Saranau Madhava Rao. They traveled by train from Karachi north to Kashmir via Rawalpindi. In the mountains, he visited the papermakers of Uri, and then retraced his steps south and changed trains at Lahore. He traveled east to Delhi and on to Agra, where he visited the Taj Mahal. At Kalpi, he met many papermakers, including a young man named Munnalal Khaddari, who was the proprietor of a papermaking school.* From there he went to Atarsi and finally to Wardha, arriving there on 25 November 1937. That evening he typed a long letter to Edith.

While this village is famous all over India there are no hotels or huts where foreigners may spend the night. . . . I have not removed my clothes, not even my shoes have been taken from my feet and yesterday I walked for many hours, ankle deep, through black dust that thoroughly choked me as we were passed by camels, ox-carts, and thousands of men and women carrying all manner of commodities upon their heads. I have tried riding in the ox-carts but I prefer to walk as the motion from side to side is most fatiguing. I can walk much faster than the ox-carts travel. The only food I have had for the past two days has been hot tea with a sort of toasted bread with [water] buffalo butter. My bottle of Vichy was broken so I have no liquid other than the tea. It would be suicide to drink the unboiled water in this place and even if it was boiled I do not think I would care for it.

We came to Wardha to see the experiments in the making of handmade paper that are being carried on under the patronage of Mahatma Gandhi, the most influential man in the Orient and one of the world's great individuals. At the papermaking school we were met by the director, Mr. J.C. Kumarappa, who had previously been informed of our coming. We spent considerable time in inspecting the school and in making photographs of the pupils at work. Gandhiji's idea is to train the young men from various parts of India so that they may go to their home states and provinces and train others, thus building up a handmade paper industry that will not only supply the local needs but put hundreds of India's idle to work. How wise a plan this is I will not attempt to say, but Mr. Gandhi has tried the same experiment with hand-weaving. In fact, he himself has devised a hand-loom that can be carried about from place to place so the worker may lose no time. Gandhiji is, of course, a sentimental dreamer, but he has a vast hold on India's millions of people.

When we reached the papermaking school Mr. Kumarappa told us that it would be impossible to see Mr. Gandhi as he had just returned from Calcutta where he had been under observation for several weeks. His blood pressure was very high and they had grave fears for the Mahatma. Mr. Kumarappa had not seen the "Master" for two months and only last week an influential Chinese gentleman had been refused an audience. I told Mr. Kumarappa that I had not come especially to see Gandhiji, that I was primarily interested in the papermaking school and I would not think of disturbing the quiet rest so needed by the Mahatma.

I was taken to see Mr. Mahadev Desai, the editor of the Congress paper "Harijan" (Untouchables) which is issued weekly by Mr. Gandhi. Mr. Desai is also Mr. Gandhi's personal secretary and his most intimate confidant. Mr. Desai also said it would be impossible to see the Master, but he would convey my greetings to him and tell him of my interest in the papermaking school which is so close to Gandhiji's heart.

We spent another half hour looking over the publications of the Congress Society and just as we were about to take our leave a message came stating that Mahatma Gandhi requested me to come to him.

Everyone about the school seemed surprised and I the most surprised of all. Mr. Desai summoned his car, an old green Ford flying the saffron, white and green flag from the radiator cap, the emblem of the Congress. I was placed in the back seat, along with a basket of eggs and a box of Dromedary dates. We were off to the secluded home of the most beloved man in all India, Mahatma Gandhi.

The antique Ford rolled over the dirt path, passed ox-carts whose drivers argued with our driver as to who had the right of way; the saffron, white and green flag seemed to mean little to the ignorant men in the ox-carts. We traveled for five or six miles over the dusty road, the entire landscape being dull and drab, just a few scrubby bushes here and there. Finally we came to a long thatched building set close to the road. I could see many men at work building fences, erecting gateways, while others were operating a great ox-driven sugar press. With reverence we alighted from the car and proceeded toward the houses within the enclosure. Mr. Desai pointed to a small plaster house set well away from the other buildings and said that the Mahatma was within. I was to wait at another house until the secretary summoned me, as it was possible, even then, that I could not see the Master. In the work shop, some distance from Gandhiji's house, I sat awaiting the signal from the secretary. In the work-shop I could hear the hum of a sewing-machine, cooking was also going on within. There were baskets of food upon the floor and the eggs that we had brought were being treated as Mr. Gandhi, I understand, will not eat an egg unless it has been rendered non-fertile. A great brown man, clothed only in a breech-cloth, sat upon the porch spinning, and another man, prone on an outdoor Indian bed, read to the spinner. The book was apparently in Hindi and the man upon the couch was translating the text into English for the benefit of the huge brown artisan who appeared rather out of place working the delicate spinning-wheel. The book was of a culinary nature and when I appeared the subject was the making of cucumber soup. I also listened all through the chapter dealing with the boiling of buffalo milk and just as I was becoming rather impatient I saw the secretary in the distance motion for me to approach. As I walked nearer the house I could see that it had one small window in the side and above the barred window, modeled in the cement, there was a replica of a fig tree. At either side of the window spinning wheels were depicted and below there was a beehive with bees flying above, all carved in the material of which the house was built. The house is one story, tile roofed and surrounded by a crude picket fence. I opened the gate and walked toward the secretary who requested that I remain in Mr. Gandhi's presence only a few moments as he was very weak. I entered the door and there was the Mahatma. He was upon the stone floor his body covered with a white sheet. His head rested upon a pillow and about his head there was a white cloth, held with a safety pin. Seven of his disciples, both men and women, all Indians, were about him, one man took notes of every word he spoke. The doorway was low and when I entered I had to stoop. Mr. Gandhi looked up at me and said in a clear, soft voice, in perfect English, "You are very tall, Mr. Hunter, you must stoop to enter my poor home." He held his hands together before his face, in the manner of India and then he extended his hand and I kneeled down and took his hand in mine. He asked me a few questions about making paper by hand and then his head seemed to relax and I could see that he was very tired. He extended his hand again to me and again I held it within mine. All was then silence and I backed out of the low doorway. I had come in contact with a truly "Great Soul," the meaning of Mahatma.

Following this extraordinary experience, Hunter traveled from Wardha to Bombay. Then turning east again toward Calcutta, he and Rao finally arrived in Secunderabad. "In alighting from the train I was quite overcome as several young Indian ladies were there to welcome me with strands of daisies and roses which were placed around my neck. I was rather glad of this attention as the garlands helped to hide a very dirty shirt that I was wearing." (plate 76) Hunter continued east, stopping in Rajahmundry, where he was greeted with more garlands and where he secretly celebrated his fifty-fourth birthday. The two weary and dirty travelers finally arrived in the teeming port of Calcutta on 2 December 1937.

Following only a few hours' rest, Hunter and Rao set off once again on what was the most arduous part of their trip. Their destination was the papermaking village of Outshasi in Central Bengal (now Bangladesh). The village, which Hunter spelled Autshasi, was so remote that it does not appear on the map that Hunter carried with him and upon which he traced his route. To reach Outshasi, they traveled by boat up the Brahmaputra River, then by launch hired at Talatalla, finally by an even smaller boat to Tarapassa. The waterway was so narrow and overgrown that Hunter had to lie down all the way to Subachani. They passed village after village where the main industry was the manufacture of pottery from the local red clay. These were the poorest and most wretched places Hunter had ever been.

There were blind people, lepers; men, women and children with bodies twisted in grotesque forms that would make the contortions of the late Lon Chaney look dull in comparison. I saw demented women chained and roped to their husbands, children picking the small-pox scabs from their faces, men with half bodies and babies whose limbs were so thin that a finger ring could have been passed over the foot and up to the hip, sights seen only in nightmares and in the paintings and etchings of such artists of the unreal as Gustav Doré and William Hogarth. On one side of the canal lived the Hindus, on the other the Mohammedans, two peoples who do not agree and who are fighting constantly. The Hindus do not eat meat and regard the cow as sacred; the Mohammedans eat meat and kill the sacred cows of the Hindus. This leads to conflict. At the edge of the canal a cow had fallen into the stream and the poor half-dead creature was surrounded by a dozen bare-necked vultures each one ripping the flesh from the bones of the limp animal. In India everything is left to Fate, there is no struggle for life and when death finally comes it is the only relief.

One hundred sixty miles from the nearest road upon which a car could travel, the party finally arrived in the papermaking village in the late afternoon. After an uncomfortable night sleeping on a hard bench, Hunter was awakened at five the next morning by the villagers eager to show their distinguished guest papermaking. He removed the bamboo mats from atop his shoes, placed there the evening before to keep out the scorpions and tarantulas, and barely had time to dress before the "entertainment" began. Considering it unfitting for a foreign gentleman to visit the papermill, the village elders had instructed that the mill be brought to him. After a few hours of demonstration and conversation with the *kagazis* (papermakers), the equipment was packed up for Hunter as a gift. Retracing their steps, he and Rao were back in Calcutta a day later.

Exhausted, Hunter took a few days to rest and catch up on his correspondence. He wrote Harrison Elliott that the Indian Industrial Commission had asked him to stay for a year to supervise the papermaking mills, but this was out of the question, "I shall never visit India again as there will be no need as I have covered every papermaking district and have done the job most thoroughly, although I now feel that I have added at least 10 years to my age." While still in Calcutta, Hunter received a letter from the Industrial Association in Rajahmundry, a school he had visited. The officials wrote that they were most grateful for the "sacrifice" Hunter had made to interview the papermakers personally, and the sympathy he had for the development

of hand papermaking as a viable industry. They announced that a new
papermaking section of the school would be named the "Hunter Section" in
his honor. One evening, he gave a short presentation about his fact-finding
trip at a public meeting, after which it was resolved that the Calcutta Hand
Made Paper Maker's Association be formed. The primary objectives of the
association were to preserve the craft by improving its quantity and quality
and by promoting its unique characteristics. They reasoned that until the
government and the public recognized that handmade paper was a valued
commodity there was little hope of expanding the industry. (While this was
a lofty goal and the interested associations had some impact, after sixty years,
little has changed.)

Traveling via the Suez Canal, Hunter arrived home in early February
1938, after more than a month at sea.

Papermaking by Hand in India

A few days before leaving on this trip, Hunter had met with Elmer Adler
about the Pynson Printers publishing his book on India. They agreed that it
would be the same style, size, edition, and price as the earlier book. Upon
his return, Hunter worked on the manuscript for *Papermaking by Hand in
India* for a few months; he sent it to Adler in May. The new book appeared
a year later in June 1939 (see plate 76).

The major difference between the first Pynson Printers book and the second was the text paper. It would have been appropriate for the book to have
been printed on Indian handmade paper, but none could be found that was
worthy. An oriental paper might have been the second choice, but Japanese
paper was ruled out because of strong anti-Japanese sentiments due to that
country's unpopular war with China. One example of this was that, in
April 1939, the Japan Paper Company changed its name to the Stevens-
Nelson Paper Company. Ultimately, Adler chose a Swedish handmade paper
because it somewhat resembled the Japanese paper used in *Papermaking
Pilgrimage to Japan, Korea and China*. As before, Gerlach bound the edition.
He used black leather for the spine and a multi-colored, block-printed
Indian cloth for the sides. Hunter later admitted that he had made a mistake
in choosing the cloth because it gave a bright, gay appearance to a book that
was, to most readers, rather depressing.

Although *Papermaking by Hand in India* was sold out within a year,
Elmer Adler had other financial problems, and by April 1940, Pynson
Printers closed its doors. Adler eventually moved to the University Press at
Princeton, New Jersey. Once Hunter's financial dealings with Adler were
concluded, the two book lovers became great friends.

Chapter 15

If I have done anything worthwhile, it is in the establishment of the Paper Museum.
Dard Hunter

The origins of Hunter's paper museum date back to his years at Marlborough. It was there that he began building a collection of books and specimens relating to papermaking, watermarks, typography, and printing. After putting together the Smithsonian Institution's papermaking and typography exhibits, he realized the importance of sharing the artifacts from his collection with others—he was already sharing his knowledge. As he broadened his research to include oriental papermaking and printing, he contacted people from around the world, who sent him books, papers, tools, and equipment.

In late 1927, Hunter wrote to Ruel Tolman, his colleague at the Smithsonian Institution.

> My "museum" is only mental so far, but I do hope to have a small room some day where I can set up the papermaking material I have collected. I also want to show, so far as possible, the uses that paper is put to, especially fine papers. It is for this that I am anxious for the Japanese [wood] blocks [which the institution exchanged for a copy of *Primitive Papermaking*].
>
> We intend starting a small paper mill in the east and I hope to have a place suitable for the papermaking material there. My idea is along the line of the typographical museum of the American Type Founders Company at Jersey City, only, of course, not so elaborate.

As we know, the museum at the Lime Rock mill never materialized, and during the first half of the 1930s, Hunter instead focused his attention on traveling, collecting, and book publishing. In August 1933, Hunter decided to catalogue his collection, which he estimated numbered about 400 objects, not including his library. During this period, he was helping other institutions develop exhibits on papermaking and the book arts, as well as exhibits of his own work. The first of these was held in January and February 1934 at the Jones Library in Amherst, Massachusetts, and titled, "Books, Written and Made by Dard Hunter." The next month, it opened in the Treasure Room of the Boston Public Library and ran until 1 May. A display of over fifty items, including "photographs, original drawings of title-pages, Ex-Libris, initial letters, pamphlets, proof-sheets, and copies of the completed books—all relating to the highly original work of Mr. Hunter," shed new light on his design work, then virtually unknown. Many collectors of his books who saw the exhibit were impressed with this aspect of Hunter's work, a part of his life about which he rarely spoke.*

Also in 1934, Hunter was asked, on behalf of Chicago's Museum of Science and Industry, to acquire equipment for a papermaking exhibit. When the Lime Rock mill was sold in November 1933, Hunter tried to buy the papermaking equipment from Mr. Weber, but to no avail. Disappointed but not dissuaded, Hunter wrote to Jack Green of J. Barcham Green asking him to search England for disused mill equipment suitable for exhibition. Such equipment was found, including a York stone vat, and after much negotiating between Green and the Chicago museum, the equipment was shipped and installed later that year. For his own collection, Hunter purchased and had shipped with the rest of that equipment seven pairs of English moulds from J. Barcham Green.

The foundation of the Dard Hunter Paper Museum was finally laid in December 1935 when Hunter invited George Houk Mead, the president of the Mead Pulp and Paper Corporation, to visit Mountain House. Like many of his generation and profession, Mead had an appreciation of papermaking history. After being shown some of Hunter's collection during the December meeting, Mead suggested that a paper museum and a hand papermaking mill be created in Chillicothe. He urged Hunter to come up with plans and intimated that the corporation might financially support the enterprise. However, in a letter to Mead written at the end of January 1936, Hunter reasoned that while Chillicothe might be a good location for the museum— the Mead Paper Mill there attracted visitors from around the world—it would be better situated nearer New York City. In fact, he wrote, he was about to purchase several acres of land within 35 miles of the city where he intended to set up a museum, papermill, and press.† Nevertheless, Hunter wrote, if Mead was serious about having the museum in Chillicothe, he would reconsider.

Mead's reply came more than a month later.

My interest in your work, and the collection you have made which is now in Chillicothe, is, indeed, a serious and deep one; and I have given the entire matter quite a little thought since our very pleasant visit together.

I am prepared in the reasonably near future to have the Mead Corporation build for you a proper building of moderate size on whatever location you may choose near your house for the purpose of properly protecting and perpetuating this very valuable work of yours. . . . Your own reputation is already both national and international, and in turn, the many interesting people who come to review your historical and artistic development will, I think, enjoy a comparison with the more modern developments by calling upon us.*

Hunter's reply was noncommittal, simply stating that he would be happy to discuss the idea further when Mead was next in town. What Mead probably did not know was that Hunter had other irons in the fire. Mead's delayed reply had prompted Hunter to write about his museum to an ardent collector of Mountain House Press books, Carl T. Keller of Boston. In turn, Keller lunched with Dr. Karl T. Compton, president of the Massachusetts Institute of Technology to broach the subject. Compton was so captivated by the idea that in May 1936, he made Hunter an offer to provide exhibit areas for his collection, which Compton suggested he lend to MIT, as well as space for a small papermill and press. Compton also offered him an unpaid position—curator or director of the Dard Hunter Museum. Hunter was not interested in an unpaid position, however, and he wrote Compton to that effect. As Compton was away from Cambridge over the summer, nothing further happened.

In the meantime, Hunter renewed negotiations with George Mead. By mid-December 1936, architects were making blueprints for the museum building to be located on Hunter's orchard to the north of Mountain House. (This property is now the home of Cornell and Irene Hunter.) The large building, about 54,250 square feet, was to be in the style of early Virginian architecture and modeled after the public library in Chappaqua, New York. In addition to the museum, the Hunters were to live in this building; Mountain House was either to be rented or sold.

Just when all seemed settled, Compton wrote Hunter with good news; he was now able to offer a stipend of $5,000 a year. The position would entail curating the collection while giving Hunter the freedom to continue his research and writings. If Hunter wanted to volunteer to teach, Compton added, that could be arranged, too. After considering the ramifications of Compton's proposal, Hunter responded:

> The plan appeals to me very much as it would give me unlimited satisfaction to work in the manner you have outlined. . . . As I would wish to devote all of my time to the Paper Museum I do not believe it would be practical for me to enter into a new arrangement until after the [India] journey was out of the way. . . . In the meantime I would be pleased to have more details relative to the proposed plan for my permanent connection with the Massachusetts Institute of Technology as I am greatly interested in just such a project as you have proposed in your letter.

As if there was not enough going on already, Hunter had another scheme to move his collection to the Museum of Science and Industry, a plan coordinated by the Chicago-based paper-trade publisher William Bond Wheelwright. The major stumbling block was that the museum could not afford to pay Hunter a stipend. To solve this problem, Wheelwright suggested organizing The Kami Club, which would publish a monthly periodical devoted to the finer aspects of papermaking. Wheelwright proposed that dues be $3 per year, and his goal was to sign up 1000 subscribers. After the expenses of the club were met, the surplus would pay Hunter's salary, as well as any other costs not covered by the Museum of Science and Industry.

Hunter was interested in this rather elaborate idea, primarily because the magazine, *KAMI*, would publish his articles on a regular basis. He also thought the selection of the name an appropriate one as it was a Japanese word for paper, but he also wondered, "are the Japanese in sufficient good grace in this country to make the title a popular one? . . . I have no animosity toward the Japanese myself, but I am aware that there is a feeling against them by those who do not know the situation in the Orient." But good idea or not, The Kami Club never materialized. A few days after presenting the idea to his friend, Wheelwright decided that he was too busy to pursue it.

Undaunted, Hunter pushed ahead with the Mead proposal. In January 1937, Mead confirmed that construction of the museum would begin in the spring. However, even though Mead and Hunter continued to correspond, ground was never broken, and the idea was finally laid to rest when Mead paid off the architects' bills later that year.

Having had both the Chicago and Mead plans dissolve into thin air, Hunter was relieved in August 1937 to hear again from Keller about MIT.

As there were only a few weeks before he was to leave for India, Hunter wanted some reassurance that the MIT plan was still viable. He wrote to Keller,

> I really would like to be connected with this fine institution in some capacity. A year or more ago I believe I told you that Mr. George Mead of the Mead Pulp and Paper Corporations was contemplating a Paper Museum to be erected here in Chillicothe where one of their largest mills is located. For the present at least this worthy project has been laid aside and when I last saw Mr. Mead he intimated that they might be interested in helping to establish such a Museum in Cambridge. Mr. Mead is an M.I.T. graduate [BS, chemical engineering, 1900]. . . . There is no reason why I should remain in Ohio, except that my Great-Grand-father was foolish to come out here from Virginia in 1812. Personally I do not care for it here and have no desire to remain, but we have real estate and a printing business of long standing and these things make it difficult to break away.

Keller promptly replied,

> I get a hint of encouragement in your letter; it looks to me possible that you might forget Great-Grandfather and do what is most satisfying to yourself, and let your boys run the newspaper. . . . For heaven's sake, be careful on these silly trips you take all around the world! You know we haven't any other Dard Hunter around.

Hunter left for India in October, and a few weeks after he sailed, a letter arrived in Chillicothe from MIT President Compton.

> I have not bothered you with letters regarding the proposed arrange-ments whereby we might offer quarters for your paper museum and some assistance to you in continuing this work, for two reasons. One of these is the fact that I dislike any attempt to exert personal pressure in a matter of this kind, believing that your own desires and good judgment in the matter must be the deciding factor. The other reason was my friendly relation with George Mead so that I did not wish to be a "com-petitor" with him but would rather leave any decision in the matter entirely up to your own best judgment.
>
> The situation here has changed in an advantageous manner since our last discussion of possibilities. We have secured funds to build a large

addition to our main building which will extend along Massachusetts Avenue and provide among other things the principally used entrance to our buildings. This new addition is primarily to house our School of Architecture, but it will contain a great deal of additional space. . . . Among other things we are reserving for the paper museum a space about 125 ft. long by 24 ft. wide [3,000 sq. ft.], and with a high ceiling, on the third floor of the new building, fronting on Massachusetts Avenue. . . . Such a space will be more conveniently located both for work and for exhibit purposes than the one which we originally talked about.

A day or two after his arrival from India, Hunter wrote Compton.

Under the conditions outlined in your previous letter I would like to be connected with the Institute provided I could continue the work I have been doing. If the Paper Museum was established under your roof it would be my desire that it be a "working museum" and not simply so many cases housing obsolete and dead material. I would wish to continue the compilation of books on the subject of papermaking as there is much to be accomplished in this particular field. Also, I would wish to continue my work in the actual making of books—papermaking by hand, type-founding, type-setting, book designing and printing—in fact complete book production. All of this could be carried on in the space you mention, 24 by 125 feet. . . . I do not care to remain longer in Chillicothe, although this out-of-the-way place has served me well as I have been able to work undisturbed. Now, however, I have reached an age when perhaps it would be well to impart to others the knowledge I have gained.

Over the next few months, Hunter and Compton exchanged letters refining an arrangement that ultimately made Hunter the director of the Paper Museum at an annual salary of $5,000 with a ten-year commitment on the part of MIT. Hunter's collection was to be packed and shipped to MIT as soon as possible at the Institute's expense, but the collection and any additions to it thereafter were to remain Hunter's property. The name, Dard Hunter Paper Museum, was actually not settled upon until early 1939. Before then Hunter referred to it variously as the American Paper Museum and the American Museum of Papermaking (the name by which it is now known).

Hunter's idea to set up a small papermill within the museum was hampered by his having no vat or paper press. As there seemed no chance of budging Weber from his "not for sale" stance regarding the Lime Rock mill equipment, Hunter again wrote to English papermills to locate used equipment for sale. A representative from the W.S. Hodgkinson Company, which owned the Wookey Hole Mill, wrote about a disused vat the company was willing to sell. After confirming that all of the component parts existed, a delighted Hunter instructed that the vat be sent to MIT as soon as possible. Later that year, he ordered a huge, 10 foot high by 6 foot wide wooden screw press from the same mill.

In addition to this equipment, Hunter began to gather even more papermaking and printing material. He was especially interested in papermaking moulds, since many of the ones he had collected over the years were in the Lime Rock mill. Even though he had sent similar requests in the early 1920s, Hunter wrote the major paper and mould-making companies in Europe and new ones in the Orient asking them to donate artifacts and paper to the new MIT museum; most sent something.

Hunter decided that the museum should not exclude high-quality, machine-made papers as that segment of the industry played an important role in the book arts. To accumulate specimens and appliances, he wrote to the major American mills making book and other fine papers, as well as to equipment manufacturers. Most were pleased to honor his requests. As one example, the Jos. J. Plank Company in Appleton, Wisconsin, eagerly agreed to make some small dandy rolls and a display of the steps in making watermarks.*

Packing Hunter's collection for the move to Cambridge was scheduled for late August 1938. Dard Jr. helped his father inventory and pack that part of the collection intended for the museum. (Cornell was attending the Radio Engineering Institute in Washington, D.C.) Soon it became apparent that Hunter had underestimated the number of items, and he wrote to Compton warning him that the cost of packing and shipping would be higher than estimated. This also meant that shipment would be delayed, but as work on the museum's home, the new William Barton Rogers Building, was also behind schedule, this was not a problem. In addition to packing, Hunter and Dard Jr. also made two scale models: one, a stamping mill in Kashmir; the other, a typical set-up for making handmade paper in Indo-China.

THE OPENING
In mid-November 1938, fifty crates insured for $25,000 were shipped to MIT. The two Dards arrived in early December and found an apartment at 302 Beacon Street, overlooking the Charles River. Hunter was pleased that it was just a short walk across the bridge to MIT. Father and son spent the

next six months unpacking, assembling the artifacts in the cases, and preparing labels.

Hunter found institutional life a difficult adjustment. A month before the official opening, he wrote a discouraging letter to Edith.

The "visiting committee" have been here and spent about 20 minutes in our place. They are all of scientific mind and I don't believe anything other than a slide-rule would appeal to them. At the dinner in the evening (a perfect bore to me) they all talked slide-rule and scientific dribble, all of which did not interest me in the least. One man dwelt for an hour on the possibility of photographing the sound waves from metal to ascertain the depth of annealing and hardening. The same scientific mind told about having a nightmare and erecting a bell over his bed for his wife to ring, in the next room, when he screamed. This occurs when he eats cheese at night. This old scientific brain cell is 71 and is head of the research department of the General Electric at Schnectady. To me he was a most developed bore. The dinner was fine, but the chatter left me cold. I think nine-tenths of this so-called "science" is nothing more than indigestion. The committee felt, I felt, that anything of an historical nature was pure bunk and therefore my exhibit little above plain drivel. Dr. Compton talked but little, as he always remains rather quiet, but takes on a wise look. I think he has many of my qualities. But, anyway, I am of the opinion that the Paper Museum did not make much of a hit with the committee.

This week, Dr. Philip Hofer, Curator of Printing and Graphic Arts of Harvard, called upon us and I am to go out to his hang-out Monday. Here is a man who was really appreciative and gave us no end of encouragement. I think Harvard would have been the place for my junk; surely M.I.T. is not the setting, of this I become more and more convinced. Dr. Hofer said that he wished Harvard could have this material. In any event, it all makes me rather uncertain as to just what the outcome will be as I am becoming more and more of the thought that the Museum is short-lived at M.I.T. I think they would keep me, but I would never feel entirely comfortable tucked away among watts, cells, ultra-violet rays, atoms, slide-rules and the like. I am out of place, and there is no use to deny it.

Of course, the visiting committee was very impressed by Hunter's museum. The Opening Tea was held on 5 June 1939, and between 500–600 people showed up for the event.* Dard Jr. wrote his mother that it had been a great success. But the euphoria did not last. That December, several Institute staff members reported to Compton's assistant, James R. Killian Jr., that Hunter was unhappy. Apparently, he had complained that most of the museum visitors were not affiliated with the Institute. Acutely aware of the rivalry between MIT and Harvard, Hunter also mentioned that a large number of the latter's students and faculty were regular visitors. Killian suggested another tea to get MIT people into the museum, but the head of public relations disagreed, "I think the old practice of measuring the buoyancy of culture by floating it on tannic acid can be overdone."

Instead, Hunter was asked to give a Society of Arts lecture, "Paper and How It Is Made." During this lecture, he utilized the Wookey Hole Mill equipment and made paper, to the delight of his audience. The strategy worked, and the lecture drew MIT people and other visitors to the museum in record numbers. Recognizing his unique knowledge and teaching abilities, Hunter was invited to be one of the instructors in an academic course, "The Art of the Book." He was responsible for covering papermaking, type making, and letterpress printing. It was hard to know who enjoyed his demonstrations and lectures more, the students or the teacher. To everyone's regret, the course was canceled after America entered World War II in late 1941.

In mid-1940, the question regarding the museum's ownership arose. The original agreement between Compton and Hunter stipulated that as long as Hunter was employed by MIT, the museum was on loan to it. Only after the museum opened, however, did MIT officials begin to understand its true value, and they must have approached Hunter with offers to purchase it. However, Hunter would not sell for two reasons: as long as he owned the collection, he felt it was unlikely that MIT would dismiss him, and if he sold the collection, the profit would be taxable. Nevertheless, he wanted his estate to benefit from the collection's worth. This dilemma was solved when his life insurance agent proposed a scheme that suited both parties. MIT agreed to pay the premiums on a $30,000 life insurance policy on Hunter. (Hunter had valued the collection for $35,000—a figure Carl Keller considered too low.) Upon Hunter's death, the Institute would give the insurance money to Hunter's heirs in exchange for the collection.

On 23 January 1941, a formal agreement was signed with a provisional understanding that a catalogue or inventory of the museum's holdings would be forthcoming. This was an important issue to the MIT officials as they wanted to ensure that nothing of value would be taken from the collection. Initially, Hunter worked diligently on the catalogue, but as time passed, he found it difficult to keep at the task. One problem was that he was constantly adding to the collection. He and Dard Jr. had put together an inventory as the collection was being packed, and there was also the catalogue that Hunter had started in the early 1930s, but neither of these was complete. A solution seemed to appear in the person of M.A. Azam. Azam, an Indian chemical engineer, cheerfully volunteered to type the information (from the two lists?) into a catalogue. In July 1942, Azam wrote that he had finished the 60-page catalogue, but he did not send a copy to Hunter. In January 1943, he wrote again and described the *Evolution of Paper Catalogue*— Azam's title—as a document that took the visitor case by case through the museum, although the pages could also be reorganized in such a way to make the information chronological. Azam wanted it printed for sale, but this was never done. Furthermore, it is not known when, if ever, this document was seen by Hunter.*

THE PAPER MUSEUM PRESS

Even before the museum officially opened, the director and his assistant set up a small private press, called the Paper Museum Press, using the Shniedewend Midget Reliance Press that was purchased some years before. As little Lime Rock paper was left over from previous Mountain House Press books on which to print the new press's projects, Hunter decided to have paper made at the Wookey Hole Mill. In June 1939, the Bull's Head and Branch watermarked moulds were sent to England, but in August, he canceled the order as he had repurchased the Lime Rock mill and all the paper in it.

In October, the Paper Museum Press began its first project, a limited edition brochure titled "Massachusetts Institute of Technology: Dard Hunter Paper Museum." From the reams and reams of Lime Rock paper, the Hunters selected a cream color, wove paper watermarked HAND MADE U.S.A., the most abundant of all of the papers made by the mill in the year following the receivership. The eight pages of text were set in Caslon. The photogravure frontispiece shows the spacious room in which the Dard Hunter Collection was displayed; artifacts covered nearly all of the wall space, and the cases were filled with wood blocks, prints, and Mountain House Press books. (plate 77) The wrapper is a blue Lime Rock paper decorated with Jost Amman's illustration of the papermaker from Schopper's 1568 *Panoplia Omnium Artium*.

Two hundred copies of the brochure were printed and bound pamphlet-style with blue linen thread. In February 1940, the brochures were distributed gratis to friends of the museum, to loyal supporters of the Mountain House Press, and to Hunter's oldest friends such as Sterling Lord. (In order for Peter Franck to receive a brochure, he had to trade for it.) As soon as the existence of the brochure was known through notices in the trade papers, Hunter received daily requests for copies, which he could not satisfy.

In a letter to a friend in late February 1940, Hunter expressed hope that the Paper Museum Press would publish a booklet every few months, and indeed, the Press's next project was already under way—a specimen sheet of Dard Jr.'s font of type.

DARD JR.'S FONT OF TYPE

The end of Dard Jr.'s stay at the Western Reserve Academy came in 1937. It was apparent that he was not suited for a traditional college education, but he was exceptionally skilled in manual work. A compromise was made, and that September, he enrolled in the Cleveland School of Art (CSA) where he could continue honing his manual skills, as well as receive instruction in design and the history of art. In his spare time, he worked in N.A. Petrone's fine jewelry studio.

Although Hunter had decided some years before that he had no wish to produce another font of type, Dard Jr. was keen on doing so. His father helped him cut his first few punches, and this work continued under the supervision of his design instructor at CSA, the well-known letter historian and collector Otto F. Ege. Although young Dard's typeface has much in common with his father's, it is more refined and uniform (see plate 54). In fact, the young man's major source of inspiration was the roman type of Nicolas Jenson, the fifteenth-century type designer. From 1937 until summer 1940, Dard Jr. cut the upper- and lowercase letters, along with the numbers and points, including the ampersand, question mark, and exclamation point. Although a punch for the ligature *fi* was cut, no matrix or type have been found. Like his father, he cut no italics or accented letters.*

Once the punches were cut, Dard Jr. struck and justified all of the matrices and hand cast his font of type using the 18-point German mould. Hunter was so proud of Dard Jr.'s achievement, he wrote to Edith from MIT that he could hardly wait to use his son's type.

To a boyhood friend, Dard Jr. wrote,

> I guess the biggest thing around here is that I have successfully completed my font of type and it doesn't look bad even if I do say so myself. Dard said that it is the finest thing that has been done in modern times but I can't tell about this. We will soon see. I haven't gotten many outside criticisms yet but when I do I can see where I stand, perhaps. However, I even haven't printed it yet—just a rough proof. It is to be just a specimen page with a reproduction photograph of all tools, punches & matrices, etc. Also an introduction and colophon in Caslon. This will all be bound in a heavy cover and the finished pamphlet put in

a slip case. There will be 150 copies & these will be sent to all libraries & perhaps some museums of the world. It isn't finished enough yet to really see the final outcome but I am hoping for the best.

In the autumn of 1940, the *Specimen of Type* was finished. (plate 78) The edition was 100 instead of 150, and no slipcase was made. In November, the *Specimen* was sent gratis to many of the same people and institutions who received the museum brochure. Except that it is a folio, *Specimen* is much like the brochure. Caslon was used for the cover and the explanatory pages; the specimen page was, of course, printed in Dard Jr.'s type in black ink with a large capital *A* printed in red. The specimen reproduces a page from a fifteenth-century book; the rough proof Dard Jr. wrote about was taken from a sixteenth-century source. While the blue wrapper paper is the same used for the brochure, the text pages were printed on the Bull's Head and Branch watermarked paper. Otto Ege sent Dard Sr. a congratulatory letter.

> Today I received the *thrilling* specimen page! ! ! Father *deserves* much praise, teacher little. Frankly Dard Jr. has the "something" that Goudy always lacked—a warmth, a craft touch—a directness—which I believe the Japs. say, "It is that that makes art." To me, it can well take its place among the faces used by the private presses of the better type—I should like to shake his hand—firmly in congratulations on a remarkable achievement!

Ege's good opinion was certainly welcome, but in March 1941, Dard Jr. gained national attention when the *Specimen* was mentioned in *The New York Times Book Review*. The "outside criticism" he had been waiting for was good: "A large page set in the new face is included and is the initial showing of this virile, handsome type, agreeably archaic and full of character." Following the issuance of the *Specimen*, Dard Jr. began receiving requests to use his font, but with one exception, these were declined.*

The exception was a broadside of Robert Frost's poem *A Considerable Speck*, which Dard Jr. printed for the Colonial Society of Massachusetts. One year before, on 21 November 1939, Frost had been a guest at the Society's annual dinner, during which he composed and delivered the poem. Bostonians Augustus Loring and his wife, the noted marbler Rosamond B. Loring, were active in the Society and great friends of the Hunters. In April 1940, Loring sent a copy of the poem to Dard Jr. asking if he would print it for the Society. Finished just after the *Specimen*, Dard Jr. sent *A Considerable Speck* to Loring in mid-December 1940. (plate 79) Loring sent a warm letter of congratulations and a $75 honorarium.

The *Speck* consists of a full sheet of paper folded once to form a folio. The wove paper again was from Lime Rock and watermarked HAND MADE U.S.A. To set off the Frost poem with a decorative border, young Dard cut a new punch—a fly. On the front of the folio was printed the title, one fly, and the poet's name. The poem was printed in black ink and enclosed in a border of fly ornaments. Appropriately, the initial *A* was printed in "speck" brown. The edition of *A Considerable Speck* was 100, and once members of the Society received their copies, Loring sent extras to prominent persons, including President Roosevelt. *A Considerable Speck* was the last project printed by the Paper Museum Press, except for exhibition labels and a lecture announcement for Miss Che-Fong Seto, a Chinese woman who assisted in the museum and who taught Dard and Edith Chinese calligraphy.

Even before the *Specimen* and the *Speck* were finished, Dard Jr. had decided he was unhappy with some of the letters. No doubt he would have cut new punches, but during the summer of 1941, he was no longer working with his father. Instead, he was the assistant in the MIT Hobby Shop, where he learned a number of different crafts including bookbinding; he taught wood- and metal-working. That summer, he gained independence from his father and confidence in his own skills. Within a few years, he and Cornell joined the armed forces to help America fight World War II.

Without Dard Jr.—his "eyes"—Hunter could not do presswork, and so he had little to do except attend to the daily routine of the museum and write books. His one great achievement during the war years was the publication of *Papermaking: The History and Technique of an Ancient Craft*, discussed in Chapter 16.

DARD HUNTER PAPER MUSEUM—FOLLOWING THE WAR

Upon the retirement of Dr. Compton in late 1947, James R. Killian Jr. succeeded him as president of MIT. Dr. Compton's influence was not gone, however, as he was chairman of the Corporation of MIT, a position he held until his death in 1954. The new dean of humanities was the ex-director of the libraries, John E. Burchard, and Dr. Vernon D. Tate was named to fill Burchard's shoes.

Librarians Burchard and Tate were acutely aware of the importance of cataloguing the Hunter collection, and to help with this task, Burchard arranged for two women to work part-time on it. In March 1948, Miss Catherine Ahearn and Mrs. Mary Lee were given the responsibility of compiling as much information as they could with their limited expertise; any remaining gaps were to be completed by Hunter. Ahearn and Lee reorganized the Museum's library alphabetically by author, described the contents of the exhibition cases as well as they could, and then tackled the solander boxes full of paper specimens in Hunter's office. To document the decorated papers, Ahearn contacted Rosamond Loring, an expert in that field. A little over a year later, Ahearn notified her superiors that the catalogue was complete, except for Hunter's input.

Hunter's ten-year tenure at MIT officially ended in November 1948, but no action was taken until 9 May 1949 when President Killian met with Burchard and Tate. The results of the meeting were:

• Hunter had to retire as of June 1949 as he was over the mandatory retirement age of 65;

• the museum was to move to the Charles Hayden Memorial Library building, which was under construction and due to open in 1950;

• Dard Jr. was to be asked to take a full-time appointment, renewable after one year, to help complete the catalogue, prepare the exhibits for the move, and help rearrange the exhibits after the move. It was to be made clear to Dard Jr., however, that he was not to do any "private" work such as the "old" techniques of printing or type-making (this made it quite clear that Killian did not want the Paper Museum Press to be reactivated);

• the acquisition of a working model of a fourdrinier paper machine was to be dropped. (William Bond Wheelwright and D. Clark Everest, both influential paper men, had gone to considerable lengths to have the model donated to the museum. Later, they were allowed to proceed, but the model was never acquired because Killian and Burchard ultimately refused to have it in the collection.)

One day after the meeting, Killian sent a letter to Hunter outlining his decisions, and added,

Dr. Tate also told me of your expressed desire to retire officially as curator of the museum. While this creates a problem for the Institute, we understand the reasons which lead you to wish to be relieved of any scheduled responsibility. If it is agreeable to you personally, we could arrange the retirement to take place as of June 30. . . . I had hoped that I might have an opportunity to see you so that I might discuss some of these matters across the table, and I take this means in lieu of the opportunity of seeing you personally. It has been a source of pride and pleasure for the Institute to have you here, and we have appreciated your services as curator, realizing full well the difficulties which it entailed because of the separation it required from your home base. Those of us here who have had the opportunity of knowing you will most certainly hope that the matter of formal retirement will not keep you away from the Institute.

Hunter's reply was swift.

Dear Dr. Killian: Your communication of the tenth was a complete surprise to me, and even after several readings I cannot detect that you have left any opening for a reply. I hope, however, that it will not be out of order for me to state my feelings in regard to your conclusive letter.

I wish to say that I have not resigned as curator of the Paper Museum, nor have I thought of resigning. If, however, it is your personal desire that I be dismissed from all connection with the Paper Museum, then I can only say that I will try to comply with your wish gracefully and without remorse. . . .

My work at the Paper Museum has not gone unnoticed, either in this country or abroad. Of this I am certain from the letters and articles that I receive. In the same mail with your letter came a communication from the American Pulp and Paper Association with the request that I become an honorary member of this wide-spread Association. Even this highly-industrialized organization has at last recognized my work as being helpful and beneficial. . . .

After devoting more than forty years to the building of a collection embracing thousands of items on one subject, it is not an easy or indifferent matter to permanently sever all connections with that assemblage. I will say that no one at M.I.T. realizes the extent of this collection, or has any conception of the work, travel, and patience that have been required to gather the material together; nor is there any realization of the thousands of dollars that have been expended in this regard. Even when I am absent from the Museum the collection is never forgotten and I am constantly gathering stray and obscure material dealing with Papermaking. Throughout my entire tenure at M.I.T. my salary has been used liberally in acquiring additional material; in fact, there has not been a single year that my "honorarium," as Dr. Compton called it, has begun to cover my Museum and living expense.

The gathering of the Museum material and the issuing of more than a dozen non-profitable limited editions has now practically exhausted what was once a comfortable estate. From a financial point of view my life has been anything but fruitful.

As stated in the second paragraph of this letter, I have not resigned from M.I.T. Had I thought of so doing I would have followed the traditional procedure of communicating with you in writing. Unless I have misinterpreted the substance of your letter, it is your wish that I be dismissed as Curator of the Paper Museum of the Massachusetts Institute of Technology. Naturally, this will mean that I must seek a teaching position in another university so that my personal income may be supplemented. This will enable me, as in the past, to print books upon which there is little or no profit, and to continue to collect "Paperiana." I would not be content unless I could pursue the work I undertook to accomplish so many years ago.

    With all kind wishes, ever. Sincerely yours, Dard Hunter.

After receiving Hunter's letter, Killian sent a memo to Burchard.

Apparently [Hunter] did not mean what he said or believe what he said in telling Vernon Tate that he wished to retire. I have called Hunter and told him to ignore my letter, and have asked him when he is in town to come in to see me so that I may explore the whole situation with him. He replied that he plans to be here some time during the month . . . [Burchard, pencil notation] Mr. JRK: The Hunter matter is indeed a contretemps; I think VDT may not have been too careful but still believe most of onus is on curious mentality of Hunter. Would you like to talk to me before you see Hunter. More than a year ago he took a different line.

Confusion reigned for a few weeks. Finally, in late July 1949, all of the parties met. It was then agreed that Hunter had officially retired on 30 June 1949, and effective 1 July, he was appointed honorary curator of the Paper Museum with an annual stipend of $5,000. His duties were essentially the same, and it was expected that he would spend at least six months of the year, preferably during the winter, at MIT. The appointment was to be renewed on 1 July each year until 29 November 1953, Hunter's seventieth birthday. It was made clear to Hunter that once he reached seventy, he could not continue to be paid by the Institute, as the rules strictly forbade it. Hunter agreed to these conditions, and over the next few months, he focused on facilitating the move of the collection. While waiting for the building to be completed, Hunter went back to Chillicothe to continue setting type for his next book *Papermaking by Hand in America*. He had also been asked to be an expert witness in the Alger Hiss treason trial. Hiss was accused of passing secrets to Whittaker Chambers, an avowed communist and courier for a group of spies. Hunter's role was to identify and date the manifold, or carbon copy, paper that was crucial evidence in the trial. Refusing to attempt a judgment based on a photograph of the paper, Hunter insisted on having a piece of the actual evidence. However, even with the sample, he could not determine the age or origin of manufacture. Much to his disappointment, he was not called to testify.

Deadlines for the museum move came and went, but finally, in April 1950, Hunter received word that the move was imminent. He and Dard Jr. drove to Cambridge and finished setting up the exhibits just in time for the dedication of the Charles Hayden Memorial Library on 19 May 1950. Practically everything from the collection was moved except the huge Wookey Hole press, which was three feet too high; three years later, it was cut down to fit.

THE DARD HUNTER PAPER MUSEUM AT IPC

On 29 November 1953, Hunter celebrated his seventieth birthday, and he was officially no longer on MIT's payroll. He had no idea what the future might hold for the collection except that Killian hoped another institution would purchase it. In May 1954, MIT received a tentative offer from the Institute of Paper Chemistry (IPC) in Appleton, Wisconsin; several years earlier, the idea of a paper museum had been advanced by IPC presidents Otto Kress and Westbrook Steele. Indeed, Steele's friend D. Clark Everest had already donated the Lime Rock mill papermaking equipment to that end. When Hunter learned of the potential move to IPC, he thought it the natural venue for his collection. The only problem was that MIT considered the offer too low. Hoping for a better deal, Burchard approached a number of universities, including Yale, Harvard, Princeton, Georgia Tech, and Columbia University (to which Harrison Elliott had given much of his paper-making equipment). While each of the institutions was interested in the collection, all politely refused either because of a lack of space or of money for Hunter's salary. Having no other option, in June 1954, MIT officially accepted IPC's offer: $16,400, the cost of Hunter's life insurance premiums.

On 12 June, Westbrook Steele sent Hunter a letter outlining the relationship between IPC and Hunter. The salient points were:
• IPC would perpetuate the name Dard Hunter Paper Museum and keep it functionally intact;
• IPC would insure the collection and keep it accessible;
• Hunter would be the director of the museum for life;
• Hunter would provide a catalogue of the collection;
• IPC would pay Hunter a stipend plus his travel expenses to Appleton for at least a year.

Hunter's appointment with IPC commenced on 1 July 1954. Steele sent a memo to IPC staff at the end of July: "With a great deal of gratification and pride we announce that The Institute of Paper Chemistry is to be the new and permanent home of the Dard Hunter Museum of Paper." In August, Hunter expressed concern over some of the points listed in Steele's initial letter, which were immediately addressed by Steele. Satisfied, Hunter signed a contract on 19 August. A comparison of Steele's letter and the contract reveals a significant omission in the latter concerning the perpetuity of the name of the museum. Why this was left out of the contract is not known, unless it was assumed by everyone that the contract merely elaborated on certain points in the original proposal and was not meant to supersede it. From other correspondence, it appears that the primary reason Hunter wanted a contract was to have written confirmation that, in addition to his salary, his Social Security tax and health insurance would be paid by IPC.

Hunter went to MIT in October 1954 to oversee the move. There he was joined by George A. Graham, IPC's administration coordinator and museum liaison. Although Hunter would have preferred to have had Dard Jr. help him, his son had a full-time job in Chillicothe; Graham proved an able alternative. In early November, three moving vans arrived safely in Appleton. When the time came for Hunter to help arrange the exhibits, he found he could not leave Chillicothe because his cousin-in-law Clara Hunter was dying of cancer. Dard Jr. went instead.

Over Christmas, perhaps brought on by Clara's imminent death, Hunter suffered a series of hemorrhages in his good eye. However, when Dard Jr. returned from Appleton, he was amazed to find his father setting type and printing labels for the new exhibits.

While attending the museum's Open House on 27 February, Hunter was delighted to discover the catalogue prepared by Ahearn and Lee. A letter to Ahearn, who was still at MIT, explained,

> What I really wanted to tell you was about the Catalogue you prepared. I had never seen this listing as it was locked in the file cabinet. I was simply amazed at the thoroughness with which you did this cataloguing and I want to tell you how grateful I am. Everyone who saw your work commented on the efficient manner in which it was accomplished; every item was described perfectly and I doubt if ever before such a perfect listing had been made of any collection. Please accept my most sincere thanks.

He was relieved to find that all he had to do was fill in the gaps, so the most demanding part of his contractual arrangement with IPC was nearly satisfied.

Hunter's yearly routine involving the paper museum was established early on. Whenever possible, he attended the executive conference, an annual event that usually took place in May. The attendees represented the pulp and paper industry, and the event gave Hunter an opportunity to show off his collection, as well as occasionally demonstrate hand papermaking. In addition to the May visit, Hunter traveled to Wisconsin from 1955 to 1959, usually in the late summer or early autumn, to work in the collection with Graham. In 1955, Hunter was pleased when IPC awarded him an annual stipend of $1,200 for life, the only stipulation being that he give no *more* than two lectures or demonstrations yearly. After 1959, Hunter was increasingly disabled by asthma, and his visits to IPC were rare. Graham left IPC in late 1959, and his place was taken by Dr. Harry Lewis, who remained curator of museum until his retirement in mid-1966, a few months after Hunter's death.* Hunter's last visit to his museum was in September 1964.

HUNTER'S GREATEST CONTRIBUTION

When asked to name his greatest contribution to our knowledge about paper, Hunter would invariably state that it was the Dard Hunter Paper Museum. Unfortunately, between opening its doors at MIT in 1939 and the opening of the American Museum of Papermaking in Atlanta in 1993, the Dard Hunter Paper Museum suffered in a number of ways.

First, the exhibits were relatively static. That is, the artifacts displayed on the walls and in the cases rarely rotated. While most of the paper on display was of excellent quality, it suffered from nearly sixty years of exposure to light, heat, pollution from gases and particulate matter, and high humidity levels.†

Second, the museum's locations almost guaranteed that limited numbers of people saw the exhibits. At MIT, it was first located on the top floor of the William Barton Rogers Building. When it was in the Charles Hayden Memorial Library from 1950 until 1954, the museum was quartered below the ground floor. While at the Institute of Paper Chemistry in Appleton from 1954 to 1989, the museum was located in the basement and sub-basement of the main building. By stark contrast, the current museum is accessible and inviting. The Robert C. Williams American Museum of Papermaking Featuring Dard Hunter's Collection—boldly announced over its entrance—is located directly off the lobby of the Institute of Paper Science and Technology (formerly IPC in Appleton). Now visitors cannot help but see it as they enter the building. Not only this, IPST staff, especially curator Cindy Bowden, have done an exemplary job of drawing in people to see the exhibits that are comprised largely of artifacts from Hunter's collection. School children routinely tour the museum, and temporary and traveling exhibits give the collection national exposure.

Third, when Hunter designed the original exhibits and labels, he assumed the audience already had some knowledge of papermaking and printing. Even if visitors were not familiar with these subjects, a tour with Hunter around the exhibits soon enlightened them. But as years passed, Hunter spent less and less time in the museum, and as the visitor's knowledge and interest in these historical subjects decreased, the exhibits became less relevant to everyday life. The situation was not helped by the fact that the pulp and paper industry was but little represented, although early machine-made papers and a model of the first paper machine were on exhibit. Industry presidents such as George Mead and D. Clark Everest were keenly interested in the history of paper, and they did not consider this lack of representation a serious drawback. Likewise, Karl Compton, Otto Kress, and Westbrook Steele were also mindful of the important role the technological history of papermaking played in their teaching institutions. Unfortunately, interest in the museum declined as these men were gradually replaced by professional administrators who were not as sensitive to its historical importance. As a consequence, the relevance of the collection to the various institutions' curricula diminished. The AMP, on the other hand, assumes that most visitors need to be informed about paper and its precursors, printing, watermarks, the modern pulp and paper industry, and the future of paper. Now visitors can enjoy and learn from exhibits that are both pertinent to their lives and accessible on many levels.

Fourth, when Hunter's museum opened in 1939, people in "the trade" knew who he was. However, after his death until the AMP opened in 1993, recognition of him as an individual, not to mention his work outside the collection, grew dim. To rectify that situation, the AMP includes a niche, almost a shrine, devoted to Hunter. This exhibit documents his accomplishments and illustrates them with examples of his books from the Roycroft period on, as well as many of his personal papermaking moulds and watermarks. Here also hangs a wonderful oil portrait of Dard Hunter by Walter Sherwood, posed in the museum at MIT in 1940. (colorplate 11) George Moore's bust of Hunter stands nearby.

Chapter 16

The edition of "Papermaking by Hand in America" has been in process of writing and production for many years and it is probable that this book will end the activities of this Private Press. Dard Hunter

Of all the books Dard Hunter wrote, probably the easiest was his autobiography. He actually wrote two, the first was published in 1941, the second, in 1958 (covered in the next chapter). In January 1940, Porter Welch of the Rowfant Club, a private literary club in Cleveland, Ohio, inquired whether fellow member Hunter was interested in writing "a comfortable little book on yourself, your thoughts, your ideals, your work and just what started you on your fascinating life's pilgrimage." Hunter was especially pleased to accept the offer as the book was to celebrate the 500th anniversary of printing from moveable type. He decided that the autobiography should be about his career before 1923, and so the title *Before Life Began* was conceived after the adage "life begins at 40."

In October, Welch received the manuscript, which he submitted to Bruce Rogers, the renowned book designer.* Upon reading the manuscript, Rogers agreed to work on the project even though he was semi-retired. In a letter to Hunter on 16 December 1940, Rogers wanted to know if there was any chance that Dard Jr.'s type could be used for the book. Father and son were, of course, very flattered by this request, but Hunter wrote that it was out of the question (Rogers chose Bulmer Roman instead). Rogers also wanted to use Lime Rock paper, and Hunter was happy to sell him about five reams. Rogers arranged to have the waterleaf paper sized and plated.

Although Welch had envisioned a small book between 25 and 80 pages, the final autobiography was considerably longer—116 pages. *Before Life Began* is a charming, humorous, and sometimes irreverent recollection of Hunter's early life. This book is somewhat frustrating to the researcher, however, because the author was little concerned with accuracy and more intent on telling a good story. Perhaps because Hunter began writing the book during

Hitler's bombing of London, it begins rather pessimistically. However, his views of the follies of modern life were long-held ones, and they did not mellow with time; he used the same opening for the second autobiography published seventeen years later.

During the past fifty years the world has undergone a more complete transformation than in any like period in history. The change is usually termed "progress," but I feel certain the historians of the future will write into their records that this word should never have been used in this connection. It has been my fortune, good or ill, to live through this half century of transformation and to see the changes that have come, one upon another. Had it been my privilege to determine the dates of my life span I should have made another choice for my birth year, and chosen a much earlier period. Having been born in the early eighties, however, the greater part of my life has been lived during the industrial revolution of the machine age, a prosaic period which has never appealed to me; the modern mechanical world has unfolded before my eyes. I have always been an advocate of honest hand work and have long struggled against the introduction of machinery, but I fear my efforts have been no more effectual than would have been the efforts of a lone termite in the petrified forest. The discovery of oil in the ground making possible the invention of the gasoline engine was the real turning point. Before the advent of the automobile—and the natural sequence of aeroplanes, tanks, and bombers—the world was more at ease. There is no gain, however, in quarrelling with machines, science, and technology, but the question persists—with all their labour saving, shorter hours of work, and abundant leisure, have they brought more happiness into the world?

Had I been given my choice I would have fixed the beginning of my life during the middle of the eighteenth century and the termination near the year 1830. This period was, to be sure, almost totally lacking in the production of fine paper, well-printed books, and achievement in the graphic arts, but it was a slow-moving, gracious period of spacious life. Had the choice of place where I could have lived this span of years also been given me, I would have selected England or Scotland, the latter country being the seat of my forebears.

Being one of those unfortunate individuals, however, who are not afforded the privilege of selecting birthday or birthplace, I came into this world in the unromantic year of 1883, in a hilly agricultural and industrial town of eastern Ohio.

In the final few pages of the book, Hunter gave an overview of his life from 1923 on, describing his books and his Asiatic pilgrimages. He devoted a long paragraph to his writing and book production.

> I have never made the slightest pretense of being a skilled or entertaining writer. I even doubt if I have an appreciation of fine literature. Poetry does not interest me and I find it impossible to grow enthusiastic over so-called pleasing word combinations or well-turned phrases after the fashion of genuine litterateurs. I have written only of papermaking, interspersed with some little account and anecdote of my experiences in various parts of the world while gathering material relating to my subject. The sort of straightforward writing I have done has not been difficult; I write without effort, but perhaps my writing is not read without effort. In producing my first papermaking books I regarded the actual compilation of the text as the easiest step in the whole procedure. The actual work came in the making of the paper, and this was an almost endless hardship for me; all of my printing has been done on handmade paper which must be printed damp to assure sincere and pleasing results. The punch cutting, matrix adjusting, and hand casting of the type required several years of toil, and when the fount was finally completed I had to overcome hardships in presswork that one never encounters in using type from the commercial foundry. Only a person who has been through the complete process of book production by the ancient hand methods and without the proper tools can possibly have a genuine appreciation of the tedious and arduous work involved. The mere writing of text was little more than play.

There are no illustrations in *Before Life Began* except for a sheet of the Large Portrait watermark bound into the book as a frontispiece. The lovely brown paste paper used on the cover was made by Veronica Ruzicka. Bruce Rogers numbered and signed each copy, and his device also was printed in red ink on the last page. The book, in an edition of 219, was distributed to the Rowfant Club members in June 1941, some copies were sent to special collectors and libraries, and there were a small number of copies for sale at $11.50.

Not surprisingly, the Rowfant Club's invitation to publish a biography of Hunter was not the first one. As early as 1925, Sterling Lord was eager to write about his friend. Hunter's reply to this idea was:

> What you say about writing a history of my life makes me laugh. You surely must be dreaming, or is it a nightmare you are having? I don't

know who in the devil would want to read a history of my commonplace life. I could cover it in one sentence, thus: Born, failed in school,
piffled at East Aurora, married and spent rest of the days in nursing
kids. I can't believe you are serious in this matter, but if you are please
erase the inky plot from your brain as it is the most absurd idea you
ever had.

Edith added to the end of the letter,

I think you should write a history of Dard's life, by all means, no matter
what he says about it. I only wish I could write but it would not look
well coming from me any way. You know him better than any one else
& can do it. Go ahead. I will do all I can to help you.

It is indeed a pity that Lord never wrote a biography, as it would have given
us invaluable information about their early years together at the Roycroft,
in Vienna, and in London.

As for Hunter's life *after* forty, he alluded to a possible sequel at the end
of *Before Life Began*: "In gathering material for the papermaking books I have
travelled more than a quarter million miles and have spent over twenty-six
solid months on steam and sailing ships—but that is another story."

Papermaking: The History and Technique of an Ancient Craft

Of all the books with which Dard Hunter is associated, *Papermaking: The
History and Technique of an Ancient Craft* made his name renowned throughout the world down to the present time.

By the end of 1938, Hunter's most successful commercial book, *Papermaking Through Eighteen Centuries*, was out of print. Eager to update that book
and to introduce information about oriental papermaking, Hunter signed a
book contract with McGraw-Hill publishers in early 1939. The publishers
thought they would receive a book-length version of Hunter's "The Story of
Paper," an article that appeared in the October 1937 issue of *Natural History
Magazine*. When Hunter submitted the manuscript in March 1940, the
editor was stunned to find that instead of a popular work about the romance
of paper, Hunter had written a scholarly, technical work on the world history of papermaking. When Hunter refused to change the tone of the book,
the contract was canceled.

Hunter immediately wrote to other publishers, including Alfred A.
Knopf, to see if any were interested in his new book. Knopf was, but he

wrote that the company could not publish it immediately because of the chronic paper shortage. In any case, Knopf thought the manuscript needed revision. He wrote that if Hunter cared to revise the manuscript over the next year, he might be in a position to proceed then. Hunter agreed, and with it in mind to expand the book, he spent the remainder of 1940 collecting even more information and illustrations. As he knew relatively little about the modern pulp and paper industry, Hunter asked Harrison Elliott to write the section on the development of papermaking fibers. Elliott was pleased when Hunter credited him in the foreword. Knopf liked Hunter's revision, and *Papermaking: The History and Technique of an Ancient Craft* was published in February 1943. Included in that edition were two samples of paper—one laid, one wove—from the Lime Rock mill, bound in between pages 102 and 103. The dust jacket was designed by W.A. Dwiggins, one of the noted book designers of the day, but Hunter did not care for it. The edition was 2,500 and the price $4.50. *Papermaking* was both a scholarly success and, despite the economic situation, a commercial success.

On its publication, Hunter received many letters from appreciative readers, such as: "I have just finished reading your fine book 'Papermaking' and wish to thank you for the part you have played in putting one of your books within reach of the average reader who like myself is interested in the history and technique of paper making." Indeed, the easy availability of information for those who could not afford his limited edition books was Hunter's primary goal, but he never found it easy to work with another publisher.

By November 1944, Knopf was planning a second printing of *Papermaking*, but Hunter had other plans. Even before he had finished the original manuscript, he knew that the book was not complete; large sections on oriental papermaking were still missing. He approached Knopf with the idea of revising and enlarging the book. Realizing that many who bought the first edition would acquire the second, Knopf readily agreed. This time, the contract stipulated that Hunter was to receive a 15 percent royalty to compensate him for the 5 percent he received on the sale of the first edition, plus he was given an advance of $750. Knopf also agreed that the dust jacket be redesigned to Hunter's satisfaction. This time the author took no chances and designed it himself.

In December 1945, the revised manuscript for *Papermaking* was sent, along with 150 new illustrations, to the Plimpton Press, Knopf's printers. A publication date of late 1946 had been set, but on account of the large number of pages—over 600—and the inevitable corrections, changes, etc., the project took much longer than expected. The book finally appeared in

November 1947 to much acclaim. No samples of paper were included in this edition. A number of unbound sets were sent to England and imprinted by the Cresset Press. That press did a second printing in 1957, and Knopf also did a second printing in 1967.

Papermaking: The History and Technique of an Ancient Craft, the first of Hunter's books carried in European bookstores, was immediately recognized by bibliographers, collectors, and historians as a remarkable achievement. Even as Hunter worked on the revision, he appreciated the importance of the book. "My plan is to make the second edition of this book much more complete and comprehensive than the first so the new edition will remain the standard work on this particular subject for many years to come." When the book was out of print, the rights were purchased by Dover Publications and a paperback reprint edition was issued in 1978. It is still in print. Just as Hunter predicted, even fifty years after its publication, *Papermaking* is still considered *the* reference book on the subject. It is doubtful that it will be entirely superseded, although a number of books have appeared over the last two decades that have expanded some subjects, such as *Japanese Papermaking* by Timothy D. Barrett.

THE HUNTER FAMILY AND WORLD WAR II

In August 1940, the Battle of Britain began. Hitler hoped that through the bombing of London, Germany could launch a successful invasion of the island and thus completely conquer Europe. In 1939, President Roosevelt ran for an unprecedented third term and won the election chiefly because voters did not want to change administrations during the crisis abroad. Although most people wanted the United States to remain neutral, everyone was aware that the country would be pulled into the conflict soon. The Selective Service Act was passed on 16 September 1940, which made it mandatory for every male between 20 and 36 to register for the draft. Nine hundred thousand men were to be selected each year for combat and non-combat service. Dard Jr. and Cornell both registered: while the former was working at MIT, the latter was a student at The Ohio State University. Cornell was more anxious to get into the war effort, however, and within the year, he was working for the Defense Department as a radio engineer.

A year later, on 7 December 1941, the Japanese attacked the U.S. base at Pearl Harbor, Hawaii, and the next day Congress declared war on Japan. On 11 December, Germany and Italy declared war on the United States, and suddenly, within a week, the attention of all Americans was focused on war. By May 1942, Cornell was in officer's training school, and Dard Jr. had left MIT to work as a toolmaker at a nearby General Electric plant. In June,

Dard Jr. was classified 1-A, which amazed all as the young man had an inoperable hernia. To everyone's relief, he was soon re-classified a "limited service man," and as such was unlikely to go into combat. Eventually, Private Dard Hunter Jr. was transferred to Wright Field in Dayton, Ohio, just 50 miles west of Chillicothe. There he worked for the army air force as a mechanical engineer; by then, Cornell was an inspector for the War Department and was stationed in Chicago, Illinois.

Because of this separation, letters between family members were exchanged almost daily. While Edith wrote notes to her boys, Dard typed letters, some two or three pages long. These letters, full of anecdotes, political observations, comments on the war, and family minutia, make wonderful reading. In their letters, the boys always referred to their father as "Dard" and to their mother as "Bunker." They, in turn, had a host of nicknames. The most popular for Dard Jr. were Dardo, Dardu, Dukie, Sgt., Doe, Dyd, Dart, and Di; while Cornell was Corn and Cornie, Joe, Josy, Jot, Cpl., and Syd.

This is a typical letter.

Friday, December 1, 1944, 8:45 AM

Dear Joe and Dard:

As you have probably experienced we are passing through a severe cold wave and it has been somewhat of a worry to your 22,207 day-old father. Last night on the porch when I was ready to retire the new mercury thermometer told me it was about 18 degrees above zero and from all appearances it was going lower. I have been afraid of the car freezing right along and I fixed the garage best I could by stopping up the cracks. Your mother tried to get additional Prestone yesterday, but as the car now stands it is about 30% Prestone and 70% C.S. [Christian Science] that is supposed to keep it fluid. Your mother says I have so much fear about it that my fear will make it freeze. In other words, if it should freeze I would naturally be to blame. I have a very decided fear about both fire and freezing and your mother says that I will meet my end, therefore, by one of these methods. It is difficult for an old infidel like me to go along with her on many of her religious views. In any event I went to the garage this morning and saw that it was all right, thus far. I also want to start the radiator in the kitchen to keep the pipes from freezing, but your mother also has that under her divine guidance and she says a final "NO," and when your mother gives such a command it is well to creep off and say nothing more. In all my 266,484 hours I have never seen so much absolute determination housed within 110 pounds. The Choates certainly are a very strong race and it is nice that both the boys have some of this robust, rich blood flowing through their flexible pipes; it would be sad if it were all Hunter blood for then you kids would be little more than gutter-snipes, like Mr. Churchill called Prof. Hitler. The disappointing feature is that your father has no Choate or Cornell plasma in his crusty arteries.

Have now a chance to do something for Doc. Holmes who hasn't sent us a doctor bill in 45 years. Other night he telephoned that he had a friend in N.Y. who wanted me to autograph a book and this I naturally agreed to do & it is being sent. I'm glad to be able to exchange my signature (not on a cheque) for so much medical service. Tomorrow I go again to Doc. Bolmer's for more spine heavings. My back is still sore from the other treatment which probably shows how rigid it was. I think it feels less like an iron poker and with faith I believe a course of treatments would actually help the nerve pressing. I look upon my back very much as I would upon any machine—if a wire is caught between two pieces of iron the only way to free the wire is to pry the irons apart—so it is with nerves and bones. . . . Determined women have their good points, but they are oftentimes hard to cope with in later life as they must have their own way. (Nothing personal intended.) We are hoping that you boys are warm of nights in your barracks as this may be a cold winter the way she is starting out. . . . This is all for today, from the Father, [signed: Pa]

While stationed in Chicago in late 1942, Cornell met Irene, and they were married on 27 February 1943. A few years earlier, Dard Jr. had met a young woman in Lime Rock, Alice L. Lukes. Assumptions were made that the two would marry, but by the middle of 1941, the romance was off.

As neither son could spend the winters with her, from 1942 until the end of the war, Edith lived with Dard in Boston, when he worked at MIT. She was delighted with the opportunity to indulge her passion for concerts, the opera, and the cinema; card-playing was not a nightly event, however. At the end of 1944, Hunter volunteered for the United Service Organizations, the USO, although it fatigued him to hand out cups of tea to servicemen after a long day at the "Musee" or "Wax Works." But while it was expected that he should do "his bit," he was not entirely happy when Edith decided to do hers. Much to his surprise, she got a job making capacitors in a factory. To the boys, he commented, "Your Mamma says she has three objects in taking on the job: (c) to help the war cause; (b) to be occupied and with other women; (a) the money. . . . [By the end of the first day] she will have learned all the swear and cuss words known by the entire 300 ladie workers."

Edith was quite adept at soldering, not surprising given the manual dexterity required to play the piano, and she did not mind the monotony of the work. One thing was soon clear to Hunter: the job gave Edith real pleasure, and however much he might joke about her work in his letters, he supported her completely. Initially, Edith wanted to use her earnings to buy a piano for the apartment, but she quickly gave that up in favor of buying furniture and *objets d'art* at auctions, events she found very exciting. She tended to bid on old, cumbersome pieces, especially oriental "stuff," and soon the apartment was overflowing with her bargains. Dard admitted, however, that for the most part her instincts for a bargain were good.

By spring 1945, the end of the war in Europe seemed imminent. Before peace came, however, President Roosevelt died on 12 April. Although Hunter did not agree with Roosevelt's decision to enter the war in the first place, he was nevertheless disheartened by this news. On Friday, 13 April, he wrote to his sons.

> The President's death has been most distressing. . . . He did a good job and I daresay it was harder on him than anyone knew. I presume some of the anti-Roosevelt crowd will blame him for dying at such a critical time! I think the war will progress as he had planned so well, but my hopes of preventing another war have been much lessened. We have no man to take his place. . . . It's a crazy world that you boys have been born into and I would not blame you for being resentful, but you both accept it so well . . . when this war is over we must all retire and have a long rest with doing the things we wish to do.

On 8 May 1945, when the Hunters were preparing to leave Boston for Chillicothe, people were celebrating Victory in Europe, V-E Day, in the streets. The Hunters celebrated, too, relieved that Dard Jr. and Cornell were safe from combat in Europe. However, fighting continued in the Pacific arena. Dard Jr.'s job at Wright Field was so important that there was no concern that he would be transferred, and by January 1946, he had accumulated enough points to be discharged.*

By contrast, Cornell's fate was in some doubt when he was transferred to Oahu, Hawaii, but he ended up as a cook—his specialty, pineapple pies. He was promoted from corporal to sergeant, but he hated Hawaii and could not wait to get home. On 6 August 1945, an atomic bomb was dropped on Hiroshima, and nine days later, V-J Day was celebrated. But Cornell had to wait several more months before he was discharged, and it was not until June 1946 that he and Irene were reunited. They made immediate plans to have him complete his college education at Ohio State.

Papermaking in Indo-China

While Hunter was revising *Papermaking: The History and Technique of an Ancient Craft*, he was also working on two other books. In January 1946, he and Dard Jr. began a five-year project to publish Hunter's last two Mountain House Press books. The first was *Papermaking in Indo-China*, a book that Hunter had begun after his trip to that part of the world in 1935. This book, as outlined in the prospectus,

> describes in detail the making of paper as the craft was practiced previous to the Asiatic conflict, and it gives an account of Daphne bark (*Daphne cannabina, Daphne involuvcrata, Daphne Gardneri*), the superior material used in Indo-China, Nepal, and Tibet as a strong and durable fiber for making paper. Also a considerable portion of the volume is devoted to the fourteen hundred mile journey to Indo-China and the amusing and tragic experiences encountered while in that exotic country. This monograph is a companion volume to "Papermaking in Southern Siam," a book that was printed at my private press in 1936, after my third voyage to the Far East in 1932 [*sic*].

Caslon was again selected as the type, and the quarto format was planned to closely resemble *Papermaking in Southern Siam* and *Chinese Ceremonial Paper*. As the Lime Rock mill had been acquired since the publication of those books, Hunter chose a wove paper watermarked along the upper edge, HAND MADE U.S.A. Two different colors of this paper were used for the text: white for about one hundred copies and the preferred cream for the last fifty-five. The collotypes were printed on the cream paper for all copies regardless of the color of the text paper.

For *Papermaking in Indo-China*, Dard Jr. cut several new type ornaments, some of which were probably designed by his father. These include a pagoda, cloud, beetle, square, flower bud, lotus flower, and leaf and buds (see plate 54). These ornaments were used singly or in pairs to form different decorative patterns for the chapter headings and borders.

By October 1946, the book was finished. Having forgotten about the problems he encountered over the binding costs of *Chinese Ceremonial Paper*, Hunter again issued the prospectus before receiving a firm quote from Franck. The book was priced at $38.50. Not including the slipcase, Franck wanted to charge $10.88 per book, a price essentially the same as he charged for the very complicated *Chinese Ceremonial Paper* ten years before. Franck explained his financial situation.

No use arguing much about the cost of living-index. The facts remind one every day that some people go to crazy lengths in taking it while the taking is good, a free for all now. A battery which I needed for my car the other day, jumped that very day from 11.90 to $21.00. Somebody, alas, always will be the poor sucker in inflation. If you "shop" yourself sometimes you will find very few things in a grocery store which are not 100 to 300 percent, like butter, higher than in 1936, cereals & bread stuffs excepted, or others yet under control. . . . My prices are not based on fluctuations. The trouble is that I have spoiled you as a client with the two books which you mention as an index, Chinese Ceremonial Papers and to a lesser extent Siam. . . . The price for CH.C.P. should have been more than twice what it was. As it was I earned $35.00 weekly less than I had at [Rudge] when employed, and this with a complete modern hand bindery on my hand. The Siam book figured at the same "wage" for myself and less for Cornelia, should have cost you $4.65.

Today material is higher and I can not and do not intend to work at such a loss and take risks on inflation besides. As to the reduction of the price: I will cut down on labor for the Indo-China, if the leather gets here in time for a leather back binding and we do not use cloth as per suggestions and samples enclosed. I would of course be blessed with a bright red leather for the rest of my days.

Although he sympathized with Franck, Hunter did not know what to do. As Franck's name appeared on the colophon and in the prospectus, Hunter was stuck with whatever price the binder wanted to charge (Dard Jr. thought Franck's estimate was reasonable). If Franck held to this charge, Hunter's profit for each book would be about $13, once all of the bills were paid. Therefore, he was relieved when a few days later, Franck reduced his cost by one dollar per book. Once a number of books were bound, however, Franck revised his price up close to the original estimate; Hunter grudgingly paid it. The binding is arguably the most beautiful of the regular bindings of Mountain House Press books. (colorplate 12)

In January 1947, the prospectus was sent out and orders flooded in, primarily from collectors who wanted to ensure that they owned this book. Many were disappointed over not receiving *Papermaking in Southern Siam* and *Chinese Ceremonial Paper*.

Surprisingly, Hunter never felt confident that his books would sell, and he did not presume anyone's purchase. Although asked repeatedly to do so, Hunter did not have standing orders, i.e., automatically sending books on publication to collectors or institutions. This practice would have saved him a great deal of trouble, but he preferred to keep a list of prospective purchasers, send out a prospectus, and wait for orders. With the exception of *Old Papermaking in China and Japan*, Hunter's fears were unfounded; Mountain House Press books usually sold out within two years of publication, some much quicker.

There was only one planned book that Hunter did not publish, because he never visited the countries in question. That book would have been devoted to Tibetan and Burmese papermaking, and it would have completed his researches in that part of the world. As late as January 1947, he had written the American Embassy in India to inquire about travel in Tibet and Burma, and although he was assured it was safe to travel in those areas, it was not until 1952 that he had time to go. By then, however, he was physically incapable of making the arduous journey. He might have considered making it with either Dard Jr. or Cornell, but both of his sons had careers and family obligations. Even though he must have made notes and possibly a rough manuscript during the war, based on material he purchased from collectors, nothing pertaining to this book has been discovered.

HUNTER'S MAGNUM OPUS, *Papermaking by Hand in America*
While printing *Papermaking in Indo-China*, Dard Jr. managed to work simultaneously on another book his father was compiling. For the second edition of *Papermaking: The History and Technique of an Ancient Craft*, Hunter had amassed information about early American watermarks. Recognizing that little had been written on the subject of American papermaking history, he wrote a well-received article in the January 1946 issue of the magazine *Antiques*, titled "Ohio's Pioneer Paper Mills." At the end of the article, Hunter included a note, "The author of this article is gathering material for a book on the early papermakers of Kentucky, *western* Pennsylvania, and Ohio. Should any reader of ANTIQUES possess watermarked papers made in pioneer days in this region, or have information relating to the early mills, please communicate with Doctor Dard Hunter, 77 Massachusetts Avenue, Cambridge, Massachusetts."

Readers did indeed send useful information, and Hunter sent additional enquiries to most of the local historical societies and libraries in those three states. Eventually, Hunter expanded the book to include a description of the first mill established in each state or colony from 1690 to 1817—from the year when the first American papermaker, William Rittenhouse, began operating his mill to the year Thomas Gilpin installed the first papermaking machine in America. As the book neared completion, however, Hunter narrowed the focus and changed the cut-off date to 1811.

For this new book, tentatively titled *Papermaking by Hand in America*, Dard Jr.'s entire font was to be used for the first time by the Mountain House Press. After the publication of *Specimen of Type* and *A Considerable Speck*, Dard Jr. wanted to re-cast his font by machine. In 1942, he purchased used casting equipment from the defunct H.C. Hansen Type Foundry in Boston. The machinery was stored there until March 1946, when it was shipped to Mountain House. According to a small envelope containing one piece of type, the first cast made on one of the Martin Torlsaas casting machines was at 6:35 P.M. on 29 May 1946. Dard Jr.'s original matrices proved unsuitable, however, and he struck and justified a second set using the Hansen machinery.

Over the next year, he worked on his font of type in readiness for printing *Papermaking by Hand in America*. In addition, he also cut punches for seventeen new type ornaments, most of which were designed by his father. On one sheet of paper, Hunter sketched ornaments for specific states; a flower for New Jersey, a fish for Massachusetts, a stylized maple leaf for New Hampshire and Vermont, and a lobster for Maine. (plate 80) The lobster was not executed, however, and instead a pine tree represented that state. Some of the ornaments were decidedly patriotic and included two versions of eagles and a shield with "stars and stripes." Hunter designed at least two other ornaments, which, it appears, were never cast: a windmill, for which a punch was cut, and a scallop shell. (Cornell also cut a punch of a flower, but it was never cast.) Judging by other sketches that appear on proofs of text pages, the ornaments were designed as printing went along. The ornaments used in *Papermaking by Hand in America* form the last two rows in plate 54. These were used either singly or in combination with other "flowers" to produce decorative chapter headings, tailpieces, and borders.

In the spring of 1947, Dard Jr. went to Lime Rock to pack and ship to Chillicothe all of the remaining paper stored there. After a careful inventory, Hunter was dismayed to find that there was not enough of one type of paper to print *Papermaking by Hand in America*. For the estimated 200 folio pages and 210 copies, at least 21 reams of paper were required, more allowing for spoilage, endpapers, guards, and fillers required for binding. In August, Hunter wrote both the Hayle and Wookey Hole Mills asking for quotes on 30 reams of paper to be made on the Bull's Head and Branch watermarked moulds. Before sending the order, however, he decided to flout convention and print on four types of the most abundant of the Lime Rock papers. This was a radical idea: the papers were all different weights, sizes, textures, and colors. However, it is precisely these differences that give *Papermaking by Hand in America* its unique visual and tactile qualities. (plate 81)

The most prevalent paper was white and modern laid. Dard Jr. later stated that this paper

> was unsuitably thin and unsized making dampening and printing most exasperating and sometimes almost impossible. The registration pins on the tympan of the press would have a good tendency to tear the dampened sheets during printing, thereby making registration on the verso page improbable. It was almost a wonder that the printing of this folio came out as well as it did considering all of the various obstacles encountered.

Papermaking by Hand in America was copiously illustrated. The frontispiece was the sepia photogravure of the 1852 lithographic view of Mountain House and Chillicothe, first used in *Primitive Papermaking*. It was hand-colored for the new book. To make facsimiles of early documents, photographs and photostats were ordered from historical societies and libraries, and line etchings were made from them. In addition, other illustrations were photographic prints, processed by Dard Jr. in his newly equipped darkroom off the studio in Mountain House. In early 1947, Hunter sent another round of letters requesting photographs of early American ream labels, with a view to reproducing some of these in the book. As if he did not have enough to do, Dard Jr. also made facsimiles of watermarked paper at the Paper Museum in 1946 and 1947.

> In reproducing these watermarks, special attention had to be given in order to imitate them to conform to the originals. Since all were of the laid variety, to accomplish this, mould screens had to be woven to duplicate the gauge of wire and number of laid and chain lines to the inch. For a number of these screens, the wire was reduced to the correct dimension through a drawplate. After approximately 5 month's labor, and with enduring patience, the task was finally concluded.

Before printing of *Papermaking by Hand in America* began in earnest, Hunter realized that two presses would greatly facilitate printing. The large Shniedewend Printers Proof Press, acquired in 1922, was ideal for printing "two-up" (two pages at once), and it was reserved for the text pages. The small Shniedewend hand press was still at MIT, and initially Hunter did not want to move it. However, when he could not locate another, it was shipped to Mountain House in August 1948. As usual the facsimiles were printed first, although the ream labels continued to be printed up until the book was ready for the binder in August 1950.

By the summer of 1947, the two Dards had their routine down. Hunter "composed at the type case . . . without the usual prepared copy customary in regular book composition, but with the aid of copious notes and myriad references gathered together during the many years of research." On a good day, Dard Jr. could proof and print two pages of text on the large press; his father printed the illustration pages on a single leaf on the small one.*

When the time came for negotiations to commence regarding the binding, Dard Jr. was delegated "manager." In October 1948, Dard Jr. informed Peter Franck that he had one or two more chapters to print, and once those were done, he could start tipping-in the illustrations and specimens for the copy to be sent for a trial binding; he expected to complete the job that winter. While Franck was delighted with the prospect of binding the book, he declined to give any estimate until he received a complete copy.

Progress was slow, however, and without finishing the type-setting, Hunter returned to MIT in December 1948. There he suffered the first of a series of severe asthma attacks and had to return to Mountain House. In many ways, his attack was fortunate, as it allowed printing to continue almost non-stop during the first six months of 1949. However, further delays were caused as more and more ream labels were discovered, and the book continued to grow. Finally, in early February 1950, Dard Jr. sent Franck a copy, still missing a few illustrations. Even though the book was incomplete, Franck was impressed.

> I am awed by the work of creation, truly to be a testimonial to the work of Dard Hunter and his disciple son. It is the BOOK PRESERVATIVE of the history of American papermaking, a story beautifully told and done into a book of beauty, interest and a charm all of its own. About the title page, I also felt the impression of great top weight and am pleased that you are reprinting it. I am not a critic of printing; often it is a matter of opinion and taste anyway but I feel that there is enough poetic charm in the book and its arrangement to outweigh any criticism which may be made.
>
> What a job you accomplished in making all the many special watermarks and papers so excellently done, and the picture gallery reproduced from old paper labels which would inspire the most commercial papermaker of our time to label-making of his own if he sees your collection in the book. The texture of most of the text paper used looks innocently delicate and refined. I hope to see a great deal of this book and have more opportunity for study and discovery of the work. . . . I can wait for the cover siding paper you are printing as I have other work at present which will keep me alive. . . .

IRISH LINEN much heavier and better than we used before is available at present. We bought a sample yard and a piece of it is included here. An early decision by you on the use of this material for the edition [and the printed side papers] would be wise. Do not be too economic minded on the binding please as the people who buy the book will and should be glad to pay for a decent binding job if it *can* be and IS produced. I would also, somehow, make the buyers sense that the books can not be run through the bindery like ordinary books and, what of it; is it not the most extra ordinary book on papermaking that ever was and is likely to be published?

Although I dislike to suggest it, a slip case seems necessary in view of the very irregular edges where dust can penetrate so easily.

I think you are to be congratulated, both of you on the conclusion of a fine job.

Dard Jr. and his father confirmed with Franck that the binding was to be similar to that used for *Old Papermaking in China and Japan*, a three-quarter linen binding with printed side papers. In early March 1950, Franck finished the trial binding at a cost of $91. In the absence of the printed side papers, he covered the book in his own marbled paper.* Franck wrote that after making some changes, he was sure he could get the cost down to about $46 with a slip case. Hunter was stunned at the price. He had envisioned charging a modest $100 for the book, although book dealer Philip Duschnes and Elmer Adler had urged him to charge at least $175. Hunter wrote a letter to Franck, above Dard Jr.'s signature, stating that if the binding was $40 then the Press would realize a very small profit once other bills were paid (including the salary paid to the pressman—Dard Jr.). Before the letter was sent, however, Hunter wrote both Gerhard Gerlach and Arno Werner asking for quotes based on a description of Franck's binding. Gerlach's response is unknown, but in early May 1950, Werner wrote from his bookbinding studio in Pittsfield, Massachusetts, acknowledging the receipt of two copies of the book sent to him for a firm quote. Within two weeks, Werner had completed the bindings. He estimated that the work including a clamshell box covered in natural buckram with a back of red leather would be $40. In the meantime, an anxious Franck wanted to know what was holding up Hunter's decision about his binding. Finally, in August, Hunter visited Franck at his studio in Gaylordsville, New York while en route to MIT. He brought with him both Franck's and Werner's trial bindings. Franck's opinion of Werner and his binding was made clear in a letter received by Hunter a few days later.

I appreciate greatly that you showed me the book-dummy which A.W. did for you. I am sure it would never have happened through A.W. directly, although he has found this an open "born" of technical information for a number of years. We were at his place Saturday afternoon, last, and took him and family up Greylock; Helen being the driver. He is getting a car himself now and hopes to be a frequent visitor here. W. can be quite generous, especially when his commercial backers the Eaton Co. prop him up. I probably told you that this concern, a few years ago, sent one of their head men around with Arno to take over, lock, stock and barrel, mortgage and all, pay me 6 mills for a year and then probably fire me again. . . . I will, of course, not mention a thing about the dummy A.W. made, to the binder. It is all in the business of life and living in a "tooth and claw" world, I suppose; anybody can draw his own conclusions regarding this relationship of business, art, the crafts, friendship, etc.

I can however see that I have to be somewhat on my guard if [Cornelia and I] should visit Europe. We may come back and find only one or two clients left. As long as there is health with me there is little to be afraid of, however.

In case you would want Werner's box—as we considered the possibility—it would be best if you ask him directly for the price on the separate item.

My price for book and box, at best could not come down to A.W. price. He has facilities which I will never have, gluing machine etc. I doubt that he ever uses homemade pastes etc. The time was too short that I could determine details like that on your dummy of his. Most of your unsized papers require special handling in pasting and he might have used something more of a "quick sticker" but I do not know. The success of a job with us was always based on principles of permanence and quality first and then came the consideration of the dollar.

And who did the binding? The Hunters compromised: the work was divided between Franck and Werner. While both Hunters thought that Franck was the better binder, Werner had a distinct advantage over him because his price was lower, and he worked faster. It is estimated that Franck bound about 45 copies while Werner bound approximately 115, for a total of the 160 copies sold by late 1953. One reason why Franck did not bind more copies was that he and Cornelia took a trip to Germany—their first since the early 1920s—from April to September 1951. Although Franck did bind a few copies of *Papermaking by Hand in America* after his return, his professional relationship with Hunter essentially ended in late 1951. (Just as had happened with Adler, as soon as Hunter and Franck's professional relationship ended, one based on friendship blossomed. This camaraderie became especially important to the two men after their wives died; Edith from a heart attack in January 1951 and Cornelia from a tragic accident in March 1953.)

Having learned from past experiences, the Hunters had waited to print the prospectus for *Papermaking by Hand in America* until they had a much better idea of who would bind the books and at what cost. Not only that, but they were still printing facsimiles of ream labels. Finally, the book was ready. Elmer Adler, in a letter dated 18 September 1950, thanked Hunter for the gratis copy of Number Two of the new book. "I am more impressed than ever. It is a remarkable accomplishment." Adler also commented that he still considered the price, $175, too low, but typically Hunter was not convinced that the book would sell at the set price, let alone an even higher one. The rush of orders took the Hunters completely by surprise. Dard Jr. had not actually completed coloring the frontispieces, tipping-in the illustrations, and collating the three hundred plus pages for all of the copies. He worked diligently, and once a month sent completed books out for binding in sets of ten.

On 29 November 1950, Hunter's sixty-seventh birthday, Elmer Adler scheduled an exhibit at Princeton University featuring the first public showing of the new book; Dard Jr.'s type appliances were also shown. It was this gesture that confirmed Alder as a loyal friend, and it was he and D. Clark Everest who were responsible for garnering the largest number of orders for the new book.

With the publication of *Papermaking by Hand in America*, Hunter decided once and for all that it would end his involvement in the Mountain House Press. His decision is reflected in the seventh leaf on the printer's mark, which flutters from the branch. (plate 82) Dard Jr., however, was interested in writing and publishing a book on decorated papers. But while information and various papers were gathered from around the world, this project did not get much beyond the planning stage, although a few line etchings were made.

OTHER HONORS

In 1947, Frederic W. Goudy, the renowned typographer, died. To honor him and other pioneer typographers, the Lakeside Press and the R.R. Donnelley & Sons Company of Chicago sponsored an exhibition, "American Type Designers and Their Work." Both Hunters' typefaces were represented. In the accompanying leaflet, Hunter's type is described as "odd but forceful," with a further note that the type was "properly cut on punches by the designer." In fact, the Hunters were the only type designers who cut their punches, justified the matrices, and cast the type by hand. For some reason, the date of Hunter's type was given as 1919; the first Chicago Society of Etchers book predates that by four years.

In all, Hunter received four honorary doctorates: Lawrence College in 1931, The Ohio State University in 1939, Wooster (Ohio) College in 1947, and Lehigh University in 1949. In 1948, he was awarded the prestigious A.W. Rosenbach Fellowship in Bibliography, and the University of Pennsylvania arranged for him to give two Rosenbach Lectures in April 1949. The first was on oriental papermaking, and the second was based on the research he had been doing for *Papermaking by Hand in America*. Although the University of Pennsylvania Press routinely published the Rosenbach Lectures, Hunter suggested that they instead publish a commercial edition of *Papermaking by Hand in America*. They agreed and *Papermaking in Pioneer America* was published in 1952 for $3; once again, Hunter ensured that the information he had so arduously gathered was readily available to all.

Chapter 17

As you know, I am constantly working on the subject of PAPER and I daresay I will continue this pursuit until the last breath. Dard Hunter

While Dard Jr. and his father worked on the last two Mountain House Press books, Cornell was back at The Ohio State University studying industrial arts education. Dard Jr. had not yet married; he was too devoted to his father's projects to pursue romantic interests, although there had been some near misses. In December 1949, Cornell graduated from college, the first in his family to do so. He sought positions in his chosen field, but as none offered a reasonable salary, he and Irene moved back to Chillicothe. There he had no option but to accept a job working for the Mead Paper Mill in the order department. Edith was sure, however, that her younger son would eventually find his niche.

On 2 March 1951, Hunter was back at MIT after a long absence because of *Papermaking by Hand in America*. In Mountain House at around 1:00 P.M. that day, Edith was cleaning house when she suddenly collapsed and died.

Dear Sterling: Again I am in Chillicothe. I came here yesterday upon the most distressing mission of my life. Edith, whom you knew so well, passed on Friday very suddenly of a heart attack. The funeral will be tomorrow at two. The boys are here of course.

I am 67 and I have felt for some time that I would prefer not to live much longer and now I am convinced that my work is finished. . . . Naturally nothing has been settled and I do not know what we will all do now. Of course, the boys have much to live for, although for myself I can see nothing ahead now. Edith, as you know, was a most noble person and one who would always be missed. I do not now feel that I can go on. My life has been full and I have accomplished something, although not always what I would wish to do.

I am depressed, disheartened, and despondent. Always, Dard.

As a memorial to Edith, Dard had two mahogany Reader chairs made for her beloved First Christian Scientist Church. On the back of one chair is an engraved silver plaque, inscribed "In Memory of Edith Cornell Hunter 1951." For special headstones, Dard contacted the well-known artist-craftsman John H. Benson, who drew a design for Dard's stone with his printer's mark; Edith's design was similar except that in place of leaves on the branch, Benson drew cornel (dogwood) blossoms with "ECH" in the shield. Although Benson also suggested a design for Edith with a musical theme, in the end a granite headstone was carved simply "E.C.H. 1951."

Following Edith's funeral, Hunter returned to Boston, where he could be distracted by demonstrating papermaking, guiding tours, and, of course, answering correspondence. Hunter wrote to Lord that "since Edith's going I have felt more and more that I would not return to the old house in Chillicothe for my retirement." However, his spirits were temporarily lifted when on 1 July 1951, he was appointed Honorary Curator of Paper Making and Allied Arts in Harvard's Department of Printing and Graphic Arts.* In Hunter's opinion one of his most prestigious honors, this one-year appointment was renewed every year until his death.

That October, he and Dard Jr. were to take a trip to England, but at the last minute, Hunter decided not to go; Dard Jr. went alone. While in England, he took hundreds of slides of mills still making paper by hand. He also spent a great deal of time browsing through antique shops. His interest in English decorative arts had grown to the extent that following his return, he took a position working on the restoration of Adena, an early nineteenth-century house located near Chillicothe and owned by the Ohio State Archaeological and Historical Society.†

On 10 May 1952, Dard Jr. married Janet Ruth Rea. She shared Dard Jr.'s interest in antiques; the couple seemed well matched. Impressed by his work at Adena, the OSAHS offered him a two-year scholarship to attend the Museum Studies Program, co-sponsored by the Winterthur Museum and the University of Delaware, with the proviso that upon graduation, he return to Adena. The newlyweds made their first home in New Castle, Delaware, and while he attended classes, she worked in the museum office.

LIFE SLOWLY RETURNS TO NORMAL

After Edith's death, Hunter seemed less able to overcome his chronic health problems—asthma and neuritis—which were particularly bad in the cold, damp winters in Boston. However, he temporarily forgot about these annoying ailments, when, in February 1952, his friend Victor W. von Hagen, the author and explorer, asked him to join an expedition to Peru. When the shipping company stipulated that the over 65-year-old Hunter prove that he was fit to travel, even he was surprised when the doctor pronounced him in excellent health for a man his age. In the end, he did not go to Peru, but some of his old *joie de vivre* returned, and he took his first airplane ride. As usual, he told Lord all about it.

I have been back about two weeks after two months in Scotland and England. I went alone and had a very pleasant sojourn, especially in the country villages of England where I stayed near the handmade paper mills—one in Somerset the other in Devon. In London I stayed at 32 Lexham Gardens where we all lived about forty years ago. London has changed so much that it is a place to remain away from now. I found the city depressing and my interest in it entirely gone. The country is lovely, if one gets away from the cities which are just as obnoxious as any American cities. . . . The getting over is expensive. I paid about $400.00 on the plane coming back, but it was an interesting trip. . . . Of course, 5 hours is gained so the flying time is about 17 hours. In going over (on a freight ship) it took about 12 days. As my time is worth nothing I shall in future go by freight, although the plane is most intriguing. My son Cornell is in the local bank and he is coming along very well indeed and in time he will be in a good position.

You may have read about the new atomic plant that is to be built 22 miles south of here [in Piketon]. It will change Chillicothe greatly and I doubt if I will wish to live here again. . . . I hate to see this development and "progress" so near here, but nothing can be done about it as the site is ideal for such a plan. Of course, Chillicothe real estate will soar and while we have several pieces, the boys do not want to sell so that does me no good as I would like to get out of here entirely. The boys, however, will continue to live here and they want the houses and land. I daresay that I will get along all right as I can live cheaply in Europe. Also, I like it better there in many ways and other ways I do not care so much for the life there. I will adjust myself to whatever comes up for me. . . . With Edith gone and both the boys married, I feel rather lost, but I will get along someway for the time I have left.

Hunter did return to Mountain House, however, when he was not at MIT. When Dard Jr. and Janet returned from Delaware, they moved in with Hunter. For the most part, everyone was content.

In the winter of 1953–54, Hunter, having retired from MIT, and Elmer

Adler went on a four-month tour of universities in the southern states sponsored in part by the American Federation of Arts. The purpose of the tour was to generate interest in the book arts and in the development of special collections in university libraries. Adler did most of the lecturing, while Hunter preferred to remain in the background. However, he was always happy to answer questions, and often showed the film *Paper: The Pacemaker of Progress*, made in the Lime Rock mill in August 1945, as well as many of the slides taken by Dard Jr. of English mills.

Hunter and Adler agreed that the most significant and surprising aspect of the tour was their stay at the Tuskegee Institute in Alabama.

Although I have found many things of interest at each university I believe that Tuskegee was the most interesting. There we also lived on the campus and for the entire time we were at the Institute we did not come in contact with a single white person. Mr. M.D. Sprague is the Librarian at Tuskegee and we found him as understanding and appreciative as any white librarian along the line. The institutions we visited and gave the seminar were: William and Mary, University of Virginia, Virginia Military Institute, Washington and Lee, University of North Carolina, Womans College of the University of North Carolina, University of South Carolina, University of Georgia, Tuskegee Institute, and next week University of Miami. It all has been rather hard work, but, at the same time, we feel we have done something worth while.

My Life with Paper: An Autobiography

While on the tour, an article about Hunter, "Paper Detective," by Neil M. Clark, appeared in the popular magazine *The Saturday Evening Post*. "Paper Detective" initiated a flood of letters from people around the world concerning such topics as the identification and dating of paper, watermarks, and inks; paper recycling; and paper restoration and preservation. Although replying was time-consuming, Hunter never failed to respond to a letter.

"Paper Detective" did more than bring Hunter's name before the general public; among his friends, it renewed an interest in his autobiography. Since *Before Life Began* appeared in 1941, he had been urged to publish his entire life's story and, indeed, was compiling notes for such a book. Hunter assumed that the Rowfant Club would publish the sequel, but after the popularity of "Paper Detective," he realized that his story might interest a larger audience. Adler thought so, too, and he wrote to Alfred Knopf about the idea. In July 1954, after he had read *Before Life Began*, Knopf wrote Hunter voicing some concerns over the project.

I don't think there is any doubt of your ability to continue this book in an interesting way. You aren't, as you state yourself with admirable frankness, a brilliant writer, and BEFORE LIFE BEGAN would have benefitted by a little judicious copy editing. However, I am sure that further memoirs would deal with rather more sophisticated happenings, and I hope you'll go right on.

Hunter replied: "Should the autobiography be continued it would be my wish that it be gone over by a trained editor, but not to extent of completely destroying my homely style, if style I have at all." Eventually, the two men agreed to pursue the project, and well into 1955, Hunter worked on the manuscript. For the first half, he slightly reworked the text of *Before Life Began*, but as he worked on the second, he became concerned that his story was too personal to be published in a trade edition.* However, both Adler and William Bond Wheelwright disagreed, and bolstered by their support, Hunter sent Knopf the completed manuscript in October 1956.

Knopf replied, "For reasons that are largely sentimental but not in the least, I assure you, commercial I would like to publish your autobiography which I have read with considerable care. But—and I must be frank with you—it is absolutely unpublishable in its present form." The blunt letter went on to outline problems that were stylistic rather than contextual or organizational. As it was the first time his writing had been so critiqued, Hunter felt disconsolate. Normally replying to letters by return of post, Hunter took over a week to write Knopf:

> Your criticism is well founded and I shall profit by what you have written, both in your letter and on the manuscript itself. I am again working on the material and I hope it will be much improved after I have done what I can. No matter how much work I may put on the manuscript I feel that it should be judiciously edited if publication is seriously considered.
>
> Many, many thanks for your exceedingly helpful comments and suggestions.

Hunter worked on revising the autobiography in Puerto Rico, where he spent the first few months of 1957. He had first traveled to San Juan in early 1956 to visit Elmer Adler, who was by then in charge of a government project to set up a graphic arts collection. Although he greatly enjoyed Adler's company, Hunter also relished the warm climate, as he was increasingly unable to cope with the bitterly cold and damp northern winters.

In July 1957, Hunter sent Knopf the 70,000-word manuscript. Knopf replied that the work still needed extensive copy-editing and that he would not guarantee to publish it, but in early December, Hunter signed a contract for the untitled autobiography. Knopf suggested that Hunter design the book, which he declined to do; eventually, Knopf asked Rudolph Ruzicka. Although very busy with other projects, Ruzicka wrote, "Anything connected with Dard Hunter is bound to be a fussy job, but this one is so enticing that I would like to undertake it."

Hunter sent Knopf about forty suggestions for the title, some of which included: Ts'ai Lun Was the Cause of It All; In the Path of a Chinese Eunuch; All the Way with Paper; A Lifelong Paper Chase; My Life with Paper; Paper, Type, and Books; I Followed Paper Everywhere; The Wasp and I; A Paper Hunter. Knopf liked none of Hunter's suggestions, and Hunter liked none of Knopf's. Having reached an impasse, Hunter wrote Ruzicka asking him for suggestions and urging him to include the word "paper" in the title.

Ruzicka responded,

> I agree that [Knopf's] "My Own Story" is flat. The word "Paper" in the title would not mean much to the general public. My wife suggests:
>> Paper Was My Fate
>> My Life, and Paper
> I think more subtle and a better title would be one along the line of:
>> In the Mould of Memory
>> My Life's Watermarks
> I wish it could be "From Rags to Riches"!
> Jacobs [of Knopf] tells me they are busy editing your MS. I hope they will not edit it too much, I like your writing immensely. I shall do my best with the book.

In the end, one of Hunter's titles was selected: *My Life with Paper: An Autobiography*. Throughout the first nine months of 1958, Knopf's staff worked with Hunter to prepare the manuscript, illustrations, and paper specimens for a press run of 4,000 copies. The two paper specimens included in *My Life with Paper* were a piece of spirit paper left over from *Chinese Ceremonial Paper* and the Lime Rock paper with the Dog and Dagger watermark (see plate 95).* *My Life with Paper* included an extensive bibliography of Hunter's books and articles, as well as a list of significant articles about him. (It should be noted, however, that there are several errors in the bibliography, for example, the publication dates of *Primitive Papermaking* and *Papermaking Pilgrimage to Japan, Korea and China*.) The only acknowledgment went to Helen V. Tooker, who was editor of *El Mundo* as well as his landlady in Santruce, Puerto Rico; she had assisted Hunter with the manuscript.

My Life with Paper arrived in American bookstores in October 1958 and retailed for $5; a few months later, it could be purchased in Europe. As usual, Hunter received a number of letters congratulating him on his latest success. But as was true with *Before Life Began*, the veracity of *My Life with Paper* is problematic. Hunter often dated events incorrectly. For example, he stated he first arrived in East Aurora in July 1903—it was 1904. This error appeared in both autobiographies. He was aware that there were some mistakes, as evidenced by his comments to Sterling Lord: "I fear you may see some flaws as it is difficult to remember so much over such a long period. . . . I found my memory a little tricky, but I doubt if there are any really serious discrepancies." It is obvious that Hunter was far more interested in getting across the richness of his life than in a strict accounting.

To Peter Franck, he wrote, "the material is somewhat more personal than I would have had it for a trade book. However, I don't suppose it makes much difference as it will not be widely read, and only by those who perhaps know something of my work anyway."

"MY LIFE WITH ASTHMA"

Soon after his seventy-fifth birthday, Hunter was to leave for Puerto Rico, but at the last minute, he realized that the high humidity in San Juan actually aggravated his asthma. While the symptoms—wheezing and fatigue—had occasionally appeared a few years before 1956, it was not until then that it became cause for concern. Indeed, it was so acute that he kept an envelope inscribed "My Life With Asthma by Dard Hunter, 1956–onward," stuffed with letters, prescription forms, brochures, and diaries documenting his fight with this debilitating disease.

In early 1957, a doctor determined that Hunter was allergic to certain molds and dusts, and he prescribed the new drug cortisone and, later, other steroids, which brought only temporary relief. In fact, they proved to have the unpleasant side-effect of muddling Hunter's mind for short periods. While in this state, he was incapable of making even the simplest decision. This proved a trial to everyone, particularly to Dard Jr. and Janet, with whom he shared Mountain House. Hunter was not happy with this living arrangement, but because of his failing health, there was no alternative. The only respite either party had from each other's company was occasional trips, but as Hunter became progressively incapacitated by shortness of breath brought on by any exertion, his excursions from home became less frequent. In late 1959, Dard Jr. and Janet toured Europe. That Thanksgiving, Hunter wrote Adler, "The Mountain House is a lonely sort of place with ghosts and spooks rattling around the rooms every night." While he worked in the house during the day and slept there at night, Hunter went down to Cornell and Irene's apartment for dinner. Hunter looked forward to these visits because he loved playing with his three-year-old granddaughter, Martha Anne. Hunter was more than delighted with his first grandchild, and he constantly bragged about her in letters to friends. One friend, upon learning of Martha's birth, congratulated Hunter, but hoped that she would not be "a limited edition." By Thanksgiving Day 1959, Irene was pregnant with their second child; Edith Cornell Hunter was born the following March.

In early December, Hunter again wrote Adler, "What you are doing is so worthwhile and so useful to the people of Puerto Rico that your entire time is well justified. I feel that my own work ceased when I gave up the curatorship of the Paper Museum and since that time I have had no real hold on anything." Earlier that year, Adler had sold his house in Princeton and was living in San Juan in La Casa del Libro—The House of the Book. Adler had donated not only the few books of his own not left to Princeton University, but contacted friends like Hunter asking them to contribute material for the collection. Appropriately, the collection specialized in Spanish incunabula. A valued colleague of Adler's was David Jackson "Jack" McWilliams, a professor of English literature at the University of Puerto Rico.

McWilliams became a close friend of Hunter's, too. But though Adler enjoyed the company of McWilliams and other young professionals he met, he particularly liked it when his old friend and traveling companion, Dard Hunter, came for a visit. Adler was upset when in December 1959 Hunter had to postpone his trip to San Juan because of poor health. Although Hunter fully intended to visit Adler later, he never saw his friend again. On New Year's Day 1962, Adler suffered a heart attack. Upon hearing the news, Hunter wrote to McWilliams.

> It was with [*The Literature of Papermaking*] that Elmer came into my life. He wrote a review of this book which was given a full page, with illustrations, in the Sunday *Times* book section. This obscure book of only 180 copies which I had printed did not warrant such publicity and only Elmer would have been granted such valuable space in the *Times*.
>
> This was the beginning of no end of help that Elmer always seemed anxious to give my struggling attempts at bookmaking. When the *Colophon* came along he promoted the Lime Rock mill, and still later he published two of my papermaking books, the finest of the entire series.

At Princeton he continued to do everything possible to help me along. It was through Elmer's efforts entirely that Alfred Knopf published the two papermaking books which were my most serious contribution to the craft of papermaking; still later Knopf issued the autobiography, also through Elmer's efforts. I do not hesitate to say that what success my books have had has been due to Elmer Adler's interest and enthusiasm. And, his influence has not been confined to me alone. He has been of decided benefit to others and their names would make an impressive list. As you know, Elmer is exceedingly modest and he would never admit that he had ever done anything for anybody.

I feel that Elmer will come out of the present difficulty and again take up his work. I have long had the belief that he would outlast me. He comes from a long-lived family; mine is the reverse. Elmer differs from most of us old men as he has work to do and he retains the ability to do it. I feel certain that he will be back at Calle del Cristo 255.

Adler did not pull through, however, and he died on 11 January 1962. McWilliams was appointed director of La Casa del Libro, but as his teaching position allowed him to be at the house only part-time, he asked Hunter to come down and help out. Knowing that the high cost of living was one reason Hunter had not visited San Juan, McWilliams offered him free accommodations at La Casa del Libro. Much to his relief, Hunter found he had few breathing problems while in San Juan; he also became convinced that despite the humidity, the warm climate did much to alleviate most of his problems, both physical and mental. But it is just as likely that the primary reason for this sense of well-being was due to his feeling useful.

Hunter also had personal reasons for wanting to get away from Mountain House during this period. Dard Jr. and Janet were not getting along, and in February 1962, a legal separation was drawn up which eventually led to their divorce later that year; they had no children.

At the end of May, Hunter returned to Chillicothe. That spring, he felt better than he had in years, and he even managed to spend a few days at the Paper Museum in Appleton early in July. Once back in Chillicothe, however, the allergy and asthma problems reappeared, as did the mental problems resulting from his medication. His letters were lucid, but they are also filled with impractical plans to live in Europe, Arizona, Wisconsin, or Maine—all to escape the mold that caused his respiratory problems.

Later that July, Henry Morris visited Mountain House. Morris had established a hand papermill, print shop, and bindery in his home in North Hills, Pennsylvania. Hunter regarded Morris's press, the Bird & Bull Press, as one of the true private presses because he published new work—if not always his own—rather than oft-printed material. Morris's visit to Mountain House was "to get some first-hand information about cutting and casting type in the old manner, but I fear he went away with the thought that it was too big a task for him to undertake."* During the visit, the two men also discussed Morris's next publishing project, eventually titled *Five on Paper*. For this book, Hunter agreed to write an essay based on his 1952 visit to the Tuckenhay Mill, titled "A Collection of Notes Written in the Vat-House of an Old Devonshire Paper Mill." The manuscript was completed in November, but the book was not published until September 1963.

The last trip Hunter made to La Casa del Libro was in January 1964, although up to two weeks before the trip, it was doubtful that he would make it. Around Christmas, he was hospitalized for ten days with pneumonia and was still in a weakened state by the first of the year. He recovered enough, however, to fly down to San Juan on 22 January, even though his feet were badly swollen. This sojourn in a warm climate did him a great deal of good, although while there he received very sad news: Sterling Lord had died on 12 March 1964. To Lord's widow, Ruth, he wrote,

> As you know, Sterling, Peter Franck and I have been friends ever since the turn of the century, almost sixty years ago; I had known Sterling longer than any other of my friends. Only Peter now remains of my contemporaries, all others have long since passed into a more tranquil world.
>
> Sterling Lord meant a great deal to me and his influence upon me in my younger years was most pronounced and I shall always be grateful to him for his help and for his encouragement. We spent many happy days together in East Aurora, Vienna and London; he was my most intimate and dearest friend. Now that he has left this troubled earth I feel quite alone!
>
> My most profound sympathy to you.†

Lord's death was a devastating blow to Hunter, but it was just one of a series that had occurred over the preceding five years. Harrison Elliott died in December 1954.‡ His cousin Junius Hunter passed away five years later. That same year, Robert Robertson passed away. In 1960, J.J. Lankes died, and a year later, John Rogers-King, the Lime Rock mill manager.

Not one to be depressed for too long, Hunter rallied as he resumed his daily routine at La Casa del Libro: reading the books in the collection, making sure that visitors left better informed about the book arts than when they entered, taking daily walks down the narrow streets of the picturesque town, and sitting in the sun in the little park nearby. When Hunter returned to Chillicothe in June 1964, he wrote to McWilliams,

> Assuming that my life was worth saving, it is my opinion that you did just that, for when I left here in January I was closer to crossing the River Styx than I had ever been before. Through all of the months of my stay in San Juan you were exceedingly kind to me and I shall always be grateful to you. . . . I seem to have adjusted myself to the decided change from the warm, sunny weather of San Juan. This morning the sky is dismal and dark, but I am hoping for a little sun later on in the day as Junior is coming to take me to "Adena" where I can walk through the grassy lanes surrounded by apple and cherry orchards. The roses and other spring flowers are most abundant this year.

This letter of appreciation was soon followed with another filled with hope for the future, as a new doctor had found the reason why he was having so many problems—it was his heart.

> After my return here I became decidedly worse and I could not breathe at all when lying down. For several nights I tried to sleep in my chair, but even this was little relief. My ankles were so swollen that I could scarcely get my shoes on. My sons insisted that I see Dr. Hoyt, the local heart specialist, and Junior made an appointment. As Dr. Hoyt was the grandson of my father's physician and friend I did not mind going to him. He gave me a rather thorough examination and concluded that my breathing trouble was due to hardening of the arteries leading to and from my heart, a condition due to age. In any event, he gave me a treatment of digitalis and it worked like magic! In two days my breathing was normal and my ankles were reduced to their original size. What a remarkable drug is digitalis, made from the powdered dry leaves of the common foxglove plant which we have in our garden. Dr. Hoyt also prescribed Vitamin C for my hands and this has helped too. I am only hoping that these remedies are more or less permanent and not simply a temporary respite from a very annoying condition.

The new treatment worked well, but it was too little, too late. As his father found it increasingly difficult to get up and down stairs, Dard Jr. fixed up a bed in the library. Hunter progressively lost his appetite, and within a few months, the six-foot tall Hunter weighed a mere 128 pounds.

McWilliams and Franck gently admonished him to eat a healthier diet, but Hunter's meals consisted primarily of milk and cereal. But even as his health failed, Hunter lost neither his mental acuity nor his sense of humor. In April 1965, he wrote McWilliams about two amusing incidents.

> Yesterday I had a visitor, a rare occasion. He was a retired librarian from the University of North Carolina, at Chapel Hill. When Elmer and I were there in 1954 we had met him, although I had forgotten. At the local hotel where he stayed over night they told him that I had died several years ago, and when he went to the bank across the street to get a draft cashed they confirmed the word that I was no longer among the living. Aside from confirming this sad news they would not cash his draft. So, you see how well known I am in the old hometown. The retired librarian then went to the First National Bank on another street with the hope of getting some cash for his draft. Here he was referred to Cornell who looks after such things. In the usual routine manner Cornell asked him if he knew anyone in Chillicothe who might identify him. The librarian said that the only person he had ever known from here was Dard Hunter, but alas, he was dead, and would be unavailable for an endorsement! My son not only enlightened him about my being alive, but cashed his draft. The old librarian told me all of his experiences in Chillicothe when he was here yesterday morning.
>
> A week or two ago I had a call from Cleveland from a man I did not know, his name being Hugo Alpers. He asked if I would autograph a book or two if he would come down to Chillicothe, about 350 miles. Of course I agreed and in a few days he arrived with two huge cartons of books, all from my private press or from the Pynson Printers. I was amazed to see what he had: three copies of *The Literature of Papermaking*, 1925, four copies of *Primitive Papermaking*, 1927, and duplicates of many of my other books, including six copies each of the two books Elmer had done, 1936 and 1939. He wanted them all autographed on the title-pages and although I objected to this particular spot, he insisted and I complied. All of the books were in mint condition. He said he would buy any books of mine that were offered. What strange turns book collecting can take!
>
> Please forgive a badly typed letter as I am not only writing in the dark, but I am using only one eye today.

Another strange, but eminently satisfying, turn in book collecting was that in February, a copy of *Papermaking by Hand in America* had sold at auction for $1,600!

Hunter spent the remaining months of 1965 answering letters and rummaging through the many bundles and boxes of stuff tucked away throughout the house. On 29 November 1965, he found the receipt for the doctor's bill rendered on the occasion of his birth exactly 82 years earlier.

THE END

Before 1962, Hunter had not kept a regular diary except to make notes during a few of his trips abroad. From that year until his death, however, he did keep journals, titled "My Life with Asthma," in which he recorded weather conditions and notes about how he felt, slept, what he ate, medications taken and when, etc. Initially, he recorded few professional or personal events; mostly a comment or two at the beginning and end of each year, and on his and Edith's birthdays and their wedding anniversary. Gradually, he began to include incidental events in his otherwise boring life. With only a few weeks to live, he penciled in contrasting views of the future.

> Friday, December 31, 1965. Another year is finished & I again wonder if I will get through the next? I rather hope not as I am so uncomfortable, especially at night. The past two years have been trying, but I have adapted myself so that I do not let the hard breathing disturb me. Old Age is a burden & one has to take it with as little complaint as possible.

> Saturday, January 1, 1966. A brand new year, but I am used to them by now. This year has started with a warm (40 degrees) rainy day, also rain throughout last night, although I slept quite well for me. Joe [Cornell] came at noon & stayed about an hour. Brought magazines & a book for his senile father. Jr. working in his shop all day. I have not been out all day; in fact not since Thanksgiving. Mild weather so far & I hope it continues. May go to [San Juan] later in the month if I feel equal to it.

Indeed, Hunter was looking forward to being in warm San Juan, but as the end of January drew nearer, he began to doubt if he would be able to make the journey. In one of his last letters, he wrote McWilliams about this prospect, as well as the troubling events in Indo-China.

> Dear Jackson: In your letter of the seventeenth you mention that you have been expecting me and that my room is all ready. How kind and thoughtful you are and how I would like to be there with all of you young folks and in the warmth and comfort of la Casa! I do hope to be able to go later if only I can gather the strength and stamina.

I have been having some difficulty the past couple of weeks, but now I am somewhat improved. It is my own opinion that nine-tenths of my trouble is nothing more than old age, too many years. The physician has me on a non-salt diet and also digitalis so I can assume that the old heart is tired and weary.

Until the past week the weather here has been delightful, sunny and bright, but on Monday the temperature dropped to zero and we had nine inches of dry snow, the deepest for more than six years. This morning the temperature is 12 degrees and the weatherman says more snow is on the way. Many of the roads are impassable. How wonderful it is to live in San Juan!

Perhaps I should not mention it, but I am worried and greatly disturbed by our involvement in Indo-China [now Vietnam, Cambodia, Laos]. I fear [President Johnson] and other officials have been led into a trap from which there is no escape. It is possible for even great governments to be ill-advised. In 1934, thirty-two years ago, I found myself in Hanoi where I had to remain much longer than I had planned. I went to Tonkin to visit the paper-villages and my trying experiences were more than I had expected. In previous journeys I had become to know something of the Japanese, the Chinese, the Siamese and the Koreans, but the people of Indo-China were unlike any other Asiatics. In no other country did I dislike the people as I did the Indo-Chinese. In both the north and south they are totally unreliable and untrustworthy. I fear that the U.S. Government has been drawn into a situation that will require years to untangle and then only to find that nothing has been gained or settled. Of course, when I was in Indo-China the French were in control and the World War was yet to be, but the people have not changed.

Best to you all. Ever gratefully, [Dard Hunter]

McWilliams immediately wrote to Dard Jr. in a last ditch effort to persuade him to prevail upon his father to come to La Casa del Libro.

Though Dard does not do much while he is here, the fact that he can get out, can go to the plaza or the little park, can sit in the sun and watch the pigeons, or occasionally takes over for one of us downstairs helps him get through the day—and I think sometimes that his worst problem is that he is either alone or is unable to get out very much there at Chillicothe.

McWilliams's strategy worked, but it was too late; Dard Hunter never again sat in the warmth of the sun. His last entry in the diary was,

> Saturday, February 19, 1966. Joe up for his weekly visit. We talked of going to San Juan, & Jr. & Joe decided I should go on the 24th. So Jr. arranged reservations for himself & for me, leaving Columbus at 8:15 A.M. so we will stay at the Holiday Inn over night, Wednesday, leaving Thursday. Jr. seems to want to go & Joe can come & get me in the spring. I have been doing poorly at night. Dr. Wood gave Jr. pills for me. Winter is not yet over, I fear.

Early the next morning, Hunter suffered a fatal heart attack, following a short but severe bout of asthma. Dard Jr. wrote in his father's diary,

> Sunday, February 20, 1966. Passed on to the other world at approximately 4:30 A.M. *God Bless His Soul*

Chapter 18

His position as a producer of beautiful books is assured, as is his standing as a pioneer in the pursuit of this particular phase of the history of technology, but it is beginning to appear that above all else it is Hunter's influence as an inspiration to the revival of a thousand-year-old craft that is most pervasive. Leonard Schlosser

Considering his close connection with his father's work, Dard Hunter Jr. (who after his father's death preferred Dard Hunter II) might have been expected to follow in Senior's footsteps. For the most part, however, this was not the case. By 1966, Dard II had a successful career as curator of the historic site Adena; his brother, Cornell, was on his way to becoming a bank president. A year after his father's death, Dard II married Janet Case Hill, who had an eight-year-old son, Chris, from a previous marriage. In April 1968, their only child Dard III was born. As the result of a car accident, Chris died that December, and soon afterward, four-year-old Eloise was adopted.

Dard II made only one major foray into authoring, printing, and publishing, when he decided in the late 1960s to write *The Life Work of Dard Hunter.** Over a fifteen-year period, he read his father's correspondence (which was scattered throughout Mountain House and in no particular order), wrote the manuscript, and printed letterpress the text using his font of type on paper made by hand in England. In addition, he printed letterpress hundreds of facsimiles of his father's early drawings and designs. When he did not have enough paper specimens to include in the book, he formed sheets on original moulds, some of which were borrowed from other collections. Dard II's primary motive in publishing this book was not, however, to satisfy any sustaining interest in papermaking, typography, or printing, but rather to pay homage to his father, arguably the most important person in his life.

Once his two-volume work was finished in 1983, the retired curator spent the rest of his life as cabinetmaker (specializing in reproduction English furniture), gunsmith, jeweler and amateur gemologist, and philatelist.

By 1988, Dard II was suffering from the effects of advanced heart disease, and realizing that he might not have long to live, he decided to take his son to Europe to retrace the footsteps of Dard I. The more he learned about his grandfather's work, the more young Dard was intrigued by it. But before Dard II could see his son fully embrace his heritage, he died on 13 September 1989 at the age of 72. Together with his mother and Elly, Dard III dealt with his father's early passing, not sure where the future would take him. In 1991, he graduated from Asbury College in Wilmore, Kentucky with a degree in business management. His first priority was to preserve Mountain House, which had been neglected for decades. Like his ancestors, Dard III proved to be a skilled craftsman, deeply interested in why and how things work, and challenged by the seemingly impossible. Even before the preservation work was finished, he set up a small paper mill in the basement and began printing on a modest basis. Recently, he established Dard Hunter Studios, a business specializing in products that incorporate his grandfather's graphic designs, as well as his own specialty watermarks and handmade papers. Sometime in the future, Dard III would like to see Mountain House become a center where people would learn papermaking, printing, and other book arts. If this plan comes to fruition, the participants will experience, as I did, the unique character of Mountain House, which is imbued with the very spirit of Dard Hunter.

HIS PAPERMAKING LEGACY

While the death of Dard Hunter did not mark the end of interest in the history of paper, it could easily have signaled the demise of its manufacture by hand in America. After all, by 1966, apart from the short-lived Lime Rock mill, no one had succeeded in establishing a viable handmade paper business since the L.L. Brown Company closed down that department in 1907. Hunter's primary motivation in setting up a mill at Marlborough in 1912 was to learn as much as he could about the materials and techniques of hand papermaking—not to mention to do something few living Americans had done. He had his share of failures at Marlborough, but from them, he accumulated invaluable knowledge about the processes of the craft.

As word of the existence of his mill spread, artists, tired of paying high prices for imported handmade papers, sought him out. Flattered by this attention and genuinely interested in trying to fill a need, Hunter attempted to operate a commercial business, but frustration soon set in. Working with limited experience, inadequate equipment, and a loathing for salesmanship, Hunter decided he could not make a go of the business alone. Ideas about expanding the mill and hiring personnel were explored, but eventually he realized that while one outcome of a successful business would be intense personal gratification, the endeavor would also be time-consuming, leaving little time for other activities, such as research and writing. And so, it became his ardent dream to establish a commercial handmade paper mill in which he would not serve as papermaker but as creative supervisor, as well as designer and maker of watermarks. Papermaking would more appropriately be left in the hands of professional vatmen, couchers, and laymen, who would employ the techniques of previous centuries. In the establishment of such a mill, Hunter would resurrect the traditional craft that had been dead in America since 1907, as well as fill the needs of artists and letterpress printers.

The problem was: Where would this mill be located? As the Marlborough site was not suitable, he searched for another. After two years, the right property had not been found, and he returned to Chillicothe in 1919. For the next ten years, he vacillated between setting up a mill nearby, joining the Butler Paper Corporation in The Hunter Mills scheme, and having paper made in England under his name. As we know, none of these plans succeeded. But in 1930, his dream finally became reality when the Robertsons made the first sheet of paper in his Lime Rock mill. Although the Great Depression certainly did not help the business, the mill could have succeeded if reliable quantities of quality paper had been made. Unfortunately, the enterprise was doomed to fail for the simple reason that the old iron foundry was a poor site for a paper mill because of the ubiquitous debris. For the same reason, Hunter's goal to resurrect this mill, following its repurchase in 1939, would also have been a disaster. He knew this but still found it impossible to let the idea go. Finally, in 1952, he faced reality and gave up the dream that had both sustained and plagued him for almost forty years.

Throughout his life, Hunter held strong views about "hobby" papermakers, including Harrison Elliott, Douglass Morse Howell, Arthur Laws, John Mason, and Henry Morris.* In Chapter XV of his *Papermaking: The History and Technique of an Ancient Craft*, Hunter described the efforts of these hobbyists, as well as his own at Marlborough: "The making of paper in limited dimensions at a small vat enables the amateur to study fibre formation, and much can be gleaned about paper and watermarking through working in this limited manner. Such procedure, however, has but little relationship to real papermaking by hand with large moulds and proper equipment." Hunter defined a papermaker as someone who had served a long apprenticeship and who could make a consistent sheet of paper over and over again, working in concert with a coucher and layman. The only persons in his circle of acquaintances he thought deserved the title of "papermakers" were Robert Robertson and his sons.

But no matter what Hunter thought of them, people like Douglass Howell played a crucial role in the renaissance of papermaking in this country. After attending a seminar taught by Howell in 1962, Laurence Barker set up a papermill at the Cranbrook Academy of Art near Detroit, Michigan, and many of his students influenced others to make paper by hand. One of the most important connections was made between Aris Koutroulis, one of Barker's students and a Tamarind master printer, who introduced Kathryn Haugh Clark to papermaking while he was printmaking instructor and she was a student at Wayne State University.

After graduation, Kathryn and husband Howard Clark, a mechanical engineer and industrial designer, moved to San Francisco, California. Nearly thirty years later, Howard recalled the moment that changed their lives.

> In the fall of 1970, I was sitting in our living room with Dard Hunter's *Papermaking: The History and Technique of an Ancient Craft* in my lap when it hit me. I looked up from the book and I remember very clearly everything that I saw in the room and the dining room beyond. I had just read Chapter XV once again, and Dard had once again admonished me for even thinking about making handmade paper on a small scale, when it struck me that things had changed, really changed.
>
> Creative energy infused in the air of San Francisco in 1970, a good deal of it came from book arts dynamo Clifford Burke, who borrowed Hunter's book from a collector and handed it to Kathryn and me saying, "You need to read this." He was right. Hunter's book revealed the world-wide scope of papermaking and that making it as a studio craft was not uncommon in other cultures, even if it was unheard of in the West. We saw, through our 1970 eyes, that handmade paper could be accepted and used in ways that would have been unthinkable in Dard Hunter's era.
>
> We began corresponding with Dard Hunter II shortly thereafter, thanks to Arnold Grummer at the Institute of Paper Chemistry. Dard encouraged us to give it a try. If our basement shop wasn't so wet, we would have framed those letters (as well as those from Henry Morris, James Lamar Weygand, Remy Green and James Yarnell). As it was, we referred to them constantly.

The Clarks were soon joined by Kathryn's twin sister, Margaret Haugh Kuehnle (now Prentice), and her husband, Kit. After Howard made the moulds, vat, and beater using Hunter's book as his guide, the other three began making paper in 1971. Kathryn recalled, "We thought . . . it will take us a couple of months to figure this out, and it took us years." Serious paper-making became possible because Kathryn was employed as a stone lithography printer at Collector's Press, a Tamarind offshoot studio. The Press's director Ernest deSoto gave them an order for a custom paper for Mexican artist José Luis Cuevas, and soon after their paper appeared in *Cuevas Comedies*, they received other orders for custom artist papers. Bolstered by this success, the Clarks and Kuehnles decided to try to make a living by the craft. Howard's family farm in Brookston, Indiana seemed the ideal place to build a mill designed especially for papermaking. In Spring 1972, Twinrocker Handmade Paper was established there.*

> When we were building the first mill, Dard [II] invited us to Chillicothe, where we spent . . . an unforgettable evening at the Mountain House. . . . To our astonishment, Dard gave us two paper moulds. They were J. B[archam] Green discards that he brought home from England . . . and were our first shadowmark and laid moulds.
>
> Dard II was quiet and introspective, not given to emotional display, but we could sense his excitement at what we were doing. This and occasional phone calls and visits helped get us through the dark days of the next few years.

Margaret and Kit left Twinrocker in 1973, and the operation could easily have ceased then, but the Clarks were determined to make their studio mill a viable business. While Howard designed and built the necessary equipment and solved most of the technical problems, Kathryn became the "master craftsman" at the vat. Because Twinrocker's clientele required relatively small quantities of paper in custom sizes and shapes, Kathryn made paper in the same way that she editioned a print: one person forming *and* couching each sheet. (Even though Twinrocker now makes stock as well as custom papers and employs a number of papermakers, this one-person technique is still practiced.)

After a year of struggling alone, the Clarks recognized, just as Hunter had done in 1917, that if the mill—and by extension, the craft—was to continue, others had to be trained to make paper. And so in 1974, the first Twinrocker apprentice, Katherine Kiddie, arrived in Brookston. She was quickly joined by a succession of talented and dedicated young people who wanted to make paper. These include Timothy Barrett, who is director of the western and Japanese paper mill at the University of Iowa and who has

written extensively on the subject; Lee S. McDonald, who runs a successful
papermaking supply and equipment business near Boston; Jennie Frederick,
an artist and teacher living near Kansas City, Missouri; Timothy Payne, who
operated the Jabberwock Mill in Tasmania, Australia; and Bernie Vinzani
and Katie MacGregor, who make paper in their mill in Maine. Other Twinrocker apprentices, while not now involved in papermaking, are artists and
educators with ongoing interests in paper. The apprenticeship program
ended in 1985, and the mill now employs people from the local community.
Shop director Travis "TJ" Becker has been trained to take over when the
Clarks retire. Although Hunter's legacy lies at the root of the revival of
papermaking in this country, Twinrocker gave the craft crucial commercial
legitimacy, as well as important technical and artistic innovations.

As early as the 1940s, artists saw beyond the use of paper in its traditional role as a support, and began using paper as a medium for the creation
of works of art. American artist Isamu Noguchi exploited the translucent
quality of Japanese handmade paper and made paper "lantern" sculptures
illuminated from within. In the early 1950s, Douglass Howell experimented
extensively with paper as an artistic medium. In the 1970s, Winifred Lutz,
another of Barker's students, began making elegant sculptures from paper
and pulp. Other people who turned from traditional media to paper pulp
to create unique works include Kenneth Noland, Robert Rauschenberg,
Frank Stella, Kenneth Tyler, and Claire Van Vliet.

There are a number of other pioneers who have worked in handmade
paper. These include: John Koller, Don Farnsworth, Robert Serpa, Helmut
Becker, Walter Hamady, and the late A. Lynn Forgach and Joseph Wilfer.
Hamady, in turn, taught many students who established their own studio
mills, including Sue Gosin's Dieu Donné Papermill in New York City. Glenn
House explored the potential of a native Alabama mulberry plant, which
yields fiber similar to Japanese *kozo*. Lilian Bell experimented with other
indigenous plants and wrote about preparing them for papermaking.

Elaine and Donna Koretsky, Tom Leech, and Dorothy Field have further
contributed to our knowledge by documenting their visits to Third World
papermaking villages, some of which Hunter visited more than a half-
century ago. Marjorie and Harold Alexander brought papermaking for the
first time to urban communities in Jamaica and Egypt. Peter Thomas has
visited and documented the few remaining European and English hand
papermaking mills. Still others have published books on the modern craft
of papermaking, notably Bernard Toale and Jules Heller. In 1987, Amanda
Degener and Michael Durgin started the journal *Hand Papermaking*.

And what about future generations? The number of graduate programs
in the book arts continues to increase. Letterpress printing, papermaking,

and bookbinding are all enjoying a slow but steady renaissance among young people, as well as older professionals embarking on new, craft-oriented careers. Because papermaking is easy, immediate, and nontoxic, it is a natural artistic medium for children. One appeal is that it creates something beautiful and useful out of common plants, recycled paper, even trash. The number of papermaking opportunities for children increases yearly; Arnold Grummer and Gloria Zmolek Smith have written books on the craft especially for children. Some of these youngsters will develop an abiding interest in the craft, as well as in the other book arts, and Hunter would have been especially pleased by this development. After all, he wrote *Paper-Making in the Classroom* more than sixty years ago.

IN CONCLUSION

I never met Dard Hunter; he died well before I developed any interest in paper or the physical book. If I had met him, no doubt, I would have found him a shy, modest gentleman who was generous with his knowledge if he sensed genuine interest, but I also know that no one knew Hunter through a casual acquaintance. There were only a handful of people who really knew him: his parents, brother Phil, wife Edith, sons Dard II and Cornell, and close friends Sterling Lord and Harrison Elliott. Nevertheless, I count myself as part of this small group because I spent several years reading his letters and his books. For almost three years, I lived and worked in Mountain House, surrounded by artifacts—from the mundane to the awe-inspiring—collected and used by him. I was charmed by his witty, often self-deprecating style; awed by his unwavering dedication to hand-crafting books and other objects; envious of his capacity for knowledge; and inspired by his sheer determination to follow his dreams, no matter what the obstacles. I also have to say that, at times, I was troubled by his occasional contradictions, but it was *all* of these traits that made Dard Hunter the unique man he was.

Some have argued that Hunter could follow his dreams because his social and economic background easily afforded him those opportunities. Certainly, his Scotch-Irish heritage resulted in a secure, lifelong income that did not emanate chiefly from his labor. However, this income benefited his family more than him. I am convinced that even without that financial safety net, Hunter would still have gone down the same paths. But the most crucial part of Hunter's ancestral inheritance was not money, it was his unfailing determination and persistence.

Upon the publication of Hunter's *Old Papermaking* in 1923, English printer James Guthrie wrote, "The place of Dard Hunter [in the book arts] is not yet so obvious."* Seventy-five years later, his place is well established, and as the millennium dawns, his legacy continues to grow.

Appendix A
Papermaking by Hand: Materials and Techniques

This topic is a vast one; indeed Dard Hunter spent most of his life researching and writing books about how it was practiced around the world. What follows, therefore, is necessarily a condensation of the basic processes in order to give those unfamiliar with the subject enough information to appreciate Hunter's story. If this whets the appetite for more information, the reader is encouraged to consult the books listed in Sources.

Tradition has it that papermaking began in China in about 105 C.E. and that the discoverer of this remarkable technology was Ts' ai Lun, a Chinese eunuch who worked at the royal court. Recent discoveries indicate, however, that papermaking is an older technology, but in either case, as soon as its significance as a writing support was appreciated, the secret of its manufacture was closely guarded in China for hundreds of years.

This early technique to make paper was quite simple. Scraps of fabric and rope, mostly hemp, were macerated with water in stone mortars with pestles until the woven or twisted characteristics of the original material were eliminated and a pulp was formed consisting of individual fibers. To form a sheet of paper from this pulp, a frame of bamboo was constructed, over which a piece of woven cloth was stretched and secured: the mould. The mould was floated in a dammed part of a stream, and the concentrated pulp was poured onto its cloth-covered surface. The water from the stream diluted the pulp, and once the papermaker distributed the fibrous mixture evenly over the surface, the mould was lifted out. The excess water drained away, leaving the fibres in a more or less even layer on the cloth. The mould was then set aside to dry, and another was used to make a second sheet, and so on. Obviously, this technique called for many moulds. Once the paper was dry, it could be peeled from the mould cover, and the mould reused (see plate 75). Eventually, virgin fibers from plants replaced cloth and ropes. A common fiber in use in Chinese hand papermaking today is bamboo.

Over many centuries, the multi-mould technique spread slowly westward into remote areas, such as Tibet and Nepal, where it is still in use today. In the more civilized parts of China, papermaking improved, and eventually, a technique involving just one mould was developed. One mould allowed the papermaker to form a sheet, which, in turn, was transferred from the mould while still wet. It was this technique that eventually found its way into Korea and Japan in the seventh century. Within a hundred years, this technique had spread west into the Arab countries surrounding the Mediterranean sea.

Nagashizuki—JAPANESE PAPERMAKING

Over the last twelve centuries, Chinese, Korean, and Japanese hand paper-making has changed little, and the techniques used in these Asian countries also show only slight variations. As more has been written about Japanese hand papermaking by Hunter and others, it will be used as the example to describe the general Asian single mould process.

In the best tradition of Japanese hand papermaking—*nagashizuki*—the raw material that yields fiber is found in one of three shrubs. In order of prevalence from very common to relatively rare, these are *kozo* (*Broussonetia kazinoki* Sieb. or *Broussonetia papyrifera* Vent.), *mitsumata* (*Edgeworthia papyrifera* Sieb. et Zucc.), and the silky fiber *gampi* (*Diplomorpha sikokiana* Nakai). The first two shrubs are easily cultivated while the third grows wild. The term "rice-paper" when applied to Japanese papers is incorrect, yet it is used everywhere in the world, including Japan. The term "paper mulberry" comes much closer to describing the most common fiber, *kozo*.

The preparation of these fibers is comparatively simple. Harvest of the year-old, inch-thick shoots of the plant occurs in the winter months. The shoots are steamed to allow easy removal of the bark from the woody core. The bark is then soaked in water and as much of the outer, or black, bark is scraped off as possible. The inner, or white, bark is then dried. When paper-making is to commence, the white bark is boiled for a few hours in a mild alkaline solution to dissolve the non-fibrous constituents. The bark, still in long strands, is rinsed in pure mountain streams to remove debris, cooking residues, and to further whiten the fiber. At this point, the strands must be carefully picked over by hand to remove all the specks of discolored bark, *chiri*. When picked as clean as is appropriate for the quality of paper desired, the strands are squeezed together to form a moist bundle. For a period of less than an hour, the bundle is beaten by hand with a mallet until strands of fiber can be easily pulled from the mass.

The second essential raw material used in *nagashizuki* is a viscous, ropy liquid, *neri*, made by soaking the pounded root of the *tororo-aoi* (*Abelmoshus manihot* Medikus or *Hibiscus manihot* L.) in water. The function of the *neri* is twofold: 1) to defloculate, or separate, the fibers in the vat, and 2) to slow the drainage of the water from the fiber thus allowing longer manipulation of the pulp on the mould. Because of the effects of *neri*, multiple dips into the vat are possible, and thus, sheets of an incredible variety of thicknesses can be produced. *Neri* is also thought to aid in the later separation of the couched and pressed but still wet sheets.

The Japanese hand mould comprises two parts: the *su* and the *geta*. The *su* is a separate mat consisting of bamboo splints, spliced and butt-joined together; these form the closely spaced, horizontal "laid" lines. These splints are secured together, vertically, at intervals of an inch or so by intertwining silk or horsehair strands, called "chain" lines, to form a flexible mould cover. Where the splicing of laid lines occurs a double row of chain lines appears on either side. When finished, the *su* resembles a *sushi* mat, an oriental roller blind, or a bamboo place mat.

The *geta* is a two-part wooden frame hinged together. The lower section is reinforced with wooden ribs that run vertically and are spaced about three to four inches apart. The upper section is a frame hinged to the lower one along the back edge. The *su* is not secured to the *geta*, but merely rests on the lower section of the *geta* when it is open. When the *geta* is closed and secured with clamps, the *su* is secured in place. The upper section of the *geta* prevents the pulp from running off the *su* during sheet-forming (in western papermaking, the deckle serves a similar purpose). When a large *geta* is used, two handles enable the papermaker to form sheets without having to over-extend his or her arms. (plate 83)

The next few steps—sheet formation, couching the sheet from the *su*, pressing, drying, and finishing—are described in Dard Hunter's *Papermaking Pilgrimage to Japan, Korea and China*.

> The equipment used in the actual formation of Japanese handmade paper comprises four essential items: The mould, in which the suspended fibres are formed into sheets; the vat (*sukibune*), which contains the macerated pulp in suspended solution; the agitator (*mase* or *sabri*), in the shape of a huge comb, used in stirring the contents of the vat; and the table or platform upon which the newly-formed sheets are laid or "couched."
>
> The vat: In Japan the receptacle for the pulp is extremely simple in construction, merely an oblong wooden tub about four feet wide, seven feet long and two feet deep, the timber about three inches in thickness. At each end of the vat are permanent wooden supports for the agitator, called *mase-geta*. The comb-like agitator is removable at will and swings easily from the tops of these supports, as is clearly shown in photo 36 [not reproduced in this book]. When not in use the *mase*, or stirring implement, hangs upon the wall. The handmade paper vat of Japan, unlike that of Europe, has no pipes, permanent agitator ("hog"), bridge, or any appurtenances whatever, save the *mase* and the *mase-geta*. Set flush with the bottom of the vat are two separate rows of tile, which serve no more important purpose than as buffers for the wooden bucket when the vat is emptied. In some vats these tiles are ornamental, but

apparently their only mission is to prevent the bailing receptacle from scraping the wooden bottom of the vat. No drains are supplied.

To commence work: The vat is filled with pure water to within about eight inches of the top. Next, the beaten pulp is added by hand, an amount sufficient for a given number of sheets. There is a definite system of regulating the amount required. The macerated pulp is moulded into square blocks by pressing it into four-sided wooden forms, much in the same manner as clay is moulded into bricks. Each of these moist blocks of pulp represents so many sheets of paper of a certain size and thickness. The method of measurement is thoroughly simple and from all indications most practical. The blocks of pulp needed are placed in the vat of water with the *nori* [*neri*], or size . . . the *mase*, or agitator, is next put in place on the supports, and the mass in the vat given a most thorough stirring. This mixes the pulp and water, forming an "emulsion" of countless individual fibres in suspension. The stirring process requires considerable time and must be done at certain intervals, as well as when new blocks of pulp are added to the diminishing stock in the vat.

The vat charged with water, pulp, and *nori* and thoroughly agitated, the worker is ready to form paper upon the mould. (Photograph 37.) [see plate 83] . . . each [large] mould is suspended from overhead by four cords, the upper end of each cord being tied to the small end of a bamboo pole, the pole giving sufficient "spring" to allow the handling of the mould and yet furnishing considerable support and balance. The mould, with its underframe and hinged deckle, between which lies the bamboo "laid" cover which in turn is covered with silk cloth, is held by two conveniently placed handles, as shown in the photograph. The mould is next skillfully tilted at the ends so that it takes up a small amount of the watery fibrous stock upon its silk cloth surface, then shaken to and fro; a portion of the pulp forms the first layer of the sheet, while the remainder of the stock floats over the newly-formed surface back into the vat. The mould is again dipped slightly into the vat of pulp and another layer formed, all the while the mould being kept in motion and the thin fibrous liquid floating over the deposited layer, the surplus being allowed to flow over the edge of the deckle, or upper *sugeta*. After several dippings and a great deal of rolling motion the sheet is practically formed, but, as if to give a last finishing touch and to cross the fibres, the worker brings the mould to the front edge of the vat which acts as a support for a sort of fanning motion which discharges the surplus stock over the back edge of the mould and completes the formation of the sheet. The moulding process is not easily described, although I have seen hundreds of sheets formed and have watched the dexterous manipulation of the moulds for hours. It is quite obvious that the entire technique is different from that employed in the formation of European handmade paper, requiring, no doubt, far more skill than the Occidental method.

The system of Japanese papermaking just described is known as *nagashizuki*, while another form, much simpler, consisting of using all of the pulp [without the addition of *neri*] lifted by the mould, is termed *tamezuki* [Hunter footnote: a lengthy description of nuances of these terms]. The work of forming paper at the vat is accomplished equally well by men or women, but women workers predominate to a marked degree. A worker can make up to five hundred sheets a day, the paper being untrimmed, about 23 by 64 inches in size.

The deposited layer of pulp lies so thin upon the silk cloth that it is scarcely discernible. The next operation is to free this filmy sheet from the mould, a process which in itself requires no mean skill. The "deckle" frame of the mould is unhooked and thrown back, the silk-covered bamboo *su* is now lifted free from the under *sugeta*, or support, and the newly-formed sheet deposited upon a cloth-covered board placed upon a table at the worker's back. (The first sheet "couched" on the board comes away from the *su* with some difficulty, but after several sheets have been laid down as a foundation the work progresses with less hardship.) The "couching" is accomplished by placing the front edge of the *su* lengthwise upon the already formed sheets, and allowing the *su* to roll slowly over the pile, thus causing the new sheet to adhere in its full breadth to the stack of paper. The *su* is next lifted from the near edge of the pile and drawn away, leaving the filmy sheet squarely upon the pile. . . . It must be understood that each sheet is laid directly upon the other, without the interleaving felts used in the European process of making handmade paper.

Pressing and drying the paper: At the end of the day's labour each worker has completed a pile of paper which contains anywhere from two hundred to five hundred sheets; the stack is called a *shito* [Hunter's footnote: *shi* - paper, *to* - layers or strata]. The following day, five or six of these piles, each supported by its board, are assembled in one straight block, and pressure applied by a huge lever upon the end of which heavy stones are hung. . . . The pressure is increased gradually by the careful addition of more stones. In no case should paper be subjected to a severe pressure at the beginning, as this would cause the sheets to adhere together. The amount of pressure and the length of time in the "press" depend upon the thickness of the paper, the size of the sheets, kinds of pulp, *nori*, and the temperature of the day. Each variety of paper demands a slightly different treatment, so it is not possible to lay down any specific rules for presssing. The piles being pressed sufficiently, each separate sheet, while still somewhat moist, is stripped from the *shito* and "pasted," or brushed, against a board for drying (Photograph 42.) [plate 84]. . . . The drying is subject to the weather, and the outdoor method is used at all times except when it rains; I have even seen rows of the boards, covered with paper, leaning against the low mill buildings when the atmosphere was quite cold and the ground covered with snow. . . . In looking down upon a papermaking village from surrounding hills, a most picturesque sight greets the eye, for wherever one may look there are hundreds of the drying boards, each with three or four sheets of paper upon it. . . . After drying, the paper is graded according to smoothness, gloss, thickness, cleanliness, and other characteristics.*

It is clear from this quote that Hunter held a deep reverence for the Japanese papermakers, especially for their skills and their commitment to the ancient traditions of the craft.

WESTERN HAND PAPERMAKING—FIBER PREPARATION

Many believe that some form of Chinese papermaking using the single mould method was being used in Arab countries as early as the eighth century. However, four centuries passed before papermaking reached Europe via north Africa. The first European mill was at Játiva, Spain and was established around 1150. From Spain, papermaking spread slowly northward over the next several hundred years. In America, the first paper was made by German-born William Rittenhouse in his mill near Philadelphia, Pennsylvania in 1690.

Wherever papermaking was practiced, the availability of materials changed the technique. Instead of bamboo or paper mulberry as the source of raw fiber, European and American papermakers had to work with a wide variety of rags of hemp, linen, and later cotton—a sometimes unsavory but plentiful source of fiber. The rags were sorted by fine to coarse weaves, dark to light whites, and weak to strong textile structures. The colored rags were separately treated. Once sorted, the rags were cut into small pieces and washed, soaked, or retted, occasionally in alkaline solutions, to cleanse and soften the woven structure. Once softened, the rags were macerated until the textile turned into individual fibers. The first of the macerating machines was called a stamper (see plate 48). This apparatus consisted of rows of large wooden hammers, the heads of which were covered with iron teeth. The action of the hammers was powered by a water wheel, and they rose and fell rhythmically into stone pits containing the rags; continuous exchanges of fresh for dirty water flowing through the pits insured the whitest possible fiber.

In the late seventeenth century, a machine called the Hollander beater, so-named because it was invented in Holland, gradually took the place of the stampers. The Hollander beater was essentially an oblong tub in which rotated a roll embedded with blades. As the roll turned, the mixture of softened rags and water was forced between the blades and a plate embedded in the bottom of the tub. By adjusting the distance between the blades and bed plate, the fibers could be primarily cut or fibrillated. The important advantage the Hollander beater had over the stamper was that it could macerate rags much more efficiently; it also engaged a washing system that continuously flushed out dirty water and introduced clean.

The primary disadvantage of the Hollander over the stamper was that if attended by an unskilled worker, the machine tended to cut the fibers rather short. However, the time the fiber stayed in the stamper pit, compared to the Hollander beater, was much less critical. Whereas an extra half day in the stamper might result in significant changes in fiber length, the same difference might be seen in an hour in the Hollander. Therefore, the beaterman was, and is, perhaps the most important worker in the mill, for as most papermakers know, paper is made in the beater, not in the vat.

Once beating was complete, the pulp, or stuff, was added to the vat and diluted to a very watery consistency, the exact dilution depending upon the thickness of paper being made. (Half-stuff is partially beaten pulp, sold either wet or as dry, thick sheets, or laps. From either state, half-stuff must be beaten to the desired extent dictated by the type of paper to be made.)

THE WESTERN MOULD

Once the pulp is diluted in the vat, papermaking can begin. Each sheet is formed on a mould not dissimilar to the Japanese mould already described. Western hand papermaking moulds have two main sections. The first is a wooden bottom frame, rigidified with vertically positioned ribs that keep the cover from sagging during papermaking. In large moulds, metal rods run perpendicularly through the ribs to further stabilize the frame. The second section is a completely separate unit called the deckle (from the German, *deckel*, meaning lid or top). The deckle, a simple frame, fits over the bottom section of the mould, and it determines the paper's size, contour, and thickness depending upon its interior dimensions and shape. In traditional hand papermaking, as practiced in the West for centuries, it was common to employ a pair of matching bottom sections and one deckle.

Although similar in many ways to the oriental *su*, the European cover differs significantly in that it is made entirely of metal wire, usually copper or brass, and is permanently attached to the bottom section. (plate 85) The wire cover is made by weaving a distinct pattern using rows of slender wires that usually run parallel to the long dimension of the mould; these constitute the "laid" wires, or lines. As each of these wires is laid in place, it is attached to the last one by two intertwined thinner wires, called chain wires. The chain wires, or lines are spaced at about one-inch intervals, and usually run parallel to the short dimension of the mould. This is called a laid and chain cover, or simply a laid mould. When completed, this wire cover is similar to a *su*, but unlike the *su*, it is permanently tacked onto the bottom frame. Usually, the chain lines are positioned directly over the ribs, and then sewn to them utilizing tiny holes drilled into the ribs along their length. Once the cover is secured to the ribs, the sharp wire ends are covered with strips of metal and tacked onto the top of the bottom frame. The deckle fits snugly over the top of each of the matching bottom frames, leaving exposed just the wire cover, a sieve-like screen through which the water from the pulp drains. This type of mould is called an antique laid, or single-face, mould. At the contact point between the chain lines and the ribs, faster drainage of water takes place. Because where water flows fibers follow, in paper formed on an antique laid mould, more fiber is deposited along the chain lines. These thicker areas, seen as shadows, are visible when the paper is viewed in transmitted light (see plates 51, 52, 60, 64, 85).

At some point early in the history of European papermaking, watermarks began to be made by bending thin wire into shapes and sewing the designs onto the surface of the cover (see plate 85). As the pulp is thinner at these raised areas, watermarks appear lighter than the rest of the sheet, when viewed in transmitted light (see plates 51, 52, 60, 64, 88, 93–95).

In England in the early 1750s, a new style of cover was devised to address a common complaint among printers: antique laid papers were not uniformly thick across the sheet. This new cover was also made with wire but woven to resemble cloth. Appropriately, this type of mould and the paper formed on it are called wove (see plates 86, 87, 89–92, 94, 96, 97). Because the first wove covers were sewn directly to the ribs as in the antique laid mould, it was soon apparent that the paper was still thicker over the ribs. To eliminate this problem altogether, an anonymous mould maker first sewed either a layer of widely spaced, laid wires or a coarsely woven wire cloth directly to the ribs; these are called backing wires or cloth. The wove cover was then sewn to the backing. As this lifted the wove cover from direct contact with the ribs, no shadows appear in paper made on this type of mould. Wire watermarks were as easily sewn to a wove mould as a laid one.

Shortly after the development of the wove mould, the antique laid mould gradually underwent a change. As old antique laid covers wore out or the moulds needed repair, the covers were removed and either reused or replaced. In many cases, the laid cover was sewn onto backing wires or cloth as described above. As the laid cover was no longer in intimate contact with the ribs, drainage was even across the cover, and no shadows appeared in the paper. This second type of laid mould is called a modern laid, or double-face, mould (see plates 88, 93, 95). Antique laid moulds never went out of fashion, however, and today both types of laid moulds, as well as wove hand moulds are available.

SHEET FORMATION

Once the pulp is prepared and the pair of moulds selected, papermaking can begin. Traditionally, three people are required to make paper (see plate 71). The vatman is the most skilled papermaker; daily, it is his (or her) responsibility to form hundreds of consistent sheets of paper by dipping the mould into the dilute solution of fiber in water. Once the dip is completed, the vatman skillfully shakes the mould, both from back to front and from side to side, to help distribute the uppermost layers of fiber evenly across the sheet before the free water drains away. (Only one dip is possible in western hand papermaking, as the *neri*, used in Japanese papermaking, is not present.)

Once the sheet is "set," the vatman passes the mould to the coucher (from the French, *coucher*, to lay down) while keeping the deckle in his hands. At this point, the coucher has already passed the other mould along the back of the vat to the vatman who then grasps it and positions the deckle on top. He begins to form the next sheet immediately.

In the meantime, the coucher takes the mould with the newly formed sheet on it and turns it upside down. Amazingly, the wet sheet continues to adhere to the surface of the mould cover until it is couched onto a piece of damp felt with an uninterrupted rocking and pushing motion, which transfers the freshly formed sheet from the mould to the felt. The coucher passes that mould back to the vatman, places another felt on top of the sheet just couched, and receives the next mould ready for couching. So the rhythmic actions of these two skilled workers continue to build a pile of paper and felts on the coucher's tray.

The third person in the team is called the layman or layboy—often an apprentice who might be promoted to coucher and after many years, to vatman. When about 140 sheets of paper and felts are built up on the coucher's tray, a so-called "post" is formed. The post is transported to the press where a large amount of water is removed from the paper and felts. After the first pressing, the layman's job is to separate the still wet, but more cohesive, sheets of paper from the felts. As he builds a pile of wet paper on wet paper, he places the felts on a board near the coucher's station.

Over the course of a day, this team could make several reams of paper, each ream made up of approximately 500 sheets. At the end of the day, the stack of paper is lightly pressed overnight; the next day, the sheets are hung in the loft to dry. Most paper was sized to make the sheet more impervious to the penetration of liquid and to add strength. Sizing involves dipping dried sheets into a dilute gelatin solution, pressing them, and loft-drying. If the paper is to be used for a water-based medium such as ink, the paper is heavily, or hard, sized. If the paper is to be used for letterpress or intaglio printing, it is lightly, or slack, sized. After the paper receives the appropriate surface finish through hand burnishing, plating, or calendering, it is inspected for defects and shipped to the customer.

Appendix B
Moulds and Watermarks Associated with Dard Hunter

Unfortunately, original research sources containing information about the many moulds and watermarks associated with Dard Hunter are sparse. This is particularly true of the moulds used at the Lime Rock mill. Nevertheless, although incomplete, the following represents the most comprehensive description of Hunter's papermaking moulds and watermarks to date.

It is not possible to reproduce in this book all of Hunter's watermarks, but most of the ones executed or designed by him are illustrated. For the remaining images, the reader might consult the following two books. Dard Hunter II's *The Life Work of Dard Hunter* not only photographically reproduces almost all of the watermarks described below, but many specimen sheets of paper are also bound-in; most of these appear in Volume 2.* As this book was published in a limited edition, a more accessible work is Douglas B. Stone and Hardev S. Dugal's *The Dard Hunter Collection at the Institute of Paper Chemistry I. Dard Hunter Watermarks* (Appleton, 1984). In the following descriptions, photographically reproduced watermarks not illustrated in this book are noted by: Hunter + illustration letter; Stone/Dugal + number. If the notation "nr" appears, the image is not reproduced in that book.

Notes:
• The moulds described below are given in chronological order as Hunter received them, as are the various watermarks attached to them.
• All mould dimensions are given height x width with the chain lines running vertically. Likewise, the paper dimensions are given height x width relative to the watermark orientation.
• A slash / in the description of a watermark denotes that what follows it is on the next line or in a space below.
• The term "watermark" is often used to refer to the entire image, words, or numbers on a mould. However, a distinction is sometimes made by using "watermark" to refer to images positioned on one side of the mould, while "countermark" refers to a series of words or numbers, positioned on the opposite, or counter, side.
• In many cases, watermarks are placed on the mould wrong-reading. The watermark then reads correctly when the front side of the paper is viewed in transmitted light. This side is called the wire side while the back of the paper is the felt side. The wire side is smoother, more compact, and easier to write on.

MARLBOROUGH MILL MOULDS, FIRST PAIR

(plate 86) Even before he purchased the Marlborough property in May 1912, Hunter wrote to English mould making firms W. Green, Son & Waite and T.J. Marshall & Co. Ltd. (the latter was where Hunter first made paper). He asked both for a quote for a pair of plain (no watermark) moulds: 6.75 x 8.75 inches, one wove and one modern laid with one deckle. As the Marshall moulds were less expensive, that firm received the order, and the moulds were delivered to Hunter in mid-August 1912.

FIRST LAID MOULD: At different periods, two watermarks were attached to this mould. The first, a light-and-shade watermark, a fleur-de-lis, appears on only one extant sheet (Hunter nr, Stone/Dugal nr). Upon this fragment is inscribed in pencil: "First sheet of paper made by Dard Hunter at his mill in America. From pulp brought from England from the Batchelor Mill in Kent, 1912." Soon after this first sheet was made, the fleur-de-lis watermark was removed from the mould; its maker and whereabouts are unknown.

Much later, the final watermark applied to this mould was in wire, a lion rampant topped by the English crown (Hunter nr; Stone/Dugal #43). As no contemporary papers have been found with this watermark, it is likely that it was either taken from one of the Palmer Mill moulds or was sent by one of the English mouldmakers, coming into Hunter's possession by early 1921.

FIRST WOVE MOULD: In the winter of 1912–13, Hunter began experimenting with light-and-shade or *chiaroscuro* watermarks, and over the period from 1913 until the late 1920s, four such watermarks can be attributed to him. Light-and-shade watermarks differ considerably from simple wire watermarks as they can produce tonal images ranging from dark to light. Light-and-shade watermarking was not possible until the invention of the wove mould cover in the mid-eighteenth century. In the mid-nineteenth century, an Englishman, William H. Smith, invented this watermark technique. Smith's technique involves a number of steps, the first of which is to carve the image into a sheet of wax on a light box using gravers, needles, gouges, etc. As the wax is sculpted, the image appears through the changing thicknesses of wax. The finished wax model is then coated with a thin layer of powdered graphite and electrotyped to produce a metal die. An annealed (softened, less brittle) woven wire cloth is then pressed into the die, and the image is formed. The cloth is then hardened and sewn onto the mould. If the depressions in the cover are very great, the layer(s) of backing wires or cloth can be cut out, or bent out of the way. The areas of the watermark that are above the surface of the cover will appear light in the paper, while the areas that are below it will appear dark, with gradations of grey in-between.

Hunter's techniques varied only slightly from Smith's. In some cases, he carved only one wax model, and in others, two: one cameo, or male, and one intaglio, or female. He then sent the wax model(s) to a manufacturer that made the dies, usually in copper. Annealing the screen to make it malleable, Hunter then pressed, or had pressed, the wove cover between the dies making the three-dimensional image. He then refined the image with hand tools such as a burnisher. In some cases, graphite-coated plaster casts of the image exist, although it is not clear from Hunter's correspondence what purpose they served. They could have been cast from the wax models and used to make the electrotypes, thus preserving the vulnerable waxes.

After hardening, the wire cover was attached to the mould. However, it is not necessary to emboss the cover in this way. Small or simple light-and-shade watermarks can be produced by annealing the wire cloth and working it with hand tools. Before such watermarks are attached to the mould, the cloth must be hardened. It is possible that Hunter made the fleur-de-lis watermark in this manner, and for some reason discarded it after making only one or two sheets.

However, the success of the light-and-shade watermark depends more on the preparation of the fiber than on the preparation of the wove cover. The secret is to cut the fibers very short (but not to bruise or fibrillate them too much, as then the paper shrinks and distorts). Short fibers conform to the different levels of the sculptured wire cloth. If the fibers are too long, they tend to tangle and drape over the various edges thus creating fuzzy, undefined images. The only problem with watermarked papers made with short fibers is that they tend to be relatively weak, unless they are heavily sized. Expensive to make, the best examples of these papers were, and continue to be, highly prized works of art, rather than utilitarian (although Hunter did use such watermarked papers for stationery, as did Elbert Hubbard, whom Hunter was no doubt emulating).

The first light-and-shade watermark Hunter executed himself depicted the Marlborough Mill with DARD / HUNTER / MILL in wire in his Viennese letter style, complete with a spiral at the end. Hunter probably carved the wax for this watermark in summer 1913. Although he probably attempted to make the dies himself, he did write to several firms asking if they could make them. The following is quoted from a draft written on the back of a letter dated 27 August 1913.

I wish to locate a firm in America where I can get my dies for making watermarks. . . . From a wax bas-relief there is a heavy copper electro type made about ⅛ inch thick. From this electro there is made another

of the same thickness, making male and female dies. The wax relief
I will make now is about 5" x 7" the thickness of the wax is about ³⁄₁₆".
If you can do this work, I would be glad to know [the cost] for each die.

It is possible that the F.A. Ringler Company made the dies for the mill
watermark, as in 1917, they made a set for another of Hunter's watermarks.
Once the dies were received, Hunter prepared the wire cloth and attached it
to the mould. He then sewed on the wire countermarks. He formed a few
sheets on this mould, but he had trouble making a clear image because the
pulp could not be beaten well enough (evidenced by the few extant pieces).
Perhaps intending to resolve these problems later, he put the mould aside.
In 1921, he may have experimented again with this mould, but he soon decided that this mould and its companion laid mould with the lion rampant
wire watermark would serve a better purpose as part of the papermaking
exhibit at the Smithsonian Institution.*

HUNTER'S LARGE PORTRAIT WATERMARK
(plate 87) Hunter's earliest fully documented foray into light-and-shade watermarking actually began in January 1913 when he wrote to the T.J. Marshall
company about having such a watermark made. They replied,

> The sample of watermarking which you send us is a portrait [uniden-
> tified] executed by the famous Italian house of Pietro Miliani [Fabriano,
> Italy]. We have seen this portrait many times in various collections of
> watermarking, it is a most unique specimen of the art and this is the
> only house we know of which can produce equal to this.
>
> We have done watermarked portraits from time to time but they
> have never been anything like the effect in the sample. Pietro Miliani
> does not supply Moulds but only supplies paper and to have a special
> portrait made would be exceedingly expensive. We do not think you
> would be able to obtain such a portrait from anywhere to attach to a
> Mould. . . . In this portrait watermarking, a great deal depends on the
> execution in wove wire of the portrait, but almost more on the special
> preparation of the stuff. The firm above mentioned, we have no doubt,
> have a special method of beating, the secret of which they do not divulge
> to anyone, and this it is which gets their remarkable effects.
>
> If you like we can send you over a mould with a sunk head (or
> relief) to experiment on & you could see how you got on without going
> to the expense first of all of a special mould.

Hunter was also corresponding with W. Green, Son & Waite on this subject. That firm forwarded some wax patterns cast from their dies, as well as a few sheets of a portrait watermark of Schiller, the German poet.

Intrigued by the thought of having his own portrait in paper just like Elbert Hubbard, Hunter sent the 1904 Roycroft photograph of him in profile to W. Green, Son & Waite requesting a quote in February 1913. They replied,

> A Mould for paper 8⅛" x 10¼" with one Embossed head about the size of photo sent would cost about £7.0.0 plus freight and duty.
> A Mould for paper 16¼ x 20½, with 4 heads, about £10.0.0 plus freight and duty.
> Yes, the die could be used for any number of embossings likely to be required.
> For this kind of making, it is necessary to cut the fibres *very, very* short, and make the pulp as much like flour & water as possible.

Hunter decided on the "one Embossed head" mould and increased the dimensions to 8.5 x 11.5 inches. By the end of May, the artist at W. Green, Son & Waite had finished making the wax model of the portrait, the die had been cast, and a wax cast from it sent to Hunter for approval. With his reply, Hunter sent them the design for the wire countermark DARD / HUNTER in his Viennese lettering style. The mould was made and three sheets, formed from different proportions of pulp to water, were sent to him. Marked A, B, C, only the latter has been found; it measures 8.25 inches x 11.5 inches.

At the end of October 1913, Hunter sent a letter to W. Green, Son & Waite confirming that he had received the mould, the original wax impression, and the die.* He also inquired as to whether pure linen or a mixture of linen and cotton pulp would serve equally well in making this type of watermarked paper, to which they replied yes, as long as the fiber was cut fine "like wet flour." They also offered suggestions in case he wanted to have more paper made from his mould.

> If it is only an occasional quantity of paper from this Portrait Mould which is wanted, say for your own letter-heads or what not, would you not obtain a better result if you placed the order for the making of the paper with the firm who made the small quantity of paper we sent to you, or with any other firm who can made as good a watermark paper as they can?

If on the other hand, you yourself want to carry on the making of hand-made paper in the U.S. it is of course a different matter, but we would point out that this particular paper, with so beautiful a water-mark, is a very, very different thing for you to start on, and it would be a very great marvel if you succeeded well.

The earliest mention of his portrait watermarked paper appears in a letter of July 1914 from the Foreign Bureau of the Internationale Ausstellung für Buchgewerbe und Graphik Leipzig granting him permission to repro-duce an interior scene of the exhibit (for an unknown purpose). "We very much admired and appreciated the splendid water-mark of your writing paper which is the best proof that you are highly interested in paper mak-ing."* This was either a sheet of paper made on this mould at his mill, or was one of the samples marked A or B, mentioned above.

In any case, after experimenting with this mould, Hunter realized that he could not beat the fiber to the correct consistency. Therefore, in early December 1914, he wrote to Perrigot-Masure—the French paper manufac-turers who had made the earlier samples—inquiring about the cost of mak-ing large quantities of paper from this mould. They quoted between $6 to $8 per ream, depending on the quantity ordered. Hunter made calculations on the bottom of the letter, but there is no indication that he placed an order then. In 1922, he sent Perrigot-Masure an order for seven reams, which was made on his mould. (There has been some confusion about whether this stationery was made on a hand mould or on a cylinder ma-chine. There is no indication in the correspondence that the latter was the case. As the fibers were beaten quite short, subtle deckle edges are pro-duced, which were often mistaken for the deckle edges seen on cylinder machine-made papers.)

Used primarily as stationery, this Large Portrait watermark paper was also a specimen in *Old Papermaking*, and the prospectus for *The Literature of Papermaking 1390–1800* was printed on it. In 1924, Perrigot-Masure made another nine reams, some of which was used for the frontispiece for *Before Life Began* (1941). When used as stationery, the sheet was folded backwards to form a half sheet, 8.25 x 5.75 inches, which, in transmitted light, shows the portrait "looking" to the right with his name correctly oriented on top of it.*

MARLBOROUGH MILL MOULDS, SECOND PAIR
(plates 88 & 89) The second pair of moulds purchased by Hunter was also made by Marshall's and measure 11 x 8.25 inches, one modern laid and one wove with one deckle. When asking for a quote in January 1913, Hunter indi-cated he wanted to make envelopes, as well as full sheets. The firm replied,

As regards the envelope it would be possible to make a Deckle to fit the pattern which you send us but it would be more or less a clumsy job and we do not think it would work satisfactorily. . . . No, the best thing to do would be to have another pair of Laid and Wove Moulds upon which you could use the Deckle belonging to the previous pair and on this pair of Moulds we should put a tearing wire the shape of your pattern. This tearing wire makes the paper much thinner in the particular place where the tearing wire comes and forms the envelope. This is how hand made envelopes are usually made.

Hunter decided he could alter his own moulds, rather than invest in a second pair.* In early March 1913, Marshall's sent a letter acknowledging the order for one pair of moulds. Separately, they dispatched

5 pieces of tearing wires and 5 pieces of silver wire for designs, all in different thicknesses. At the same time we are sending a sunk portrait which you will be able to fix to a Mould yourself, together with 2 other samples of embossed watermarking which we think might be useful to you in your experiments. As the pieces of wire are such a small matter we gladly send these without invoice. We have consigned the parcel as "samples of no value" as suggested, and we hope they will reach you without trouble.

SECOND LAID MOULD: Hunter made two watermarks for this mould. The earliest was DARD HUNTER / paper press enclosed in a circle / 19 MILL 13 (Hunter nr; Stone/Dugal #42, envelope). All of the pieces were cut from sheet brass and soldered to the laid cover. In 1914, the press and MILL were replaced with a DH-in-a-heart watermark. The outline of the heart is wire, the center is a woven screen, and the DH was cut from sheet brass and all were sewn to the cover. The date 1913 was left on this mould to commemorate the year his mill commenced operations.

Paper made on this mould was used by Hunter as letterhead and for larger envelopes (using a tearing wire). In the DHAMH, there are a few pieces of paper made on this mould that were experiments or samples of pulp "marbling," perhaps intended as decorative endpapers. Although the base paper of these sheets was often cream, the colored pulps—brown, yellow, blue, and green—were also used in combination. This marbling effect was probably made by first forming the base sheet on the mould, and before couching it, colored pulp was carefully swirled into the wet sheet.

SECOND WOVE MOULD: In 1914, Hunter began work on designing his most elaborate watermark, called the Papermaking Commemorative, using both light-and-shade and wire techniques.* He carved two wax models: one intaglio and one cameo. In an oval, the image depicts a vatman, dressed in Colonial costume, standing at the vat forming a sheet of paper. In the background is a heavy wooden press with the inscription "1690," denoting the year the first American papermill began operations.

The rest of the design, painstakingly done in wire, gives homage, on the left, to the first English papermaker, John Tate, and to the first printer to use Tate's paper, Wynken De Worde. On the right, the watermark and initials of the first American papermaker, William Rittenhouse, appear; the first printer to use his paper was William Bradford. In between these pioneers is Dard Hunter, identified by a DH in a scroll at the top of an architectural enclosure. Within the plinth are the words, "DARD HUNTER MILL *makers of* HANDMADE PAPER." (This enclosure is strikingly similar to the cover design of the early issues of Frederic Goudy's journal, *Typographica*.)

The uppercase letters, except for the DH-in-a-scroll and the papermakers' initials, are in Hunter's Viennese lettering and a sans serif roman. The cursive letters DH-in-a-scroll are very similar to the uppercase *D* and *H* used on one of the third laid moulds described below.

When the first Chicago Society of Etchers project commenced in 1915, Hunter set this mould aside before finishing the cover, although he had probably formed all of the wire watermarks by then. In the fall of 1917, it seems that he decided to finish the mould, because that September, the F.A. Ringler Company made dies from his wax models, and it is assumed that these dies were made for the Papermaking Commemorative watermark. The copper dies are identical to the ones made for the earlier watermark of Hunter's mill (see description of first wove mould, above). Once Hunter had received the dies, the oval design was embossed into a wire screen, the cover attached to the mould, and the wire watermarks sewn on.

As Hunter was no longer making paper in his mill by late 1917, it is doubtful that he had a chance to make paper on this mould until late 1920 or early 1921. That year, for the 21 June issue of *Paper*, he wrote "Watermarking Hand-Made Paper," and the Papermaking Commemorative mould was used as an illustration. The caption reads: "WOVE MOLD FOR MAKING SHEETS OF PAPER IN TWO COLORS. The oval is made in a different color from the margin of the sheet by stenciling out each in turn; the two portions of the sheet are united while still in the wet pulp state." In the DHAMH, there are a few sheets of paper made by Hunter illustrating this technique. The center oval paper is light blue while the remainder of the sheet is off-white. While Hunter experimented with stencils, he also used a mould fragment to which a second oval light-and-shade watermark was attached.

Rather than ruin one of his moulds for this second oval, Hunter probably sacrificed one of the Palmer Mill wove moulds, received in late 1920. Using a makeshift deckle for the fragment, Hunter had to carefully pour blue pulp onto the surface. He then experimented by either couching it directly onto a full sheet or couching it into a void created when the oval on the whole mould was masked out.

As he did not have a mill at the time, it is possible that he set up the small beater, a wash tub, and the laying press—normally used for bookbinding—in an arrangement similar to the one pictured on page 65 in *Paper-Making in the Classroom.*

This second pair of Marlborough Mill moulds, as well as the copper dies for the Papermaking Commemorative, are in the AMP. The intaglio and cameo waxes, graphite-coated plaster casts, another oval in wire cloth, and a photograph of the mould were all part of Hunter's exhibit given to the Smithsonian Institution in 1921.*

MARLBOROUGH MILL MOULDS, THIRD PAIR

By early 1914, Hunter decided he needed a large mould on which book papers could be made. Such a mould would yield a sheet that could be used in a variety of formats; full size or folded in the following configurations: a folio (folded once, two leaves, four pages), a quarto (folded twice, four leaves, eight pages), an octavo (folded three times, eight leaves, sixteen pages), etc. With the use of tearing wires, a large mould could also be separated into many sections, thus producing, with one dip, a number of smaller, individual sheets. On a large mould could also be made two or more envelopes using tearing wires. In January 1914, Hunter ordered a pair of laid moulds with one deckle, to measure 16 x 23 inches, from W. Green, Son & Waite. They acknowledged receipt of the order and asked,

> Will you kindly send us a sample to show the laid lines required, saying at the same time whether you require the paper to look like that you have written on, (that is, darker by the chain lines and lighter between the chain lines), or whether you require it to look level as per sample A herewith. Will you please say if we are to make any allowance for shrinkage; and if so, how much both ways of the Mould.

The question regarding the level vs. the uneven "darkness" of the laid paper refers to modern laid vs. antique laid paper, as described in Appendix A. Hunter chose modern laid. He also took Waite's advice and allowed for shrinkage by increasing the inside deckle measurement by half an inch in both dimensions, 16.5 x 23.5 inches.* Together with the deckle, this pair of moulds is in the DHAMH.

THIRD LAID MOULD A: To this mould, a large wire watermark, *Dard Hunter Mill*, in cursive script was applied, running horizontally in the center of the mould (Hunter E; Stone/Dugal #5).† This mould was also used extensively to create decorative endpapers in the same colors described for the second laid mould and in additional colors of purple, grey, and pink.

THIRD LAID MOULD B: This mould may have been used without a watermark for a number of sheets, predominately in a deep yellow, before the DH-in-a-heart watermarks were applied in two diagonally opposite corners, each heart running parallel to the chain lines. While waiting for the antique laid moulds he ordered to make paper for *The Etching of Figures,* Hunter experimented with this mould.

ROYCROFT WATERMARKS

It is possible that in mid-1914, Hunter made, or at least experimented with making, paper for the Roycroft. The author has examined a small private collection of sheets in a variety of colors and sizes, probably formed on all of the laid moulds Hunter had at that point, using tearing wires to create odd-sized sheets. While some of the thick sheets appear to have no watermark, others are watermarked ROYCROFT in wire with the letters positioned in between two chain lines, running parallel to them. While there are several beige sheets, most of the papers are in vibrant or deep colors of purple, green, blue, yellow, and rust. Turquoise and mauve note cards, 3.75 x 6.75 inches, are also included in the collection; these are quite thick and no watermark can be detected. For the most part, these sheets are formed from under-beaten pulp, and the formation is poor.

A second wire (or light-and-shade) watermark on a laid mould is also in this collection, but it is difficult to describe the design as, again, the formation of the beige paper is poor. This indistinct watermark, enclosed in a double-line border, is located in one corner and includes a small star.

MARLBOROUGH MILL MOULDS, FOURTH PAIR

(plates 51, 52, 60, 64, 85) The pair of 16.5 x 23.5 inch antique laid moulds, ordered for *The Etching of Figures* in March 1915 from W. Green, Son & Waite, arrived in October, after having been lost for months.

FOURTH LAID MOULD A: This mould was watermarked with the DH-in-a-heart in one corner and, in the diagonally opposite corner, the seal of the Chicago Society of Etchers made of wire, wove screen, and sheet brass

(Hunter B & D; Stone/Dugal #2a & b). Paper made on this mould constitutes most of that used for *The Etching of Figures, The Etching of Contemporary
Life*, and the J.C. Vondrous Folio.

FOURTH LAID MOULD B: As far as can be determined, this mould was
not used at Marlborough.

These moulds were first used as a pair in 1922 when Hunter was planning to print *Old Papermaking* (1923). As he had no mill, he decided to have
the paper made in England. He removed the old watermarks and sent the
pair to W. Green, Son & Waite whose artisans made four wire watermarks
after Hunter's design, the 1922 Branch watermark. These were placed in two
diagonal corners on both of the moulds and each runs parallel to a short side.
J. Barcham Green's Hayle Mill made the paper, which was used as the text
paper for *Old Papermaking* and *The Literature of Papermaking 1390–1800*.

In October 1926, Hunter needed more paper to print *Primitive Papermaking*. As he still had no mill, he again shipped the pair of moulds to
W. Green, Son & Waite. The 1922 Branch watermarks were removed, and
new watermarks based on Hunter's printer's mark, the Bull's Head &
Branch, were attached in the same two corners on each mould. Again, the
paper was made at Hayle Mill.

Paper made on the Bull's Head & Branch watermarked moulds were
also used at the Lime Rock mill for *Old Papermaking in China and Japan,
Papermaking in Southern Siam*, and *Papermaking by Hand in America*. When
Dard Hunter II decided to print his *The Life Work of Dard Hunter*, he sent
these moulds to the Wookey Hole Mill in Wells, Somerset, England. The
Bull's Head & Branch watermarked moulds remain in the DHAMH.

VOJTECH PREISSIG: PAIR OF MOULDS AND WATERMARKS
In January 1920, Czechoslovakian Vojtech Preissig of the Wentworth Institution, School of Printing and Graphic Arts in Boston, Massachusetts, wrote
Hunter asking if he could make a special, watermarked paper for an unidentified book to be printed in a limited edition of 150 copies. Preissig sent
Hunter a dummy sheet with the watermark drawn—with the notation to
retain the crooked quality of the lines—: VOJTECH PREISSIG DARD HUNTER,
a squat brick house with a prominent roof line, and 1920 (Hunter nr; Stone/
Dugal #33). Assuming that he would soon have a mill through his association with the Butler Paper Corporation, Hunter ordered a pair of antique
laid moulds, approximately 18.75 x 23 inches and the wire watermarks from
W. Green, Son & Waite that November; Preissig reminded him to change
the watermark date to 1921.

Well into 1921, Hunter kept Preissig apprised of developments concerning The Hunter Mills, but by September, it was obvious that the mill was not to be. Preissig suggested that Hunter set up an experimental paper-mill and teach at the Wentworth Institute. Intrigued by this idea, Hunter sent course information, floor plans, and a list of equipment and supplies to Preissig. The Institute's principal interviewed Hunter, but according to Preissig, it did not go well. Preissig was so upset by the perceived slight to his friend, he wrote that his own future at the Institute was in doubt, and he urged Hunter to dismiss any idea of joining the staff.

Finally, in December 1921, Hunter ordered seven reams of Preissig's watermarked paper, dated 1922, from J. Barcham Green's Hayle Mill; the paper arrived early the next year. Hunter took two of the seven reams for his own use. Later, he used this paper to print some of the illustrations for *Old Papermaking*. The moulds remained in England in case more paper was to be made, but eventually Preissig had them sent to the State Printing Office in Prague. Preissig remained at the Wentworth Institute until 1924, after which he set up a press in his home. In 1930, he returned to his native Czechoslovakia and died in a concentration camp in 1944.

HUNTER'S SMALL PORTRAIT WATERMARK

In March 1921, Hunter designed a similar watermark to the Large Portrait for a second stationery sheet. This paper was intended for use with a typewriter, while the Large Portrait folded format was more suitable for handwritten letters. With perforations under the watermark, this paper also served as a personalized check. Compared with the Large Portrait, Hunter's profile is considerably smaller and shifted to the top left of the 11 x 8.25 inch sheet with the words, DARD HUNTER, in lettering similar to his typeface, to the right (Hunter nr; Stone/Dugal #25).

Hunter sent the lettering design and his 1904 Roycroft photograph to Enrico Toniolo of Italy and ordered the watermarks and a mould. Later, Toniolo mentioned that the wax was modeled by an artist at Pietro Miliani in Fabriano. The letters were cut from sheet metal and sewn to the cover. The wove mould and wax model were sent to Hunter in May 1921.* In February 1922, after receiving several quotes for paper to be made on his Large and Small Portrait watermarked moulds, Hunter decided to have Perrigot-Masure make seven reams of the Large Portrait, and five of the Small Portrait.† The two hand moulds were sent to France.

Nothing so immediately impressed Hunter's correspondents as the receipt of one of these portrait sheets. Most people had never seen anything like it, and even if they had, certainly not in ordinary stationery. One person remarked, "The letterhead you sent up with the watermark certainly was the most beautiful thing I have ever seen." However, Hunter was not entirely pleased with either of his portrait watermarks. He particularly disliked the Small Portrait, as evidenced by a letter to Sterling Lord written in early January 1923, where he wrote "Rotten" across the portrait and crossed through his name. Apparently, the paper was not *too* bad because in 1924, Hunter ordered another six reams of the Small Portrait paper from Perrigot-Masure; in 1929, from the same mill operating under the name, Papeteries d'Arches, he ordered another twenty-four reams.

LORD BYRON

(plate 90) The portrait watermark of Lord Byron was the third of the light-and-shade type watermarks that Hunter carved in wax. "Lord Byron" was first mentioned in an early 1915 letter from Alfred Fowler, who queried, "Do you make the white stationery with the head (of Byron, is it not?) watermark for sale?" Of course, Fowler was looking at Hunter's Large Portrait watermark. However, the observation gave Hunter the idea of making a watermark of Byron. He modeled the wax after a portrait of the poet by Jules M. Gaspard, the Roycroft artist.

It is not known when Hunter commenced work on this watermark, but it is first mentioned in his October 1921 article in *The Inland Printer*, "The Watermarking of Portraits, Ancient and Modern."

> In recent years most excellent portraits have been made of Schiller, Lord Byron, Pope Benedict, the King and Queen of Italy, the ex-Kaiser of Germany, Theodore Roosevelt, as well as many other notable personages. The late Elbert Hubbard used a portrait of himself in the upper right corner of his letter paper, and as there were many thousands of these sheets made this mark is perhaps more familiar in this country than any other portrait watermark that has been made.
>
> When it is necessary to make large quantities of these portrait watermarks it is the custom to make four sheets on a mold. The mold is crossed both ways with a square wire, which cuts the sheet as it is being couched, thus giving two genuine and two imitation deckles on every sheet.

In this article, Hunter was referring to his wax model of "Lord Byron," not the mould, which had yet to be made. At the end of 1921, Hunter sent his wax model to W. Green, Son & Waite with an order to attach the resulting cover to a new mould. A few test sheets of this paper were made and sent to Hunter for his approval. The sheet measures 11.75 x 9 inches. On 23 January 1922, Hunter sent a letter to Ruel Tolman at the Smithsonian Institution using one of these trial sheets as stationery. The letter also contains Hunter's surprisingly critical comments regarding this type of watermarking.

> The sheet upon which I am writing came in this morning from France where it was made from a mould I completed over a year ago. I have no mill myself now so sent it abroad to have it tested.... [in ink] This is supposed to be Lord Byron. I do not think he would feel flattered; but then I do not regard these watermarked portraits as artistic as the material is not suited to the effort. That is, I feel it is stretching a point to produce a portrait watermark; the medium is not proper for the result desired.

Shortly after the test sheets were received, Hunter sent off inquiries about having large quantities made. He received quotes for various sizes of paper from a mill in Germany, but eventually, he arranged for W. Green, Son & Waite to handle the order for the paper. They sent the mould to Perrigot-Masure. That mill added the words "ARCHES" in wire in the lower right corner. (The ARCHES no longer appears on the mould, as it was removed by Dard Hunter II before he made specimens of this paper for *The Life Work of Dard Hunter*.) Although no invoice for the paper exists, it is likely that no more than 250 sheets, or half a ream, were made. This paper was included as a specimen of modern watermarking in *Old Papermaking*, printed in an edition of 200. As was common practice, the mould was retained by the mould maker in case it was needed again, but in December 1926, the "Wove Mould Lord Byron" was returned to Hunter. The mould is now in the collection of the AMP.*

PAPER MAKERS CHEMICAL CO. WATERMARK

In early 1924, the Paper Makers Chemical Co. asked Hunter to mount an exhibit of watermarking and demonstrate hand papermaking at their booth during the Second Paper Industry Exposition scheduled for 7–12 April in New York City. He was happy to oblige and altered an English mould from an unidentified source, adding new countermarks for souvenir sheets. On the left half of the paper, the watermark reads: COMPLIMENTS OF / device (irregular shape with CHEMICALS inside) / PAPER MAKERS CHEMICAL COMPANY / WESTERN PAPER MAKERS CHEMICAL CO / NEW YORK / 1924. On the right half, it reads: DARD HUNTER / device (Britannia with Crown) / HAND MADE PAPER. (The only reproduction of this watermark is the right half,

Stone/Dugal #47; with some alterations, it is probably the same paper as Hunter N; Stone/Dugal #46 and #50. A full, unprinted sheet, 12.75 x 20.75 inches, is in the AMP.*

HARRY WORCESTER SMITH

By 1926, Hunter had received many requests from prominent and not-so-prominent people for watermark portraiture. These requests invariably followed the person having seen Hunter's portrait stationery. With one exception, however, all failed to follow through once the cost estimates were received. The exception was Harry Worcester Smith. In July 1926, Smith accepted Hunter's quote of $500 for the watermark and mould, and between $25 to 30 per ream for the paper, 11.25 x 8.75 inches. Smith was a wealthy gentleman and an important inventor in the textile industry, as well as a financier, sportsman, and author.

He had a series of photographs taken and sent to Hunter. A pose show-ing Smith in profile dressed in a coat and tie was selected and sent to Paris to Paul Couvez, one of Europe's most respected makers of "filigranes artis-tiques." A few sample sheets were made from the trial watermark and sent to Hunter for his approval. The only known image of this first watermark appears in an undated photograph of Hunter holding the sheet up to the library windows at Mountain House. Hunter sent a sheet to Smith, who con-sidered the pose and dress too formal. In September 1927, Smith sent Hunter another series of photographs, with a note that he preferred the one posed casually in an open-necked shirt (obviously Smith was a man comfortable with himself and his position in life). Hunter sent this photograph to Couvez, who modeled a second watermark. Trial sheets were made, which received approval from both Smith and Hunter. Hunter drew the lettering for Smith's full name, positioned along the top edge, in a round version of his Viennese style. In the lower right corner, Hunter signed it D.H. (Hunter nr; Stone/Dugal #31).

W. Green, Son & Waite in London were prepared to make the hand mould in July 1928 as per Hunter's order, but Couvez instructed Perrigot-Masure to make the mould. When the mistake was discovered, the cover was removed from the French mould and sent to the English mould makers, who sewed it to their mould. There is no period after the H of D.H., and it was probably lost when the cover was removed from the first mould. The period is neither present on any of the watermarked paper examined by this author nor on the mould, although its sewing holes can be clearly seen.

It was almost a year later, in May 1929, when Papeteries d'Arches finally billed Hunter for twenty-six reams of the Smith paper. As Smith ordered only twenty, Hunter kept six reams for his own use. The mould is now in the AMP.*

HUNTER COAT OF ARMS

(plate 91) The last light-and-shade watermark executed by Hunter was for his family's coat of arms. Rather than for stationery, however, it is likely that this sheet was to be a sample of one of the many services the not-yet-functioning Lime Rock mill could provide. In March 1928, Hunter was having problems electrotyping the wax model, and he asked the Van Bolt-Kreber Co. in Columbus, Ohio, if he could make dies from plaster casts of the wax models. Even though the answer was yes, he ordered copper male and female dies from the company in June.†

Once the dies were made, Hunter embossed a wove screen and temporarily whipstitched it to a mould to make trial sheets. A few of these specimen sheets were recently discovered in the Melbert B. Cary Graphic Arts Collection at the Rochester Institute of Technology, and the marks made by the temporary stitches can be easily seen.‡ This paper measures 9.5 x 13.5 inches, and the tall watermark is positioned horizontally on the paper. The RIT papers are cream color, and the formation is very uneven although the fiber length is relatively short. Perhaps Hunter made these sheets in his new mill in 1930 to test out the watermark, but he did not like the horizontal orientation of the image on the mould. He either cut down the cover to make it vertical, or made another cover and sewed it to another mould. A few more sheets, measuring 10.5 x 7.75 inches, were formed on this second cover. After troubles began at the mill, the mould was set aside. The Coat of Arms was made as both a dark image against a light background (see plate 91), or vice versa by inverting the cover so that the high points are reversed, creating a light image against a dark background.

No further mention was made of this watermark until January 1932, when Hunter received a letter from Paul Couvez thanking him for sending the sketch of the Coat of Arms. Couvez included a quote for paper made from *his* watermark, along with the suggestion that the height of the sketched image be reduced from ca. 6.75 to 5 inches. He also confirmed that the words "Dard Hunter" were to be added to the scroll at the bottom of the image. However, no evidence has been found to indicate that Couvez ever modeled this watermark.

MATURE PORTRAIT

(plate 92) Perhaps prompted by Harry Worcester Smith's order, in 1927 Hunter decided to update his own portrait. He was no longer the long-haired bohemian pictured in his watermark stationery, but a respected author and scholar; it was time to reflect that in his correspondence. Interestingly, he did not contact Couvez to do his portrait, probably because the French artist was too expensive. Among other people recommended to him was a German, Andreas Kufferath of Mariaweiler, near Durën. Hunter had several photographs taken by John Hathaway of Chillicothe and sent them to Kufferath in March 1928 for an estimate. Kufferath's price was $225 for the watermark and mould, which Hunter approved in October. The first attempt was a three-quarter view of Hunter's head and shoulders, the wax of which Kufferath forwarded in December 1928, together with a revised quote of $175 for a completed mould.*

In June 1929, Hunter wrote that the wax did not look enough like him. Kufferath had already started a second wax using the same view and had also asked another artist to make a third wax from one of Hunter's other photographs, a profile. As soon as these waxes were finished, Kufferath had some trial sheets made for Hunter's approval. In October, Kufferath acknowledged the receipt of yet another photograph, and he wanted to know how Hunter liked the paper samples he had already sent. The very small number of sheets made by Kufferath indicate that Hunter rejected both. A profile made either by Kufferath or by the unidentified artist proved the most acceptable. Extant are a few trial sheets, measuring 13.25 x 10.5 inches, made in a variety of paper colors: a warm and a cool grey, and cream.† Hunter gave a few of the trial sheets to close friends as souvenirs. However, as no further correspondence has been found relating to this watermark, it appears that it did not please Hunter enough to warrant an investment in the mould or paper.

COLORED "WATERMARKS"

Intrigued by Sir William Congreve's work in the early nineteenth century, in which he developed techniques to watermark currency papers so that they could not be counterfeited, Hunter decided to experiment similarly. Actually, Hunter had already "played" with two Congreve techniques—double couching and stenciling—when he experimented with the Paper-making Commemorative mould. To further familiarize himself, he experimented with a third variation of Congreve's processes in 1928. Photographing a variety of images, from coats of arms to his printer's mark from *Primitive Papermaking*, he had line etchings made. He then printed these in black ink on tissue. Each was colored by hand with waterproof inks or colored pencils. Once the medium was dry, the tissue was then moistened to expand it and laid onto a freshly couched, thin, white sheet. A second sheet was then formed and couched over the first sheet, sandwiching the "watermark." Once the paper was pressed and dried, the "watermark" is somewhat visible in normal light, but more easily seen in transmitted light. In the AMP, there are five versions of these "watermarks" (Hunter nr; Stone/Dugal #35–39). While intended primarily as experiments, these "watermarks" would have been marketable as stationery, although very labor-intensive and expensive. It is not known if such services were offered, and if so, if any orders were received and filled by the Lime Rock mill.

LIME ROCK MILL MOULDS AND WATERMARKS
(plates 85, 93-97) Most of the moulds used at the Lime Rock mill came from the Palmer Mill in Downton, England. In 1920, Hunter made a list of Palmer Mill moulds on the back of a letter. The names and sizes of the moulds were (in inches, width x height): sheet & half: 25.25 x 14.25; sheet & half: 23 x 13.5; medium: 22 x 17.75; double cap: 27 x 17⅛; [illegible]: 24⅜ x 19.75; note foolscap: 17 x 13.5; and double demy: 32⅛ x 20. It is not certain whether this was a complete inventory of the Palmer Mill moulds he purchased; there might have been others.

Most of the papers made at the Lime Rock mill have image watermarks in the center of the right half. These existed on the original Palmer Mill—and possibly other—moulds. These images were traditional English symbols that indicated paper sizes: Britannia (a woman with a spear in one hand and an olive branch in the other, enthroned on a war wagon upon the sea, and all enclosed in an oval usually topped with a crown); a shield topped by a fleur-de-lis; and a fleur-de-lis in a shield topped by a crown.

New countermarks—words and dates—were applied both to the left and right halves of the moulds in different combinations: DARD HUNTER, HAND MADE, SUPERFINE, LIME ROCK CT, and 1930. When the mill went into receivership in 1931, Hunter's name was removed from the moulds along with some of the image watermarks. The countermark HAND MADE was often retained, or new countermarks were made and attached to otherwise plain moulds (Hunter A, D–L, O–R, AA–EE; Stone/Dugal #7, 9–12, 14, 21, 23–24, 45–47, 50).

The most distinctive of the Lime Rock watermarks—and one probably made by Hunter himself—was made in wire in the shape of a greyhound from the Hunter coat of arms with a dagger (Hunter II called it a cloverleaf)—poised on the back of the animal and a lively *DH* to the right. The laid wires of this modern laid mould were thicker and more widely spaced than on other covers, and the resulting sheet has more character than any of the other papers made at Lime Rock. In a letter from dandy-roll manufacturers Jos. J. Plank, dated 30 March 1928, a reference is made to this design: "Wonder how the 'DOG' design would appear if made in your stock and with your mould." This suggests that Hunter may have designed the Dog and Dagger watermark for the Plank company to attach to an exhibition dandy-roll. If this was the case, Plank may have made an additional watermark that was attached to a newly woven laid mould cover. In any case, many reams of paper were formed on this mould, as well as envelopes (Hunter M; Stone/Dugal #13). The whereabouts of the mould and watermark are unknown.

During 1930, Hunter, with help from George Moore, made a number of custom watermarks, in light-and-shade and wire, for personalized stationery. They include ones for Edith: ECH, two designs; Beach: HB; William Edwin Rudge: printer's mark (?), 1873; artist Troy Kinney: TK; Pynson Printers: printer's mark, Mercury and Pegasus; and Roycroft: trademark, the cross and orb (Hunter S–Y; Stone/Dugal #15–20, 22, 44, 49).

In addition, two sisters, Mrs. Metcalf and Mrs. Sharp, from Providence, Rhode Island, ordered stationery for their husbands' Christmas presents (LDSM and HDS, respectively). In early November 1930, Hunter was finishing up these light-and-shade watermarks, and Carmelita Gomez attached them to the moulds. The paper still had to be made, sized, and plated in time for the holidays, and at the last minute, John Rogers-King drove to Providence to deliver part of the orders.

The names of the papers produced at the Lime Rock mill varied according to the mould used, the color, sizing, and the final surface finish, e.g., plated vs. not plated. Local town and village names were used such as Salisbury, Norfolk, Taconic, Sharon, Lenox, Stockbridge, and for old time's sake, Marlborough.

While some of the Lime Rock moulds are in the collection of the AMP, the whereabouts of others are unknown.

WATERMARKS USED FOR *Papermaking by Hand in America*

The papers used in Hunter's last Mountain House Press book were made at the Lime Rock mill on a variety of moulds (see Appendix C). The facsimile watermark and document illustration papers were made by Dard Jr. in the museum at MIT in 1946 and 1947. In order to make the facsimile watermarks, Dard Jr. substantially altered moulds (possibly those used at Lime Rock and whose whereabouts are unknown). However, one of the moulds employed to make paper for a number of the document facsimiles still exists in the AMP. It measures approximately 13.5 x 16 inches. The antique laid mould is in four sections, presently with no tearing wires, with a script *DH* watermark in the center of each section (Hunter nr; Stone/Dugal nr).

Appendix C
A Descriptive Bibliography

The following bibliography consists of all of the books published by Dard Hunter and the Mountain House Press: 1915–1950. At the end of this appendix, the reader will also find descriptions of four important books that were written by Hunter and published by others. These include the two Pynson Printers books designed by Elmer Adler, Hunter's first autobiography designed by Bruce Rogers, and his second autobiography designed by Rudolph Ruzicka.

Notes:
- Unless otherwise noted, the author of the following books is Dard Hunter.
- All dimensions are given in inches, height x width.
- A slash / in a caption, watermark, or stamp denotes that what follows it is on the next line or in a space below.
- Many of the watermarks are illustrated in both Dard Hunter II, *The Life Work of Dard Hunter*, Volume 2 and in Douglas B. Stone and Hardev S. Dugal, *The Dard Hunter Collection at the Institute of Paper Chemistry I. Dard Hunter Watermarks*. As Stone/Dugal is more accessible, it is referenced below; also see Appendix B.
- Dard Hunter signed all of the books made at his press in Chillicothe, Ohio, on the colophon page. None of the Marlborough books examined by this author were signed.
- At the beginning and end of every book, there are a number of un-printed pages, called endpapers; these are not included in the descriptive bibliography.
- The predominate color of printing ink is black. Other colors are noted when used.
- The binding described is the one that appeared on most copies in the edition. Special bindings are described where appropriate.
- Hunter's primary binder was Peter Franck, who often signed his work with a black stamp featuring a reversed *P* conjoined with *F* within a triangle.
- Side paper is a term that Hunter and Franck used; a more common term is cover paper.
- They also used the term back instead of spine; to avoid confusion, spine is used below.

MARLBOROUGH-ON-HUDSON, NEW YORK

William Aspenwall Bradley

The Etching of Figures (plates 51, 52, 55)

Publisher; imprint: Chicago Society of Etchers; Dard Hunter

Year of publication: 1915 (colophon: MCMXV–MCMXVI; distributed March 1916)

Printer's mark: none

Typeface: Dard Hunter Sr.

Printer: Dard Hunter Sr.

Format: quarto

Text paper: off-white, antique laid and modern laid, ca. 16.5 x 23.5

Watermarks: DH-in-a-heart in one corner (parallel to chain lines), seal of Chicago Society of Etchers in diagonally opposite corner

Mill: Dard Hunter's Mill, Marlborough-on-Hudson, NY

Frontispiece: *Torah* by William Auerbach Levy, etching on Japan vellum?

Front matter: title page, foreword (2 pages)

Pages of text: 7

Back matter: colophon

Illustrations: line etchings: 2 (title page, label)

Original specimens: none

Edition: 250

Price: copies distributed as 1915 keepsake to members of CSE, $5 to non-members

Binder: Oakwood Binders, Pittsfield, Massachusetts (Sterling Lord and Peter Franck)

Binding: One-quarter vellum with side papers; label: on cover, printed in red; spine titling: none

Side papers: commercial handmade, gray, laid

Enclosure: none

Prospectus: none found

Comments: Accompanying the book was a notice from Oakwood Binders announcing the availability of a permanent binding designed by Hunter: full limp vellum with linen ties at extra cost of $10.00. This notice was was printed in brown ink on beige, wove paper, probably by the Roycroft job press. "List of Active Members of Chicago Society of Etchers" was also inserted. The list was printed at the Roycroft on laid paper, watermarked: Roycroft Made in Italy.

Frank Weitenkampf

The Etching of Contemporary Life (plates 51, 52, 56)

Publisher; imprint: Chicago Society of Etchers; Dard Hunter

Year of publication: 1916
Printer's mark: none
Typeface: Dard Hunter Sr.
Printer: Dard Hunter Sr.
Format: quarto
Text paper: off-white, antique laid, ca. 16.5 x 23.5. (It is possible that earlier modern laid paper might be found in this book.)
Watermarks: DH-in-a-heart in one corner (parallel to chain lines), seal of Chicago Society of Etchers in diagonally opposite corner
Mill: Dard Hunter's Mill, Marlborough-on-Hudson, NY
Frontispiece: *Our Neighbor's Yard* by Ernest D. Roth, etching on Japanese medium weight paper
Front matter: title page, foreword
Pages of text: 7, no pagination
Back matter: colophon
Illustrations: line etchings: 4 (title page, label, chapter heading, initial *A*)
Original specimens: none
Edition: 250 (number of etchings made was 270)
Price: copies distributed as 1916 keepsake to members of CSE, $5 to non-members
Binding: one-quarter vellum with side papers; label: on cover, printed in red; lettering: none
Side papers: commercial handmade, brown, laid
Enclosure: none
Prospectus: none found
Comments: Accompanying the book was a notice from Oakwood Binders announcing the availability of a permanent binding designed by Hunter: full brown pigskin, blind stamped on front and spine, finished with blind tooling; with slipcase [box] at extra cost of $10.00. The notice was printed in black ink on white wove paper, possibly by the Roycroft job press. The press might have also printed the inserted "List of Active Members of Chicago Society of Etchers 1916" on wove paper, no watermark.

Bertha E. Jaques
[*J.C. Vondrous Folio*] (plates 51, 52, 57)
Publisher; imprint: Chicago Society of Etchers; none [Dard Hunter]
Year of publication: 1917
Printer's mark: none
Typeface: Dard Hunter Sr.

Printer: Dard Hunter Sr.

Format: folio (from half of a full sheet)

Text paper: off-white, antique laid, ca. 16.5 x 23.5

Watermarks: DH-in-a-heart in one corner (parallel to chain lines), seal of Chicago Society of Etchers in diagonally opposite corner

Mill: Dard Hunter's Mill, Marlborough-on-Hudson, NY

Frontispiece: *The Old Town [Prague] Bridge Tower* by J.C. Vondrous, etching on wove, machine-made? paper

Front matter: none

Pages of text: 2, no pagination

Back matter: none

Illustrations: line etchings: 2 (initial *T* plus first two lines of text, tailpiece)

Original specimens: none

Edition: 250

Price: unknown

Binder: none

Binding: none

Enclosure: none, see Comments below

Prospectus: none found

Comments: According to 25 September 1917 letter from Jaques to Hunter, "[The etching] is to be matted, enclosed in a heavy paper folder stamped with the seal of our Society, and enclosed with the etching will be a very brief account of the etcher and his work." This author has examined only two copies of the *Folio* and only one of Vondrous's etchings; neither had the original mat or folder.

CHILLICOTHE, OHIO

Old Papermaking (plates 60, 62)

Publisher; imprint: Dard Hunter; none

Year of publication: 1923

Printer's mark: Bull's Head & Branch, three leaves

Typeface: Dard Hunter Sr.

Printer: Dard Hunter Sr.

Format: quarto

Text paper: white, antique laid, ca. 16.5 x 23.5

Watermark: 1922 Branch

Mill: J. Barcham Green, Hayle Mill, Maidstone, Kent, England

Frontispiece: *Dard Hunter's Mill* by Ralph M. Pearson, August 1914, photogravure based on the original etching

Front matter: half title, dedication, title page, copyright, colophon, preface (2 pages), contents (2 pages)

Pages of text: 104
Back matter: none
Illustrations: line etchings: 78 (most of the ones not printed with the text are in color); photographs: 7
Illustration papers: watermarks and mills: DH-in-a-heart watermark, Marlborough Mill; VOJTECH PREISSIG DARD HUNTER [a squat brick house with a prominent roof line] 1922, see Stone/Dugal #33 and Appendix B, antique laid, Hayle Mill; no watermark, Japan vellum, mill unknown; no watermark, modern laid, mill unknown
Original specimens: paper: 11
Edition: 200
Price: $25
Binder: Supervised by Charles Youngers, Roycroft bindery, East Aurora, NY
Binding: Three-quarter text paper with paste papers; label: none; spine titling: printed in black
Side papers: Paste papers by Hunter in a variety of colors: blue, reddish-pink, green, and purple
Enclosure: Two-piece box covered in text paper; label: red-brown ink on Japan vellum
Prospectus: quarto, text paper, printed by Norman T.A. Munder

The Literature of Papermaking 1390–1800 (plate 60)
Publisher; imprint: Dard Hunter; none
Year of publication: 1925
Printer's mark: Bull's Head & Branch, four leaves
Typeface: Dard Hunter Sr.
Printer: Dard Hunter Sr.
Format: folio
Text paper: white, antique laid, ca. 16.5 x 23.5
Watermark: 1922 Branch
Mill: J. Barcham Green, Hayle Mill, Maidstone, Kent, England
Frontispiece: *DARD HUNTER'S MILL* | *Marlborough · on · Hudson*, photogravure, based on a photograph by Boston photographer Charles Kingsbury, 1913
Front matter: half title, title page, copyright, dedication, colophon, prefatory note
Pages of text: 40
Back matter: none
Illustrations: line etchings: 44; photographs: 2

Illustration papers: watermarks and mills: DH-in-a-heart, Dard Hunter Mill (cursive) watermarks, Marlborough Mill; 1922 Branch, Hand with clover leaf from middle finger watermarks, Hayle Mill; unidentified, poor quality straw paper; unidentified, variety of old and modern papers

Original specimens: none

Edition: The colophon indicates that the edition was 190. The sales record numbers up to 183, but no names were entered after number 180.

Price: $30

Binder: Peter Franck, New York, NY

Binding: Portfolio, three-quarter natural linen fabric with gray laid side papers, linen tape ties at each open edge; label: none; spine titling: none. Initially, a few copies were bound with paste papers, but Hunter directed Franck not to use them as they were "too gay."

Enclosure: none

Prospectus: folio, Hunter's Large Portrait watermark stationery, printed by Will Ransom

Primitive Papermaking (plates 64–66, 85)

Publisher; imprint: Dard Hunter; MOUNTAIN HOUSE PRESS

Year of publication: 1927

Printer's mark: Bull's Head & Branch, 5 leaves

Format: folio

Typeface: Dard Hunter Sr.

Printer: Dard Hunter Sr.

Text paper: off-white, antique laid, ca. 16.5 x 23.5

Watermark: Bull's Head & Branch

Mill: J. Barcham Green, Hayle Mill, Maidstone, Kent, England

Frontispiece: *The Mountain House overlooking Chillicothe | from a print of 1852 | Dard Hunter's Private Press*, a sepia photogravure based on an original chromolithograph *View of Chillicothe, O.* by James T. Palmatary and published by E. Sachse

Front matter: half title, title page, copyright, dedication, colophon, "A Note . . ." (2 pages)

Pages of text: 38

Back matter: bibliography

Illustrations: line etchings: 42; photographs: 10

Illustration paper: same as text

Original specimens: *tapa*: 22; bark: 2

Edition: 200

Price: $75

Binder: Peter Franck, Mt. Vernon, NY

Binding: Portfolio, three-quarter natural linen fabric with gray laid side papers, linen tape ties at each open edge; label: line etching in brown and black ink: PRIMITIVE PAPERMAKING BY DARD HUNTER; spine titling: none. (Hunter designed a more elaborate label printed in brown ink with a figure in a South Sea Island landscape, but there is no evidence that it was used.)

Enclosure: none

Prospectus: quarto, either text paper or 1922 Branch watermarked paper, Caslon Oldstyle No. 471 (American Type Founders Company), printed by Dard Hunter

Comments: This book was printed in two inks: the normal black and a warm, brown ink, formulated by Hunter, which he called "Tonga brown."

Old Papermaking in China and Japan (plate 64, 85)

Publisher; imprint: Dard Hunter; MOUNTAIN HOUSE PRESS

Year of publication: 1932

Printer's mark: Bull's Head & Branch, six leaves

Format: folio

Typeface: Dard Hunter Sr.

Printer: Dard Hunter Sr.

Text paper: off-white, antique laid, ca. 16.5 x 23.5

Watermark: Bull's Head & Branch

Mill: Hunter's Lime Rock mill, Lime Rock, CT (1931)

Frontispiece: *Papermaking in China | from a coloured drawing by an unknown native artist | circa, 1800 | Victoria and Albert Museum*, photogravure

Front matter: half title, title page, copyright, colophon, "A Note . . ."

Pages of text: 60

Back matter: none

Illustrations: woodcuts: 7; line etchings: 29; photogravures: 5

Illustration papers: text paper, Japanese handmade paper, possibly other Lime Rock mill papers

Original specimens: old paper: 16; bark: 3

Edition: 200

Price: $75

Binder: Peter Franck, Gaylordsville, CT

Binding: three-quarter natural linen cloth with side papers; label: letterpress on bluish-gray dyed text paper; spine titling: none

Side papers: These were made by first coating Bull's Head & Branch paper with a wash or two of waterproof India ink. Using a large line etching made up of a pattern of the Chinese characters for "paper" and "book," Hunter printed the design in "gold" bronze powder ink for the first few copies. For an unspecified number after that, he printed the design only in a Chinese red (vermilion?) ink. Lastly, and for most of the books, he used both gold and red, slightly offset.

Enclosure: none

Prospectus: quarto, text paper, printed by Will Ransom

Comments: Julius J. Lankes cut the large Chinese-style initial *A* as well as the cartouche above it. He also made woodcuts for illustrations of two Japanese plants used for papermaking fibers, paper mulberry [*kozo*] and *mitsumata*, as well as the title and the printer's mark. Previous printer's marks were line etchings.

Papermaking in Southern Siam (plate 64, 85)

Publisher; imprint: Dard Hunter; none [Mountain House Press; from prospectus: The Private Press of Dard Hunter]

Year of publication: 1936

Printer's mark: none, see Comments below

Format: quarto

Typeface: Caslon Oldstyle No. 471

Printer: Dard Hunter Sr.

Text paper: off-white, antique laid, ca. 16.5 x 23.5

Watermark: Bull's Head & Branch

Mill: Lime Rock mill

Frontispiece: *Khoi*, woodcut, hand-applied color. Note: The caption and the relief print were both printed on a lightweight Japanese paper.

Front matter: half title, title page, copyright

Pages of text: 21

Back matter: description of illustrations (2 pages), description of moulds (2 pages), colophon

Illustrations: woodcut: 1 (frontispiece); line etchings: 3; photogravures: 17

Illustration papers: frontispiece: lightweight Japanese; plated text paper

Original specimens: paper: 3; bark: 1; mould cloth: 1

Edition: According to the colophon, "Due to my strong aversion to the monotony of press-work only 115 copies of this book have been made." Of this number, 99 were offered for sale.

Price: $27.50

Binder: Peter Franck, Gaylordsville, CT

Binding: one-quarter black leather with side papers over vellum corners;
    label: none; spine titling: gold

Side papers: printed on India ink-coated text paper by Hunter in red and
    gold inks from old Siamese woodcuts purchased in Bangkok

Enclosure: none

Prospectus: quarto, text paper, Caslon Oldstyle No. 471, printed by Dard
    Hunter

Comments: There is no printer's mark on the title page as this and the fol-
    lowing two books were not printed with either Hunter or Dard Jr.'s type.

Chinese Ceremonial Paper

Publisher; imprint: Dard Hunter; none [Mountain House Press]

Year of publication: 1937

Printer's mark: none

Format: quarto

Typeface: Caslon Oldstyle No. 471

Printer: Dard Hunter Sr.

Text paper: Japanese handmade, "Shogun" heavyweight, 17.5 x 22.5

Watermark: none

Mill: unknown, purchased through Japan Paper Co.

Frontispiece: *A FURNACE FOR BURNING SACRED PAPER*, photo-
    gravure. In some copies, the frontispiece was hand-colored. The caption
    is printed on a separate sheet.

Front matter: half title, title page, copyright, contents, introduction (4 pages)

Pages of text: 77 (includes plate descriptions interspersed)

Back matter: colophon, bibliography (2 pages)

Illustrations: line etchings: 6; photogravures: 8; collotypes: 2 (facing pages 40
    and 64)

Illustration papers: plated and unplated Bull's Head & Branch, Lime Rock
    mill

Original specimens: ceremonial "money," prints, etc.: 49

Edition: 125

Price: $37.50

Binder: Peter Franck, Gaylordsville, CT

Binding: one-quarter red or black leather with side papers over vellum
    corners; label: none; spine titling: gold

Side papers: For approximately 50 copies, Hunter printed side papers in gold
    and red inks on brown, persimmon juice-dyed Japanese paper ("Omi"?).
    The design in gold was printed from an old Chinese woodcut of a five-
    clawed dragon used to make ceiling paper decorations for the Imperial

Palace in Peking; the underlying red design was the "endless world" motif. The remaining copies have only the dragon design printed in gold on text? paper coated with India ink.

Enclosure: no slipcase for the red binding has been examined; for the black binding, a slipcase with black buckram spine and black and gold side papers was made

Prospectus: quarto, illustration paper, printed by Dard Hunter

Papermaking in Indo-China (colorplate 12, plate 94)

Publisher; imprint: Dard Hunter; none [Mountain House Press]

Year of publication: 1947

Printer's mark: none

Format: quarto

Typeface: Caslon Oldstyle No. 471; type ornaments cut and cast by Dard Hunter Jr., see Comments below

Printer: Dard Hunter Sr. and Dard Hunter Jr.

Text paper: ca. two-thirds of the edition was printed on white wove paper, while one-third was on the preferred cream color, wove paper. Although both papers were made on the same mould, the sheet size varies from 15.5 x 23.5 to 15 x 22.75. This probably accounts for the fact that twenty-eight copies of this book are 3/16 of an inch shorter than the rest of the edition.

Watermark: HAND MADE (upper left) USA (upper right)

Mill: Lime Rock mill

Frontispiece: none

Front matter: title page, foreword (2 pages)

Pages of text: 59

Back matter: description of illustrations (4 pages), specimen description, colophon

Illustrations: woodcut: 1 ("Foo Dog" on the title page); collotypes: 18

Illustration paper: exclusively, the cream text paper

Original specimens: paper: 2

Edition: 182

Price: $38.50

Binder: Peter Franck, Gaylordsville, CT

Binding: one-quarter red oasis goatskin with side papers over vellum corners; label: none; spine titling: gold (see colorplate 12)

Side papers: Dard Jr. printed the side papers using a variation of his father's earlier technique. A Lime Rock paper was coated on one side with India ink.* A seventeenth-century North Chinese woodcut was printed with a transparent ink lightly pigmented with red. When the ink was slightly tacky, the whole sheet was wiped with a cloth dipped in "gold" bronze powder. The powder adhered to the ink and was also trapped in the slight texture of the paper giving the black background a warm, lustrous tone. Red halos and green lotus and drapery were overprinted with two tint blocks.

Enclosure: none. Note: Five slipcases were made for Hunter's personal copies. The slipcases are covered with the side papers, reinforced on the sides and back with red buckram and red leather tips at the head and tail.

Prospectus: quarto, cream text paper and white, modern laid paper, watermark: HAND MADE; Caslon Oldstyle No. 471, probably printed by Dard Jr.

Comments: For this book, Dard Jr. cut several new type ornaments some of which were probably designed by his father (see plate 54). Along with the fly ornament, these were often used in pairs to create different decorative patterns for the chapter headings and borders. As the end of printing the title page neared, Hunter changed the design. He arranged a decorative border made up of ascending and descending pagodas and clouds around the title. He also tightened the spacing of all of the elements. Only 24 copies were printed with this border.

Papermaking by Hand in America (plates 64, 80-82, 85, 93, 94)
Publisher; imprint: Dard Hunter; MOUNTAIN HOUSE PRESS
Year of publication: 1950
Printer's mark: Bull's Head & Branch, seven leaves (six on branch, last flutters off)
Format: folio
Typeface: Dard Hunter Jr. (cut and cast by machine by him); poem on page 74 set in Dard Sr.'s type
Printers: Hunter Jr. printed text, Hunter Sr. printed most of the illustrations
Text papers: 1. white, modern laid, full sheet ca. 19.5 x 23.5, trimmed at top and bottom; 2. white and cream (preferred), antique laid, 16.5 x 23.5; 3. white, cream, dark cream, plated and unplated, wove, ca. 15.5 x 23.5
Watermarks, text: 1. HAND MADE, see Comments below; 2. Bull's Head & Branch; 3. HAND MADE USA
Mill: Lime Rock mill
Frontispiece: *The Mountain House overlooking Chillicothe / from a print of 1852 / Dard Hunter's Private Press*, sepia photogravure, hand-colored. (This is the same photogravure used for *Primitive Papermaking*.)

Front matter: half title, title page, copyright, foreword (3 pages), contents

Pages of text: 318

Back matter: index (4 pages), colophon

Illustrations: photogravure: frontispiece; woodcut: printer's mark; cut sheet brass, mounted type-high: all initials; line etchings: 101 (66 tipped-in text and 35 ream labels); photographs: 44 (36 tipped-in text and 8 ream labels; all taken and processed by Dard Jr.)

Illustration papers: 1. cream, beige, dark brown, various weights, antique laid; 2. beige with flecks, plated, modern? laid; 3. white, also dyed; 4. white, modern? laid, badly ruffled laid lines; 5. white cream, dark cream, various weights; 6. modern? laid, dyed with coffee or chicory, probably one of above papers; 7. gray, white, medium and heavyweight, wove; 8. blue, heavyweight, wove?; 9. yellow, wove; 10. pink and magenta, wove?

Watermarks, illustration: 1. *DH* script (four countermarks on the mould, 13.5 x 16, AMP #2817); 2. none found; 3. DARD / HUNTER / SUPERFINE / HAND MADE (left), [Britannia] (right), see Stone/Dugal #12; 4. none found; 5. Bull's Head & Branch, DARD HUNTER; 6. none found; 7. none found; 8. DARD HUNTER / HAND MADE, see Stone/Dugal #14; 9. none found; 10. none found

Mill: probably all from Lime Rock mill except illustration paper #1, which was made by Dard Jr. at MIT or at Mountain House in the late 1940s.

Facsimile specimens: watermarks: 25 (old moulds rewoven and facsimile watermarks made by Dard Jr.)

Original specimens: watermarks: 2 (made on original moulds by Dard Jr.)

Edition: The prospectus states that while 210 copies were printed, only 180 copies were available to collectors. However, the colophon states that of the 210 copies printed, 200 were for sale. It is possible that fewer than 210 complete copies were made.

Price $175

Binders: Arno Werner, Pittsfield, MA (ca. 65% of copies) and Peter Franck, Gaylordsville, CT (ca. 35% of copies)

Binding: from the Prospectus: ". . . [three-quarter binding] in heavy bevelled boards with Irish linen back and corners, covered with a patterned paper composing of type ornaments [by Dard Jr.]. . . . The bound book measures twelve by seventeen inches, the thickness of the volume is three and a quarter inches, and the weight, fourteen pounds." Spine label: paper, printed in red and black

Side paper: printed by Dard Hunter Jr. on gray (and in at least one case, a grayish green) paper in red and black inks

Enclosure: clamshell box in half red leather binding with natural fine linen
  cover, see Comments below
Prospectus: printed by Dard Hunter Jr. on Bull's Head & Branch paper,
  Caslon Oldstyle No. 471
Comments: The text paper watermarked HAND MADE was originally, on
  left: DARD HUNTER / LIME ROCK / CT. / U.S.A.; on right: [a device of a
  fleur-de-lis over a shield] / HAND MADE, see Stone/Dugal #11. After the
  mill went into receivership, all of the watermark except HAND MADE
  was removed from the mould, see Stone/Dugal #21. (Note: Stone/Dugal
  incorrectly state that #21 was a detail of their #10; it is their #11.)

  Franck's bindings differ slightly from Werner's in that the former
  was instructed to inlay a black (or very dark blue) leather label into the
  red leather spine of the box. However, Franck did not do this in all
  cases and many of his boxes display the lettering in gold stamped in the
  red leather. His stamp, sometimes flanked with *D* and *H*, is often found
  on the bottom turn-in area of the inside back cover of the book or on
  the inside of the box.

  Werner used at least two different blind stamps: his full name on
  the leather turn-in on the box spine, interior; and a circle with FINE /
  BINDINGS / BY / HAND in the center encircled with ARNO WERNER ·
  PITTSFIELD · MASS found on the pastedown on the inside back tray of
  the box. Werner's stamps have not been found in the book. This author
  has also examined several unsigned copies.

LIMITED EDITION BOOKS AUTHORED BY HUNTER, BUT NOT PUBLISHED BY HIM

A Papermaking Pilgrimage to Japan, Korea and China
Designer: Elmer Adler (his signature and Hunter's on colophon page)
Publisher; imprint: Pynson Printers, New York, NY; Pynson Printers
Year of publication: 1936
Frontispiece: photogravure, no caption
Printer's mark: on colophon page: Mercury and Pegasus
Format: quarto
Typeface: Baskerville Monotype
Printer: Pynson Printers
Text paper: Japanese handmade, "Shogun" heavyweight, wove, 17.5 x 22.5
Watermark: JAPAN
Mill: unknown, purchased through the Japan Paper Co.
Front matter: title page, copyright, contents, introduction (6 pages)
Pages of text: 137

Back matter: checklist of Hunter's books, colophon, description of specimens

Illustrations: photogravures: 66; woodcuts (by J.J. Lankes): 4

Illustration paper: Japanese handmade, "Shizuoka Vellum" No. 2 weight, wove, 22 x 28

Original specimens: 51

Edition: 370

Price: $36

Binder: Gerhard Gerlach, New York, NY

Binding: One-quarter black leather with side papers; label: none; spine titling: in red and gold

Side papers: printed in red and gold on black paper by Pynson Printers

Enclosure: slipcase covered in "Omi V," a Japanese paper dyed with brown persimmon juice

Prospectus: quarto, on a similar paper to text paper, printed by Pynson Printers; written by Alfred Stanford and dated November 1935

Papermaking by Hand in India (plate 76)

Designer: Elmer Adler (his signature and Hunter's on colophon page)

Publisher; imprint: Pynson Printers, New York, NY; Pynson Printers

Year of publication: 1939

Frontispiece: none

Printer's mark: on colophon page: Mercury and Pegasus

Format: quarto

Typeface: Baskerville Monotype

Printer: Pynson Printers

Text paper: Swedish handmade, "Orebro," all rag, wove, heavyweight, ca. 18 x 23

Watermark: HANDMADE / [trademark: beehive and 1719 in cartouche in a double circle topped with a crown] / SWEDEN, see Stone/Dugal #40

Mill: Lessebo Mill, Lessebo, Sweden (purchased through the Stevens-Nelson Paper Company, formerly the Japan Paper Company)

Front matter: title page, copyright, contents, foreword (3 pages)

Pages of text: 111

Back matter: index (9 pages), check list, colophon, list of specimens

Illustrations: photogravures: 85 (including one on the title page)

Illustration paper: same as text, but plated

Original specimens: 27

Edition: 370

Price: $36

Binder: Gerhard Gerlach, New York, NY

Binding: one-quarter black leather with multi-colored, block-printed cloth from India; label: none; spine titling: in gold and blue

Enclosure: slipcase covered in an unidentified handmade paper

Prospectus: quarto, on text paper, printed by Pynson Printers

Before Life Began 1883–1923 (plate 87)

Designer: Bruce Rogers (signature appears on last page)

Publisher; imprint: The Rowfant Club, Cleveland, OH; The Rowfant Club

Year of publication: 1941

Frontispiece: Hunter's Large Portrait watermark stationery, folded and bound-in

Printer's mark: Rogers's device, winged satyr with a scythe cutting down a thistle with his name and the motto, "Il tempo passa," printed in red on last page; Hunter's printer's mark with three leaves appears on title page

Format: octavo, ca. 8.75 x 6

Typeface: Bulmer

Printer: A. Colish, New York City

Text paper: white, lightweight, handmade, modern laid paper, ca. 19.5 x 23.5. Hunter supplied the unsized paper to Rogers, who had the paper lightly sized and plated.

Watermark: HAND MADE, see *Papermaking by Hand in America*, Comments

Mill: Lime Rock mill

Front matter: title page

Pages of text: 114

Back matter: colophon

Illustrations: none

Original specimens: see frontispiece

Edition: 219

Price: The book was distributed to The Rowfant Club members in June, some copies were sent to special collectors and libraries, and there were a small number of copies for sale at $11.50.

Binder: unknown

Binding: one-quarter vellum with brown paste paper; label: none; spine titling: gold tooling

Side paper: brown paste papers made by Veronica Ruzicka

Enclosure: slipcase covered in a complementary brown laid paper; spine label: paper; spine titling: same as on the book printed in black

Prospectus: none found

My Life with Paper: An Autobiography (plate 95)

Designer: Rudolph Ruzicka

Publisher; imprint: Alfred A. Knopf, New York, NY; Borzoi Book
   (published in Canada by McClelland & Stewart Ltd.)

Year of publication: 1958

Printer's mark: running borzoi against a laid and chain design

Format: octavo, 8.5 x 5.75

Typeface: Fairfield Linotype, designed by Ruzicka

Printer: Kingsport Press, Inc., Kingsport, TN

Text paper: off-white, laid, machine-made

Watermark: WARREN's / OLDE STYLE

Mill: S.D. Warren Company, Boston, MA

Frontispiece: none

Front matter: books by author published by Knopf (note: the first edition
   of *Papermaking: The History and Technique of an Ancient Craft* given as
   1942; actually 1943), half title, title page, copyright, foreword (2 pages),
   contents, list of illustrations (5 pages), half title

Pages of text: 222

Back matter: bibliography (10 pages), index (7 pages), note on the author,
   colophon

Illustrations: halftones, black and white: 58

Original specimens: paper: 2 (Lime Rock mill paper with Dog and Dagger
   watermark—not all specimens have a section of the paper with the
   watermark—and a piece of "spirit-paper" from South China)

Edition: 4,000

Price: $5.00

Binder: Kingsport Press, Inc.

Binding: Full, light red buckram; "label": blue, stamped into the front cover
   and spine; spine titling: gold; head edge: light blue

Dust jacket: light gray paper, printed in black and red

Prospectus: none?

Chronology

1710s Members of the Hunter family, originally from Scotland, left Ulster in northern Ireland for Virginia (eventually moved to Pennsylvania in the 1760s)

1816 Hunter's great-grandfather moved his family to Ohio

1852 Father William Henry Hunter was born in Cadiz, Ohio

1855 Mother Harriet Rosamond Browne was born in Fairview, Ohio

1876 William and Harriet married in Cadiz and lived in Steubenville, Ohio; he was editor and co-owner of the Steubenville *Gazette*; the Centennial Exhibition was held in Philadelphia, Pennsylvania

1879 Wife Helen Edyth Cornell was born in Williamsport, Pennsylvania, 24 March

1881 Brother Philip Courtney Hunter was born in Steubenville, 12 December

1883 William Joseph "Dard" Hunter was born in Steubenville, 29 November

1891 Lonhuda Art Pottery officially began business

1893 The World's Columbian Exposition was held in Chicago

1894 William Hunter sold his interest in the Lonhuda Art Pottery

1898 Edith graduated from Miss Bennett's School, moved to New York City; pupil of pianist Henry Huss

1899 William Hunter joined brother George in the purchase of Chillicothe, Ohio's *News-Advertiser*

1900 Philip graduated from Steubenville High School; family moved to Chillicothe

1901 Philip toured as The Buckeye Wizard and spent the next two years on the road; occasionally, Dard accompanied him as assistant and "chalk talker"

1902 Florentine Pottery Company in Chillicothe began operations; Dard and Philip designed the first circular for The Phil Hunter Company

1903 Ohio's Centennial Celebration held in Chillicothe; Philip diagnosed with tuberculosis; Dard and Philip designed a second circular for The Phil Hunter Company; Dard attended The Ohio State University as a special student, September–November; without Phil, Dard went on the road with the company to California; Dard visited the New Glenwood Hotel in Riverside and decided to make furniture

1904 Dard returned to Chillicothe; made Old Mission furniture including a chair, metal fittings for the cupboard in dining room, and perhaps the Iris Vase; wrote Elbert Hubbard asking for a position as a Roycrofter, ca. June; Hubbard replied in the negative, and so, Dard left for East Aurora, New York to attend the Roycroft Summer School, 12 July; made a book-case, the Papyrus Vase, and a few graphic designs; wrote a long article about the Roycrofters for the *News-Advertiser*, 2 August; spent a month as an apprentice at the J. & R. Lamb Company, New York City to learn stained-glass techniques, September–October; returned to East Aurora as an employee and was put in charge of designing and making stained-glass windows for the Roycroft Inn

1905 Hubbard's *Man of Sorrows* was published with Dard's title page, his first design for the Roycroft Press, January; other Roycroft Press books with Dard's designs: *Rip Van Winkle*, *Nature*, the keepsake for Thomas W. Lawson, *Aurora Colonial Catalogue*, *A Catalogue of Some Books and Things*; Dard designed lighting fixtures and windows for Hubbard Hall and the Roycroft Inn; destroyed the first set of windows and installed new ones (possibly in 1906); his studio was in the cottage at the rear of the Inn

1906 William Henry Hunter died, 20 June, aged 54; Roycroft Press books with Dard's designs include: *Love Life and Work* and *Justinian and Theodora*; stained-glass projects: Emerson Hall lamps, the Dutch Lamp, the Ship Lamp, the Piano Floor Lamp, and the Inn's library windows; pottery experiments: a variety of vases and the Salamander Lamp; Dard, Philip, and Harriet spent the winter in Cuernavaca, Mexico; Dard perhaps made the Salamander Vase there and saw *amatl*, beaten bark "paper," made by Otomi Indians

1907 Dard returned to the Roycroft as the head of the Art Department, January; his new studio was at the top of the Print Shop tower; began windows for the Reception Room, Roycroft Inn, March; Edith Cornell hired as a new Roycroft pianist, June; Harriet and Philip visited East Aurora, July and August; Philip and Clara Ragna Johnson fell in love; Clara visited the Hunters in Chillicothe, September; Dard thought seriously of leaving the Roycroft to go to Europe, September; worked on important graphic designs for *Woman's Work*, *The Philistine*, *Book of the Roycrofters*, *Get Out or Get in Line*, *Catalogue of Books and Things Crafty*, and *The Complete Writings of Elbert Hubbard*

1908 Important graphic designs include: *The Fra*, *Little Journeys*, *Rubaiyat of Omar Khayyam*; Philip Hunter died of heart failure, 21 February, aged 27; Dard and Edith married in Williamsport, Pennsylvania, 24 March; left for European honeymoon; arrived in Vienna, 12 May; Dard visited the K.K. Graphische Lehr- und Versuchsanstalt, June; drew designs for stained glass windows and glass mosaic panel; he and Edith left for home via Gmunden, Austria where they stayed for three weeks, then to Germany, Netherlands, and Belgium; arrived in New York City, 11 October

1909 Back at the Roycroft, Hunter made important graphic designs including: *Little Journeys*, *Life Lessons*, *The Roycroft Leather Book*, *Roycroft Catalogue*, as well as commissioned bookplates; began the Dard Hunter School of Handicraft; *Instructions* copyrighted, March; first ad for school appeared in *The Philistine*, April; made jewelry; with Karl Kipp, began designing and manufacturing a line of copperware; they began collaborating on the Chapel lanterns, the Salon Lamp, and the Chandelier

1910 Important graphic designs include: *Roycroft Catalogue*, *Leland Powers School Boston*, *Manhattan*, *The Mintage*, *Interior Decorations and Furnishing*, and *The Standard Oil Company*; his alphabet and drawing of *Salome* published in French's second edition of *Essentials of Lettering*; second version of the Dard Hunter School of Handicraft—*Things You Can Make*—advertised,

Kipp became a partner; made designs for several German-language titles to take to Vienna; Dard, Edith, and ex-Roycroft binder Sterling Lord left the Roycroft for good and arrived in Vienna, September; with Lord, Hunter enrolled as a special student in the K.K. Graphische Lehr- und Versuchsanstalt, 20 October

1911 Hunter's design appeared on the cover of the *Pacific Printer*, January; Dard and Sterling receive diplomas from the Graphische, 10 February; Dard and Edith arrived in London, 18 February, Sterling stayed in Hamburg to study bookbinding; Hunter found work at the Carlton Studio and then at the Norfolk Studio, April; important advertising for Norfolk included: Green's Wines, Spirits and Cigars; Siddeley/Deasy Motor Cars; Napier Motor Cars, and designs for *Penrose's Pictorial Annual 1911–1912*; Edith left for home and Lord arrived in London, early May; Hunter attended Technical College, Finsbury for a month, taking enameling and cloisonné classes; saw hand papermaking moulds and typecasting appliances at Science Museum; made paper for the first time, June; spent half-days at British Museum Reading Room, summer; Hunter and Lord took a walking tour of Cotswolds and western England, June-July; mother and friends arrived for extended tour of England and Ireland; they and Hunter sailed back to America, November; Hunter started cutting punches for type; began search for farm where he could also make paper

1912 Dard and Edith spent a month or two in East Aurora when he possibly designed the Colgate Company box cover; purchased Wolfert's Roost (he later renamed the house Mill House), an historic house and farm in Marlborough-on-Hudson, New York, May; began building his papermill, summer; began experimenting in papermaking and watermarking, winter

1913 Made stained-glass windows and room dividers for the house; completed the mill; purchased the beater; continued papermaking experiments

1914 Filled small orders for stationery; papermaking and typefounding experiments continued; had letterhead printed with his type; World War I began, August

1915 First article published, "Lost Art of Making Books," in *The Miscellany*, March; commissioned by the Chicago Society of Etchers (CSE) to print end-of-the-year keepsake, March; Elbert and Alice Hubbard perished on the *Lusitania*, 7 May; Hunter purchased a large Hoe Washington handpress; spent the rest of the year making paper and finishing his font of type

1916 Finished printing *The Etching of Figures* and sent it to Lord and Peter Franck, The Oakwood Binders, March; Clara Ragna Johnson married Dard's cousin, Junius Hunter, October; Dard finished his second CSE book, *The Etching of Contemporary Life*, November

1917 United States joined the fighting in World War I, April; Dard Hunter Jr. born in Mill House, 15 May; the Hunters decided to sell Mill House and moved into an apartment in Newburgh, New York, September; Hunter completed his third and last CSE project, the *J.C. Vondrous Folio*, November

1918 Mill House sold, May; Hunter advertised for suitable mill property; Armistice signed on 11 November just before Hunter was to start serving in the armed forces

1919 Cornell Choate Hunter born in Newburgh, 3 February; Hunter family returned to Chillicothe, where Hunter purchased Mountain House, began renovations, March; made stained-glass window of "The Papermaker" for the library; continued searching for paper-mill property

1920 Left for England to tour hand papermills, April; purchased used mill equipment and many pairs of moulds from Palmer Mill, Downton, Wiltshire, May; arrived home, June; began negotiations with Butler Paper Corporation to form The Hunter Mills as soon as suitable property was found

1921 Briefly corresponded with Robert Parry Robertson, English hand papermaker, about working in U.S.A.; The Hunter Mills project collapsed; organized a papermaking exhibit from his collection and donated it to the Division of Graphic Arts, Smithsonian Institution, March; organized a second exhibit of his type-making appliances and lent—later donated—it to the Division of Graphic Arts, August; made concrete plans to write and print a book on papermaking; demonstrated papermaking at Chicago Graphic Arts Exposition

1922 Prepared the printing studio in Mountain House; bought a rebuilt Shniedewend Printers Proof Press; ordered handmade paper with 1922 Branch watermark from J. Barcham Green's Hayle Mill, Maidstone, England, for the upcoming book; borrowed type-making appliances from Smithsonian to cast more type; began printing illustrations, May–June

1923 *Old Papermaking* published; as co-owner of *News-Advertiser* with Junius Hunter, he supervised the renovation of the office building, for which he made three stained-glass roundels

1924 Began work on *The Literature of Papermaking*; suffered hemorrhage in left eye and lost sight, November

1925 Harriet Hunter died, 25 January, aged 69; *The Literature of Papermaking 1390–1800* published; traveled east, stayed in northwest corner of Connecticut, near Lime Rock, for an extended rest; made at least three small stained-glass panels commemorating pioneer papermakers (including himself) and a large panel "PAPYROMYLOS 1662" in anticipation of his papermill

1926 Left for the South Sea Islands to gather information for new book, February; returned home, May; ordered more paper with a new watermark, the Bull's Head and Branch, from Hayle Mill; started printing illustrations

1927 Borrowed appliances from Smithsonian Institution to cast more type, February; finished printing *Primitive Papermaking*, August; Mountain House Press's imprint appeared for the first time on the title page; with Harry Beach, looked for mill property in the East, Lime Rock, Connecticut property mentioned but not pursued; Beach failed to negotiate a deal with the Butler Paper Corporation to finance a papermill "proposition"

1928 Hunter purchased property in Lime Rock for the papermill for $3,000, 23 May; Dard Hunter, Incorporated established, 18 July; much of Hunter's papermaking equipment moved from Chillicothe to Lime Rock, August; Hunter spent most of this year in Lime Rock refurbishing the brick building that he intended as living quarters and a paper museum; conveyed all Lime Rock property except brick building to corporation for $1.00, 3 August (this action was later deemed illegal); renewed correspondence with Robert Robertson, English vatman, and arrangements commenced to bring the Robertson family over to make paper, October

1929 Started work on his first trade edition books: *Papermaking Through Eighteen Centuries* and *Paper-Making in the Classroom*; King brothers—John, Peter, and Hugh—hired as mill hands, August; financial problems began to take a toll on the relationship between Beach and Hunter, from September on; stock market crashed, Black Tuesday, 29 October; Hunter conveyed all Lime Rock property except brick building to Dard Hunter, Inc., December

1930 Robert Robertson and son Thomas arrived in United States, 6 March; first sheet of paper was made at mill, 5 May; Hunter spent most of the year at Lime Rock, and Edith, Dard Jr., and Cornell visited in August; the remaining Robertson family members arrived, August; Beach sold some of his shares to keep the mill solvent, and the name of the corporation was changed to Dard Hunter Associates, Inc.; with George Moore and others, Hunter finished the hand papermaking model for Crane & Co.'s new museum in Dalton, Massachusetts, October; deeded the brick building to Edith to keep it out of the control of the corporation, October; *Papermaking Through Eighteen Centuries* published by William Edwin Rudge

1931 Began work on a book about traditional oriental papermaking and ordered paper from the Lime Rock mill made on his Bull's Head & Branch watermarked moulds, February; Dard Hunter Associates, Inc. went into receivership, 15 May; received the Medal of the American Institute of Graphic Arts, May; received honorary Litt.D. from Lawrence College, Appleton, Wisconsin, June; began printing illustrations, September; important autobiographical article, "Peregrinations & Prospects," appeared in *Colophon*, September; Hunter released from all financial obligations of Dard Hunter Associates, Inc. in exchange for deed to brick building, 11 December; *Paper-Making in the Classroom* published by the Manual Arts Press

1932 John Rogers-King and Albert Stettner, mill foreman, left Lime Rock mill, January; George Moore finished bronze bust of Hunter and was killed in a car accident, March; the Great Depression strengthened its grip on Americans; Dard Jr. enrolled in Western Reserve Academy; mill carried on making paper, but hardly any was sold; Robertsons quit, November; *Old Papermaking in China and Japan* published

1933 Left for Japan, Korea, and China, March; returned home, June; began preparing text for next book; made his last stained glass panel, "Japanese Woman Making Paper"; began cataloguing his collection, August; Lime Rock mill—buildings, land, paper, and equipment—sold at auction to William J. Weber for $2500, 4 November; arranged with Elmer Adler for the Pynson Printers to publish Hunter's book on modern oriental papermaking, November

1934 Exhibition of Hunter's designs and books held at Jones Library, Amherst, Massachusetts, January–February and at Boston Public Library, March–April; bought used English papermaking equipment for Chicago's Museum of Science & Industry for a papermaking exhibition, and for his own collection, he bought used moulds from J. Barcham Green; Weber refurbished Lime Rock mill for papermaking, but nothing came of it

1935 Left for Indo-China and Siam, January; returned home, May; began preparing texts for three books based on the trip; met with George H. Mead about building a paper museum in Chillicothe, December

1936 *Papermaking Pilgrimage to Japan, Korea and China* published by Pynson Printers, May; Dr. Karl T. Compton, president of Massachusetts Institute of Technology, offered Hunter a place for museum at MIT, 29 May (no action taken); *Papermaking in Southern Siam* published, July; blueprints for museum in Chillicothe drawn up, December

1937 Plans for Chillicothe museum fell through; Edith traveled to Austria for an extended trip, summer; *Chinese Ceremonial Paper* published, late summer; Dard Jr. enrolled in the Cleveland School of Art where he continued working on his typeface under the supervision of Otto Ege, September; Hunter arranged with Pynson Printers to publish his next book and left for India, October; Compton wrote again making a firm offer to house Hunter's paper museum at MIT, late October

1938 Arrived home from India, February; wrote Compton accepting offer, 7 February; began work on a new book; Cornell graduated from high school; Dard Jr. and Cornell go on a grand tour of Europe, June–August; Cornell enrolled at Radio Engineering Institute, Washington, DC, late August; Dard and Junius Hunter sold their interests in the *News-Advertiser*, November; Hunter and Dard Jr. inventoried and packed collection for move to MIT, mid-November

1939 Opening of the Dard Hunter Paper Museum, 5 June; *Papermaking by Hand in India* published by Pynson Printers; received honorary doctorate from The Ohio State University, June; repurchased Lime Rock mill for $6,500, late August, and removed some of the paper to MIT; war declared in Europe, September

1940 Paper Museum Press (Hunter's press at MIT) published a limited edition museum brochure, February; started work on a commercial book about the history of papermaking, and Alfred A. Knopf agreed to publish; finished manuscript for autobiography, *Before Life Began*; Adler closed Pynson Printers and moved to the University Press at Princeton; Battle of Britain began, August; Dard Jr.'s *A Specimen of Type* published by the Paper Museum Press, November; Robert Frost's *A Considerable Speck* appeared in mid-December

1941 *Before Life Began* published by the Rowfant Club, June; U.S. declared war on Axis powers, December

1942 Dard Jr. and Cornell joined the armed forces

1943 Cornell and Irene Rider married in Chicago, 27 February; Hunter leased the Lime Rock mill buildings to John J. Cunningham, a retired papermaker, for seven years (Cunningham never lived or worked in the mill); *Papermaking: The History and Technique of an Ancient Craft*, first edition, published by Knopf

1944 Ohio State Museum held exhibit of Hunter's papermaking and printing accomplishments, February–March; received Ohioana Library Career Award, October

1945 War in Europe ended, 8 May; war with Japan ended, 15 August; Springer Films produced *Paper: The Pacemaker of Progress* in Lime Rock mill with Hunter, August

1946 Dard Jr. and Cornell discharged from military service; Cornell re-enrolled in The Ohio State University; Hunter, with Dard Jr., began printing book on Indo-China, February; at Dard Hunter Paper Museum, Dard Jr. made facsimile paper and machine-cast another font of his type for the upcoming *Papermaking by Hand in America*; Hunter worked on the revision for an enlarged, second edition of *Papermaking: The History and Technique of an Ancient Craft*

1947 *Papermaking in Indo-China* published; Dard Jr. packed and shipped the remaining paper in the Lime Rock mill to Chillicothe; Hunter received an honorary doctorate from Wooster

(Ohio) College, June; exhibit, "American Type Designers and Their Work," Chicago; Knopf published the second edition of *Papermaking*

1948 Smaller handpress, Shniedewend Midget Reliant, used at Paper Museum Press, shipped to Mountain House to print illustrations for *Papermaking by Hand in America*; awarded the A.W. Rosenbach Fellowship in Bibliography, University of Pennsylvania; Lime Rock mill property transferred to Dard Jr. and Cornell; cataloguing of museum begun by Ahearn and Lee

1949 Delivered two Rosenbach lectures, April; Cornell graduated from The Ohio State University with a degree in industrial arts education and was hired by Mead Paper Mill, Chillicothe; Hunter received honorary doctorate from Lehigh University, October

1950 Dard Hunter Paper Museum moved to the new library at MIT, May; Lime Rock mill was sold to D.C. Everest for $12,500, September; Adler arranged an exhibit at Princeton to celebrate the publication of *Papermaking by Hand in America*, late November

1951 Edith Cornell Hunter died of heart attack, 2 March, aged 71; Hunter named Harvard's Honorary Curator of Paper Making and Allied Arts, July, renewed every year until his death; Dard Jr. toured English papermills without his father, October; Dard Jr. secured position at Adena, an historic house near Chillicothe

1952 Dard Jr. married Janet Ruth Rea, 10 May and attended the Museum Studies Program at the Winterthur Museum for two years; Hunter spent the summer in England; *Papermaking in Pioneer America*, text based on *Papermaking by Hand in America*, published by the University of Pennsylvania Press

1953 D.C. Everest deeded the Lime Rock mill property to the village and donated the paper-making equipment to the Institute of Paper Chemistry, Appleton, Wisconsin, for its new museum; at age seventy, Hunter retired from MIT, 29 November; MIT began a search for an institution to purchase the museum; with Adler, Hunter made an extended tour of southern universities to promote the acquisition of rare books and special collections

1954 Institute of Paper Chemistry purchased Hunter's museum from MIT for $16,400, 1 July, and Hunter was named director; Harrison Elliott died, 7 December

1955 Cousin-in-law Clara Hunter died, 13 January; Dard Hunter Paper Museum at IPC officially opened, 27 February; Hunter began writing an extended autobiography to be published by Knopf; spent the summer in England and Scotland; flood left the Lime Rock mill buildings in ruin and eventually all of the buildings were torn down to make way for a new bridge

1956 Made his first visit to Adler in San Juan, Puerto Rico, February–April; began to suffer severely from asthma; Martha Anne born to Cornell and Irene Hunter, 7 August; continued to work on the autobiography

1957 Submitted manuscript for the autobiography to Knopf, July

1958 *My Life with Paper: An Autobiography* published by Knopf, October

1959 Cousin Junius Hunter died, 4 December

1960 Edith Cornell born to Cornell and Irene Hunter, 5 March

1961 With Dard Jr., Hunter traveled to Ireland and England, April–May

1962 Elmer Adler died, 11 January; Dard Jr. divorced Janet Rea Hunter, no children; Hunter finished writing his last article, published in *Five on Paper* by Bird & Bull Press, 1963

1964 Made his last trip to San Juan, January–June; made his last trip to the paper museum at IPC, July; Sterling Lord died, 12 March

1966 Dard Hunter died, 20 February, aged 82

1967 Dard Jr. married Janet Case Hill, 28 February

1968 Dard Hunter III born, 11 April

1989 Dard Jr.—Dard Hunter II—died, 13 September, aged 72

1999 Cornell Hunter died, 11 April, aged 80

Sources

The Dard Hunter Archives at Mountain House, Chillicothe, Ohio, was the primary research source for this book

BOOKS AND PAMPHLETS BY DARD HUNTER
Make Arts-and-Crafts Things at Your Home. East Aurora: Dard Hunter, 1909.
Handmade Paper and its Watermarks: A Bibliography. 1917. Reprint, New York: Burt Franklin, 1967.
One of the Most Unique & Historical Homes in America Offered for Sale. Marlborough-on-Hudson: Dard Hunter, 1917.
Old Papermaking and *Prospectus.* Chillicothe: [Dard Hunter], 1923.
The Literature of Papermaking 1390–1800 and *Prospectus.* Chillicothe: [Dard Hunter], 1925.
Primitive Papermaking and *Prospectus.* Chillicothe: Mountain House Press, 1927.
Papermaking Through Eighteen Centuries. New York: William Edwin Rudge, 1930.
Paper-Making in the Classroom. Peoria: Manual Arts Press, 1931.
Old Papermaking in China and Japan and *Prospectus.* Chillicothe: Mountain House Press, 1932.
A Papermaking Pilgrimage to Japan, Korea and China. New York: Pynson Printers, 1936.
Papermaking in Southern Siam. Chillicothe: [Mountain House Press], 1936.
Chinese Ceremonial Paper. Chillicothe: [Mountain House Press], 1937.
Papermaking by Hand in India. New York: Pynson Printers, 1939.
Before Life Began 1883–1923. Cleveland: Rowfant Club, 1941.
Papermaking: The History and Technique of an Ancient Craft. New York: Alfred A. Knopf, 1943.
Papermaking: The History and Technique of an Ancient Craft. 2d ed., revised and enlarged. New York: Alfred A. Knopf, 1947.
Papermaking in Indo-China. Chillicothe: [Mountain House Press], 1947.
Papermaking by Hand in America and *Prospectus.* Chillicothe: Mountain House Press, 1950.

Papermaking in Pioneer America. Introduction by Leonard Schlosser. 1952. Reprint, New York: Garland Publishing, Inc., 1981.

My Life with Paper: An Autobiography. New York: Alfred A. Knopf, 1958.

SELECTED ARTICLES BY DARD HUNTER

"The Lost Art of Making Books." *The Miscellany* 2, no. 1 (March 1915).

"Ancient Paper-Making." *The Miscellany* 2, no. 4 (Winter 1915).

"Seventeenth-Century Type-Making." *The Quarterly Notebook* 1, no. 3 (October 1916).

"Watermarking Hand-Made Paper." *Paper* 18, no. 17 (29 June 1921).

"The Watermarking of Portraits, Ancient and Modern." *Inland Printer* (October 1921).

"A Modern Printer-Craftsman." *American Printer* 73, no. 12 (20 December 1921).

"A Maker of One-Man Books." *The Mentor* (March 1922).

"The Story of Dard Hunter." *Ben Franklin Monthly* 21, no. 3 (March 1923).

"Peregrinations & Prospects." *Colophon* pt. 7 (September 1931).

"The Story of Paper." *Natural History* 40, no. 3 (October 1937).

"Ohio's Pioneer Paper Mills." *Antiques* 49, no. 1 (January 1946).

"Fifty Years a Binder, The Story of Peter Franck." *Print* 4, no. 4 (1946).

"Elbert Hubbard and 'A Message to Garcia.'" *New Colophon* 1, no. 1 (January 1948).

"A Collection of Notes Written in the Vat-House of an Old Devonshire Paper Mill." In *Five on Paper*. North Hills: Bird & Bull Press, 1963.

OTHER PRIMARY SOURCES

Barrett, Timothy. *Japanese Papermaking: Traditions, Tools, and Techniques*. New York: Weatherhill, 1983.

Bennett, Henry H. *The County of Ross*. Madison: Selwyn A. Brant, 1902.

Bradley, William Aspenwall. *The Etching of Figures*. Marlborough: Chicago Society of Etchers, 1915.

Clark, Neil M. "Paper Detective." *The Saturday Evening Post* (27 February 1954).

Crawford, Nelson Antrim. "The Books of Dard Hunter." *The American Mercury* 2, no. 8 (August 1924).

Curtis, Natalie. "An Historic House on the Hudson: The Silent Witness of the Growth of American Freedom." *Craftsman* 17, no. 1 (October 1909).

De Vinne, Theodore Low. *The Practice of Typography. A Treatise on the Processes of Typemaking, the Point System, the Names, Sizes, Styles and Prices of Plain Printing Types*. New York: Century Co., 1902.

"English Craftsmen to Apply Skill in Lime Rock Mill." *Waterbury Republican* (15 June 1930).

French, Thomas E. and Robert Meiklejohn. *The Essentials of Lettering. A Manual for Students and Designers*. 2d ed. Columbus: Varsity Supply Co. Publishers, 1910.

Guthrie, James. "A Note on Dard Hunter." *The Scottish Nation* (14 August 1923).

Hackleman, Charles W. *Commercial Engraving and Printing*. Indianapolis: Commercial Engraving Publ. Co., 1924.

"An Historic American House Restored." *Christian Science Monitor* (20 April 1917).

Huhner, Leon. *Gomez, The Indian Trader*. New York: n.p., 1915.

———. "Daniel Gomez, A Pioneer Merchant of Early New York." *Proceedings of the American Jewish Historical Society* 41, no. 2 (December 1951).

Hunter, Dard II. *The Life Work of Dard Hunter*. 2 vols. Chillicothe: Mountain House Press, 1981, 1983.

Hunter, Robbins. *The Judge Rode a Sorrel Horse*. New York: E.P. Dutton & Co., 1950.

Hunter, William H. *The Pathfinders of Jefferson County Ohio*. Columbus: Ohio Archaeological and Historical Society, 1898.

Jaques, Bertha E. [*J.C. Vondrous Folio*]. Marlborough: Chicago Society of Etchers, 1917.

Lord, Sterling and Peter Franck. *The Oakwood Binders*. Pittsfield: n.p., n.d.

The Mark of the Maker: The Fine Art of Papermaking at Twinrocker. Produced and directed by David McGowan and Laurie Kennard. 28 minutes. Direct Cinema Limited, 1995. Videocassette.

"The Mill House." *Christian Science Monitor* (27 November 1916).

Rollins, Carl Purlington. *American Type Designers and Their Work*. Chicago: The Lakeside Press, R.R. Donnelley & Sons Co., 1947.

Scott, Patricia. "Dard Hunter and the Personal Ideal: 1883–1966." In *The Compleat Bookman*. Columbus: The Ohio State University Libraries, 1983.

Scott, Patricia. Unpublished manuscript, n.d. [1989]. Ohio University-Chillicothe Library.

Stone, Douglas B. and Hardev S. Dugal. *The Dard Hunter Collection at the Institute of Paper Chemistry I. Dard Hunter Watermarks*. Appleton: Institute of Paper Chemistry, 1984.

Via, Marie and Marjorie Searl, eds. *Head, Heart and Hand: Elbert Hubbard and the Roycrofters*. Rochester: University of Rochester Press, 1994.

Weitenkampf, Frank. *The Etching of Contemporary Life*. Marlborough: Chicago Society of Etchers, 1916.

Wright, Helena E. "Dard Hunter at the Smithsonian." *Printing History* 14, no. 2 (1992).

JOURNALS *Alfelco Facts, American Printer, British and Colonial Printer and Stationer, Colophon, Deutsches Kunst und Dekoration, The Fra, Inland Printer, The International Studio, New Colophon, Pacific Printer, Paper, Paper Mill, Paper Trade Journal, The Philistine, Printing Art, Il Risorgimento Grafico, Scientific American*, and *The Studio*.

NEWSPAPERS *Chillicothe News-Advertiser, Chillicothe Gazette, Steubenville Gazette, Cadiz Sentinel, East Aurora Advertiser, Lakeville Journal*, and *Waterbury Republican*.

Notes

People, works, and collections frequently cited are identified by the following abbreviations:

BLB   Dard Hunter. *Before Life Began 1883–1923*. Cleveland, 1941.

CCH   Cornell Choate Hunter

CNA   *Chillicothe News-Advertiser*

DH   Dard Hunter

DH2   Dard Hunter Jr., Dard Hunter II

DHAMH   Dard Hunter Archives at Mountain House, Chillicothe, Ohio

DHRC   Dard Hunter Research Center at the Robert C. Williams American Museum of Papermaking, Institute of Paper Science and Technology, Atlanta, Georgia

ECH   Edith Cornell Hunter

HBH   Harriet Browne Hunter

LWDH   Dard Hunter II. *The Life Work of Dard Hunter*. 2 vols. Chillicothe, 1981, 1983.

MLWP   Dard Hunter. *My Life with Paper: An Autobiography*. New York, 1958.

NMAH   National Museum of American History, Smithsonian Institution, Washington, District of Columbia

PCH   Philip Courtney Hunter

PF   Peter Franck

PHT   Dard Hunter. *Papermaking: The History and Technique of an Ancient Craft*. 2d ed. New York, 1947.

S/D   Stone, Douglas B. and Hardev S. Dugal. *The Dard Hunter Collection at the Institute of Paper Chemistry I. Dard Hunter Watermarks*. Appleton, 1984.

SG   *Steubenville Gazette*
SL   Sterling Lord
WHH   William Henry Hunter

ix   *To be able* . . . PHT, 202.
 1   *His life-long* . . . Patricia Scott, "Dard Hunter and the Personal Ideal: 1883–1966," in *The Compleat Bookman* (Columbus: The Ohio State University Libraries, 1983), 16–17. Published with the permissions of David Stone and The Ohio State University Libraries.
 2   [*The Scotch-Irish*] . . . WHH, *The Pathfinders of Jefferson County Ohio* (Columbus: Ohio Archaeological and Historical Society, 1898), 100.
 3   [*They were*] . . . Robbins Hunter, *The Judge Rode a Sorrel Horse* (New York: E.P. Dutton & Co., 1950), 20.
 4   *Dear Will* . . . Joseph R. Hunter to WHH, 10 February 1876, DHAMH.
 4* Long thought to have been demolished, the house is still standing. Although rather run down, it has survived with few exterior or interior changes. It is now part of a nursing-home complex.
 4† As strange as this story may seem, it happened more than once. Recently, using the Internet, Dard Hunter III located other "Dards" in the United States and asked how each got that name. While most were named after his grandfather, one Dard, a woman, was named after an aunt who had acquired the nickname when she was a baby, also because a sibling could not say darling!
 5* See also Cathleen A. Baker, "The Lonhuda Art Pottery at Steubenville," *Style: 1900* 12, no. 2 (Spring/Summer 1999):53–57.
 6   *Dear Maw* . . . DH to HBH, 5 January 1893, DHAMH.
 7   *when the care* . . . MLWP, 6.
 7   *Dear Phillip* . . . Harry Gladfelter to PCH, 23 January 1894, DHAMH.
 7   *I can't think* . . . Mrs. Gladfelter to DH, 28 November 1927, DHAMH.
 7   *There is* . . . WHH, editorial, SG, 12 May 1883, DHAMH.
 8   *I am fearful* . . . William C. Browne to WHH, 17 December 1895, DHAMH.
 8   *MY BEST FRIEND* . . . PCH, typescript, n.d. [1897?], DHAMH.
10* This house, 46 Highland Avenue, is only a few doors away from the imposing Mountain House, which Dard Hunter bought in 1919.
10† Chalk plate technique: This easy and inexpensive technique could be done entirely in-house. A polished steel plate was coated with a composition of chalk and liquid gelatin to a depth of about one-sixteenth of an inch. Onto the surface of the hardened composition, the artist lightly scratched the design (right-reading). Then, using special chalk gravers, the design was cut away entirely, revealing the smooth steel plate below. Occasionally a blower was used to keep the chalk dust from obscuring the work.

   When finished, heated stereotype metal was carefully poured into the warmed plate. After the metal cooled, the stereotype was removed from the mold and tacked onto a wooden base so that it was type-high, ready for printing. As the steel plate was unaffected by this technique, it could be re-coated and used again. From Charles W. Hackleman, *Commercial Engraving and Printing* (Indianapolis: Commercial Engraving Publ. Co., 1924), 382–83. This is an excellent reference book describing all aspects of print media and techniques, and includes actual examples of the various techniques discussed.
13   *This hotel* . . . DH to PCH, 25 November 1903, from Riverside, California, DHAMH.
13   *COMING SOON!* . . . Pamphlet, n.d. [November 1897], DHAMH.
14   *there was* . . . CNA, 19 October 1900, in the archives of the *Chillicothe Gazette*.
14   *With square sticks* . . . MLWP, 23–24.

14 *had been . . .* Ibid., 25.

15 *Dear Bill . . .* PCH to DH, 13 November 1902, DHAMH.

15 *Am feeling . . .* PCH to WHH, n.d. [ca. 18 November 1902], from Hart, Michigan, DHAMH.

16 *Mr. Dard Hunter . . .* CNA, 15 April 1903, DHAMH.

17 *I don't think . . .* DH to PCH, 13 November 1903, from Oakland City, Indiana, DHAMH.

17 *Mr. Hunter . . .* Brochure, Star Entertainment Course, Young Men's Christian Association, Oakland, California, November 1903, DHAMH.

18 *This hotel . . .* DH to PCH, 25 November 1903, from Riverside, California, DHAMH.

18 *Came to . . .* DH to PCH, 15 January 1904, from Lead, South Dakota, DHAMH.

20 *If you . . .* DH, "Elbert Hubbard and 'A Message to Garcia,'" *New Colophon* 1, no. 1 (January 1948): 27.

20 *The Philistine . . .* WHH, "Ostentatious Waste," CNA, 7 June 1904, DHAMH.

21 *Dear Mr. Hunter . . .* Elbert Hubbard to DH, 21 June 1904, DHAMH.

21 *Daily concerts . . .* Advertisment, *The Philistine* 19, no. 2 (July 1904): back section.

22* There is speculation that some of the family letters from this period were later taken and subsequently destroyed by Clara Johnson Hunter.

22 *If you would . . .* PCH to DH, 26 July 1904, DHAMH.

22 *[The Roycrofters] . . .* DH, CNA, 2 August 1904, DHAMH.

23 *I was fearful . . .* WHH to DH, 12 August 1904, DHAMH.

23 *Drawing . . .* WHH, editorial, SG, 17 November 1883, DHAMH.

23* A year after it was drawn, the advertisement for Hubbard's *Essay on Silence* was published in *A Catalogue of Some Books & Things . . . in 1905 & 6.* The cover of the catalogue is a delightful mixture of Hunter's earlier designs, but the row of trees at the bottom makes this one of the most successful designs Hunter did in 1905. In the catalogue, there are several of Hubbard's mottoes and ads, although not all were designed by Hunter. All of his carry his monogram, with one exception: "Special Ukase No. Two to Life Members Only." Although not signed, the lettering style and the hearts indicate it as his. In one of the mottoes, Hunter introduced a geometric border. Its bold lines intersect at right angles to form a framework for the fluid and organic letters, but the two are not at odds. Hunter incorporated these geometric elements into many mottoes years before they appeared in more monumental works.

23† Line etching: The method by which Hunter's drawings were made ready for the press were multi-stepped and an advancement over the comparatively crude chalk plate technique. Using black India ink, Hunter drew the design, much larger than the final image, on a white background, usually a commercially available illustration board. If color was part of the design, he used watercolors. Corrections were made by either scratching out or by over-painting with a white lead ink. Like most artists and designers, Hunter preferred white lead over Chinese or zinc white because of its greater covering power. In many of his drawings where white lead watercolor or ink was used, those areas have turned a dark grey, or sometimes a salmon-color (see plate 27). This color shift occurs because of a chemical reaction that takes place whereby the white basic lead carbonate changes to an orange, grey, or black lead sulfide due to exposure to sulfur dioxide, one component of air pollution.

Once the drawing was finished, it was sent to the photographer who made a negative. If different colors were to be printed, a negative was made for each, using filters. A one-sixteenth inch thick plate of zinc (or copper, if very fine lines were to be reproduced), somewhat larger than the final image, was prepared by carefully polishing one surface. That surface was then coated with a photo-sensitive, bichromated glue emulsion and dried. The sensitized plate was contacted directly with the negative within a printing frame and exposed to light. The exposed areas of the photo-sensitive emulsion—the clear parts of the negative which constitute the black areas of the design—hardened and remained on the plate during developing, while the unexposed, soft areas washed away. In these latter places, the metal was revealed. The plate was then immersed into an acid bath, and the exposed metal was partially eaten away. After etching and removal of the emulsion, the resulting plate surface had high and low areas. After tooling off surplus metal in the lower, non-printing areas and strengthening the higher, printing areas by soldering, the plate was mounted onto a wooden block to be type-high. This printing block could be placed within the text and printed, or printed separately. When color printing, line etchings, one for each color, were printed successively. All of the work to prepare line etchings was done in the Roycroft Print Shop by the time Hunter arrived.

23‡ It is also possible that Hunter made this vase while at The Ohio State University in 1903. The Iris Vase was heavily used, and as a consequence, the glaze has been affected by water and is crazing and spalling. It is now in the collection of the Metropolitan Museum of Art, accession number 1982.311.5.

24* An article in the 3 March 1905 issue of *The East Auroran* reported that there were about 1300 volumes in the Roycroft Library and that five or six new books arrived weekly.

25 *A Roycrafter* . . . CNA, 14 November 1904, DHAMH.

25* Like the Iris Vase, the Papyrus Vase is in the Metropolitan Museum of Art, accession number 1982.331.6. Unlike the Iris Vase, this vase seems not to have been used, at least not extensively. As a result, the glaze is intact, although there are some fly specks and white splotches near the base. In the center of this vase, there are two fingerprints.

26 *In regard* . . . DH to Lois C. Levison, 23 October 1927. Elmer Adler Papers, Box 29, Folder 4, Manuscripts Division, Department of Rare Books and Special Collections, Princeton University Library. Published with permission of the Princeton University Library.

26 *It is a costly* . . . In *Freeborn County Standard*, Albert Lea, Minnesota, 19 July 1905.

27* The Lawson souvenir book measures approximately 13.5 x 11 inches; it is in a private collection. For Hunter's description of another calligraphed book, see Chapter 13 and "Peregrinations & Prospects," *Colophon* pt. 7 (September 1931): [4].

27 *there were eight* . . . MLWP, 33.

27 *When* . . . Miriam Hubbard Roelofs, "The Broken Windows," *East Aurora Advertiser*, 5 February 1951. Published with permission of Gilmore Stott.

28 *conventionalized roses* . . . MLWP, 35.

29 *[Hunter's] pet* . . . Felix Shay, "The Only One That Doesn't Give a Dam!" *The Fra* 19, no. 4 (July 1917): 117.

29* The woman was Dolores Dale Kelly. She wrote Hunter on 7 October 1949 and asked if he remembered a Roycroft girl nicknamed Daley, "who helped [him] fit pieces of glass together" in 1904–05.

30* After the photograph used as plate 19 was taken, Dard Hunter II sold the pieces, some of which are now in the Metropolitan Museum of Art (MMA) and the Roycroft Arts Museum.

Top row, left to right (Roman numerals denote mold numbers): Tree Vase, porcelain, white glaze and unglazed versions, height: 9 inches, on base: [Roycroft trademark] CH; MMA #: 1982.311.3 and Roycroft Arts Museum. Mug, porcelain, unglazed, height: 4.75 inches, two-part mold, on base: [Roycroft trademark] 1906 Roycroft VII CH; Roycroft Arts Museum. Tall Tree Vase, porcelain, unglazed, height: 13.25 inches, two-part mold, on base: TM or KM; not by Hunter; MMA #: 1982.311.2 and Roycroft Arts Museum.

Bottom row, left to right: Candlestick, porcelain, unglazed, height: 4 inches, base diameter: 7.5 inches, two-part mold, on base: [Roycroft trademark] 1906 CH Roycroft.

Mushroom Vase, porcelain, unglazed, height: 3.25 inches, diameter: 13.75 inches, two-part mold, on base: [Roycroft trademark] Roycroft CH; MMA #: 1982.311.4. Although this piece looks quite flat in the photograph, the modeling of the mushroom gills and the stalks are nicely done. Dragonfly Vase, porcelain, unglazed, height: 5 inches, diameter: 6 inches, two-part mold, on base: Roycroft VIIII (partially obliterated) 1906 IX CH; MMA #: 1982.311.1 and Roycroft Arts Museum.

31* Both the Salamander Lamp and the matching ceiling shade belong to Gilmore Stott. His late wife, Mary Roelofs Stott, was the daughter of Miriam Hubbard Roelofs, the only child of Alice and Elbert Hubbard. The ceiling shade was later used on a floor lamp. On the base: CH III. The diameter of the lamp shade is 19 inches and the base is 12.5 inches high. The ceiling shade diameter is 22 inches.

31† In *Deutsches Kunst und Dekoration*, 4 (1900): 342, there is a similar design by Paul Bürck of Munich: a stylized flower on a long stem with tiny leaves. The flower petals are orange, the rest, black; all elements are outlined in white. The designs found in *Justinian and Theodora* were modified slightly and used again in Hubbard's *The Doctors* (1909). Instead of orange and black, this book was printed in red and black, a combination not nearly as appealing as the original. After Hunter left the Roycrofters in 1910, the title page design was used for the covers of at least two small publications: *Pickwick Ticks* (1914) and *The Homecoming* (1915). In each case, the flowers were printed in light blue while the leaves were in lime green.

32 *Dard Hunter . . . East Aurora Advertiser*, 21 March 1907.

32 *I now think . . .* DH to PCH, 15 November 1907, DHAMH.

33 *I think . . .* DH to HBH, 18 May 1908, DHAMH.

35* The letterforms Hunter used in this series were undoubtedly derived from ones in "Behrens initialen, originalerzeugnis de Rudhard'schen Giesserei, Offenbach A.M.," in *Petzendorfer Schriftenatlas Neue Folge* (Stuttgart: Verlag Julius Hoffmann, 1903–04). Jean-François Vilain in "The Roycroft Press: Books, Magazines and Ephemera" states that all but the last volume of *The Complete Writings of Elbert Hubbard* used Hunter's designs (Marie Via and Marjorie Searl, eds., *Head, Heart and Hand: Elbert Hubbard and the Roycrofters* (Rochester: University of Rochester Press, 1994), 50). For volume 20, printed the year Hubbard died, the press returned to the traditional Roycroft initial capital letters. Does this mean that while Hubbard liked Hunter's modern style, his son and successor, Bert, did not? There are other examples of departures from Hunter's designs during 1915. However, for example, after a brief absence from the pages of *The Fra*, Hunter's designs were reinstated.

35 *Philip Courtney Hunter . . .* CNA, 21 February 1908. McKell Library.

36 *Phil drew up . . .* MLWP, 44

36 *Bunny . . .* DH to HBH, n.d. [6 April 1908], DHAMH.

36 *the most graceful . . .* DH to HBH, 13 April 1908, DHAMH.

37 [*The train compartment . . .* DH to HBH, 12 May 1908, DHAMH.

37 *We get breakfast . . .* DH to HBH, 16 May 1908, DHAMH.

38 *Tomorrow . . .* DH to HBH, 17 May 1908, DHAMH.

38 *I think . . .* DH to HBH, 18 May 1908, DHAMH.

39* Metropolitan Museum of Art, Department of Drawings, Prints and Photographs, Accession number 1982.1136 (A–C). The card catalogue reads, "Design for a three-part window in the style of Mackintosh. Watercolor and ink on blue paper, ca. 1909." The drawing consists of three separate panels. On the verso of the central panel is a partial design with many of the same elements of the finished drawing, except that this earlier design consists of a triangular pattern in two colors, orange and a light green. The jardiniere was drawn as a simple checkerboard pattern in black and purple. On the verso of the right hand panel, there are five small pencil sketches of what look to be title pages, return address labels, or business cards.

40 *I find* . . . DH to HBH, 1 July 1908, DHAMH.

40 *people in school* . . . DH to HBH, 7 July 1908, DHAMH.

41 *I would* . . . DH to HBH, 16 July 1908, DHAMH.

41 *I think now* . . . DH to HBH, n.d. [10 August 1908], DHAMH.

43 *Hand-made things* . . . DH, *Make Arts-and-Crafts Things at Your Home* (East Aurora: Dard Hunter, 1909), n.p. [1].

44* An unilluminated copy of this leaflet is in the DHAMH, and an illuminated copy is DHRC #1981.1.4.

44 *MOST everybody* . . . DH, *Make Arts-and-Crafts.*

46 *In Vienna* . . . Advertisement, *The Philistine* 28, no. 5 (April 1909).

46* Part of a listing of materials and suppliers found in Hunter's Roycroft notebook.

47* Information from the Proceedings [of the] Board of Directors, Roycroft Corp., 1902–20, 28–29, Elbert Hubbard-Roycroft Museum.

47† For more on the history of the Roycroft blacksmith and copper shops, see Robert Rust, et al., "Alchemy in East Aurora: Roycroft Metal Arts" in *Head, Heart and Hand.*

48* I am indebted to an unidentified woman for pointing out the two Ks on the occasion of a lecture I presented at a symposium for the exhibition, *Head, Heart and Hand: Elbert Hubbard and the Roycrofters* held at the Memorial Art Gallery, Rochester, New York in November 1994.

49* Among the advertisements in the September 1910 issue of *The Philistine* appears: "Roycroft Artcraft Jewelry . . . All Roycroft Jewelry, and there is precious little of it, is made in The Roycroft Shop by one man, Fra Winchewonder, an Aztec who has wandered out of the past into the present." From Vienna on 2 October 1910, Hunter wrote home, "[Kipp] says Winche's is going. Felix [Shay] has gone." Some Roycroft scholars believe that Hunter was "Fra Winchewonder," but Hunter's comment indicates that this "Fra" was someone else. Winche, or any name similar to it, does not appear in the extant names of the students of the 1909 Dard Hunter School of Handicraft.

49 *He . . . could* . . . Elbert Hubbard, *Roycroft Catalog. Books, Leather, Copper, Mottos 1910* (East Aurora: Roycroft, 1910), 91.

49† Kipp temporarily left the Roycroft from 1912 to 1915 to run his Tookay Shop, which continued even after his return to the Copper Shop. Kipp and Hunter remained in contact, and in early 1922, Hunter designed desk hardware, which Kipp made for the Leopold Desk Company, whose employee was Sterling Lord. On 4 March 1931, Edna, Karl's wife, wrote Hunter, "I have always felt that Kippy should if possible be near you for he needs you. He is really lonely when it comes to congenial or kindred spirits for you know that here in East Aurora he 'walks alone' in spite of his many friends."

Boice Lydell published a reprint of Kipp's catalogue of ca. 1914, entitled *Karl Kipp and His Work at the Tookay Shop East Aurora New York* (East Aurora, New York: Roycroft Arts Museum, 1992). On the back inside cover, Lydell included a chronology of Kipp's life, and he says that Kipp left the Roycroft Shop sometime in 1937–38. The Roycroft Shop was sold in 1938. Kevin McConnell, in his book *Roycroft Art Metal* (Atglen, Pennsylvania: Schiffer Publishing Co., 1990), states on page 22 that Kipp "retired from the Copper Shop in the early 1930s." In any case the Kipps eventually moved to Olean, New York, where he designed metal furniture for the Daystrom Corp. Kipp died in 1954.

50 *Let us* . . . Advertisement, *Craftsman* 19, no. 2 (November 1910): v.

50* Once he arrived in Vienna, Hunter wrote Clara Johnson asking her to write anonymously to Kipp as if she were a prospective student, presumably to see what Kipp would do. It is not known what came of her request.

50 *We did considerable . . .* MLWP, 42–3.

51* The fact that the prints were made from wood blocks, rather than line etchings, was stated in an article about Hunter's work in *The British and Colonial Printer and Stationer* (9 March 1911): 18.

51† A.S. Levetus, "The Imperial Arts and Crafts Schools, Vienna," *The International Studio* 30 (February 1907): 323–34. *The Studio* and *The International Studio* were essentially the same journal; the former was published in London, while the latter was published in New York. *The International Studio* contained all of the text of the London publication, as well as an additional section with advertisements for American readers.

52* According to Hunter II in LWDH, vol. 1, 139, *Im Land* was published in "Wien by Hugo Heller und Sohn in 1909, in a twelve part German serial publication." The published page format was given as 9 x 5 inches. Hunter, using information obtained from his father, also states that all of the other designs were published, including the "Flaubert." To date, I have found none of these Hunter-designed title pages in contemporary books or periodicals. It is possible that Hunter Senior meant that the designs were published as article illustrations in trade journals such as the *American Printer*.

52† The drawing for *Der Kampf* is in the DHAMH. It measures 8.75 x 4.25 inches. The background paper has discolored to a light beige color, the black lines were drawn in India ink, and red and green watercolors were used in the flowers.

53 *Dard Hunter . . .* "Dard Hunter, of the Roycrofters," *American Printer* 51, no. 2 (October 1910): 228.

54 *In my portfolios . . .* Walter B. Gress, "The Modernistic: What Well-known Typographers Think of the Trend," *American Printer* 88, no. 3 (March 1929): 34.

54 *Mr. and Mrs. . . .* CNA, 26 August 1910.

54 *One could never . . .* DH to HBH, 24 December 1910, DHAMH.

55* This information was given to me by Dr. Werner Sobotka, director of the Höhere Graphische Bundes Lehr- und Versuchsanstalt, the present day K.K. Graphische Lehr- und Versuchsanstalt.

55 *I'm not much . . .* DH to HBH, 11 October 1910, DHAMH.

55† In the Graphische's 1910 *Katalog für Schulejahr*, both Hunter and Lord incorrectly listed their names on the forms, writing their forenames first. Thus their forms are bound in alphabetical order under "Dard" and "Sterling," catalogue numbers 12 and 68, respectively.

55 *Nobody . . .* DH to HBH, 20 October 1910, DHAMH.

55 *For years . . .* BLB, 78–9. Published with permission of the Rowfant Club.

56 *[on my return] . . .* Ibid., 81–3.

57* It is known that Hunter made at least one other etching during this period, a bookplate made for his father-in-law, Edward Cornell. It is dated in the plate "1909." During this same period, he may have also made a bookplate for Clara Johnson. This was slightly more complicated in that two etchings were made, one printed in black, the other in orange. Hunter also etched two small cityscapes, one inscribed 1905. However, given Hunter's tendency to inaccurately date drawings many years after the fact, it is possible that both of these etchings were also made in 1909, especially as they depict European streets he and Edith would have walked down in 1908.

58 *Another Step . . . Pacific Printer and Publisher* 5, no. 1 (January 1911). Clipping, DHAMH.

59 *Am much . . .* DH to HBH, 8 February 1911, DHAMH.

59 *I think . . .* DH to HBH, 26 January 1911, DHAMH.

59 *Monk . . .* DH to HBH, 2 February 1911, DHAMH.

59 *To-day at school . . .* DH to HBH, 10 February 1911, DHAMH.

60 *This one . . .* DH to HBH, 7 April 1911, DHAMH.

61* Norfolk Studio, *CH Two Hundred Million Times* (London: Norfolk Studio, 1911), 2–3. This circular is printed in blue and black ink on a light straw color paper. Folded, it measures 5 x 4 inches.

61 *Monk is* . . . DH to HBH, 3 May 1911, DHAMH.

62 *from the labels* . . . BLB, 89–90, 93–4. Published with permission of the Rowfant Club.

62* DH to HBH?, n.d. [ca. 11 June 1911], DHAMH. At the end of this note is written, "This [invitation to celebrate Dominion Day 1911] is from Lady Coscaret, wasn't it just too dear in [*sic*] her to send it. Dreadfully sweet, wasn't it, huh?" Also inscribed is: "HELL! DAM ROT" and "I say so too, SL."

63 *[We] have* . . . S.H. O—, Director, H.W. Caslon & Co. Ltd. to DH, 10 July 1911, DHAMH.

63 *We passed* . . . DH to HBH, 20 June 1911, DHAMH.

63 *This is* . . . postcard, never mailed, n.d., DHAMH.

64 *I am beastly* . . . DH to ECH, n.d. [16 July 1911], DHAMH.

64 *[The] respect* . . . Patricia Scott's interview of Mrs. Van Rosen Barber, daughter of Charles "Cy" Rosen, in unpublished manuscript. Published with permission of Ohio University —Chillicothe Library.

64* Hunter may have also designed the Roycroft Inn's china, which was made by the Buffalo Pottery Company. The geometric design in green and rust has long been attributed to Hunter, but no evidence has been found to support this.

65 *The secession* . . . Edmund G. Gress, "Letterheads and Envelopes," *American Printer* 48, no. 3 (May 1909): 306.

65 *Dard Hunter* . . . *American Printer* 52, no. 4 (June, 1911): 477.

65 *I think it's* . . . DH to HBH, 18 May 1908, DHAMH.

66* Editor of *Il Risorgimento Grafico* to DH, 14 September 1911, DHAMH. This periodical did reproduce Hunter's design for *Penrose's Pictorial Annual* in the May 1912 issue.

67 *Even these* . . . DH, "A Maker of One-Man Books," *The Mentor* (March 1922): 31.

67 *My mind* . . . DH to HBH, 31 January 1911, DHAMH.

68 *[They] were* . . . DH, "Elbert Hubbard and 'A Message to Garcia,'" *New Colophon* 1, no. 1 (January 1948): 35.

68* Natalie Curtis, "An Historic House on the Hudson: The Silent Witness of the Growth of American Freedom," *The Craftsman* 17, no. 1 (October 1909): 3–11. Between the year this article appeared and 1913, when the back of the house was photographed, the hill, into which the two back rooms of the first storey were built, was cut back. Four windows were installed, two each in the dining room and in the library. Arches were cut into the walls, opening up the ground floor rooms. It is not known which of the three owners did the work. A contemporary book and two articles about the house appeared during Hunter's stay: Leon Huhner, *Gomez, The Indian Trader* (New York: n.p., 1915); and in the *Christian Science Monitor*: "The Mill House," 27 November 1916 and "An Historic American House Restored," 20 April 1917. A later article also by Huhner is "Daniel Gomez, A Pioneer Merchant of Early New York," *Proceedings of the American Jewish Historical Society* 41, no. 2 (December 1951).

68 *During* . . . DH, *One of the Most Unique & Historical Homes in America Offered for Sale* (Marlborough: Dard Hunter, 1917), 2–5.

69* This information was mentioned in a letter from Staples to Ernest R. Acker, 22 November 1926, courtesy Mildred Starin. The Craftsman furniture included an elegant, high-back settle located in the living room. A similar settle with butterfly splines, made for Stickley, was pictured in *Craftsman* in 1903. Perhaps as a reminder of their years with the Roycrofters, the Hunters installed a front door knocker, a cast iron sea horse, designed by W.W. Denslow and made by the Roycroft blacksmiths. Denslow—the illustrator of Frank Baum's *The Wizard of Oz*, published in 1900—worked for Hubbard before Hunter arrived; the sea horse was Denslow's trademark.

69† These textiles are "Notschrie," "Backhausen #5226," and an unidentified pattern, all dating ca. 1904.

70 *oak beams* . . . BLB, 102. Published with permission of the Rowfant Club.

71* This stamp was used almost exclusively to identify Hunter's collection of books and papers. Another stamp existed, "Dard Hunter Museum," but this has been found in only one book in the DHAMH. There is also a rare Dard Hunter bookplate, drawn by an unidentified artist (Ralph Pearson?), showing Hunter in a smoking jacket reading a book in his library, probably in Mill House.

72* Specifications of this beater are: tub, 56.5 inches long x 27 inches wide, with depths of 10 inches and 8 inches at opposite ends; cast iron with a red enameled interior; the roll is 12-inch diameter with a 12-inch face, and a 14-inch pulley wheel; the knives and bed plate were initially steel but were replaced by Hunter with brass to minimize rust stains in the paper. Initially, the Mills firm applied a white enamel paint, but warned that it might not last. From later correspondence, it appears that Hunter eventually had to apply the existing red enamel finish. According to the manufacturer, the capacity of this beater was 10–15 lbs of dry fiber depending on the shortness of fiber required. A cylinder washer was also supplied by the Mills firm.

72† Examples of these sheets are in the DHAMH and the DHRC. At the time, Hunter also made inquiries about the price of marbling colors, but there is no evidence that he ordered the materials or that he marbled paper.

72‡ This sketch was found in the February 1912 issue of *Il Risorgimento Grafico*, the copy of which Hunter did not receive until a year later.

73 *Austria* . . . "Europe and Good Printing in the Days of Peace," *American Printer* 59, no. 4 (December 1914): 455. This quote is from extracts by A.S. Levetus whose comments were originally published in "The Art of the Book," a special issue of *The International Studio*, which appeared earlier that summer.

74* Fowler operated out of Kansas City, Missouri. Interestingly, he was the American representative of Lucien Pissarro's, London-based Eragny Press.

74 *I have* . . . H. Alfred Fowler to DH, 13 January 1915, DHAMH.

74 *The Lost Art* . . . DH, "The Lost Art of Making Books," *The Miscellany* 2, no. 1 (March 1915): 6.

76* For example, "Ancient Paper-Making," *The Miscellany* 2, no. 4 (Winter 1915): 67–75, and in *Northern Lights* (1915): 8–12, as well as the third in the series of articles for Fowler, "Seventeenth-Century Type-Making," *The Quarterly Notebook* 1, no. 3 (October 1916): 49–54.

77* Pearson, a prominent Chicago printmaker, first learned about Hunter's mill on a visit to the nearby Elverhöj Colony in Milton, New York. Hoping to buy handmade paper from Hunter, Pearson visited and sketched the mill in August 1914. By March 1915, the etching, which depicted the scene in reverse, was ready. It is the etching referred to by Fowler in the editorial note at the end of "The Lost Art of Making Books."

77 *[You] boiled* . . . Charles Drury Jacobs to DH, 12 April 1915, DHAMH.

78 *During* . . . BLB, 103–5. Published with permission of the Rowfant Club.

78 *It did not* . . . Bertha E. Jaques to DH, 16 October 1915, DHAMH.

79 *[I heard]* . . . Jules Maurice Gaspard to DH, 18 October 1915, DHAMH.

80* Inscribed on the flyleaf is: Dard Hunter 1908. Hunter also purchased two other books in De Vinne's series on typography: *A Treatise on Title-Pages* (1904), inscribed: Dard Hunter 1904; and *Correct Composition* (1904), inscribed: Dard Hunter 1910.

80 *The modern* . . . Theodore Low De Vinne, *The Practice of Typography* (New York: Century Co., 1902), 11.

80   *was the smallest* . . . LWDH, vol. 2, 20.

80† Making type by hand: The first step is to make a punch—a tool steel bar, about .25 inch square and 2.5 inches long—onto the end of which is lightly incised the shape of the letter in reverse. (Interestingly, Hunter's punches are quite a bit shorter than this.) If there is a void in the letter, such as in the *O, P, R, a,* and *q,* a counterpunch is often made, the end of which is filed into the shape of the void. After the counterpunch is hardened and tempered, it is driven into the face of the punch. To further shape the letter, files and gravers are used. Smoke proofs are made to check progress.

Once the punch is cut, it is hardened, tempered, and struck into a bar of copper. This impresses the letter, right-reading, into the softer metal. This bar is called the matrix, or mat, for short. As striking displaces metal and creates distortion in the bar, the matrix has to be justified to make all sides parallel; the correct depth of the impression is established by taking trial castings. Many consider the justification of the matrix to be the most frustrating operation in making a font of type by hand. This probably explains why, in the machine age, only a handful of people attempted it.

The next step is to cast pieces of type, also called sorts, using the matrices and the hand mold. Hunter stated that he prepared his type metal—lead, tin, antimony, copper, and iron—using a recipe from Joseph Moxon's *Mechanick Exercises: Or, the Doctrine of Handy-Works. Applied to the Art of Printing* (London: Joseph Moxon, 1683). The hand-held mold Hunter used was an 18-point one he made himself, modeled after the 20-point mold given to him by the Caslon company in 1911. The hand mold is in two parts. When held in place by a spring clamp, the matrix is at the end of a funnel-shaped opening. The mold is held in one hand while the molten metal is ladled into the opening at the top. Nearly simultaneously, the mold is jerked upwards, ensuring that the metal flows all the way into the impression in the matrix. The metal cools quickly enough so that the mold can be opened immediately, and the rough piece of type with its long tail, or jet, removed. The mold is then closed and another sort is made. An experienced type-caster can produce between 2,000 and 4,000 pieces of type a day.

To finish the cast type, the jet is snapped off and thrown back into the pot. The type is lightly rubbed to remove any burrs. A plane (or file) is used to make a groove in the bottom of the type, which removes all traces of the rough join between the jet and the body of the type. The final step is to dress the type by planing the sides and bottom to make each piece square and type-high.

The letter on the top, or face, of the sort is wrong-reading. The experienced type setter, commonly called the compositor, can easily read the backward letter, but as an additional aid, as well as to distinguish between fonts, points, and/or foundries, a nick is cast into the side of the type, which corresponds to the bottom of the letter. The nick aids the compositor in placing the type correctly in the composing stick. As soon as the stick is full, the set type is transferred to a galley, a metal tray. Large blocks of type, or individual pages, are then tied up with string. As even the most experienced compositor makes mistakes, a so-called galley proof is made. Once proofed and corrected, the block of type, also called a form, is locked into position on the press bed, inked up, and printed.

81   *a freedom* . . . DH, *Prospectus, Old Papermaking* (Chillicothe: Dard Hunter, 1923), [4].

81* In 1918 or 1919, this press was traded by Hunter to Ralph Pearson for a gold ring for Edith, made by one of the Elverhöj Colony jewelers. The press remained in the Pearson family until it was donated to the Penland School of Crafts, Penland, North Carolina.

82   *This book* . . . Promotional leaflet, The Oakwood Binders, n.d. [March 1916?], DHAMH.

82   *In an* . . . DH, foreword in *The Etching of Figures,* by William A. Bradley (Marlborough:

Chicago Society of Etchers, 1915).

83 *full pigskin* . . . Promotional leaflet, The Oakwood Binders, n.d. [December 1916?], DHAMH.

83 *I do not* . . . Bertha E. Jaques to DH, 13 April 1917, DHAMH.

84 *This year* . . . Bertha E. Jaques to DH, 25 September 1917, DHAMH.

85 *For myself* . . . DH to SL, 21 November 1919, DHAMH.

85 *Dear Mother* . . . DH to HBH, n.d. [16 May 1917], DHAMH.

86 *His mother* . . . BLB, 108. Published with permission of the Rowfant Club.

86 *This bibliography* . . . DH, *Handmade Paper and its Watermarks: A Bibliography* (1917; reprint, New York: Burt Franklin, 1967), 3.

87* DH, *Most Unique & Historical Homes . . . for Sale,* 8. Perhaps hedging his bets in case the house did not sell, in November 1917, Hunter wrote to the Fitz Water Wheel Company asking about a steel wheel. At this time, he also wrote to Samuel Porritt & Sons, Ltd., woolen manufacturers in Lancashire, England, inquiring about hand papermaking felts. A notation on this letter indicates that 50 yards of 60-inch wide, type "H" felt were ordered on 24 December 1918. On 31 December 1917, he wrote W. Green, Son & Waite inquiring about a vat and mixing box.

87 *The acreage* . . . DH to "Mr. Real Estate Dealer," mimeographed, n.d. [ca. April 1918], DHAMH.

88* Agreement between DH and Martha Gruening, 30 April 1918. In March 1921, Mrs. Gruening informed Hunter that she was selling Mill House for $38,000. It is doubtful that she got this price because in 1923, Frederic W. Goudy, who lived nearby in "Deep-dene," wrote Hunter that when Bruce Rogers looked into purchasing Mill House, the price was little more than Hunter received for it in 1918.

89* Information gathered by deeds and plat maps in the DHAMH. On 8 March 1919, Hunter bought a parcel of land, Lot 6, in the center of his acreage. However, he could not gain control of Lots 1–30 as the Hertenstein family had only recently erected a house there, and they did not want to move. The street and alley that bisected the other lots were grassed over, and the Hertensteins bought a right of way from Hunter for $1 so that they would have a driveway from Main Street to their house; otherwise, they were completely surrounded by Hunter's property. Much later, Hunter bought the Herten-stein lots, rented the house for a while, but eventually Dard Hunter II sold the lot upon which only the remodeled Hertenstein house now stands. The home of Cornell and Irene Hunter is now located on the lots farthest away from Mountain House.

89† DH to SL, 6 and 9 November 1919, DHAMH. The letterhead, not in Hunter's typeface, reads: DARD HUNTER / PUBLISHER OF LIMITED EDITIONS ON ART AND TECHNICAL SUBJECTS. In addition to his Chillicothe address, he listed the Vanderbilt Studios in New York City (an apartment house owned by friends of his and Edith's) and the Norfolk Studio in London. Hunter remarked to Lord in this letter: "You will note by the letter-head that I am trying to kid myself as usual."

89‡ Henry H. Bennett, *The County of Ross* (Madison: Selwyn A. Brant, 1902), 78. In Bennett's book, there is a description of Mountain House in which he states that it was built by Dr. Xavier Faller. This is an error, as county records indicate that "Haver [sic] Faller" did not own various parts of the property, the house, and the vineyards until 1865.

90 *The library* . . . DH to SL, 6 November 1919, DHAMH.

91 *I have just* . . . DH to SL, 19 September 1919, DHAMH.

91* The Oakwood Binders prospered in the pre-war years. In about 1914, Hunter designed stationery and a guest book for his friends. The Oakwood Binders were also agents for Karl Kipp's Tookay Shop, the Elverhöj Colony, and Dard Hunter's papermill. By the end of the war, however, the bindery had closed. For more information, see Sterling

Lord and Peter Franck, *The Oakwood Binders* (Pittsfield: n.p., n.d.); and Dard Hunter, "Fifty Years a Binder, The Story of Peter Franck," *Print* 4, no. 4 (1946): 29–36.

92 *To-night* . . . DH to ECH, 30 April 1920, DHRC, MS 1, Addendum. Published with permission of the Robert C. Williams American Museum of Papermaking, Institute of Paper Science and Technology.

93 *I told* . . . R.H. Lunnon to DH, 25 May 1920, DHRC accession no. 1988.2267 (Box 98). Published with permission of the Robert C. Williams American Museum of Papermaking, Institute of Paper Science and Technology.

93 *various sizes* . . . F.H. Palmer to DH, 14 May 1920, DHAMH.

94 *a vatman* . . . DH to ECH, 12 May 1920, DHRC, MS 1, Addendum. Published with permission of the Robert C. Williams American Museum of Papermaking, Institute of Paper Science and Technology.

94 *You will* . . . John A. Poland to DH, 11 January 1921, DHAMH.

95* Eric Warne to DH, 20 September 1920, DHAMH. In this letter, Warne also mentioned some designs that Hunter had sent him. Warne replied, "You may call it junk, but all's grist that comes to the mill—or maw—of yours truly." Warne also mentioned Hunter's plans to come to England that autumn to start up another Roycroft!

95 *I understand* . . . Robert P. Robertson to the Butler Paper Corp., 11 January 1921, DHAMH. A transcription of the original letter was made for Hunter.

96 *suitable for* . . . [Mr. Berlein of] Nathan & Berlein to Mr. Quinn, Butler Paper Corp., 10 January 1921, DHAMH. A transcription of the original letter was made for Hunter.

96 *We had* . . . DH to SL, 28 December 1920, DHAMH.

97 *By the by* . . . DH to SL, n.d. [October 1921?], DHAMH.

97 *Books Made* . . . *Philadelphia North American*, 6 September 21, clipping, DHAMH.

98 *The N.Y. Herald* . . . DH to SL, n.d. [September 1921], DHAMH.

98 *an exhibit* . . . Ruel P. Tolman to DH, 11 August 1920, DHAMH.

98 *Beside the moulds* . . . DH to Ruel P. Tolman, 17 September 1920, collection, Smithsonian Institution, National Museum of American History, accession file 66,264.

99 *it certainly* . . . Ruel P. Tolman to DH, 22 March 1921, DHAMH.

99 *I would be* . . . Ruel P. Tolman to DH, 29 April 1921, DHAMH.

99 *All of the* . . . DH to Ruel P. Tolman, 5 May 1921, collection, Smithsonian Institution, National Museum of American History, accession file 66,548.

99 *I well realize* . . . DH to Ruel P. Tolman, 17 August 1921, collection, Smithsonian Institution, National Museum of American History, accession file 67,052.

99 *got it some* . . . Ruel P. Tolman to DH, 13 September 1921, DHAMH.

100 *One is a bamboo* . . . DH to Ruel P. Tolman, 23 September 1921, collection, Smithsonian Institution, National Museum of American History, accession file 67,905.

101 *In a venture* . . . DH to Alexander Green (a Chicago bookseller), 9 August 1923, DHAMH.

101* Some of these early articles include: "Paper for Artistic Printing," *Scientific American Supplement* no. 2119 (12 August 1916): 108; "An American Handmade Paper Mill," *Paper* 18, no. 24 (23 August 1916): 11–13; "Ancient Paper Making," *Paper* (21 July 1920): 18–19; "Development of the Beating Engine," *Paper Trade Journal* (4 November 1920): 36, 38, 40; "Watermarking Hand-Made Paper," *Scientific American* 124, no. 13 (6 March 1921): 248, 259; "A Bibliography of Marbled Paper," *Paper Trade Journal* (28 April 1921): 52, 54, 56, 58; "Ulman Stromer—First Chronicler of Paper Making," *Paper* (4 May 1921): 12–14; "Old Watermarks of Animals," *Paper* 28, no. 25 (24 August 1921): 12–15, 25; and "Laid and Wove," *The Printing Art* (September 1921): 33–40.

102 *It seems* . . . Ruel P. Tolman to DH, 25 June 1921, DHAMH.

102 *It has always* . . . DH to Ruel P. Tolman, 29 June 1921, collection, Smithsonian Institution, National Museum of American History, accession file 67,052.

102 *better* . . . DH, "A Modern Printer-Craftsman," *American Printer* 73, no. 12 (20 December 1921): 36.

102 *You ask* . . . DH to Elbert Hubbard II, 17 December 1921. Published with permission of the Roycroft Arts Museum, Boice Lydell.

103 *Thank you* . . . DH to SL, 28 January 1922, DHAMH.

103 *some* . . . W.H. Smith to DH, 6 May 1922, DHAMH.

104 *The studio* . . . DH to Elmer Adler, 2 October 1950, Elmer Adler Papers, Box 29, Folder 6, Manuscripts Division, Department of Rare Books and Special Collections, Princeton University Library. Published with permission of the Princeton University Library.

105 *Having finished* . . . DH to Ruel P. Tolman, 24 May 1922, collection, Smithsonian Institution, National Museum of American History, accession file 67,052.

106* DH to Ruel P. Tolman, 13 June 1922, collection, Smithsonian Institution, National Museum of American History, accession file 67,052. Dard Hunter II, in 1977 correspondence with curator Elizabeth Harris, concluded that his father had indeed made the composing stick.

107* DH to SL, n.d. [19 November 1922], DHAMH. For a full description of both Hunters' methods for dampening paper, see LWDH, vol. 2, 88–9.

In this letter, Hunter also mentioned "gimcracks." This referred to a request from a novelty store for an estimate to make molded handmade paper lampshades. Because Hunter's quote was too high, the store dropped the idea.

108 *Your book* . . . Burton Emmett to DH, 28 May 1923, DHAMH.

109 *I envy you* . . . W. Arthur Cole to DH, 13 June 1923, DHAMH.

109 *[Old Papermaking]* . . . Nelson Antrim Crawford, "The Books of Dard Hunter," *American Mercury* 2, no. 8 (August 1924): 471–72.

110 *This book* . . . DH, "The Story of Dard Hunter," *Ben Franklin Monthly* 21, no. 3 (March 1923): 56.

110 *'Old Papermaking'* . . . DH, *Prospectus, Old Papermaking* (Chillicothe: Mountain House Press, 1923).

111 *after this plant* . . . DH to SL, n.d. [ca. October 1923], DHAMH.

111 *The book looks* . . . DH to SL, 24 April 1923, DHAMH.

112 *[I was recently* . . . PF to DH, 23 November 1923, DHAMH. Published with permission of Yanna F. Masters and Helen Schubert.

113 *With the right* . . . PF to DH, 16 July 1924, DHAMH. Published with permission of Yanna F. Masters and Helen Schubert.

113* DH to Frank J. Lankes, 25 April 1924. Published with permission of the Grosvenor Rare Book Room, Buffalo and Erie County Public Library. The new mould mentioned was 18-point, purchased from the Küstermann & Company, Berlin.

114* This book was printed in Chicago and copyrighted by Ransom in 1923; the edition numbers 220.

114 *proud to* . . . Will Ransom to DH, 4 October 1924, DHAMH. Published with permission of the Newberry Library.

114 *I like it* . . . Will Ransom to DH, 11 February 1925, DHAMH. Published with permission of the Newberry Library.

115 *I want* . . . DH to SL, 3 December 1925, DHAMH.

115 *Dear Teddy* . . . DH to SL, n.d. [ca. September 1924], DHAMH.

118 *when I* . . . MLWP, 72.

118* This conclusion was reached after the author discussed the circumstances of Hunter's eye problems and his "flying spike" explanation with Richard Lockwood, D.O., Chillicothe and Wesley DuBose, M.D., Tuscaloosa, Alabama. Both concluded that while Hunter was renovating Mountain House, he probably came in contact with the fungus, *Histoplasma capsulatum*, which is carried in the dust of bird droppings. Histoplasmosis most commonly appears in the Ohio and Mississippi river valleys where as much as eighty percent of the population may have the disease.

As the first case of ocular histoplasmosis was not documented until 1977, it is not surprising that the real cause of Hunter's vision problems was never diagnosed. From Marvin Walker, "Presumed Ocular Histoplasmosis Syndrome (POHS)," photocopy, 23 February 1983, source unknown.

118   *Dear Sterling* . . . DH to SL, 26 January 1925, DHAMH.

119   *In one* . . . DH to Charles Brigham, 6 April 1925, DHAMH.

120   *Elliott and I* . . . DH to SL, n.d. [ca. 10 October 1925], DHAMH.

120* The Rittenhouse and Hunter mill panels, each measuring 17 x 12 inches, are now in the Roycroft Arts Museum. Hunter II made replicas of them, and they now hang in the hallway at Mountain House, as does the original Tate mill panel, 13 inches square.

120   *I am making* . . . DH to SL, n.d. [ca. 12 November 1925], DHAMH.

121* In LWDH, vol. 1, 195, Hunter II inadvertently switched the sizes of the two stained glass panels. He also dated this panel 1930; it is possible that it was begun in late 1925 but not finished until 1930.

121   *I do have* . . . DH to SL, 3 December 1925, DHAMH.

122   *Dear Edith* . . . DH to ECH, 24 February 1926, DHAMH.

122* DH to ECH, n.d. [ca. 20 February 1926], DHAMH. Hunter occasionally smoked a pipe. In this letter, he was referring to his success in meeting people on the train.

124* Hunter did not have to rely on his memory to recount his adventures, later published in *Primitive Papermaking* and MLWP, as long articles by him were published in the *Chillicothe News-Advertiser* in the 22 April, 15 May, and 18 May 1926 issues.

124   *I now find* . . . DH to Ruel P. Tolman, 28 February 1927, collection, Smithsonian Institution, National Museum of American History, accession file 67,052.

125   *During* . . . LWDH, vol. 2, 25–6.

126   *What a work* . . . PF to DH, 13 October 1927, DHAMH. Published with permission of Yanna F. Masters and Helen Schubert.

126   *Have been* . . . Ralph M. Pearson to DH, 25 October 1927, DHAMH. Published with permission of the Estate of Ronald H. Pearson.

127   *"Primitive Papermaking"* . . . Katherine White to DH, 22 November 1927, DHAMH. Published with permission of Dawson's Book Shop.

128   *After* Primitive Papermaking . . . MLWP, 98.

128   *SCHEME* . . . Harrison Elliott to DH, 5 November 1925, DHAMH.

128   *something* . . . DH to HBH, n.d. [after May 1917], DHAMH.

129* Harrison Elliott to DH, 7 April 1926, DHAMH. The paper demonstration and exhibit turned out to be a non-starter because of lack of support from the industry.

129   *Some time* . . . Isabella Beach to DH, 17 May 1926, DHAMH. This letter was written on paper watermarked: Rye Mill England.

130* This information is contained in a letter from Richard Armstrong to DH2, 6 February 1978, DHAMH. The letter continues, "After [the Guild] had some orders they were going to shift their operations to Lime Rock. The great depression of 1929 ended all that. Their venture collapsed then."

130   *Although* . . . Harry Beach to DH, 1 December 1926, DHAMH.

131   *We are still* . . . DH to SL, n.d. [27 January 1927], DHAMH.

132   *Even if* . . . Harry Beach to DH, 10 January 1928, DHAMH.

133   *won't you* . . . Harry Beach to DH, 18 January 1928, DHAMH.

133   *the attorney* . . . Harry Beach to DH, 14 May 1928, DHAMH.

135   *Dard Hunter* . . . "Week's News From Lime Rock," *Lakeville Journal*, 9 August 1928,

DHAMH. Published with permission of the *Lakeville Journal*.

135   *the whole* . . . DH to PF, 29 July 1928. Published with permission of the Estate of Georg H.T. Mandl.

136* This beater, made by the Emerson Manufacturing Company, was described in detail by Frederic Clark in a letter written to Emerson's in 1928. The beater was a wooden tub 12 feet long by 44 inches wide inside, and approximately 20 inches deep. The return passage was 18 inches wide and the roll passage was 24 inches wide. The roll was 30 inches in diameter with a 20-inch face. There were 40 bars in the roll. The bed plate was of the elbow type, 20.25 inches long by 7 inches wide at the end. There were sixteen bars in the bed plate with a quarter-inch wood filling. The beater had a maximum volume of 55 cubic feet equivalent to about 200 lbs. of air dry fiber.

In 1928, the beater was refitted at a cost of $700 with the following new parts: a bronze bed plate, a set of bronze beater bars, two new worms and a cross rod to mesh with the worm gears on the lighter bar, an elevating screw, and a cylinder washer with the necessary gearing and elevating device.

136   *I am very* . . . Robert Robertson to DH, 15 October 1928, DHAMH. Published with permission of Mrs. Leonard Godding.

137* This information was reported in "English Craftsmen to Apply Skill in Lime Rock Mill," *Waterbury Republican*, 15 June 1930.

139   *I'm glad* . . . Harry Beach to DH, 10 January 1930, DHAMH.

139   *The two Englishmen* . . . DH to PF, n.d. [ca. 15 March 1930], DHAMH.

140   *It is a white* . . . DH to DH2, n.d. [ca. 8 August 1939], DHAMH.

140* The only place any date appears is in LWDH, vol. 2, 58.

140   *The mill* . . . DH to DH2, 12 May 1930, DHAMH.

141   *The paper* . . . DH to ECH, n.d. [ca. 19 May 1930], DHAMH.

141   *Last night* . . . Ibid.

142* During an interview with the author in June 1995, Gladys Robertson Godding said that neither she nor her mother had worked in the mill.

143* "English Craftsmen to Apply Skill in Lime Rock Mill," *Waterbury Republican*, 15 June 1930. In the article, Robertson said that an uncle of his grandfather had come to America in the 1880s and worked in a mill where paper was made by machine.

144* Apparently Zacchio also made or repaired—it is unclear which from his bill of 29 August—some of the papermaking moulds for the mill.

144   *[George and I]* . . . DH to ECH, n.d. [ca. 10 October 1930], DHAMH.

145   *personality* . . . William Harper to DH, 15 August 1930, DHAMH.

145* DH to ECH, n.d. [ca. 20 September 1930], DHAMH. This letter is on paper watermarked: DARD HUNTER MILL 1913, a mould first used in Marlborough. Other letters from this period are on paper with the Papermaking Commemorative watermark, also made in the Lime Rock mill at this time.

145   *Our great* . . . DH to ECH, n.d. [ca. 16 October 1930], DHAMH.

146* *Quarto Club Papers 1928 : 1929* (New York: Quarto Club, 1930). The paper in this book is still white although often stained with irregularly shaped brown spots, probably due to poor sizing or poor dampening procedures. The watermark, S/D #9, is: (on left half) DARD HUNTER HAND MADE, (on right half) Britannia.

147   *Things look* . . . John Rogers-King to DH, 9 December 1930, DHAMH.

148   *American understanding* . . . Frederic Melcher to DH, 9 April 1931, DHAMH.

148   *but if it is* . . . DH to Frederic Melcher, draft, 17 April 1931, DHAMH.

149   *Beach had gotten* . . . DH to ECH, n.d. [ca. 2 August 1931], DHAMH.

150* DH to George Macy, 23 May 1932, DHAMH. Hunter added to the end of the letter, "I feel, as you do, that there should be a hand-made paper mill in America and I have every reason to believe that in time such a mill will be established." Actually, Hunter had already decided to revert back to his 1920 plan to provide printers with first-class paper by having it made in England. He wrote to his colleague, Jack Green of J. Barcham Green with a proposition that Hayle Mill make paper to his specifications to be marketed by the Japan Paper Company under the Hunter name. Although all of the parties were very interested in the scheme, it was Hunter's inability to make the necessary commitment that prevented it from materializing.

151* DH to John Rogers-King, carbon, 13 January 1934, DHAMH. Isabella King Beach had landed a radio job in New York City, and her weekly salary was $150, a considerable amount of money during the Great Depression.

152 *Now, what* . . . DH to DH2, n.d. [8 August 1939], DHAMH.

154 *It is my* . . . DH to T. Venkajee, carbon, 25 March 1934 (on verso of 20 February 1934), DHAMH.

155* The sewn but unbound books were sent to George McKibben for binding and distribution. Bibliographers should note that the binding of these books differs slightly from the earlier one. "RUDGE" was eliminated from the bottom of the spine and the buckram is more grey-brown than brown. The surplus leather spine labels were used on the first lot of books bound by McKibben, but at some point, another die had to be made to reproduce the label. There was an original dust jacket, probably of heavy glassine; this paper was also used for the later bindings.

155 *Several years* . . . DH, *Paper-Making in the Classroom* (Peoria: Manual Arts Press, 1931), 3.

155 *While the* . . . Ibid.

156* DH to John Rogers-King, carbon, 9 September 1931, DHAMH. It is also possible that Hunter may have been referring to the paper used for an article he wrote for *Colophon* pt. 4 (December 1930). That paper has the Bull's Head & Branch watermark.

156 *I do not* . . . DH, "Peregrinations & Prospects," *Colophon* pt. 7 (September 1931): [1].

156 *One of my earliest* . . . Ibid., [4].

157 *You ask* . . . DH to Geoffrey Hellman, 17 November 1931, DHAMH.

160 *I [want]* . . . DH to PF, 23 May 1932, DHAMH.

161 *[Dard Jr.'s]* . . . DH to SL, 10 August 1932, DHAMH.

162 *While I* . . . DH to F.J. Lankes, 21 August 1933. Published with permission of J.B. Lankes.

162 *I rather* . . . DH to PF, 12 January 1933, DHAMH.

163 *cherry blossoms* . . . DH to ECH, n.d. [1 March 1933], DHAMH.

163 *Yesterday* . . . DH to ECH, 22 March 1933, DHAMH.

164 *it is possible* . . . DH to SL, 17 April 1933, DHAMH.

164 *Yesterday* . . . DH to Harrison Elliott, 23 April 1933, DHAMH.

165 *showing* . . . Exhibition leaflet, 15 January 1936, DHAMH.

166* In 1937, Hunter bought the few remaining copies of *Papermaking Pilgrimage to Japan, Korea and China* from Pynson Printers and sold them himself.

166 *I learned* . . . PHT, 146–9.

168 *I traveled* . . . DH, *Papermaking in Southern Siam* (Chillicothe: [Mountain House Press], 1936), 14.

168 *I consoled* . . . DH, *Papermaking in Indo-China* (Chillicothe: [Mountain House Press], 1947), 32.

169 *The normal* . . . DH, *Siam*, 13–14.

170 *a monograph* . . . DH, *Chinese Ceremonial Paper* (Chillicothe: [Mountain House Press], 1937), subtitle.

171 *It worries* . . . PF to DH, 4 September 1937, DHAMH. Published with permission of Yanna F. Masters and Helen Schubert.

172 *During* . . . CCH, "Recollections of My Father, Dard Hunter," *Bull & Branch* 13, no. 1

(March 1994): 5–7.

173* In her book *Off the Deckle Edge: A Paper-Making Journey Through India* (Bombay: Ankur Press, 1995), Neeta Premchand describes a visit she made to Kalpi, where she met Munnalal Khaddari sixty years after Hunter's visit. Khaddari told her that he regretted that Hunter had not written a book about his journey through India. Premchand was pleased to tell him about *Papermaking by Hand in India*. The old man was delighted. He also encouraged her to write a book about her travels. When she returned to Kalpi to show him the first proofs of her book, Premchand learned that Khaddari had passed away shortly after their meeting.

173 *While this* . . . DH to ECH, 25 November 1937, DHAMH.

176 *In alighting* . . . DH to ECH, 28 November 1937, DHAMH.

177 *There were* . . . DH to ECH, 4 December 1937, DHAMH.

177 *I shall never* . . . DH to Harrison Elliott, 9 December 1937, DHAMH.

179 *If I have* . . . DH to SL, 29 June 1963, DHAMH.

179 *My "museum"* . . . DH to Ruel P. Tolman, 15 November 1927, collection, Smithsonian Institution, National Museum of American History, accession file 99,500.

180 *photographs* . . . "A Dard Hunter Exhibit," *Bulletin of the Boston Public Library* 9, no. 4 (April 1934): 137.

180* One enthusiast in particular was Lloyd Emerson Siberell of Cincinnati, Ohio. Siberell wrote occasional articles about Hunter. Siberell's most important project was to be a complete bibliography of all of Hunter's Roycroft designs and private press books, but it is not known whether he completed it.

180† This property was located in Haines Corners in the Town of Bedford in Westchester County, north of New York City. It was purchased and sold with no developments made on the property.

181* George Mead to DH, 3 March 1936, DHAMH. Published with permission of the Mead Corporation. At this same time, Hunter was corresponding with a real estate agent in Petersborough, New Hampshire, and he must have mentioned his plan to establish a museum. Apparently, the agent related this to the interested historical society and to the town fathers. The parties entered into a correspondence, but the idea was eventually dropped.

182 *The plan* . . . DH to Karl T. Compton, 28 December 1936. Courtesy MIT. Office of the President, 1930–1958 (Compton-Killian) AC 4. Box 11. Folder 1. Institute Archives and Special Collections, MIT Libraries, Cambridge, Massachusetts.

182 *are the Japanese* . . . DH to William Wheelwright, carbon, 28 December 1936, DHAMH.

183 *I really* . . . DH to Carl Keller, carbon, 27 August 1937, DHAMH.

183 *I get a hint* . . . Carl Keller to DH, 30 August 1937, DHAMH.

183 *I have not* . . . Karl T. Compton to DH, 20 October 1937. Courtesy MIT. Office of the President, 1930–1958 (Compton-Killian) AC 4. Box 11. Folder 1. Institute Archives and Special Collections, MIT Libraries, Cambridge, Massachusetts.

184 *Under* . . . DH to Karl T. Compton, 7 February 1938. Courtesy MIT. Office of the President, 1930–1958 (Compton-Killian) AC 4. Box 11. Folder 1. Institute Archives and Special Collections, MIT Libraries, Cambridge, Massachusetts.

185* On the fourdrinier paper machine, the pulp is sprayed onto a fast-moving, "endless" loop of web through which the water drains. The primary function of the dandy roll is to squeeze more water from the wet sheet before it leaves the web to be picked up by the felts. The dandy roll is a cylinder covered with a wove or laid screen. If a "watermark" is desired, several designs are soldered onto the screen. As the wet paper passes under the dandy roll, the marks on the screen are pressed into the sheet; this is not considered a true watermark. For more information, see PHT, 400–8.

186 *The "visiting . . .* DH to ECH and CCH, n.d. [6 May 1939], DHAMH.

186* The invitation to the tea was not printed by Hunter, but he did supply a thin Lime Rock mill paper for it. After the event, he drafted a letter to the unidentified printer complaining about the poor presswork.

187 *I think . . .* John Rowlands to James Killian, 9 December 1939. Courtesy MIT. Office of the President, 1930–1958 (Compton-Killian) AC 4. Box 11. Folder 1. Institute Archives and Special Collections, MIT Libraries, Cambridge, Massachusetts.

188* "A Collection of Material relating to Papermaking gathered together by Dard Hunter during the past 25 years. This list does not include books, pamphlets or photographs as these are listed separately," copy of a typescript, Harrison Elliott Papers, Folder 45 Hunter Museum, Rare Books Collection, Library of Congress. It is assumed that this carbon copy version is not the one Azam prepared. This typescript consists of 49 pages on Hunter's Small Portrait paper. It describes 578 items. Although undated, one of the last entries is a description of 18 examples of decorated endpapers given to the collection by Peter Franck in September 1940.

189* See also Cathleen A. Baker, "The Typefaces of Dard Hunter, Senior and Junior," *American Proprietary Typefaces*, ed. by David Pankow (New York: American Printing History Association, 1998). It should be noted that this article was written in early 1995 and much additional material about Hunter Jr.'s typeface was subsequently discovered in the DHAMH.

189 *I guess . . .* DH2 to Theodore Spetnagel, 8 May 1940, DHAMH.

190 *Today . . .* Otto Ege to DH, 14 December 1940, DHAMH.

190 *A large page . . .* Edward Larocque Tinker, "New Editions, Fine & Otherwise," *New York Times Book Review*, 30 March 1941.

190* Among these declined requests was one from Hunter's cousin, Junius, asking if Dard Jr. would print a booklet on the occasion of the June 1941 dedication of the new building for the *Chillicothe Gazette & News-Advertiser*.

   Hunter's contribution to the building was a papermaking and printing display in the lobby. In the two wall cases, oriental and occidental papers are displayed, as well as printing blocks from Hunter's collection. Also included in the display was a leaf from Gutenberg's 42-line Bible with the bull's head watermark, purchased for the newspaper by Hunter. In the accompanying booklet, *The Story of Early Printing*, Hunter described the artifacts in the cases and the three additional framed specimens. Hunter's display, now quite deteriorated after more than a half-century on display, can still be seen in the *Gazette* building on Main Street.

192 *Dr. Tate . . .* James R. Killian Jr. to DH, 10 May 1949, Courtesy MIT. Office of the President, 1930–1958 (Compton-Killian) AC 4. Box 11. Folder 2. Institute Archives and Special Collections, MIT Libraries, Cambridge, Massachusetts.

193 *Dear Dr. Killian . . .* DH to James R. Killian Jr., stamped "COPY," 16 May 1949. Courtesy MIT. Office of the Dean of Humanities, 1933–1965. AC 20. Box 4. Folder 191. Institute Archives and Special Collections, MIT Libraries, Cambridge, Massachusetts.

194 *Apparently . . .* James R. Killian Jr. to John Burchard, 19 May 1949. Courtesy MIT. Office of the Dean of Humanities, 1933–1965. AC 20. Box 4. Folder 191. Institute Archives and Special Collections, MIT Libraries, Cambridge, Massachusetts.

196 *With a great . . .* Westbrook Steele memo to Institute of Paper Chemistry staff, 30 July 1954, DHRC, Folder VIII, 1954–55. Published with permission of the Robert C. Williams American Museum of Papermaking, Institute of Paper Science and Technology.

196 *What I really . . .* DH to Catherine Ahearn, 11 March 1955. Courtesy MIT. Office of the Dean of Humanities, 1933–1965. AC 20. Box 4. Folder 191. Institute Archives and Special Collections, MIT Libraries, Cambridge, Massachusetts.

197* From 1954, Graham became increasingly knowledgeable about the collection, and from Hunter, he gradually took over answering queries. In 1959, he and Hunter planned an extensive trip to England, Italy, Switzerland, and France to make a motion picture of the extant hand papermaking mills and the paper museum at Basle. Hunter was content to cover his own costs, but the Institute would not pay Graham's expenses. To remedy this, Milton Roberts of the St. Regis Paper Company raised over $1,600 from the executives of paper companies. At the very last moment, however, the trip was cancelled. In preparation for the trip, Hunter had started receiving steroid injections to alleviate his breathing difficulties. Unfortunately, a side effect of this powerful drug caused him severe mental confusion, and he simply could not make up his mind to leave. Dard Jr. sent his father's apologies to Graham and Roberts. It is tragic that this trip never took place, as the proposed visual record of the few existing European hand papermills would have been invaluable.

In August 1959, Graham resigned from the Institute and took a job in New York City. Hunter regretted his leaving as Graham was a valued colleague, but their friendship continued. Graham's position was first filled by Edwin Schoenberger, who died suddenly in March 1960. Eugene Bunker, the Institute's librarian, then added the museum to his responsibilities. By September, Bunker had also left, and the museum was not attended by anyone until spring 1961, when Dr. Harry Lewis took over. Lewis was a respected author of technical books on paper, as well as the Institute's vice president and dean of students. Graham wrote Hunter on 2 March 1961 that he had talked with Lewis at a conference and was pleased with the news of his becoming curator, "he is a ball of fire and I am sure will bring the museum out of its doldrums that it has been in since I left."

Lewis and Hunter became good friends, as well as mutually respected colleagues, but they saw each other infrequently. In early 1964, Lewis and his secretary, Karen Bartz, began updating the catalogue compiled by MIT's Catherine Ahearn and Mary Lee. They worked on it for two years. Lewis, who was in bad health, resigned in mid-1965 but continued to work part-time on this project. Hunter never saw this catalogue, however, as it was completed shortly after his death. The next curator, Arnold Grummer, sent the catalogue to Dard Jr., who wrote in the valuations that were used to purchase insurance.

197† In 1980, a small group of "paper people" met to discuss this problem, and a year later, the Friends of the Dard Hunter Paper Museum was formed. The primary purpose of the FDHPM was to lobby the Institute for the preservation of the collection, then in Appleton. The FDHPM achieved success in this regard, especially after the museum moved to Atlanta. In 1992, the organization was renamed the Friends of Dard Hunter and its primary function is to provide a forum for the exchange of information among its members through its newsletter, *Bull & Branch*, and an annual conference.

199 *The edition* . . . DH, *Papermaking by Hand in America* (Chillicothe: Mountain House Press, 1950), colophon.

199 *a comfortable* . . . Porter S. Welch to DH, 19 January 1940, DHAMH.

199* The manuscript was returned to Hunter. Although Welch wanted it for the Rowfant Club archives, Hunter gave the corrected typescript to Elmer Adler in 1954. Adler gave it to Princeton University.

200 *During* . . . BLB, 3–5. Published with permission of the Rowfant Club.

201 *I have never* . . . Ibid., 112–13.

201 *What you say* . . . DH to SL, n.d. [ca. 6 November 1925], DHAMH.

202 *In gathering* . . . BLB, 113. Published with permission of the Rowfant Club.

203 *I have just* . . . John F. Adie to DH, 27 April 1945, DHAMH.

204 *My plan* . . . DH to Alfred A. Knopf, carbon, 9 April 1945, DHAMH.

205 *Dear Joe* . . . DH to DH2 and CCH, 1 December 1944, DHAMH.

206 *Your Mamma* . . . DH to DH2 and CCH, 21 December 1944, DHAMH.

207 *The President's* . . . DH to DH2 and CCH, 13 April 1945, DHAMH.

207* During a two-week furlough in the summer of 1945, Dard Jr. completed a large stained glass panel that hangs in the library window in Mountain House. It depicts in remarkable detail another of Amman's illustrations, the type-caster. The panel, "TYPO-GRAPHICAE 1568," measures 32.5 x 21 inches. The full-scale pattern was drawn by Hunter while Dard Jr. cut the glass pieces and put the panel together. Later, Dard Jr. designed and made a companion piece depicting Amman's printer, "IMPRIMATUR 1568." This panel is slightly larger than the previous one, measuring 35 x 23 inches, and it also hangs in the library window.

208 *describes* . . . DH, *Prospectus, Papermaking in Indo-China* (Chillicothe: [Mountain House Press], 1947), [2].

209 *No use* . . . PF to DH, 23 November 1946, DHAMH. Published with permission of Yanna F. Masters and Helen Schubert.

210 *The author* . . . DH, "Ohio's Pioneer Paper Mills," *Antiques* 49, no. 1 (January 1946): 66.

212 *was unsuitably* . . . LWDH, vol. 2, 116.

212 *In reproducing* . . . Ibid., 115.

213 *composed* . . . DH, *Papermaking by Hand in America*, foreword, [3].

213* This leaf measured 15 x 11.5 inches—half of the full sheet, 15 x 23 inches. Because there was no fold through which to sew, the binder had to adhere a strip of paper, called a guard, to the binding edge. The guard was then folded for sewing; this left a tab, which can be seen in the gutter of the book.

213 *I am awed* . . . PF to DH and DH2, 17 February 1950, DHAMH. Published with permission of Yanna F. Masters and Helen Schubert.

214* The trial binding is in the collection of Edwards H. Metcalf, The Huntington Library.

215 *I appreciate* . . . PF to DH, 30 August 1950, DHAMH. Published with permission of Yanna F. Masters and Helen Schubert.

216 *I am more* . . . Elmer Adler to DH, 18 September 1950, DHRC, MS 1, Series 1, Folder 21. Published with permission of the Robert C. Williams American Museum of Paper-making, Institute of Paper Science and Technology.

216 *odd but* . . . Carl Purlington Rollins, *American Type Designers and Their Work* (Chicago: The Lakeside Press, R.R. Donnelley & Sons Co., 1947), 4.

218 *As you know* . . . DH to Robert Booth, carbon, 3 May 1954, DHAMH.

218 *Dear Sterling* . . . DH to SL, 4 March 1951, DHAMH.

219 *since Edith's* . . . DH to SL, 9 May 1951, DHAMH.

219* Rosamond B. Loring died in September 1950. Until her death, she had held the honorary curatorship.

219† Adena was designed by Benjamin Latrobe (the architect of the nation's capitol) and built for Thomas Worthington, Ohio's governor from 1814–18. In 1946, Adena was given to the Ohio State Archaeological and Historical Society.

220 *I have been* . . . DH to SL, 17 August 1952, DHAMH.

221 *Although* . . . DH to Robert Booth, carbon, 13 April 1954, DHAMH.

222 *I don't think* . . . Alfred A. Knopf to DH, 20 July 1954, DHAMH. Published with permission of the Harry Ransom Humanities Research Center, The University of Texas at Austin.

222 *Should* . . . DH to Alfred A. Knopf, carbon, 21 July 1954, DHAMH.

222* Hunter did write to the Rowfant Club about a limited edition, and although interest was shown, the club's representative, Richard Douglas, doubted that it could afford to produce a large book.

222   *For reasons* . . . Alfred A. Knopf to DH, 8 November 1956, DHAMH. Published with permission of the Harry Ransom Humanities Research Center, The University of Texas at Austin.

222   *Your criticism* . . . DH to Alfred A. Knopf, carbon, 17 November 1956, DHAMH.

223   *Anything* . . . Rudolph Ruzicka to Sidney Jacobs of Alfred A. Knopf, Inc., copy, 23 January 1958, DHAMH.

223   *I agree* . . . Rudolph Ruzicka to DH, 17 February 1958, DHAMH.

223* In June 1949, Hunter learned that the W.D. Harper Paper Company, which had been involved in the Lime Rock mill, had a quantity of the mill's paper in storage. Eventually, Hunter bought thirteen reams of eight different papers for $200. Among this were eight reams of Sharon (cream) and a half ream of Taconic (white), both with the Dog and Dagger watermark (see Appendix B and plate 95).

224   *I fear* . . . DH to SL, 17 November 1958, DHAMH.

224   *the material* . . . DH to PF, 8 November 1958, DHAMH.

225   *The Mountain House* . . . DH to Elmer Adler, 26 November 1959, DHAMH.

225   *a limited edition* . . . William Wheelwright to DH, 14 August 1956, DHAMH.

225   *What you* . . . DH to Elmer Adler, 3 December 1959, DHAMH.

225   *It was* . . . DH to D. Jackson McWilliams, carbon, 9 January 1962, DHAMH.

227* DH to D. Jackson McWilliams, carbon, 20 August 1962, DHAMH. I have to say that I think Hunter probably did all he could to dissuade Morris from cutting a font of type and thus, nipped in the bud any possibility that Morris might eclipse him in the creation of one-man books.

227† DH to Ruth Lord, carbon, 17 March 1964, DHAMH. With the exception of family letters, the correspondence between Dard Hunter and Sterling Lord constitutes the most personal. A few months after Sterling's death, Hunter asked Ruth Lord to return the letters he had written to his dear friend, and she complied.

227‡ In February 1955, Harrison Elliott's sisters wrote Hunter asking if he wanted the paper-related material in their brother's estate. He gratefully accepted the gift and asked to have the material sent to Mountain House at his expense. Once he had sorted through Elliott's "paperiana," he sent the bibliographic material to Graham at the museum with instructions to store it away until it could be catalogued.

      The material Hunter kept seems to have consisted of Elliott's correspondence over a thirty year period, as well as many of the Mountain House Press books that Hunter had given to Elliott. As there are so few letters from him to Elliott in the DHAMH, it is possible that Hunter may have destroyed most of them. Extant letters include ones from Robert Robertson and several others, whom Hunter knew professionally. While reading these letters, Hunter discovered that Elliott had been "bad-mouthing" him to others for years. One point of contention was that while Elliott had been specifically acknowledged in the 1943 edition of Hunter's *Papermaking: The History and Technique of an Ancient Craft*, he was not singled out in the 1947 edition. This and other perceived slights led to an estrangement between the two men in the late 1940s and early 1950s, although they did reconcile shortly before Elliott's death.

228   *Assuming* . . . DH to D. Jackson McWilliams, carbon, 5 June 1964, DHAMH.

228   *After my* . . . DH to D. Jackson McWilliams, carbon, 17 June 1964, DHAMH.

229   *Yesterday* . . . DH to D. Jackson McWilliams, 30 April 1965, DHAMH.

230   *Friday* . . . DH, 1965 diary, DHAMH.

230   *Saturday* . . . DH, 1966 diary, DHAMH.

230   *Dear Jackson* . . . DH to D. Jackson McWilliams, carbon, 26 January 1966, DHAMH.

231   *Though Dard* . . . D. Jackson McWilliams to DH2, 14 February 1966, DHAMH. Published with permission of La Casa del Libro, San Juan, Puerto Rico.

232 *Saturday* . . . DH, 1966 diary, DHAMH.

232 *Sunday* . . . DH2, Ibid.

233 *His position* . . . Leonard Schlosser, introduction to *Papermaking in Pioneer America*, by Dard Hunter (1952; reprint, New York: Garland Publishing, Inc., 1981). Published with permission of the Estate of Leonard B. Schlosser.

233* In 1987, Dard Hunter II published the miniature, four-volume work, *The Making of Books*, a compilation of his father's three essays that appeared in *The Miscellany* and *The Quarterly Notebook* in 1915 and 1916. Hunter II set the original texts and printed them letterpress. These pages were then made into line etchings and printed on Lime Rock mill paper. Marlborough mill paper specimens comprise the fourth volume. Gray Parrot bound the volumes in full brown Morocco leather.

235* Elliott was the oldest of this group. He started making paper using equipment donated to the Japan Paper Company by Winifred Bird, manager of the English Eynsford Paper Mills, after she demonstrated hand papermaking at the JPC in 1931. Interestingly, a year later, Hunter corresponded with Miss Bird about the quality of Lime Rock mill papers. Much impressed by her knowledge and the fact that she was a papermaker, he was surprised to find out that she was not a member of her country's Original Society of Papermakers. He wrote to the Society's secretary, A.H. Smith to ask why. In a letter dated 29 May 1932, Smith replied that Miss Bird could be an honorary member of the Society. However to qualify, she would have to be able to make five and a half quires (one quire comprises twenty-five sheets) per post, twenty posts, or 2,750 sheets in a day —a feat that Smith suggested could only be accomplished by a man.

Elliott continued making paper throughout the war years, published numerous articles in trade journals, and befriended Douglass Morse Howell, then a young, ardent papermaker. In 1952, Elliott retired and donated most of his papermaking equipment to Columbia University; much of the remainder was left to the Library of Congress. His bibliographic collection is in the DHRC.

Douglass Howell gained a deserved reputation as a teacher and original thinker, as well as an innovative papermaker. He died in Long Island, New York in February 1994. Arthur Laws of Avon Falls, Ohio died in 1959; he experimented with handmade paper for only a few years.

John Mason and Henry Morris were the two papermakers for whom Hunter had the highest regard. When Mason retired from the Leicester College of Art, England, his papermaking activities were curtailed as a result. He died in 1980. Henry Morris continues his Bird & Bull Press, although he no longer makes paper.

235 *The making* . . . PHT, 452.

236 *In the fall* . . . Howard Clark, facsimile transmission to author, 30 July 1997.

237 *We thought* . . . Kathryn Clark, *The Mark of the Maker: The Fine Art of Papermaking at Twinrocker*, prod. and dir. by David J. McGowan and Laurie Kennard, 28 min., Direct Cinema Limited, 1995, videocassette. The film was made in 1991 and was nominated for an Academy Award as Best Documentary Short. Published with permission of David J. McGowan and Kathryn Clark.

237* Both sisters owned Lincoln rocking chairs, which gave rise to the name "Twinrocker." The mill's watermark is back-to-back rocking chairs.

237 *When we* . . . H. Clark, facsimile, 30 July 1997.

239* James Guthrie, "A Note on Dard Hunter," *The Scottish Nation* (14 August 1923): 12. Guthrie was proprietor of the Pear Tree Press in Flansham, Bognor, Sussex in England. He and Hunter were regular correspondents and often commiserated with each other on the difficulties of earning respect—not to mention a living—by making good books by hand. Guthrie owned one of the presses used by William Morris's Kelmscott Press, the Albion no. 6551. When money was tight, Guthrie asked Hunter if he wanted to buy the press. Hunter declined, but he did offer to contact likely institutions and people, including Frederic Goudy.

The Goudy-Hunter correspondence began in late June 1923, when Goudy wrote about the events leading up to the purchase of "Deepdene" in Marlborough. Apparently, the Mill House property was for sale when Goudy was looking for a home and studio, but Hunter's mill was too small to house the latter. It was through this correspondence that Goudy learned of Guthrie's Albion, which he purchased in March 1924. For a history of this press, see J. Ben Lieberman, *The Liberty Bell on the Kelmscott Goudy Press*, Council Bluffs, Iowa: The Yellow Barn Press, 1996.

246* DH, *Papermaking Pilgrimage to Japan, Korea and China* (New York: Pynson Printers, 1936), 59–66. There are two footnotes that were not included in this quote. One is a lengthy note discussing the nuances of the terms *nagashizuki* and *tamezuki* (western hand papermaking).

251* When there were not enough originals to be included as specimens in LWDH, Hunter II made paper from the original moulds or from moulds that he altered.

253   *I wish to . . .* DH, draft, n.d., on verso of 27 August 1913 letter, DHAMH.

254* The pair of moulds and deckle are NMAH #12,411 and #12,412. The two copper dies for the Dard Hunter Mill light-and-shade watermark are DHRC #974 and #975.

254   *The sample . . .* T.J. Marshall & Co. to DH, 20 January 1913, DHAMH.

255   *A Mould . . .* W. Green, Son & Waite to DH, 25 February 1913, DHAMH.

255* The mould, #964; deckle, #965; and one plaster cast, #963 of this watermark are in the DHRC. In the 1966 catalogue of the Dard Hunter Paper Museum, one wax model (DHRC #962) for this watermark is listed, but the author has not been able to examine it, as its present location is not known. A pair of casts, male and female, is NMAH #12,418. The location of the original die is not known.

255   *like wet . . .* W. Green, Son & Waite to DH, 5 November 1913, DHAMH.

255   *If it is . . .* Ibid.

256* G.A. Braendlin, Auslands-Bureau, Leipzig to DH, 23 July 1914, DHAMH. Examples of the Large Portrait made by Hunter at Marlborough are very rare; one is NMAH #12,424.

256* In early articles about Hunter's work, illustrations of this watermark frequently appear. In some cases, the portrait faces left, the wrong way, and the name is superimposed below its correct position, so that it does not obscure the portrait as it does normally.

257   *As regards . . .* T.J. Marshall & Co. to DH, 20 January 1913, DHAMH.

257* According to Hunter II, his father purchased two pairs of moulds of this size at this time. He stated in LWDH, vol. 2, 16–17 that the watermark: DARD HUNTER / a paper press enclosed in a circle / 19 MILL 13 was applied to the laid mould of one of the pair (Hunter A; s/D nr), and that this mould was used to make envelopes, using both tearing wires and a shaped deckle. However, only one pair of moulds was purchased. Hunter II probably mistook the estimate for two pairs for the final order for only one pair. It is likely that envelopes with this watermark were actually made on the first laid mould, between the application of the fleur-de-lis and the lion rampant watermarks.

257   *5 pieces . . .* T.J. Marshall & Co. to DH, 6 March 1913, DHAMH.

258* Hunter II (LWDH, vol. 2, 60–2, 64) mistakenly dates this mould from the Lime Rock mill period. Presumably, he based this on a number of off-white sheets made on this mould by his father in the Lime Rock mill in 1930.

258   *WOVE . . .* DH, "Watermarking Hand-Made Paper," *Paper* 18, no. 17 (29 June 1921): 13.

259* The modern laid mould with the watermark: DARD HUNTER / DH-in-a-heart / 1913, is DHRC #2780. It is marked with the T.J. Marshall number: A2710. The Papermaking Commemorative mould and deckle are DHRC #953 and 953a. The dies are DHRC #945 and 955. The waxes, #12,416; plaster casts, #12,417; and the oval wire cloth, #21,419.4 are in the NMAH.

259 *Will you kindly* . . . W. Green, Son & Waite to DH, 26 February 1914, DHAMH.

260* Compared with paper made from cotton fibers and/or moderately beaten pulp, paper made from fibers containing high percentages of hemicellulose, such as those from linen rag, and/or from well beaten pulp have a tendency to shrink considerably upon air drying. This accounts for the dimensional ranges of paper formed on the same mould and deckle.

260† There has been some confusion over the fact that examples of paper with this water-mark have the *t* crossed and uncrossed, see S/D #5. In his copy of S/D, Hunter II wrote that the crossbar of the *t* had simply fallen off. There was only one mould, which was laid, with this watermark.

262* This mould is made of a rather poor quality wood that looks like pine; normally, mahogany or oak would have been used. The mould and deckle are DHRC #964 and 965. The 1966 museum catalogue lists both the wax model and the plaster of paris "die," both DHRC #962, but neither have been located.

262† Perrigot-Masure referred to these two moulds by number: 2056A for the Large Portrait, 2056B for the Small. On the Large Portrait mould, there is a painted "724" and "a."

263 *The letterhead* . . . N.A. Altmann, Butler Paper Corp. to DH, 8 January 1923, DHAMH.

263 *Do you make* . . . H. Alfred Fowler to DH, 13 January 1915, DHAMH.

263 *In recent years* . . . DH, "The Watermarking of Portraits, Ancient and Modern," *Inland Printer* (October 1921): 53.

264 *The sheet* . . . DH to Ruel P. Tolman, 23 January 1922, collection, Smithsonian Institution, National Museum of American History, Graphic Arts Collection Subject File: Hunter, Dard (1883–1966) Original Correspondence, Clippings.

264* Mould and deckle, DHRC #958 & 959. This mould is marked: W. Green, Son & Waite 30303. A plaster cast of the wax or die, coated with graphite (now badly broken) is DHRC #957.

265* DHRC #5001.49 (1993.006.78). Hunter II stated that this sheet, known as Avon, was made in the Lime Rock mill after all of the watermarks on the left half were removed and replaced by a DH-in-a-heart. The Britannia on this sheet is very similar to Hunter L; S/D #46. As sheets from these two moulds are about the same size, they are probably a pair of moulds from the Palmer Mill. The "V" under the second Britannia stands for King George V (reigned 1910–1936).

266* The mould and deckle are DHRC #960 and 961 and marked: W. Green, Son & Waite 35431.

266† These dies are DHRC #939 and 940. The image measures approximately 7 x 5.5 inches. In the 1966 DHPM catalogue, the wax model is listed as #938, but it has not been located.

266‡ These sheets have no accession number.

267* This wax model, the image measuring 6 x 3.5 inches, is DHRC #1993.005.550. In the DHRC, there is a sheet of white paper measuring 13.25 x 10.5 inches, #1984.2.2a. This watermark is positioned in the center of that sheet.

267† Sheets of all three portraits are DHRC #440. The 1966 DHPM catalogue erroneously stated, "Portrait of D.H. in 7 different modeling . . . 13 inches x 10½ inches." In order of execution, S/D #27 is the second portrait, and #29 is the third. S/D also erroneously states that the moulds for the first and third portraits were made by E. Amies of Maidstone, Kent, England and dates these watermarks, 1920. This mistake is under-standable because one of the sheets was inscribed by Hunter, "To Harrison Elliott from Dard Hunter 1920." Other sheets in the DHRC are inscribed, "1942."

269 *Wonder . . .* Jos. J. Plank Co. to DH, 30 March 1958, DHAMH.

274 *[The etching] . . .* Bertha E. Jaques to DH, 25 September 1917, DHAMH.

276 *too gay . . .* DH to PF, 1 July 1924, DHAMH.

280* Franck returned one unused piece of the side paper to Hunter, which has a woodcut on the verso. The scene depicted is thought to be the marriage of Romeo and Juliet, officiated by the Friar and witnessed by the Nurse. This print has been discovered in a number of collections of Lime Rock mill paper and, in one case, on nearly a ream of paper. It is printed in a pale ochre ink as a quarto page. Presumably, there were to be additional blocks overprinted in additional colors, but it seems that the project was abandoned. Nothing else is known about the print, including the name of the artist. It might have been a project of Dard Jr.'s while he was at the Cleveland School of Art. It can be dated prior to mid-1946.

Acknowledgments

The following have generously given their permission to use quotations from copyrighted works, letters, and images, as well as photographs: Richard Blacher; Grosvenor Rare Book Room, Buffalo and Erie County Public Library; La Casa del Libro; Dawson's Book Shop; Mr. and Mrs. Christopher Forbes; Mrs. Leonard Godding; Harry Ransom Humanities Research Center, The University of Texas at Austin; the late Cornell Hunter; Dard Hunter III; *Lakeside Journal*; J.B. Lankes; the Estate of Georg H.T. Mandl; Institute Archives and Special Collections, MIT Libraries; Yanna F. Masters; David J. McGowan; Mead Corporation; Memorial Art Gallery, Newberry Library; The Ohio State University; Ohio University-Chillicothe Library; the Estate of Ronald H. Pearson; Manuscripts Division, Department of Rare Books and Special Collections, Princeton University Library; Robert C. Williams American Museum of Paper-making, Institute of Paper Science and Technology; Rowfant Club; Roycroft Arts Museum, Boice Lydell; Roycroft Inn; the Estate of Leonard B. Schlosser; Helen Schubert; Edgar O. Smith; Smithsonian Institution, National Museum of American History; David Stone; Gilmore Stott; Department of Rare Books and Special Collections, University of Rochester Library; University of Rochester Press; and Jean-François Vilain & Roger S. Wieck.

PHOTOGRAPHY CREDITS:
Grosvenor Rare Book Room, Buffalo and Erie County Public Library: plate 46
Robert C. Williams American Museum of Papermaking: colorplate 11
Department of Rare Books and Special Collections, University of Rochester Library: plate 45
James M. Via: colorplates 3, 5–8; plates 8, 14, 16–17, 30, 32
Remaining photography by the author.

Index

ERRATA

23, for "Sit down and rest . . . ," read "Sit down & rest . . ."
39, for K. Heller, read H. Heller
188, 191, 208, for HAND MADE U.S.A., read HAND MADE USA
190, for *Specimen of Type*, read *A Specimen of Type*
198, Sherwood's portrait of Hunter is dated on the back "1946"
320, acknowledgment also to Thomas Lord

This edition is reproduced from the original handmade book.
Many people helped create the Red Hydra Press limited edition of 155 copies.
John DePol cut the Hunter portrait in wood, Michael and Winifred Bixler cast the Dante types,
Kathryn and Howard Clark and Travis Becker of Twinrocker Handmade Paper made the paper,
Dard Hunter III made the endsheets at Mountain House using his grandfather's
Bull's Head & Branch watermarked mould. R. Stanley Nelson cut the punches for and cast
by hand the special CH monogram found in the text. The book was designed
and printed on a Vandercook 4 Proof Press by Steve Miller, aided and abetted by
the magnificent printer's devil Cathleen Baker, and the plates
were printed by Meriden-Stinehour.

The Plates

Plates denoted "LWDH" indicate that the image was taken from Dard Hunter II's, *The Life Work of Dard Hunter*, volume 1 (1981) or volume 2 (1983). For *The Life Work*, Hunter Sr.'s original drawings and published designs were printed letterpress as facsimiles by Hunter II, many in color; others of these were hand-colored. Objects, such as lamps, were commercially printed. Plates of watermarked papers, usually designated "LWDH, 2" are either original sheets or were made by Hunter II from the original moulds and included in his book as specimens. All LWDH images are used courtesy of Dard Hunter III as are all other plates, except where noted. ¶ Plates denoted "HHH" indicate that the photograph originally appeared in the exhibition catalogue: Marie Via and Marjorie Searl, eds. *Head, Heart and Hand: Elbert Hubbard and the Roycrofters* (Rochester, NY: University of Rochester Press, 1994) and used with permission. ¶ Unless noted otherwise, photography is by the author. ¶ Whenever possible, dimensions are given for original or very rare works. They are in inches and in the order: height x width x depth. ¶ Inadvertently, two plates "42" were printed in the text on pages 52 and 58. In this Plates section, they are both denoted "42," and the relevant text pages are referenced.

1. Dard Hunter, Roycrofter, 1904–05, ca. 4 x 1½.
Courtesy Richard Blacher.

2. Title page, Elbert Hubbard, *The Man of Sorrows* (East Aurora, January 1905). Collection of the author.

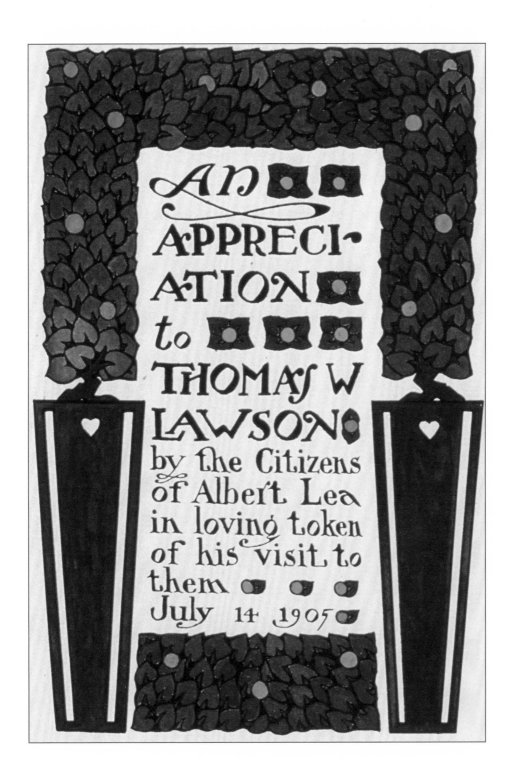

AN APPRECI-ATION to THOMAS W. LAWSON by the Citizens of Albert Lea in loving token of his visit to them July 14 1905

3. Page, Thomas W. Lawson Souvenir Book, 1905. Black ink and watercolor, 13⅝ x 11. Courtesy private collection, Boston, MA. Photograph by James M. Via.

4. Title page, Elbert & Alice Hubbard, *Justinian and Theodora: A Drama* (East Aurora, 1906). Collection of the author.

5. Stained glass window, Reception Room, Roycroft Inn, 1907. Courtesy Roycroft Inn, East Aurora, NY. Photograph by James M. Via.

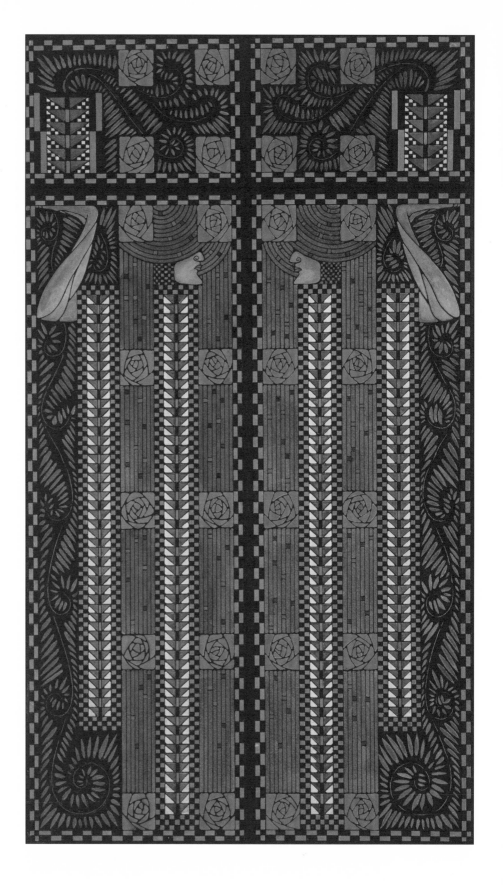

6. Drawing, glass mosaic panel for a Viennese café, 1908. Black ink, gouache, and shell gold on blue paper on board, 15¾ x 9¼. Courtesy Roycroft Arts Museum, East Aurora, NY, Boice Lydell. Photograph by James M. Via.

7. Drawing, "The Printer..," signed and dated "1904" (probably 1908). Black ink and gouache, 12½ x 9¾.
Courtesy Roycroft Arts Museum, Boice Lydell. Photograph by James M. Via.

8. Salon Lamp, with Karl Kipp, 1909–10. Stained glass, hammered copper, brass rods, 23 x 17¼. Courtesy Roycroft Arts Museum. Photograph by James M. Via. ʜʜʜ

9. Entrance to the Roycroft Inn, one of a series of
six cards printed for a promotional brochure (East
Aurora, 1910). LWDH, I

10. Library, Mountain House, Chillicothe, OH, showing five stained glass panels, most of which were designed and executed by Hunter. Left to right: "The Papermaker," 1919, 21½ x 18¼; "TYPOGRAPHICAE 1568," executed by Dard Jr., 1945, 32½ x 21; "PAPYROMYLOS 1662," 1925, 46 x 25¾; "IMPRIMATUR 1568," designed and executed by Dard Jr., date unknown, 35 x 23; and "Japanese Woman at Vat," 1933, 37 x 22.

11. Walter Sherwood, *Portrait of Dard Hunter*, 1946 (see *Errata*). Oil on canvas, 27¼ x 23. The setting is the paper museum at MIT. Photography and permission courtesy of the Dard Hunter Research Center at the Robert C. Williams American Museum of Papermaking.

12. *Papermaking in Indo-China* (Chillicothe, 1947). Side
papers by Dard Jr., binding by Peter Franck.

1. Display of Lonhuda Art Pottery at the Chicago's
World Fair, 1893.

2. Dard and Philip, ca. 4 and 6 years of age.

3. Detail, page written and designed by Dard and Philip, titled "Chilikofa Nus-Advertiser." *Chillicothe News-Advertiser*, 20 May 1903.

4. Masthead, editorial by William H. Hunter, "Ohio History, Notes and Comments." *Chillicothe News-Advertiser*, 20 May 1903. LWDH, 1

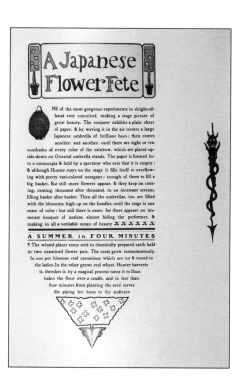

5. Page, *A Phantastic Evening with Hunter the Wizard* (Chillicothe, 1902).

6. Page, *Phil Hunter, The Wizard* (Cincinnati, 1903).

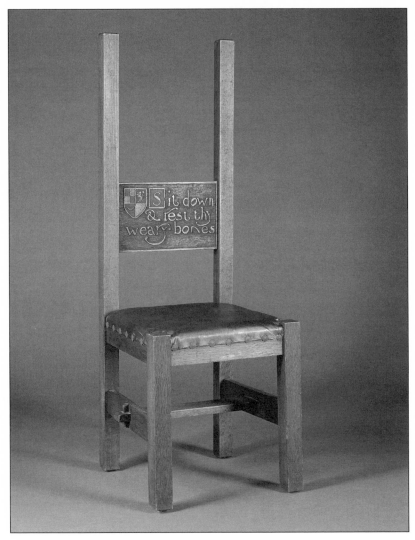

7. Footstool, probably 1904. Quarter-sawn white oak with a dark stain, 16 x 20 x 13.

8. Chair, "Sit down & rest thy weary bones," 1904. Oak and mahogany, paint, red leather, iron tacks, 51¼ x 20 x 18½. Courtesy Mr. and Mrs. Christopher Forbes. Photograph by James M. Via. ʜʜʜ

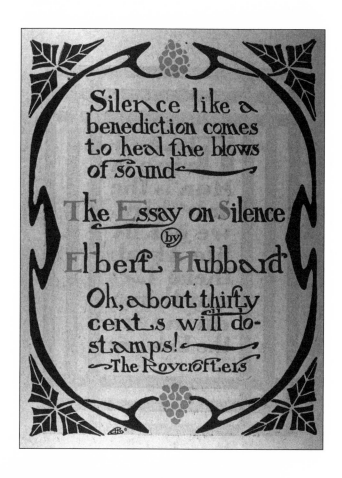

9. Advertisement in *A Catalogue of Some Books & Things…1905 & 6* (East Aurora, 1904). Collection of the author.

10. Left: Papyrus Vase, 1904. Porcelain with green glaze, height: 9⅞. Right: Iris Vase, 1904. Porcelain with green glaze, height: 6⅞. LWDH, 1. Now in the collection of The Metropolitan Museum of Art.

11. Bookcase, 1904. Fumed oak, 45⅝ x 32⅝ x 11⅞.
Courtesy Edgar O. Smith. LWDH, 1

12. Photograph by Clara Ragna Johnson, late 1904,
6½ x 4.

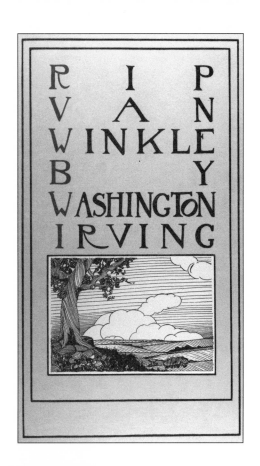

13. Title page, Washington Irving, *Rip Van Winkle* (East Aurora, February 1905). LWDH, 1

14. Drawings, chapter initials for *Rip Van Winkle*. Black ink and red watercolor, each 4½ x 4½. Courtesy Jean-François Vilain and Roger S. Wieck. Photograph by James M. Via. HHH

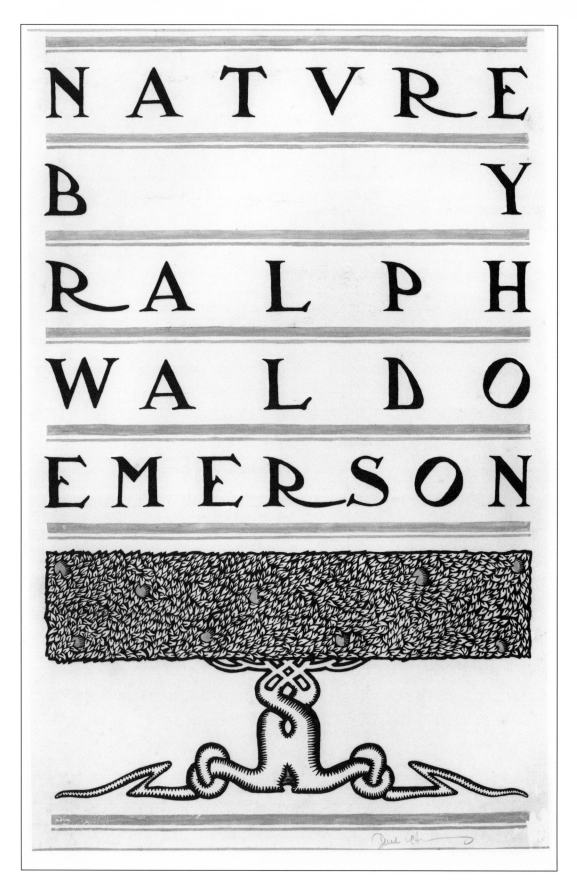

15. Drawing, title page, Ralph Waldo Emerson, *Nature* (East Aurora, 1905). Signed, black ink and red watercolor, 14⅝ x 10⅜. Courtesy Roycroft Arts Museum, Boice Lydell. Photograph by James M. Via.

16. Stained glass window, Hubbard Hall, Roycroft Inn, 1905–06. Courtesy Roycroft Inn, East Aurora, NY. Photograph by James M. Via.

17. Leaded window, Library, Roycroft Inn, 1905–06. Courtesy Roycroft Inn, East Aurora, NY. Photograph by James M. Via.

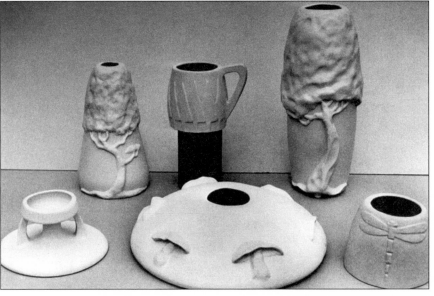

18. Piano Floor Lamp, 1906. Whereabouts unknown.

19. Ceramics, glazed and unglazed, 1906. Left to right, top row: Tree Vase, Mug, Tall Tree Vase (not by Hunter); bottom row: Candlestick, Mushroom Vase, Dragonfly Vase. For a full description of each, see endnote for text page 30. LWDH, 1. Now in the collections of The Metropolitan Museum of Art and the Roycroft Arts Museum.

20. Salamander Lamp, 1906. On bottom rim: DH monogram, III. Ceramic base, height: 12½; stained glass shade, diameter: 19. Courtesy Gilmore Stott. LWDH, I

21. Salamander Vase, probably 1906–07. Terra cotta, height: 6¼.

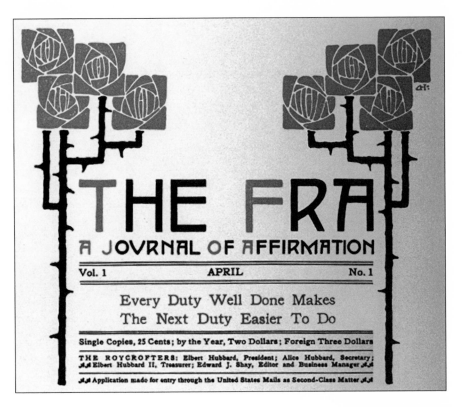

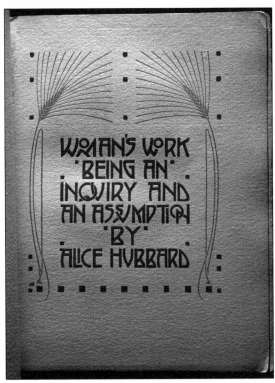

22. Cover, inaugural issue of *The Fra* (East Aurora, April 1908). LWDH, I

23. Title page, Alice Hubbard, *Woman's Work* (East Aurora, 1908). Collection of the author.

24. Title page, Elbert Hubbard, *Complete Works of Elbert Hubbard* (East Aurora, 1908–15). LWDH, I

25. Chapter initials, *Complete Works of Elbert Hubbard*. LWDH, I

26. Jules M. Gaspard, portraits of Dard Hunter and
Edith Cornell, dated January 1908. Conté crayon and
white chalk, each ca. 22 x 10.

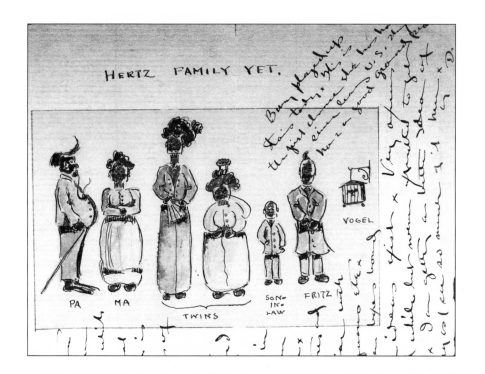

27. Sketch, Otto Hertz family, in a letter from Vienna, not dated [17 May 1908]. Ink and watercolor, 4 x 6¼.

28. Design for a stained glass window for an unidentified Viennese café, 1908. LWDH, I

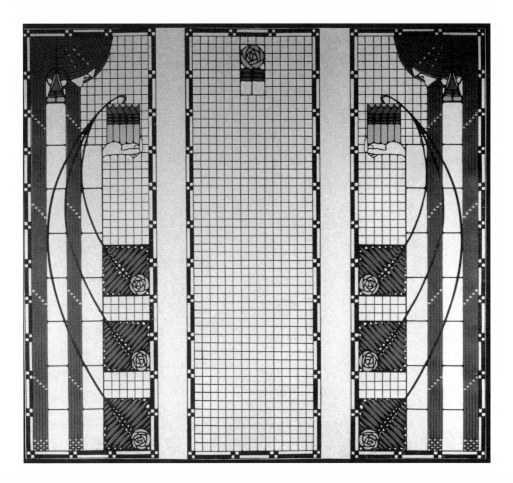

29. Design for a stained glass window for an unidentified mausoleum, Vienna 1908. LWDH, 1. Drawing now in the collection of The Metropolitan Museum of Art.

30. Cover designs for Elbert Hubbard's *Little Journeys* series. Left to right: Samuel Warner design (June 1902); Hunter (August 1908 and May 1909). Courtesy Memorial Art Gallery. Photograph by James M. Via. HHH

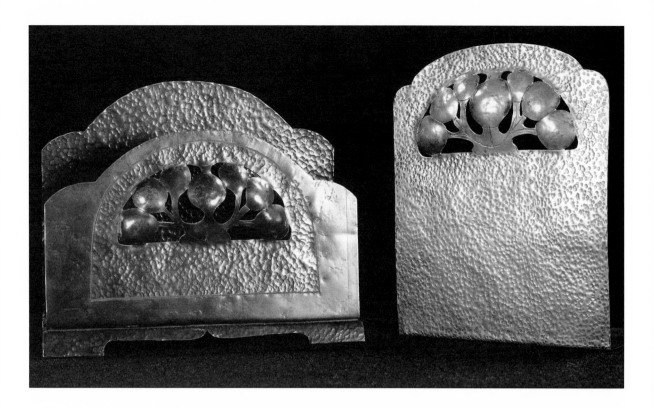

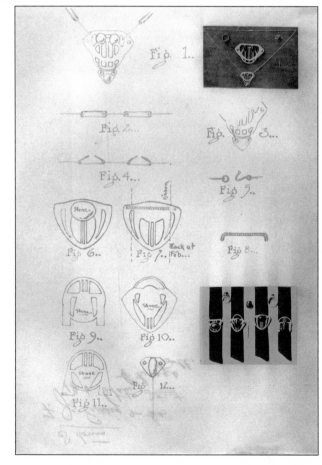

31. Letter holder and a bookend, one of a pair,
1908–09. Hammered and repoussé copper. Letter
holder: 5 x 7 x 2½; bookends, each: 6¾ x 5 x 2½.

32. Last page, *Instructions for the Making of Hand-
Made Jewelry*, March 1909. Ca. 13 x 8. Courtesy
Roycroft Arts Museum, Boice Lydell.

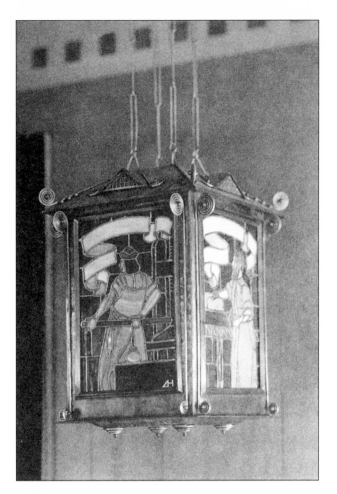

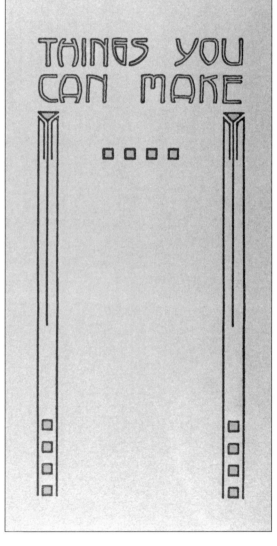

33. The Chandelier, with Karl Kipp, 1909–10. Left panel: The Printer; right: The Bookbinder. Stained glass, copper, brass, 19 x 13 x 13. Undated photograph, before electrification. LWDH, 1

34. Cover, *Things You Can Make*, 1910. LWDH, 1

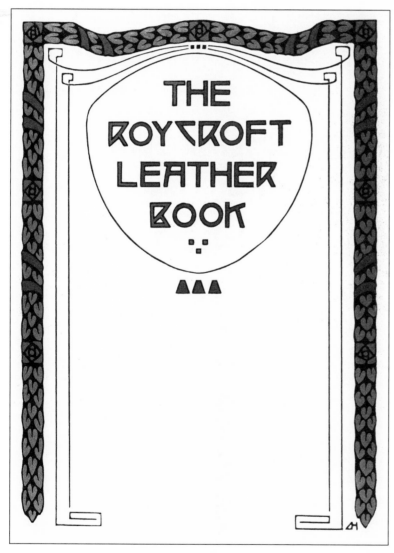

THE
ROYCROFT
LEATHER
BOOK

35. Jewelry box, probably 1909–10. Belonged to Edith Cornell Hunter. Red leather, hammered silver hinges and escutcheon, inset with repoussé copper hearts and turquoise, 4½ x 9 x 6½. Courtesy of the late Cornell Choate Hunter.

36. Cover, *The Roycroft Leather Book* (East Aurora, 1909). LWDH, I

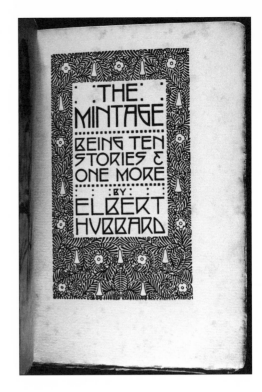

37. Title page, Elbert Hubbard, *The Mintage* (East Aurora, 1910). Collection of the author.

38. Cover, Elbert Hubbard, *The Standard Oil Company* (East Aurora, 1910). LWDH, I

39. Drawing for double title page for Carl Larsen, *Poetische Reisen in deutschen Landen…*, 1910. Black ink, each panel: 7½ x 4. Courtesy Roycroft Arts Museum, Boice Lydell. Photograph by James M. Via.

40. Drawing for double title page for Carl Larsen, *Im Land des Weins und der Gesänge…*, 1910. Black ink, each panel: 9¾ x 6⅞. Courtesy Roycroft Arts Museum, Boice Lydell. Photograph by James M. Via.

41. Drawing for bookplate for William Jordan Howard, signed and dated "1910." Black ink, 11¼ x 8⅛.
Courtesy Roycroft Arts Museum, Boice Lydell. Photograph by James M. Via.

42. (page 52) Title page, Gustave Flaubert [Ernst
Hardt], *Aus den Tagen des Knaben*, 1910. LWDH, I

42. (page 58) Double title page, Oscar Wilde, *Salome,
Tochter der Herodias*, 1910–11. LWDH, I

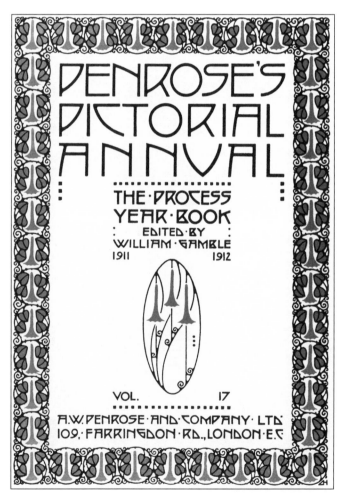

43. Cover, *The Pacific Printer* (January 1911). LWDH, 1

44. Title page, *Penrose's Pictorial Annual, 1911–1912*
(London, 1911). LWDH, 1

45. Hunter's property in Marlborough-on-Hudson, NY, ca. 1913. Left: Paper Mill and dam; right: Mill House. Original photograph by Charles H. Kingsbury, signed. Photography and permission courtesy Department of Rare Books and Special Collections, University of Rochester Library.

46. Paper Mill at Marlborough. Original photograph by Charles H. Kingsbury, signed and dated "1913." Photography and permission courtesy Grosvenor Rare Book Room, Buffalo and Erie County Public Library.

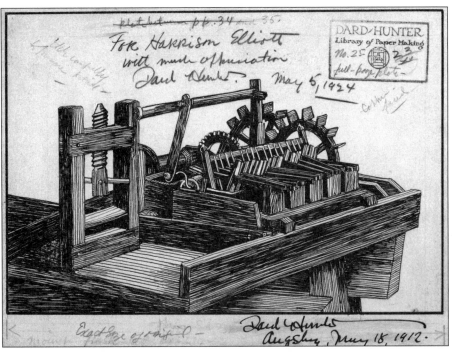

47. Library, Mill House, ca. 1913. Original photograph by Charles H. Kingsbury.

48. Drawing of a stamper (used as an illustration in 1923 *Old Papermaking*) and Hunter's library stamp, 1912. Black ink, 4½ x 8.

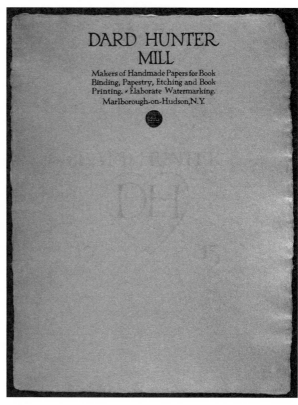

49. "Marbled pulp" papers for stationery and endsheets, 1913–15.

50. Letterhead, Dard Hunter Mill, ca. 1914. On paper
watermarked: Dard Hunter, DH-in-a-heart device,
1913. LWDH, 2

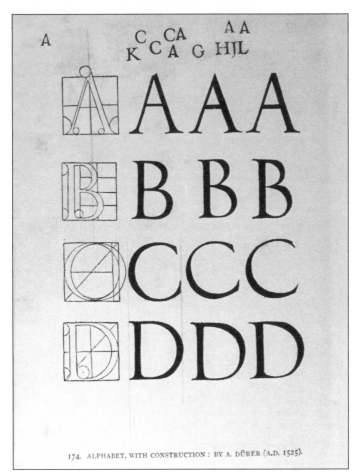

51. & 52. Watermarks in paper made for William A. Bradley, *The Etching of Figures* (Marlborough-on-Hudson, 1915–16).

53. Smoke proofs, 1912–15. On page of Dürer's designs for uppercase letters, ca. 1525, in Edward Strange, *Alphabets. A Manual of Lettering* (London, 1907).

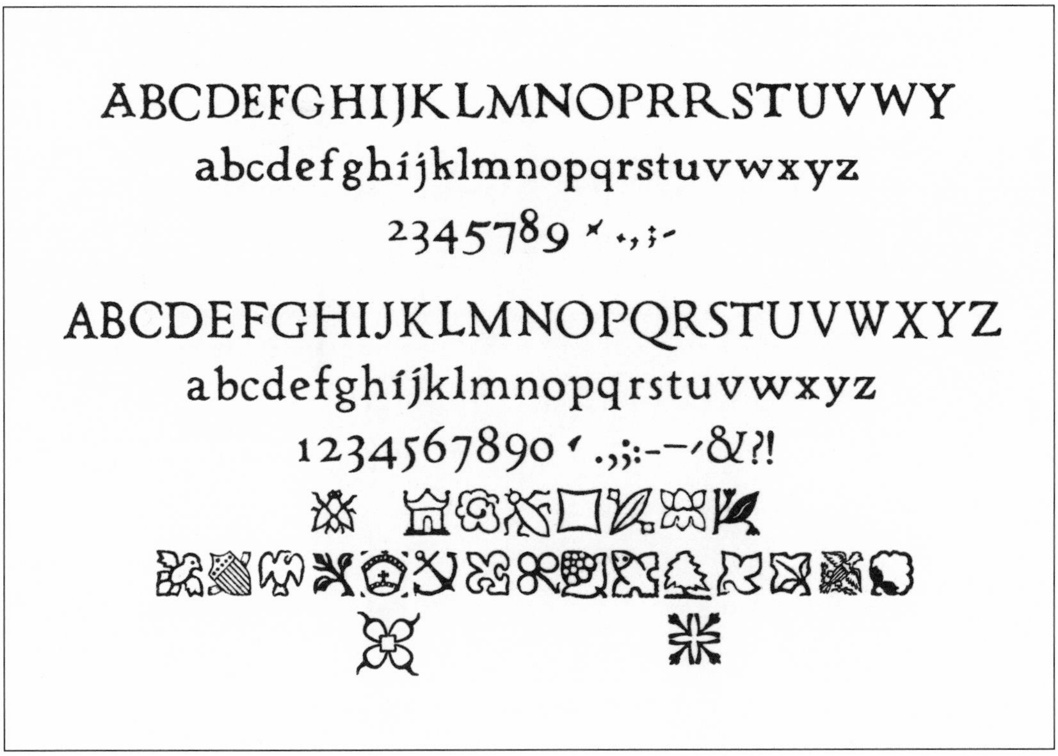

ABCDEFGHIJKLMNOPRRSTUVWY
abcdefghijklmnopqrstuvwxyz
2345789 ⸓ ·,;⁃

ABCDEFGHIJKLMNOPQRSTUVWXYZ
abcdefghijklmnopqrstuvwxyz
1234567890 ⸌ .,;:–-⸌&?!

54. Rows 1–3: Dard Hunter's typeface. Rows 4–9: Dard Jr.'s typeface. Actual size. The type shown represents extant punches and mats; not shown are additional punches cut but not cast. The version of Dard Jr.'s typeface including the ornaments, shown here, is the final one used in *Papermaking by Hand in America* (1950).

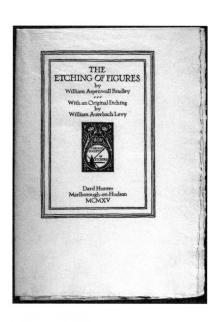

55. Title page, William A. Bradley, *The Etching of Figures* (Marlborough-on-Hudson, 1915–16).

56. First text page, Frank Weitenkampf, *The Etching of Contemporary Life* (Marlborough-on-Hudson, 1916).

THE CHICAGO SOCIETY OF ETCHERS SENDS greeting to its Associate Members in this, the eighth year of its existence, and as an expression of the appreciation its one hundred and fifteen Active Members feel for their encouraging interest, the enclosed etching of "The Old Town Bridge Tower" in Prague is presented. J.C. Vondrous of New York was invited to make this plate for the Society, two hundred copies printed and the plate destroyed. No prints are available except through membership. Mr. Vondrous should depict scenes in Bohemia with keener insight than anywhere else since he was born there in 1884; but he expresses with equal sympathy the fascinations of Italy or the rugged grandeur of our own New England coast. This is but fair as his training began in the National Academy of Design in New York and his first steps in etching were directed by one of America's veterans of the needle, James D. Smillie. The eye of any artist must rest with interest upon architecture that has strength and endurance, matured and enriched by the wisdom and beauty of ages, such as is found in the view of the Old Town Bridge Tower in Prague. In this, as well as his other etchings, Mr. Vondrous has preserved the spirit of Bohemia without insisting upon too literal expression, and his accomplishment reflects credit upon a technique that serves but does

not master. Mr. Vondrous has written the following description of his subject: "Old Town is one of the several municipalities which make up the city of Prague, and the Bridge Tower is one of the many characteristic Gothic towers of Old Prague. Begun in the fourteenth century, during the reign of Charles Fourth, the greatest of the kings of Bohemia, on the Old Town side of the famous bridge of Charles Fourth, it was not fully completed until 1451. On the left is the church of Saint Francis, a late renaissance building of 1679 to 1688, with the adjoining monastery of "The Order of The Cross with the Red Star". Between these two is the church of San Salvador, 1653-1659, its façade showing marked influence of the Italian renaissance, a style noticeable in many other buildings of that period in Prague."

Bertha E. Jaques,
Secretary and Treasurer.

Otto J. Schneider,
President.
Thomas E. Tallmadge,
Vice-President.

Dard Hunter, Junior.
May 15, 1917

Edith and Dard Hunter
The Mill
Marlborough-on-Hudson, N.Y.

57. *J.C. Vondrous Folio* (Marlborough-on-Hudson, 1917).

58. Dard Hunter Jr.'s birth announcement, 1917. LWDH, 2

59. Façade, Mountain House, Chillicothe, OH, undated photograph (after 1934).

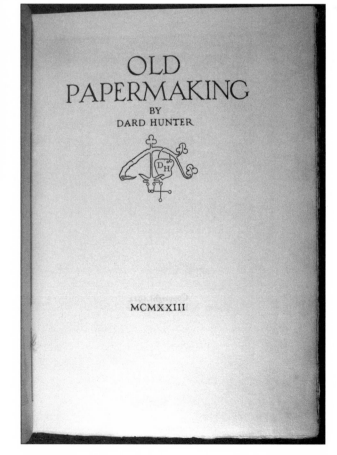

60. 1922 Branch wire watermark, one of four on two antique laid moulds.

61. Hunter printing *Old Papermaking*, ca. 1922.

62. Title page, *Old Papermaking* (Chillicothe, 1923).

63. Hunter examining *tapa*, 1926.

64. Bull's Head & Branch wire watermark, one of
four on two antique laid moulds.

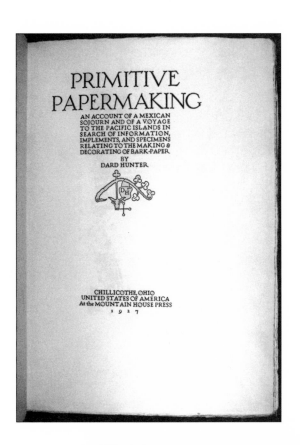

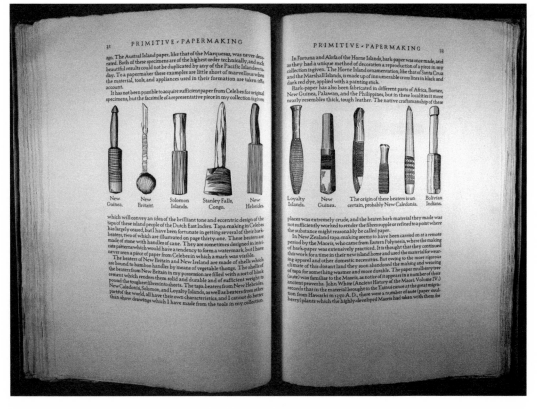

65. & 66. Title and text pages, *Primitive Papermaking*
(Chillicothe, 1927).

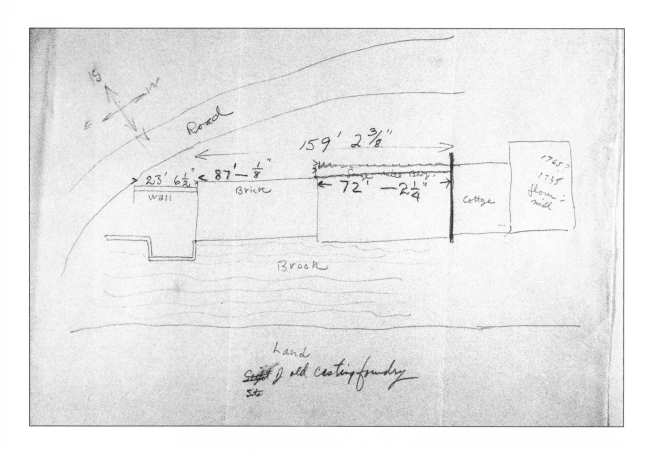

67. Pencil sketch, Lime Rock mill buildings, ca. 1928.

68. The mill at Lime Rock from upstream, late 1930s.
Brick building is far left, mill in center, top of the
dam in foreground.

69. Left to right: Thomas and Reginald Robertson,
Leonard Godding, Gladys Robertson, Harry Beach,
Emily and Robert Parry Robertson, ca. 1930.

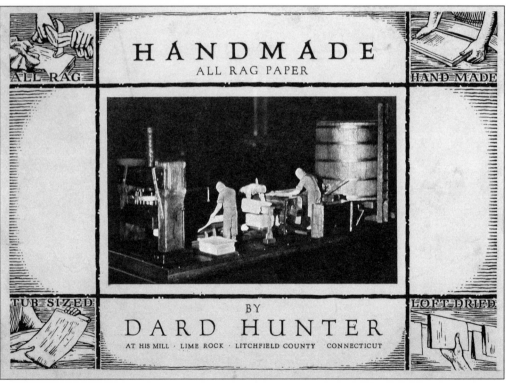

70. Hunter's drawing for remodelling the brick building at Lime Rock, view from the road, ca. 1930. (The Architects' Guild was made-up by Hunter.)

71. Label, Lime Rock mill stationery box, 1930. The Crane Museum papermaking model is pictured.

72. Dard Jr. and Cornell making paper in the summer house, Chillicothe, ca. 1930.

73. J.J. Lankes, *The Critic*, 1931. Wood engraving, 4½ x 3.

74. Hunter in Japan, 1933.

75. Hunter and Tym Niltongkum, 1935. In
Papermaking in Southern Siam (Chillicothe, 1936).

76. Title page, *Papermaking by Hand in India* (New York, 1939).

77. Dard Hunter Paper Museum in the William Barton Rogers Building, MIT, 1939.

78. Dard Hunter Jr., *A Specimen of Type*, 1940.
Collection of the author.

79. Robert Frost, *A Considerable Speck*. Printed by
Dard Hunter Jr., 1940.

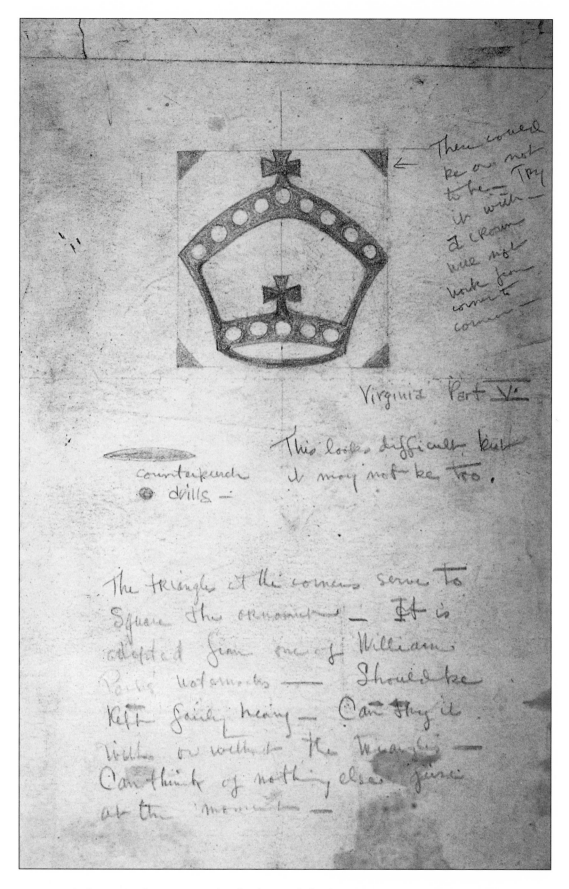

80. Hunter's drawing and notes to Dard Jr. for the punch for the Virginia type ornament used in *Papermaking by Hand in America* (Chillicothe, 1950). See plate 54.

(2) Two Rittenhouse watermarks found in the paper used in printing
"The American Weekly Mercury," a newspaper that was established
in Philadelphia, December 22, 1719, by Andrew Bradford, the son of
William Bradford, one of the partners in the original Rittenhouse
paper mill. These two watermarks are in the paper of the issue for
Thursday, March 17th, 1720, Number 13, the sheets of paper being
approximately thirteen by sixteen inches. The watermark "KR,"
for Klaus (Nicholas) Rittenhouse, occupies the left half of the
paper and the clover-leaf the right half of the sheet. According
to Francis Daniel Pastorius, the clover-leaf, or "klee-blatt,"
was the original mark or seal of Germantown, the locality of
the Rittenhouse mill. The chain-lines are spaced about an
inch apart, with about twenty-five laid-lines to the inch.

[23]

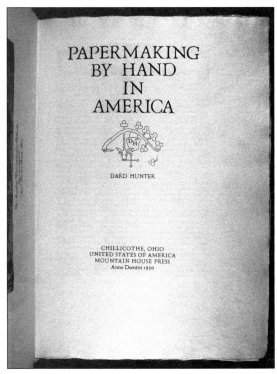

81. & 82. Text and title pages, *Papermaking by Hand in America*. Shown also are two Rittenhouse Mill facsimile watermarked papers made by Dard Jr.

83. Forming and couching paper, photograph 37 from *Papermaking Pilgrimage to Japan, Korea and China* (New York, 1936).

84. Drying paper, photograph 42, *Papermaking Pilgrimage to Japan, Korea and China*.

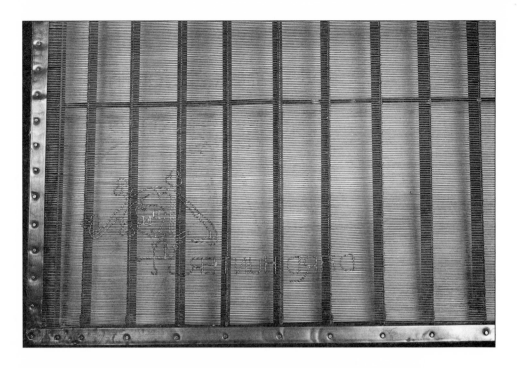

85. Detail, one of a pair of antique laid moulds with Bull's Head & Branch wire watermark. Deckle not shown. Mould size: 16½ x 23½.

86. Mould and deckle, Dard Hunter Mill, light-and-shade & wire watermarks, wove, 1913–21. Mould size: 6¾ x 8¾. Courtesy Smithsonian Institution, National Museum of American History, Graphic Arts Collection. LWDH, 2

87. Large Portrait watermark, stationery, 1913,
8½ x 11½.

88. Dard Hunter Mill watermark, stationery, 1913,
11 x 8¼. LWDH, 2

89. Mould and deckle, Papermaking Commemorative, light-and-shade & wire watermarks, wove, 1914–21. (Photograph reversed for easier reading.) Mould size: 11 x 8¾. Courtesy Dard Hunter Research Center, Robert C. Williams American Museum of Papermaking. LWDH, 2

90. Lord Byron, light-and-shade watermark, wove, 1921, 11¾ x 9. LWDH, 2

91. Hunter Coat-of-Arms, light-and-shade watermark, wove, 1928, 10½ x 7¾. LWDH, 2

92. Mature Portrait, light-and-shade watermark, executed by Andreas Kufferath (?), 1928–29, 13¼ x 10½.

93. Half of a sheet of Lime Rock mill paper watermarked, HAND MADE. Full sheet ca. 19½ x 23½. Used extensively in *Papermaking by Hand in America*. LWDH, 2 (Note: This sheet was unevenly sized with gelatin.)

94. Detail of the Lime Rock mill paper watermarked on left: HAND MADE; on right: USA (not shown). Full sheet ca. 15½ x 23½. LWDH, 2

95. Half of a sheet of Lime Rock mill paper water-marked with Dog and Dagger. Full sheet ca. 20¼ x 26½. LWDH, 2

96. Detail of watermarked stationery for Edith Cornell Hunter made at the Lime Rock mill. Full sheet ca. 7¾ x 11. LWDH, 2

97. Detail of watermarked stationery for a Mrs. Metcalf made at the Lime Rock mill, late 1930. Full sheet ca. 7½ x 10¾. LWDH, 2

Dard Hunter's Family & Friends

Harriet and William Hunter, ca. 1876.

Phil Hunter, The Buckeye Wizard. On the slate:
"Spirit World 1901."

Edith Cornell, age about 18.

Edith with Dard Jr. and Cornell at Mountain House, 1922.

Dard Hunter at the Chicago Graphic Arts Exposition, 1921. Courtesy Newberry Library.

The Hunter family with notations by Dard Jr., undated. Left to right: Dard Hunter, his cousin Florence Hunter Hale, Dard Jr., Junius Hunter and his wife Clara "Kitty" Johnson Hunter, Cornell, Florence and Junius's mother Elizabeth Hunter (wife of George Hunter), and Edith Hunter.

Irene and Cornell, undated, ca. 1945.

Edith and Martha Hunter, ca. 1963.

Dard Hunter at typewriter, undated.

Dard Jr., Chris, and baby Dard III, 1968.

Janet Hill Hunter with Dard and Eloise in front of Mountain House, ca. 1970.

Dard Hunter III at the press, 1995.

Cornell making paper with Kathryn Clark and
Charles Brownson looking on during the 1994
Annual Meeting of the Friends of Dard Hunter,
Chillicothe, OH.

Sterling Lord, ca. 1910, East Aurora, NY. Courtesy
Thomas Lord.

Peter Franck, undated.